T0393895

Rome in the Eighth Century

This book addresses a critical era in the history of the city of Rome, the eighth century CE. This was the moment when the bishops of Rome assumed political and administrative responsibility for the city's infrastructure and the physical welfare of its inhabitants, in the process creating the papal state that still survives today. John Osborne approaches this using the primary lens of 'material culture' (buildings and their decorations, both surviving and known from documents and/or archaeology), while at the same time incorporating extensive information drawn from written sources. Whereas written texts are comparatively few in number, recent decades have witnessed an explosion in new archaeological discoveries and excavations, and these provide a much fuller picture of cultural life in the city. This methodological approach of using buildings and objects as historical documents is embodied in the phrase 'history in art'.

JOHN OSBORNE is a Distinguished Research Professor and Dean Emeritus in the Faculty of Arts and Social Sciences at Carleton University, Ottawa. He is a cultural historian of early medieval Italy with a focus on the material culture of Rome and Venice. His publications include studies of medieval use of the Roman catacombs, murals in churches such as San Clemente and Santa Maria Antiqua, cultural contacts between Rome and Constantinople, and the medieval understanding of Rome's heritage of ancient buildings and statuary.

British School at Rome Studies

Series editors

Barbara Borg
Chair of Publications of the British School at Rome

Rosamond McKitterick
Chair of the Faculty of Archaeology, History and Letters and member of the Council of the British School at Rome

Stephen J. Milner
Director of the British School at Rome

British School at Rome Studies builds on the prestigious and long-standing *Monographs* series of the British School at Rome. It publishes volumes on topics that cover the full range of the history, archaeology and art history of the western Mediterranean both by the staff of the BSR and its present and former members, and by members of the academic community engaged in top-quality research in any of these fields.

Roman Port Societies: The Evidence of Inscriptions
Edited by Pascal Arnaud and Simon Keay

The Basilica of St John Lateran to 1600
Edited by Lex Bosman, Ian Haynes and Paolo Liverani

Rome, Pollution and Propriety: Dirt, Disease and Hygiene in the Eternal City from Antiquity to Modernity
Edited by Mark Bradley, with Kenneth Stow

Old Saint Peter's, Rome
Edited by Rosamond McKitterick, John Osborne, Carol M. Richardson and Joanna Story

The Punic Mediterranean: Identities and Identification from Phoenician Settlement to Roman Rule
Edited by Josephine Crawley Quinn and Nicholas C. Vella

Turin and the British Age of the Grand Tour
Edited by Paola Bianchi and Karin Wolfe

Rome in the Eighth Century

A History in Art

JOHN OSBORNE
Carleton University, Ottawa

CAMBRIDGE
UNIVERSITY PRESS

University Printing House, Cambridge CB2 8BS, United Kingdom

One Liberty Plaza, 20th Floor, New York, NY 10006, USA

477 Williamstown Road, Port Melbourne, VIC 3207, Australia

314-321, 3rd Floor, Plot 3, Splendor Forum, Jasola District Centre, New Delhi - 110025, India

79 Anson Road, #06-04/06, Singapore 079906

Cambridge University Press is part of the University of Cambridge.

It furthers the University's mission by disseminating knowledge in the pursuit of education, learning and research at the highest international levels of excellence.

www.cambridge.org
Information on this title: www.cambridge.org/9781108834582
DOI: 10.1017/9781108876056

© The British School at Rome 2020

This publication is in copyright. Subject to statutory exception and to the provisions of relevant collective licensing agreements, no reproduction of any part may take place without the written permission of Cambridge University Press.

First published 2020

A catalogue record for this publication is available from the British Library

Library of Congress Cataloging in Publication data
Names: Osborne, John, 1951– author.
Title: Rome in the eighth century : a history in art / John Osborne, Carleton University, Ottawa.
Description: Cambridge ; New York, NY : Cambridge University Press, 2020. | Series: British School at Rome Studies British School at Rome Studies | Includes bibliographical references and index.
Identifiers: LCCN 2020007252 | ISBN 9781108834582 (hardback) | ISBN 9781108819527 (paperback) | ISBN 9781108876056 (ebook)
Subjects: LCSH: Rome (Italy) – History – 476–1420. | Rome (Italy) – Description and travel. | Rome (Italy) – Antiquities.
Classification: LCC DG811 .O83 2020 | DDC 945.6/3201–dc23
LC record available at https://lccn.loc.gov/2020007252

ISBN 978-1-108-83458-2 Hardback

Additional resources for this publication at www.cambridge.org/

Cambridge University Press has no responsibility for the persistence or accuracy of URLs for external or third-party internet websites referred to in this publication, and does not guarantee that any content on such websites is, or will remain, accurate or appropriate.

Contents

List of Figures [*page* vi]
List of Plates [ix]
Acknowledgements [x]
List of Abbreviations [xii]
Preface [xiii]

1 Rome in 700: 'Constantinople on the Tiber'   [1]

2 Pope John VII *servus sanctae Mariae*   [22]

3 Clerics, Monks and Pilgrims   [67]

4 'The City of the Church'   [88]

5 The Chapel of Theodotus in Santa Maria Antiqua   [95]

6 Pope Zacharias and the Lateran Palace   [137]

7 Rome and the Franks   [159]

8 Paul I   [171]

9 Hadrian I *dux Dei*   [194]

10 Leo III and Charlemagne   [219]

Afterword   [231]

Bibliography [239]
Index [287]

Colour plates are to be found between pp. 172 and 173.

Figures

All photographs are by the author unless otherwise indicated.

2.1. Saint Peter's, Rome: Oratory of John VII, as recorded by Giacomo Grimaldi, BAV, Barb. Lat. 2732, fols 76v–77. Photo: by permission of the Biblioteca Apostolica Vaticana with all rights reserved   [*page* 28]

2.2. Saint Peter's Rome: Oratory of John VII, mosaic fragment (heavily restored) depicting John VII, now in the Vatican grottoes. Photo: with kind permission of the Fabbrica di San Pietro in Vaticano   [29]

2.3. Santa Maria Antiqua, Rome: palimpsest wall detail of 'Maria regina'.   [34]

2.4. Santa Maria Antiqua, Rome: *ambo* of Pope John VII (705–7).   [38]

2.5. Santa Maria Antiqua, Rome: ground plan. Drawn by Michelle Duong.   [39]

2.6. Santa Maria Antiqua, Rome: right side of apsidal arch wall with figures of Saints Basil and John Chrysostom.   [44]

2.7. Santa Maria Antiqua, Rome: sanctuary and apsidal arch wall (John VII).   [46]

2.8. Santa Maria Antiqua, Rome: Adoration of the Crucified Christ (J. Wilpert 1916, pl. 155).   [47]

2.9. Santa Maria Antiqua, Rome: detail of fictive curtains (*vela*) on sanctuary wall (John VII).   [50]

2.10. Santa Maria Antiqua, Rome: medallion of Saint Andrew on sanctuary wall (John VII).   [51]

2.11. Santa Maria Antiqua, Rome: Christological scenes on east wall of sanctuary (John VII).   [52]

2.12. Santa Maria Antiqua, Rome: Chapel of the Holy Physicians (west wall).   [56]

2.13. Santa Maria Antiqua, Rome: Anastasis (John VII).   [60]

3.1. San Saba, Rome: Healing of the Paralytic. Photo: Giulia Bordi.   [77]

List of Figures   vii

3.2. Saints Cornelius and Cyprian, Catacomb of San Callisto, Rome: Tomb of Pope Cornelius. Photo: © foto Pontificia Commissione di Archeologia Sacra   [81]
5.1. Santa Maria Antiqua, Rome: Theodotus chapel, detail of fictive curtains (*vela*).   [98]
5.2. Santa Maria Antiqua, Rome: Theodotus chapel, cycle of Quiricus and Julitta (east wall).   [100]
5.3. Santa Maria Antiqua, Rome: Theodotus chapel, detail of scene in which Quiricus speaks to the judge after his tongue has been removed.   [101]
5.4. Santa Maria Antiqua, Rome: Theodotus chapel, Quiricus and Julitta in prison (detail).   [102]
5.5. Santa Maria Antiqua, Rome: Theodotus chapel, Quiricus and Julitta tortured in the *sartago*.   [102]
5.6. Santa Maria Antiqua, Rome: Theodotus chapel, martyrdom of Quiricus.   [103]
5.7. Santa Maria Antiqua, Rome: Theodotus chapel, altar wall. Photo: Giulia Bordi.   [104]
5.8. Santa Maria Antiqua, Rome: Theodotus chapel, Theodotus with model of chapel. Photo: Giulia Bordi.   [105]
5.9. Santa Maria Antiqua, Rome: Theodotus chapel, Crucifixion. Photo: Giulia Bordi.   [108]
5.10. Santa Maria Antiqua, Rome: Theodotus chapel, family of Theodotus.   [109]
5.11. Santa Maria Antiqua, Rome: Theodotus chapel, Theodotus kneeling. Photo: Giulia Bordi.   [110]
5.12. Santa Maria Antiqua, Rome: Theodotus chapel, four saints 'whose names God knows'.   [112]
5.13. Santa Maria Antiqua, Rome: atrium niche, Saint Abbacyrus.   [127]
6.1. Lateran Palace, Rome: substructures below the Sancta Sanctorum, drawing of figure of Saint Augustine (?) (J. Wilpert 1916, pl. 141.2).   [145]
6.2. Capitoline Museum, Rome: *Lupa*.   [149]
6.3. Capitoline Museum, Rome: bronze head and hand from an imperial statue.   [152]
6.4. Capitoline Museum, Rome: *Spinario*.   [154]
8.1. Santa Maria Antiqua, Rome: left aisle, Christ and saints.   [188]

List of Figures

9.1. Santa Maria Antiqua, Rome: atrium, 'Maria *regina*' with Pope Hadrian I (J. Wilpert 1916, pl. 195). [195]

9.2. Santa Susanna, Rome: reconstructed mural with 'Maria *regina*'. Photo: Giulia Bordi. [201]

9.3. Sant'Adriano, Rome: murals now in the Museo Nazionale Crypta Balbi. Photo: Giulia Bordi. [207]

9.4. Mola di Monte Gelato: marble altar frontal (?) with '*Agnus Dei*'. Photo: Tim Potter. [216]

10.1. Lateran Palace, Rome: Triclinium of Leo III, facsimile of apse mosaic. [222]

10.2. Lateran Triclinium of Leo III: BAV, Barb. Lat. 5407, fol. 97r. Photo: By permission of the Biblioteca Apostolica Vaticana with all rights reserved [224]

11.1. Biblioteca Apostolica Vaticana, cod. gr. 1666, fol. 3r: initial introducing Book I of the Greek translation of the *Dialogues* of Pope Gregory I. Photo: By permission of the Biblioteca Apostolica Vaticana with all rights reserved [237]

11.2. Biblioteca Apostolica Vaticana, cod. gr. 1666, fol. 136v: initial introducing Book IV of the Greek translation of the *Dialogues* of Pope Gregory I. Photo: By permission of the Biblioteca Apostolica Vaticana with all rights reserved [238]

Plates

1. Santa Maria Antiqua, Rome: right side of apsidal arch (palimpsest wall).
2. Santa Maria Antiqua, Rome, right wall of the sanctuary: Saint Anne with the infant Mary.
3. Santa Maria Antiqua, Rome: Sickness of King Hezekiah.
4. Santa Maria Antiqua, Rome: niche with Madonna and Child.
5. Santa Sabina, Rome: narthex mural of Madonna and Child with saints and donors. Photo: Peter Coffman.
6. Santa Maria Antiqua, Rome: Theodotus chapel, general view. Photo: Gaetano Alfano/Soprintendenza Speciale per il Colosseo e l'area archeologica centrale di Roma/Electa.
7. Santa Maria Antiqua, Rome: Theodotus chapel, detail of Christ from scene of Quiricus and Julitta tortured in the *sartago*.
8. Santa Maria Antiqua, Rome: Theodotus chapel, family of Theodotus on right wall, detail of boy.
9. Santa Maria Antiqua, Rome: Theodotus chapel, family of Theodotus on right wall, detail of girl.
10. Santa Maria Antiqua, Rome: right aisle, painted niche with the three 'holy mothers'.
11. Santa Maria Antiqua, Rome: atrium, Pope Hadrian I and his 'guarantor'.
12. San Clemente, Rome: right aisle of lower church, Madonna and Child in the niche.

Acknowledgements

My foremost debt is to the British School at Rome, which has welcomed me enthusiastically for more than four decades. Over that time, I have benefited from conversations with a number of the directors, and a great many of the residents; and the library, expertly directed by Valerie Scott, remains my favourite place in the world in which to read and to write. Indeed, the creation of this book began there in the spring of 2018, facilitated by the award of a Balsdon fellowship.

No scholar works in isolation, and over the years I have enjoyed the friendship and counsel of many who share my fascination with early medieval Rome. Sadly, some are no longer with us, among them Leonard Boyle, Caecilia Davis-Weyer, Richard Krautheimer, Tim Potter, and David Whitehouse. But I continue to rejoice in the friendship of many others who have contributed to my understanding in ways large and small, and in that regard I shall single out for mention Maria Andaloro, Antonella Ballardini, Claudia Bolgia, Giulia Bordi, Tom Brown, Robert Coates-Stephens, Marios Costambeys, Sible de Blaauw, Judson Emerick, Julian Gardner, Manuela Gianandrea, Federico Guidobaldi, Alessandra Guiglia, Ingo Herklotz, Lesley Jessop, Gregor Kalas, Dale Kinney, Rosamond McKitterick, Gillian Mackie, Maria Laura Marchiori, Maya Maskarinec, John Mitchell, Giuseppe Morganti, Tom Noble, Éamonn Ó Carragain, Valentino Pace, Jo Story, Alan Thacker, Erik Thunø, Ann van Dijk, and Vera von Falkenhausen. I am grateful to Michelle Duong for the plan of Santa Maria Antiqua included in this volume, to Peter Coffman and Giulia Bordi for their kind assistance in providing photographs, and to Angela Roberts for her meticulous care in catching numerous typographical errors and inconsistencies. Special thanks go to Claudia Bolgia, Rosamond McKitterick, and Tom Noble, whose excellent comments and suggestions have improved the text enormously. We did not always agree on every detail, but as Richard Krautheimer once memorably said to me, 'I don't like it when you agree with me, as then I can't learn from you.'

Last but in fact foremost, Per Jonas Nordhagen has served as my unofficial guide and mentor since my first encounter with his work. His ground-breaking research on the painted decorations of Santa Maria Antiqua provides the foundation on which this book has been constructed, and over the years he has been unfailing in his encouragement and generosity. In return I offer this small gift in the year of his ninetieth birthday.

Abbreviations

BAV	Biblioteca Apostolica Vaticana
BNFr	Bibliothèque Nationale de France
CBCR	R. Krautheimer *et al.*, *Corpus Basilicarum Christianarum Romae*, 5 vols. (Vatican City: Pontificio Istituto di Archeologia Cristiana, 1937–77).
CCSL	Corpus Christianorum Series Latina
CT	*Codice topografico della città di Roma*, R. Valentini and G. Zucchetti (eds.), 4 vols. (Rome: Istituto Storico Italiano per il Medio Evo, 1940–53).
LP	*Le Liber Pontificalis: texte, introduction, et commentaire*, ed. by L. Duchesne, 2 vols. (Paris: Ernest Thorin, 1886–92). *Tome troisième. Additions et corrections par Cyrille Vogel* (Paris: E. de Boccard, 1955).
LTUR	*Lexicon Topographicum Urbis Romae*, ed. by E.M. Steinby, 6 vols. (Rome: Edizioni Quasar, 1993–2000).
MGH	Monumenta Germaniae Historica
ODB	*Oxford Dictionary of Byzantium*, A. Kazhdan (ed.) (New York and Oxford: Oxford University Press, 1991).
OR	*Les 'Ordines Romani' du Haut Moyen Age*, M. Andrieu (ed.), 5 vols. (Louvain: Spicilegium sacrum Lovaniense, 1931–61).
ÖstNB	Österreichische Nationalbibliothek
PL	*Patrologiae cursus completus, Series Latina* (Patrologia Latina), J.-P. Migne (ed.), 221 vols. (Paris: Garnier, 1841–64).

Preface

The seeds for this study were sown some three decades ago over convivial dinner conversations with Richard Hodges, then Director of the British School at Rome. Our views of what the city of Rome might have looked like in the early Middle Ages differed considerably: mine based largely on the compilation of papal biographies known as the *Liber pontificalis* and some remaining fragments of mosaic and mural painting, and his on the evidence of archaeology. I saw a city in which the arts and culture clearly flourished, at least in comparison to most other parts of contemporary western Europe and Byzantium, and he saw an impoverished and largely depopulated post-Roman urban wasteland that was conspicuously lacking any archaeological footprint, an 'invisible city' (*'città invisibile'*) in the words of Riccardo Santangeli Valenzani.[1] In retrospect, I think we were both wrong. I relied too heavily on a written text that presented a very one-sided picture, compiled primarily for the purpose of self-promotion; and Hodges's conclusion perhaps was based not so much on the analysis of surviving evidence, but rather on an almost total absence of evidence. Today a more nuanced reading likely falls somewhere in the middle of those extremes.[2]

What has changed? Primarily the archaeology. Thirty years ago, apart from a handful of excavated churches, for example, Santa Maria Antiqua, San Saba, San Crisogono, and San Clemente, the archaeological evidence for life in early medieval Rome was virtually non-existent. Excavators of a previous age had rarely stopped to study or even record the medieval layers in their rush to get down to levels deemed to be historically more important. But this situation was altered irrevocably beginning in the decade of the 1980s, with important excavations taking place in numerous locations in the city centre, including the imperial *fora* and, perhaps most significantly, at the Crypta Balbi.[3] We now have vastly more information at

---

[1] Santangeli Valenzani 2003: 115.
[2] For a thoughtful analysis of the situation, although perhaps still overemphasizing the 'collapse' scenario: Hodges 1993.
[3] For the Crypta Balbi: Santangeli Valenzani 2003 and Vendittelli 2004. For an overview of early medieval Rome seen through the lens of recent archaeology: Paroli 2004. For the contribution of recent archaeology to our understanding of the broader situation across Italy: Wickham 1999.

our disposal than we did four decades ago; and there is probably no more dramatic testimony to the advances made in our understanding of the early medieval city than the opening in the year 2000 of the Museo Nazionale Romano at that latter site. At the same time, the evidence provided by archaeology has permitted a much more informed reading of the few surviving written sources, as well as abetting increased contextual analysis of surviving fragments of architecture along with work in media such as mosaic, painting, and sculpture. As Kyle Harper has put it so succinctly: 'Archaeology provides a continuous stream of random data to correct the lapses and distortions of the textual record.'[4] That said, however, archaeology on its own also presents a distorted picture. If we measured early medieval Rome only through the changes documented in the excavation of the site of the Crypta Balbi, we might conclude that the first half of the eighth century was an era of complete catastrophe (*'una vera catastrofe'*).[5] But that too would be inaccurate.

The other significant change has been the growing acceptance by historians that 'documents' are not only comprised of writing on parchment or paper. Chris Wickham has observed that 'Roman documents hardly exist for the eighth and ninth centuries',[6] but that remark applies only to a certain class of document. Archaeological materials, along with standing remains, in other words buildings and their decorations, are also 'documents', and speak volumes about life in the early medieval city. In 1980 Richard Krautheimer took an important and impressive step in this new direction with his book *Rome: Profile of a City, 312–1308*; but his focus was on the periods for which documentable activity was most intense, and surviving buildings and their decorations were most prevalent, and thus the eighth century received almost no attention whatsoever in comparison to what came immediately before and after. This book will attempt to fill in that particular crack.

The subtitle, 'a history in art', is intended not merely to be descriptive but also to signal a difference in methodological approach. Over the years I have attempted to build a case for what I have come to call 'history *in* art', as opposed to 'history *of* art'. The term is not my invention: credit for that goes to an architectural historian named Alan Gowans (1923–2001), who understood precociously that material culture could be used more broadly as documentation for history, and he passionately promoted this methodology at a time when most 'art' historians were engaged almost exclusively with what is generally called 'fine art'. Gowans was a proselytizer for this

---

[4] Harper 2011: 500.   [5] Santangeli Valenzani 2003: 125.   [6] Wickham 2015: 8.

approach to historical study, at the time profoundly novel in anglophone universities, preferring in his own research to engage with what he deemed 'popular and commercial' architecture rather than buildings of a more elevated level of patronage; and he chose this name for the academic department he founded at the University of Victoria (British Columbia) in the early 1970s, with the wording consciously intended to signal a fundamental difference from more traditional art history programmes. I was exceptionally fortunate to be offered my first academic appointment in his 'Department of History in Art', and I instantly discovered an intellectual home.

My graduate student sojourns at The British School at Rome also played an important role in this regard, introducing me to the methods and approaches of archaeology. David Whitehouse, the director at that time, was himself a medieval archaeologist, and he employed the evidence unearthed in his excavations to shed light on larger historical issues. Indeed, the sites he chose to excavate were often determined by the desire to answer specific puzzling questions. Archaeology was thus regarded very clearly as a means to an end, not the end itself. It produced grist for the historian's mill, and I came to regard the history of art in a similar light. Many mornings he would conduct what amounted to an informal seminar over the course of our communal British School breakfasts, presenting the issues being tackled in his own current research and exploring questions of methodology. These discussions certainly helped to shape my doctoral dissertation, and the same approach was further honed in subsequent studies of the medieval use of the Roman catacombs and the atrium of the church of Santa Maria Antiqua.[7] These latter projects were intended as integrated historical studies balancing the evidence provided by various classes of document, in the fervent belief that the whole would be greater than the sum of the individual parts.

One of the most difficult issues for the 'historian in art' is the determination of basic facts about the 'document' in question, in the same way that more traditional historians need to know the date and circumstances of production of the written sources that they study. Context is essential. It is one thing to say that murals on the walls excavated beneath Roman churches such as San Clemente or Santa Maria Antiqua are 'medieval', or even 'early medieval', and quite another to determine whether you are dealing with a document of, say, the eighth century or the eleventh. And of course the difference is vitally important if one wants to bring this evidence

---

[7] Osborne 1985; and Osborne 1987.

to bear on the exploration of any larger cultural issue. Dating early medieval painting in Rome, particularly in the absence of a known patron, has been enormously problematic, and until the second half of the twentieth century it was based almost exclusively on stylistic analysis, itself a highly subjective process and one frequently prone to considerable error. In attempting to develop a better understanding of the chronology of my 'documents', I have been enormously fortunate to have had a mentor who pioneered the development of more objective approaches to dating, again with one foot planted squarely in the discipline of archaeology: Per Jonas Nordhagen. Nordhagen's detailed documentation and analysis of the early medieval murals in the church of Santa Maria Antiqua constituted the methodological model to which I aspired. His work constitutes the foundation for this study, and it will feature prominently in what follows.

Andrea Augenti has recently made an eloquent plea for archaeologists and art historians to work together, in effect treating their approaches to material culture as a single endeavour, as has long been the case for the study of classical antiquity;[8] and at a broader level, over the course of the twentieth century this same thinking led to the emergence of a new academic discipline calling itself 'medieval studies', reflected in the title of the journal published by the Pontifical Institute of Mediaeval Studies in Toronto.[9] 'Medieval studies' implies an integration of the disparate disciplines of history, art history, archaeology, palaeography, codicology, diplomatics, epigraphy, numismatics, theology, and much more; and to my mind it offers the most useful lens with which to shape our understanding of people, places and events from this period.

This book thus proposes to take a more integrative approach to the history of the city of Rome than has hitherto been attempted, particularly with respect to the evidence of 'material culture', here broadly defined. The eighth century should be seen as an exceptionally critical moment in the long history of the city of Rome, a time of considerable change encompassing politics, economics, religion, social and cultural practices, and even language, from the upper echelons of political and ecclesiastical life to the lowest strata of daily existence. More importantly, perhaps, this is the moment when Rome redefined itself in a way that would condition life in the city, and establish its role in the larger world, for at least another millennium. All those changes, and in some instances also certain

[8] Augenti 2016: 276–84.
[9] For an analysis of the particular Canadian contribution to the development of 'medieval studies': Reynolds 1991.

continuities, can be documented through the approaches of archaeology and history in art. Despite often being viewed, and all too frequently dismissed, as a 'dark age',[10] the eighth century has in fact left us with a substantial and very tangible record of achievement. My aim is to collect and present some of that evidence; and my hope is that in doing so I can add more colour to a picture that has hitherto been much too stark.

Although the primary focus will be on the evidence of material culture, with the intention to rectify an imbalance in many earlier studies, this does not mean that written sources will be ignored; indeed, to the contrary. The *Liber pontificalis* remains our single most valuable document for early medieval Rome, and an indispensable tool for historians of any persuasion hoping to understand the city in this era.[11] Its evidence can be supplemented and at times corrected by a broad variety of other sources, ranging from surviving epigraphic inscriptions to a compendium of papal correspondence to the Frankish kings (the so-called *Codex epistolaris carolinus*),[12] to authors and historians based elsewhere who comment on matters 'Roman', among them Gregory of Tours, Bede, and Theophanes. If material culture constitutes the 'warp', then written documents provide the 'weft', the aim being to weave the two strands together in order to provide a single 'text', in the original meaning of that word as constituting a woven object.

In attempting to draw together these disparate strands of evidence, I have constructed this narrative chronologically. It is a story with a beginning, a middle, and an end. Rome in 800 was a vastly different entity than Rome in 700, or even in 750, and the intention is to document that change as it happened, a process of continual evolution not a dramatic revolution, and if possible also to obtain some understanding of how and why it occurred. And because so much of our evidence, both written sources and material culture, is associated with the names of individual popes, the episcopal reigns of these principal actors in our drama will be used to create an overarching matrix, with Sergius I (687–701) and Leo III (795–816) serving as useful and appropriate bookends. We begin with Sergius, because his apparent opposition to the religious policies of Emperor Justinian II may be seen with hindsight as initiating the political

---

[10] This common trope underlies the title of Peter Llewellyn's *Rome in the Dark Ages*. The notion goes back at least as far as the fourteenth century: see Mommsen 1942.

[11] For the nature, function and importance of the *Liber pontificalis*, see most recently Capo 2009: 3–109; McKitterick 2011; Gantner 2014a: 16–38; and McKitterick 2015. Examples of its use as a source for art historical terminology include Moretti 1997 and Martiniani-Reber 1999.

[12] Preserved in a single manuscript in the Österreichische Nationalbibliothek in Vienna, MS lat. 449; see Gantner 2014a: 38–43. For a broader discussion of papal letters in this period, see Noble 2001a: 183–96.

process that ultimately detached Rome from the empire to which it had given its name. And to avoid confusion, I shall generally use the anachronistic but broadly understood term 'Byzantine' as it has normally been used by art historians, which is to say more broadly in a cultural sense of the 'Christian eastern Mediterranean' where Greek was the common language used in religion, politics and commerce, and not only in the narrow political sense of the bits of the 'Roman Empire' that remained after its frontiers were dramatically curtailed in the seventh century. The story will end with Pope Leo III, because his coronation of Charlemagne as *imperator* in December 800 can be regarded as a useful marker for the conclusion of the development of a new alliance with the Franks and a shift in the papal world view from one centred on the Mediterranean to one encompassing primarily western Europe. The eighth century is also very conveniently bookended by two important mosaic projects in Rome: the funerary chapel of Pope John VII (705–7) in Old Saint Peter's, and Leo III's Lateran triclinium. Both make impressive statements about their time; and while neither survives intact, both are extensively documented, and thus we can speak of their nature and import with considerable assurance.

This book is certainly not the first to survey the history of the city of Rome in the eighth century, the moment when the papal state is born. Many others have trodden this path previously, among them Peter Llewellyn, Thomas Noble, Paolo Delogu, Federico Marazzi, and most recently Clemens Gantner. But their endeavours have been focussed primarily on politics and economics, using the evidence of written documents. In that process, comparatively little attention has been paid to material culture, so the approach here is fundamentally different. This is not to say that material culture has been ignored entirely, I hasten to add. Both Thomas Noble and Paolo Delogu have been valiant in their attempts to expand their reach in this regard, but material culture has rarely been their primary concern. What is intended here is not so much a *political* history, although to some extent it cannot escape being such, but rather a *cultural* history, in the broadest possible sense of that term, and with the focus squarely on buildings and their decorations, and what these can tell us about those who spent their time, energy, and above all their money, on such projects. In looking at the evidence of wall-paintings and mosaics we shall consider a broad variety of topics, including subject matter, patronage, audience, style, technique, and more broadly what Gowans termed their 'social function'. The intention in each instance will be to use the 'artefact' as an historical 'document', not merely to supplement the *Liber pontificalis* but rather to speak in its own voice.

This approach will also lead to some diversion from previously accepted wisdom, most notably with regard to the characterization of the ruling élite in the city at this time of dramatic economic, political, and social change. Noble and Gantner, among others, have stressed the emergence of a Latin-speaking nobility which brought the run of 'Greek' popes to an end in 752 at the death of Zacharias; but this study will suggest a somewhat different understanding of that new ruling class, based largely on the evidence of their religious practices and patronage, viewed through the lens of the buildings, and above all their decorations, for which this new élite was responsible. These reveal some hitherto unexplored continuities in cultural practices that persisted in the city despite the obvious political changes. Rather than a 'Greek' élite being replaced by a new and ethnically different 'Latin' one, it will be proposed that the individuals and families remained largely unchanged, but instead chose very deliberately to 'reinvent' themselves as 'Romans' in the light of changing political realities, and at a moment when the adjective 'Greek' was acquiring pejorative implications in Rome. Most controversially, perhaps, I shall contend that even Pope Hadrian I (772–95) came from a family with hellenophone cultural roots.

There can be little doubt that the city of Rome changed over the course of the eighth century, and political actions were both the catalyst for that evolution and its primary theatre. The seventh-century losses of Egypt, Palestine, Syria, North Africa, and parts of Anatolia had opened the door to the possibility that the Christian *oikoumene* need not be co-terminal with the frontiers of the Empire ruled from Constantinople, so this mental hurdle had already been overcome. Cultural practices, on the other hand, including religious practices, were much more deeply embedded, and here change was very much slower to develop. In this regard Rome appears to have remained a 'Mediterranean' or 'Byzantine' city far longer than many have realized.[13] Even the political break between Rome and Constantinople, when it came, was anything but sharp and decisive, and I shall attempt to demonstrate this broader cultural continuity primarily through an examination of buildings and their decorations. For the most part, these structures are of a religious nature, as that is quite simply the evidence that we currently have; but it should be remembered that buildings were first and foremost stage sets for events that were considered necessary or important in the lives of those who built and used them, and churches in particular were constructed and decorated to frame the various religious practices, both individual and collective, and above all the

---

[13] This point has also been made forcefully by Maskarinec 2017: 338.

Christian liturgy, undertaken in that space. Over and above those 'contextual' and 'functional' aspects, however, at what Sible de Blaauw has termed the 'spiritual or abstract level' they also 'performed' the liturgy in their own right, a 'visible manifestation of the invisible'.[14]

This book has three principal ambitions. The first is to survey what we know about the material culture of Rome from the period of the eighth century. The second, more methodological, is to make a case for viewing buildings, their decorations, and physical objects more generally, as important historical 'documents' which go far beyond merely supplementing written sources. They are worthy of examination in their own right, and can be usefully employed even in the absence of chronicles, letters, charters, and the like. And the third is to offer a different view of élite Roman society in the eighth century, based on the cultural 'baggage' inherent in the spaces they created, the mural decorations they chose, and the objects they used. Perhaps most importantly, however, my overarching intention is not only to demonstrate that, despite some significant challenges, life in the city remained vibrant and active and anything but 'invisible', but in addition to advance the seemingly preposterous claim that the eighth century might be regarded as the most important in the entire history of the city of Rome, measured by the subsequent longevity of the institutions and practices which evolve in that time.

Additional notes for readers

Where standard English forms exist for place names, these have been preferred (e.g. Naples, not Napoli). For churches, following what has now become a standard practice, Italian names are used with the exception of Saint Peter's.

In transcribing inscriptions, I have used square brackets to suggest letters where the originals have been lost, and round brackets for the expansion of abbreviations in the Latin original, in other words where the letters are known to have been understood.

The secondary literature dealing with early medieval Rome is substantial, much of it written in the last few decades, and the 'Bibliography' at the end of this volume makes no claim to be exhaustive. It represents only those items that I have found most important and/or useful, and to which reference is made in the text.

---

[14] De Blaauw 1991: 32–4; see also Osborne 2004.

1 | Rome in 700: 'Constantinople on the Tiber'

Any attempt to chart the history of Rome over the course of the eighth century must begin by establishing a point of departure, and consequently the aim of this initial chapter is to paint a picture of political and cultural life in the city in or about the year 700, a 'launching pad' or foil against which to measure the continuities and changes that will follow. The overarching premise in this regard is that Rome in that year still functioned as an integral part of the Empire to which it had long ago given its name, even if the political capital had been moved to Constantinople (formerly Byzantium) some four centuries earlier. As yet, no one seriously questioned the existing political order. This continued integration can also be documented extensively in the sphere of material culture, as revealed through both archaeology and the analysis of buildings and their decorations.

Many of the ivory diptychs created for the Roman consuls in Late Antiquity featured personifications of 'Old Rome' and 'New Rome', the twin poles of the Empire's constructed identity. And although its geographic extent was fractured in the seventh century by the dramatic loss of Egypt, North Africa, and the Levant to the Arabs, in addition to being divided by deep theological differences regarding the nature of Christ, if there had been consuls to issue diptychs in 700 the traditional formula would probably still have been regarded as appropriate. There can be no doubt that the importance of 'Old Rome' had dwindled mightily over the course of the sixth and seventh centuries, particularly in political terms. The city was no longer a place of authority where important decisions were made, but the name alone still carried enormous *cachet*, and would in fact be used by the emperors in Constantinople until their conquest by the Ottomans in 1453. Nevertheless, 'Old Rome' remained a part of its homonymous Empire in much more than name. In 700 it still exercised considerable influence in the sphere of religion, and, despite some opposition from other senior patriarchs, its bishop, the pope, was broadly considered to wield substantial influence in matters of the faith, a position reaffirmed by the success of the Roman delegation to the Sixth Ecumenical Council that had met at Constantinople in 680–1 CE. There the opposition of the Roman church to the 'heresy' of Monotheletism received formal approval.

At the end of the seventh century the imperial capital on the Bosporus was no longer a youthful upstart, fashioned in the shadow of 'Old Rome' which initially it had sought to emulate. It had long since overtaken and surpassed its parent as a political, economic and cultural centre. In fact, by 700 their relative position had been largely reversed in broadly cultural terms, with the result that 'Old Rome' could now be aptly described as a 'Constantinople on the Tiber'.[1] Per Jonas Nordhagen, who coined that phrase, was thinking primarily in art historical terms, and indeed the Roman monuments dating from the years around 700 may have been little different from work being undertaken at the same time in Constantinople, and, as we shall see, possibly even executed by the same workshops of painters and mosaicists. Of course the question is complicated enormously by the Byzantine imperial policy of Iconoclasm,[2] in effect over much of the eighth and early ninth centuries, with the result that almost nothing now survives of the pictorial arts in the city of Constantinople from the years before 843. But we can nevertheless assess the situation in the capital from two directions. The first is the scattering of contemporary buildings in 'Byzantium' about which something is known, for example, the mosaic decorations of the Church of the Dormition at Nicaea (modern Iznik in Turkey);[3] and the second is art in Constantinople from the years immediately after Iconoclasm. While the latter does not provide reliable testimony for questions of pre-Iconoclastic style or technique, the overall schemes of decoration and the iconographic formulas employed appear substantially unchanged after the hiatus in image production, where these can be assessed. All told, enough evidence survives, in Rome and elsewhere, to suggest that Nordhagen presents a highly plausible case.

This chapter will propose that Rome in the year 700 was a 'Byzantine' city in many if not most other respects as well, from politics and economics to language and culture. This is not to say that early medieval Rome remained unchanged from Late Antiquity. To the contrary, it had changed dramatically, particularly in the areas of demographics and social practices; but, if anything, this period of transformation had served to bring it closer to the world of the contemporary eastern Mediterranean rather than pushing the two regions farther apart. That break would indeed come, but at the dawn of the eighth century it still lay somewhere in the future. In

---

[1] Nordhagen 2000.   [2] *ODB*: 975–7.
[3] Underwood 1959; Barber 1991; and Brubaker and Haldon 2001: 21–3.

700 there was no substantial dichotomy between the notions of 'Rome' and 'Byzantium', either in conception or reality.

In order to understand Rome in the year 700, we need to begin by looking briefly at the previous two centuries, and in particular the devastating effects of the calamitous Gothic wars on the city, its population, and its administration. The period of the sixth and seventh centuries was not the best of times for the broader fortunes of the Roman Empire in general, and the Italian peninsula in particular.[4] It suffered an endless series of conflicts, plagues, famines, and natural disasters for which we have very scant records of their consequences for daily life; but for the period of the Gothic wars (535–53 CE), and for their effects on Rome in particular, we have an observant eyewitness in the person of the historian Procopius, albeit writing only some years later. He provides, for example, a lengthy and vivid account of the situation in the city during the year-long Gothic siege from March 537 to March 538. And so we shall begin with him.

Following a successful campaign to retake North Africa from the Vandals, in 535 Justinian had sent his foremost general, Belisarius, to reconquer Italy from the Ostrogoths. Belisarius landed in Sicily and moved north, eventually reaching Rome in December 536; but then the Ostrogothic king Vitiges counter-attacked, and laid siege to the city. Vitiges did not have sufficient strength to break through the city's Aurelian walls, but the outnumbered imperial forces wisely resisted all attempts to lure them into an open battle, resulting in a prolonged period of stalemate. At first this was a mere inconvenience to the populace, with the cutting of the aqueducts resulting in the necessary closure of the baths, but it was not long before famine and disease began to take a significant toll.[5]

The 'Gothic War' would drag on over almost two full decades, with first one side and then the other gaining advantage, before the final defeat of the Ostrogoths by Narses at the battle of Mons Lactarius in Campania. Over that period, the city of Rome would suffer a number of sieges, being occupied first by one side and then the other; and slowly but surely the population was severely reduced. In the 546 siege by the Ostrogothic king Totila we are told that the inhabitants were reduced to eating nettles and their own dung. Procopius reports that 'there were many too, who, because of the pressure of the famine, destroyed themselves with their own hands; for they could no longer find either dogs or mice or any dead animal of any

---

[4] For a recent survey of the evidence for the collapse of 'social cohesion' in sixth-century Italy, see Pohl 2018.
[5] Procopius, *History of the Wars* 5.20.5, 6.3.1–22; trans. Dewing III: 195, 309–15.

kind on which to feed.'[6] When Totila's army eventually occupied the city, apparently only some 500 men remained, the rest having either fled or succumbed to starvation;[7] and when the Ostrogothic army moved on, they took the last remnants of the population with them, 'refusing to allow a single soul in Rome, but leaving it entirely deserted'.[8]

Procopius's dismal picture is corroborated fully by the sequence of papal biographies known collectively as the *Liber pontificalis*.[9] During the siege by Totila, for example, we are told that 'Such a famine occurred in Rome that they even wanted to eat their own children'. Our text goes on to report that 'some of the senators – the patricians and exconsuls Cathegus, Albinus, and Basilius – escaped, reached Constantinople and were presented before the emperor Justinian in their affliction and desolation'.[10] Understandably enough, there is no evidence that they ever returned.

Justininian's 'Pragmatic Sanction' (554 CE) brought a new civil-military administration, headed by an exarch resident in the Adriatic port city of Ravenna; but political upheaval continued to plague the Italian peninsula, culminating in the invasion in 568 of the Lombards, who quickly occupied north and central Italy, establishing their capital in the Po Valley at Pavia. War was not the only affliction to be suffered by the populace of Rome: time and again we hear of the devastating effects of famine, disease, and the flooding of the Tiber river (*LP* 64.1, 65.1, 69.1; ed. Duchesne I: 308, 309, 317). The most obvious result was that the city became severely depopulated, although the decline in numbers had already started in the fifth century.

Various historians have attempted to calculate an approximate figure for the city's remaining inhabitants. Richard Krautheimer, for example, estimated a population in the mid-sixth century of about 30,000,[11] which would represent a decline of some 97 per cent since the era of Constantine (r. 306–37) when it is thought to have been about one million. Although one scholar has expressed the view that Krautheimer's figure may actually be too high,[12] most others who have tackled this topic are slightly less pessimistic; Ludovico Gatto, for example, has argued that the population probably did not dip below 100,000,[13] although Riccardo Santangeli Valenzani prefers a figure of

---

[6] Ibid., 7.17.19; trans. Dewing IV: 299–301.   [7] Ibid., 7.20.19.
[8] Ibid., 7.22.19; trans. Dewing IV: 349.
[9] For the origin and nature of this important and influential text, first compiled in the sixth century using models such as Suetonius, Pseudo-Aurelius Victor, and the *Historia Augusta*, see McKitterick 2011 and McKitterick 2015: 226–7. For a survey of the various manuscript recensions, see most recently Capo 2009: 58–88; and Gantner 2014a: 302–14.
[10] *LP* 61.7, ed. Duchesne I: 298; trans. Davis 2010: 57.   [11] Krautheimer 1980: 65.
[12] Hodges 1993: 356.   [13] Gatto 1998.

50,000–60,000.[14] Given the lack of hard evidence, all such figures must necessarily be guesswork, however 'educated' on the basis of data such as the figures for pork distribution;[15] but regardless of the precise number, and even accepting the most conservative estimates, the effect on life in the city will certainly have been dramatic. Large areas within the perimeter of the third-century Aurelian walls were no longer inhabited, and would be re-deployed for agriculture, interspersed with little islands of population. Wickham envisages 'as many as a dozen "urban villages" scattered across the vast area inside the perimeter of the Aurelian walls'.[16] Unfortunately, very little is known about the nature of domestic housing in this period, until the reappearance in the ninth century of newly constructed residences in areas like the Forum of Nerva.[17] A similar picture of what Hodges deems 'staggering depopulation' characterized the rural hinterland outside the city, and he notes that the 'population passed below any threshold that is readily identified by field archeology'.[18] By the beginning of the seventh century, daily life in 'Old Rome' and its environs would no longer have been recognized by those who had lived there in the years before 500 CE; but from the ashes a new city slowly but surely emerged, albeit one very different in a great many respects except for the institution of the papacy with its stout adherence to what it defined as orthodox Christianity, as well as the physical urban landscape created by the buildings and monuments inherited from a previous age.

These dramatic developments did not pass unremarked by contemporary authors, and perhaps most notably by the pope whose reign ended the sixth century and inaugurated the seventh, Gregory I (590–604).[19] Two passages from his writings paint a bleak picture of the situation in his time. In his homily on the Old Testament Book of Ezekiel, Gregory observes: 'Everywhere we see lamentation, on all sides we hear groans. Cities lie in ruins, fortresses are razed, fields are deserted, the earth is returned to solitude. No countryman has remained in the fields, hardly any inhabitant in the towns. . . . For where is the Senate? Where now are the people? Rome, though empty, already burns.'[20] And a similar sentiment is expressed in his *Dialogues*: 'Now the cities have been depopulated, fortresses razed, churches burned down, monasteries and nunneries destroyed, the fields abandoned by mankind, and destitute of any cultivator the land lies empty and solitary.

---

[14] Santangeli Valenzani 2004a: 23. [15] Whitehouse 1988: 29–30. [16] Wickham 1999: 15.
[17] Santangeli Valenzani 1997.
[18] Hodges 1993: 356–7. For the broader Italian context, see also Valenti 2018.
[19] For Gregory and his world view, as expressed in his numerous books and letters, see Markus 1997 and Neil 2013.
[20] Gregory I, *Homil. in Ezechielem* VI.22 (*PL* 76: 1010); trans. Gray, 228–9.

No landholder lives on it; wild beasts occupy places once held by a multitude of men.'[21]

Gregory can perhaps be seen as a sort of Janus figure, with two heads. One head looked backward and lamented what had been or was being lost.[22] It was in his time, for example, that the last recorded meeting of the Roman Senate took place, on 25 April 603;[23] and perhaps a sign of things to come may be discerned in the location chosen for this gathering: the Lateran Palace, the papal residence. But the other head looked forward, to a new place for the Christian church in the lives of western Europeans, and to a prominent role in that process for the bishops of Rome. In his time the popes became much more active 'players' in events taking place in the world around them, including the city of Rome itself. It was Gregory who organized a public penitential procession with the aim of ending the plague devastating the city in 590, with seven different groups starting from seven different churches, and meeting at Santa Maria Maggiore.[24] Another similar procession, the 'Major Litany' ('*letania maior*') from the church of San Lorenzo in Lucina to Saint Peter's via the Milvian Bridge, was celebrated annually on 25 April. It was clearly intended to replace the pagan *Robigalia* festival, given that it took place on the same date and followed much the same route.[25] These public events should be viewed as furthering an ongoing process of ecclesiastical appropriation of the physical landscape of Rome, also manifested in the concurrent development of the stational liturgy, a unifying factor that incorporated large areas of the city and large numbers of its lay inhabitants.[26] Gregory I is also the pope who initiated the Roman church's active outreach efforts in terms of evangelization, beginning with campaigns to eradicate remaining vestiges of paganism in Sardinia and Corsica, followed shortly thereafter by Augustine's mission to Kent in the year 597 to convert the Anglo-Saxons (*LP* 66.3, ed. Duchesne I: 312).[27]

---

[21] Gregory I, *Dialogues* III, 38, ed. Moricca: 226–7; English translation from Brown 1984: 40.

[22] McNally 1978. For Gregory's sense that these events were signs that the Apocalypse was not far off, Markus 1997: 51–4. Humphries (2007) takes a less dramatic view, arguing that evidence for some continuity in the fourth and fifth centuries should be extended to the end of the sixth.

[23] Chastagnol 1996; Burgarella 2001; and Humphries 2007: 21.

[24] Gregory of Tours, *Historia Francorum*, ed. Krusch and Levison, I.1: 477–8; trans. Dalton II: 427–8. For the development of the 'seven-fold litany' (*letania septiformis*) processions and their implications, see Baldovin 1987: 158–9; and Latham 2009.

[25] Dyer 2007.

[26] Baldovin 1987: 268; Quattrocchi 2002; Romano 2014: 54–62, 109–39; and De Blaauw 2017: 24–7. For the influence of imperial ceremonial on emerging papal practices, Humphries 2007: 51–3.

[27] Richards 1980: 228–50; Markus 1997: 80–2, 177–87; and Ricci 2013. The position of Rome as the source for all aspects of Christian theology and liturgy in Anglo-Saxon England permeates the writings of authors like Bede; see Hilliard 2018: 41–2, 45–7.

Gregory has long been seen by historians as a pivotal figure in the history of the papacy, someone from a distinguished and wealthy family who began his career in the secular administrative system, including a precocious stint as the Urban Prefect of Rome in 573 CE, but who then moved into ecclesiastical life, founding some seven monasteries on his family estates (six in Sicily and one in Rome), and also serving as the papal *apocrisarius* to Constantinople before being elected pope in September 590, apparently against his will and while still only a deacon.[28] The use of the term 'consul of God' ('*consul Dei*') in his funerary inscription is telling, as it suggests that this melding of civic and ecclesiastical duties and responsibilities was ultimately a conscious decision. Richards sees in him 'the deep intertwining of *Christianitas* and *Romanitas*'.[29]

The full papal exercise of authority over the city of Rome still lay somewhere in the future, however. When Pope Boniface IV (608–15) wanted to convert the abandoned and presumably derelict structure of the Pantheon into a new church, he first sought and obtained permission from Emperor Phocas (*LP* 69.2, ed. Duchesne I: 317), and at the same time the imperial *patricius* Smaragdos erected an honorific column to the emperor in the Roman Forum.[30] Public monuments and public spaces were clearly still controlled by the civil administration. A few decades later, Pope Honorius (625–38) similarly obtained the permission of Emperor Heraclius to remove bronze roof tiles from the temple 'that is called of Rome' ('*qui appellatur Romae*') in order to re-cover the roof of Saint Peter's (*LP* 72.2, ed. Duchesne I: 323). Public buildings and monuments were evidently still regarded as imperial property in 663 when the Emperor Constans II decided to strip the city of its bronze, including the Pantheon's roof tiles (*LP* 78.3, ed. Duchesne I: 343),[31] but these first inklings of papal interest in the urban architectural fabric would continue to develop as time passed. It would be interesting to know if Pope Honorius also sought imperial permission when he converted the Curia Senatus building in the Forum into the church of Sant'Adriano. Presumably he did, but in this instance no mention is made in our only source for this action, the *Liber pontificalis* (*LP* 72.6, ed. Duchesne I: 324).

Of all the social customs that were significantly disrupted by prevailing political circumstances, the most readily documentable through archaeology is undoubtedly burial practice. Roman law dating back to the fifth century BCE had prohibited burial within the *pomerium*, which in Late

---

[28] Richards 1980: 25–43; and Markus 1997: 7–14. [29] Richards 1980: 50.
[30] Taddei 2014a; and Kalas 2017. [31] Coates-Stephens 2017.

Antiquity had become more or less synonymous with the circuit of the Aurelian walls. As a result, the major cemeteries were situated along the roads leading outwards from that perimeter, both on the surface and, from the beginning of the third century CE onwards, below ground in subterranean passages that have come to be known as the catacombs. With very few exceptions, extramural burial remained normative until the first half of the sixth century, at which time a dramatic change occurred. Dated catacomb burials cease fairly abruptly at this moment, and at the same time we find the earliest evidence of burials inside the city walls. This change may have been prompted initially by the sheer impossibility of gaining access to the cemeteries in times of siege,[32] and indeed two sources record this circumstance explicitly, albeit anecdotally. The first is Zosimus's account of the unsuccessful siege of Rome by Alaric and the Visigoths in 408: 'And when there was no means of relief, and their food was exhausted, plague not unexpectedly succeeded famine. Corpses lay everywhere, and since the bodies could not be buried outside the city with the enemy guarding every exit, the city became their tomb.'[33] Just over a century later, we find a similar situation during the twelve-month Ostrogothic siege of 537–8. When a deputation of citizens came to the imperial commander, Belisarius, to voice their complaints, the inability to follow the normal practice of burying their dead outside the walls was singled out for specific mention.[34] In such circumstances it is not difficult to imagine that new solutions must necessarily have been sought, and in recent years the written accounts have been fully confirmed by the discovery of many dozens of intramural graves datable to the sixth and seventh centuries, beginning with Marina Marcelli's excavation of the Porticus Liviae on the Oppian hill. This site included some fifteen tombs, cut into a late fourth- or early fifth-century mosaic floor, constituting a useful *terminus post quem* for the interments; and the few objects of glass and other materials found in the graves suggested a date near the end of the sixth century.[35]

---

[32] Osborne 1984b.

[33] Zosimus, *New History* 5.19; trans. Ridley, p. 120. Zosimus was writing a century later, and in Constantinople, but his account of the years 407–10 CE is heavily dependent on the earlier work of Olympiodorus of Thebes, who is generally considered to have been well-informed, although not himself an actual eyewitness; see Matthews 1970 and *ODB*: 1524, 2231. For the impact on burial: Meneghini 2013.

[34] Procopius, *History of the Wars* 6.3.19; trans. Dewing III: 312–3. Procopius too was writing later in life, and in Constantinople, but had accompanied Belisarius in Italy, and thus had first-hand knowledge of the events in question.

[35] Marcelli 1989.

In subsequent years, Roberto Meneghini and Riccardo Santangeli Valenzani collected and analysed evidence from some 85 burial sites within the walls of Rome, totalling some 500 graves, and proposed dates in either the second half of the sixth century or the seventh century on the basis of stratigraphy and articles found in the tombs, primarily glass and ceramics, although finds of any objects were quite rare. These graves were not elaborate, often in simple trenches or reusing earlier materials.[36]

Rossella Rea has used this data to propose a typology of urban burials, dividing them into three groups that succeeded one another in approximate chronological sequence.[37] The earliest are what can be termed 'casual' burials, usually found in isolation and devoid of formal organization. For Meneghini and Santangeli Valenzani these represent the *'momenti di emergenza'* recorded by Zosimus and Procopius,[38] when traditional extramural burial was simply impractical. By the middle of the sixth century, however, a practice that had been born of necessity now became more systematic, with burials laid out in a more orderly fashion and comprising larger groups, no doubt reflecting the simple reality that large areas of the city lay derelict, and thus were available to be put to new uses. And in the final phase, these urban burials began to be clustered around the city's churches, for example, Santa Maria Antiqua in the Roman Forum.[39] Marios Costambeys has suggested that the development of ecclesiastical graveyards might be associated with an attempt by the clergy to reclaim some measure of control over this important social practice.[40]

Perhaps fortuitously for the future of the city of Rome, the seventh century also witnessed enormous disruption in the eastern quadrant of the Empire, with the conquests undertaken by first the Persians and then the Arabs, the former ephemeral and almost immediately reversed by the Emperor Heraclius, but the latter permanent and still a defining factor for the political geography of the Middle East today. This turmoil resulted in a significant displacement of population, best documented for male religious communities at least some of whom made what was presumably a conscious choice not to live outside the now diminished frontiers of Christendom. A number of 'refugees' and other peripatetic monks and clergy, both individuals and groups, found their way westwards, many apparently preferring Rome to Constantinople.[41] Among them, for example, was John Moschus, author of

---

[36] Meneghini and Santangeli Valenzani 1993; Meneghini and Santangeli Valenzani 1995; and Meneghini 2004b.
[37] Rea 1993. [38] Meneghini and Santangeli Valenzani 1993: 106.
[39] Augenti 1996: 163–8. See also Coates-Stephens 2020. [40] Costambeys 2001.
[41] Bréhier 1903; Sansterre 1983 I: 17–20; Dagron 1988: 48–9; and von Falkenhausen 2015: 44–9.

the *Pratum spirituale*, who came to Rome along with his disciple Sophronius, a future patriarch of Jerusalem. Moschus would end his days in the city in 619.[42] Some two decades later, a community of Greek-speaking monks from Cilicia established itself outside the walls at Acuas Salvias, now the site of the Cistercian community of Tre Fontane.[43] This latter group brought with them the head of Anastasius the Persian (martyred in 628), and this relic is listed in the more-or-less contemporary guide for pilgrims to Rome, the *De locis sanctis martyrum*.[44] Other ascetic communities would soon follow, perhaps most notably a group from the monastery of Saint Sabas outside Jerusalem, also refugees from the Arab conquest, who settled on the 'little' Aventine hill in the 640s, naming their church San Saba after their original founder.[45] We shall return to this building and its decorations in a subsequent chapter. And in the reign of Pope Donus (676–8) a group of Syrian monks who had migrated to Rome were discovered to be Nestorian heretics, necessitating their dispersal among other houses in the city (*LP* 80.2, ed. Duchesne I: 348). Communities of hellenophone monks would remain a feature of religious life in Rome through to at least the eleventh century.[46]

Not all the religious 'refugees' were monks. Others were or would become regular clergy, and they soon found a place among the ranks of Rome's ecclesiastical establishment. One such was Theodore, whom we are told was born in Greece, the son of a bishop from Jerusalem (*LP* 75.1, ed. Duchesne I: 331). He was the first of a line of hellenophone *émigrés* or their offspring to reach the top of the church hierarchy in Rome, becoming pope in the year 642. Many more would follow. Of the thirteen bishops who occupied the seat of Saint Peter from the election of Agatho in 681 to the death of Zacharias in 752, only two are described in their *Liber pontificalis* biographies as 'Roman': Benedict II (684–5) and Gregory II (715–31). Among the other eleven there are five 'Syrians', four 'Greeks', and two Sicilians, the last presumably also Greek-speaking. This statistic is rather stunning, and despite what must presumably have been a fair degree of 'Italianization', the prolonged dominance of individuals whose cultural and religious background was grounded in the eastern Mediterranean must have been significant.[47] As Jean-Marie

---

[42] Sansterre 1983 I: 57–60.   [43] *Ibid.*, I: 13–17.
[44] *CT* II: 109; and Bertelli 1970. In the autumn of 713 CE this relic effected the cure of the daughter of Theopemptos, an *émigré* bishop from Syria who had sought refuge in Rome, as recorded in a contemporary text, composed in Greek and later translated into Latin: Smith 2018.
[45] Sansterre 1983 I: 22–9.
[46] Sansterre 1988. For a more general introduction to monasticism in early medieval Rome: Ferrari 1957, and Costambeys and Leyser 2007.
[47] For a fuller documentation of the Greek presence in the city, see Mango 1973: 695–714; Burgarella 2002; von Falkenhausen 2015: 44–57; and especially Sansterre 1983. Thomas Noble

Sansterre has aptly observed, in a largely depopulated city their numbers need not have been enormous to have exerted a substantial impact.[48]

Nor were all the newcomers religious. In his seminal study of the population of early medieval Italy, with the principal focus on Ravenna and the territories of the Exarchate, Thomas Brown has documented the total disappearance of the 'old order' of noble families, many of whom had either perished in the Gothic wars or fled to the safety of Constantinople, and their replacement in the seventh century by a new cohort of land-owning magnates: 'gentlemen and officers' drawn primarily from the senior ranks of the army who chose to settle in the more stable 'garrison' environment of the post-conflict era. Upward social mobility was most easily obtained through military service, and many senior positions were held by 'Easterners', appointed either directly from Constantinople or by the imperial exarch in Ravenna.[49] This group had the means to purchase land in what Brown has aptly described as 'a buyer's market'.[50] Before long they started to use the term 'noble' ('*nobilis*') and attempted to make their titles hereditary.[51] As we shall see, in eighth-century Rome these two streams – clergy and military – began to merge, with élite families often having a foot in both. Some may indeed have been recruited locally, but prosopographical and other evidence strongly suggests that much of the 'new nobility' was ultimately of 'Byzantine' background, at least in the case of Rome, however 'Italianized' these individuals may have become by the second or third generation. The evidence to be gleaned from the realm of material culture certainly supports such a view. And the imperial bureaucracy will also have made a contribution, for example, Pope John VII (705–7), son of the '*curator palatii*' Plato.

Pilgrimage was also beginning to draw new arrivals to the city, albeit primarily from another direction, attracted by the presence of the relics of Saints Peter and Paul, and the tombs of many other early martyrs, located either in purpose-built shrine churches or still resting in their original

---

remains sceptical of 'an eastern domination of Rome's intellectual life' (Noble 1995: 84), observing that by the time of their election most of the individuals concerned would have been in Rome for at least a decade, and hence thoroughly 'Roman' (Noble 2014: 82). Writing about Ravenna in this period, Thomas Brown acknowledges the difficulty of determining ethnic origin on the basis of names, preferring evidence such as the Latin inscriptions written using the Greek alphabet that were appended to numerous documents; see Brown 1984: 67–8.

[48] Sansterre 1983 I: 21.
[49] Brown 1984: 61–9. By contrast, Costambeys (2000: 390–3) argues for greater continuity in the composition of the Roman aristocracy.
[50] Brown 1984: 105. An example is provided by the soldier Tzitas, recorded in a Ravenna papyrus of 591 CE as having married locally and purchased land (Brown 1988: 134).
[51] Brown 1984: 63.

graves in the extramural cemeteries (catacombs).[52] That this already had become a going concern in the second half of the sixth century is readily documented in our sources, and the work of numerous pontiffs to repair and restore graves situated in the catacomb cemeteries is recorded in the *Liber pontificalis*, beginning with the entry for John III (561–74): 'He loved and restored the cemeteries of the holy martyrs' (*'Hic amavit et restauravit cymiteria sanctorum martyrum'*; LP 63.1, ed. Duchesne I: 305). Furthermore, this same pope made provision for Sunday services at the subterranean shrines, with the Lateran providing both the liturgical instruments and the necessary lighting.

Other popes were even more ambitious Pelagius II (579–90) constructed a new extramural shrine church for St Lawrence on the Via Tiburtina (*LP* 65.2, ed. Duchesne I: 309), situated directly over the saint's grave; and Honorius I (625–38) did the same for the tomb of Saint Agnes on the Via Nomentana (*LP* 72.3, ed. Duchesne I: 323). Both structures still survive, with some of their original mosaic decorations intact, including images of the papal donors bearing models of their new buildings. Both also signal the primary motives in the early Middle Ages for much of the construction of new architecture, or the adaptation of older buildings: namely, to serve as appropriate architectural settings for the performance of the liturgy, the central practice of the Christian religion in which Christ's sacrifice was commemorated and ritually re-enacted, and secondly to house the remains of the saints, whose intercessory powers were seen increasingly as relevant to salvation.

The Constantinian shrine church of Saint Peter's was also growing rapidly in importance,[53] and Gregory of Tours records the practice of creating 'contact relics' for visiting pilgrims by lowering small pieces of cloth into Peter's tomb, where they came into contact with his saintly remains. It was believed that if these *palliola* acquired sanctity and became true relics, they would gain weight in the process.[54] A similar account is preserved additionally in both Georgian and Arabic sources.[55] The dramatic growth in the number of pilgrims soon began to disrupt the performance of the liturgy in Saint Peter's, necessitating a major restructuring of the area of the high altar about the year 600. A semi-circular crypt was installed, with an entrance in the south transept and an exit on the north

---

[52] Colgrave 1969; and Llewellyn 1993: 173–98. For a succinct introduction to the geography and architecture of 'Rome of the pilgrims', see Thacker 2014.
[53] See the useful overview in Liverani 2013.
[54] Gregory of Tours, *De gloria martyrum*, ed. Krusch, 54; trans. Van Dam: 45–6.
[55] Sauget 1973.

side; and the altar was newly reconfigured above it, thus allowing pilgrims to venerate Peter's grave without creating any disruption to services.[56]

In terms of the promotion of hagiographic cults, however, the overwhelming emphasis for new dedications between the mid-sixth and mid-eighth centuries seems to have been on imported rather than indigenous Roman saints, including Cosmas and Damian, Sergius and Bacchus, Cyrus and John, the Forty Martyrs of Sebaste, and numerous others whose images we shall encounter on the walls of churches such as Santa Maria Antiqua. Maya Maskarinec has thoroughly documented this phenomenon in the centre of the city, in the area of the Forum, the Palatine, the Aventine, and the Tiber bend.[57] These cults all originated in the eastern Mediterranean, and simply reflect the cultural and religious background of those who wielded power during this period, or who came to the city bearing relics. After 750, as we shall see, the focus on 'Byzantine' saints will disappear dramatically.

An enormous quantity of evidence regarding the economic situation in early medieval Rome came to light in the years following 1981 through the excavation of the site in the centre of the city known as the Crypta Balbi, a porticoed courtyard adjacent to the theatre built in 17–13 BCE by Lucius Cornelius Balbus.[58] A deposit in the building's *exedra*, datable to about the year 700, revealed that a flourishing system of Mediterranean commerce and trade remained in place through to the end of the seventh century, attested principally by large quantities of ceramics imported from southern Italy, the eastern Mediterranean, and especially North Africa. The presence of copious amounts of coinage demonstrates that it was also a monetized economy;[59] and the Crypta Balbi had apparently itself become a site for the manufacture of luxury goods for export, since among the finds were both objects, and moulds for the production of objects, similar to those from the supposedly 'Lombard' cemeteries excavated at Castel Trosino and Nocera Umbra.[60] The sheer number of finds in this one deposit was extraordinary, including some 460 coins, 700 metal objects, more than 100 pieces of bone or ivory, more than 10,000 glass objects, and roughly 100,000 ceramic sherds, including 1,150 lamps and some 3,000 fragments of African red slip ware ('*sigillata africana*') from the region of Carthage. The last datable coin was a *solidus* from the first reign of Emperor Justinian II (685–95).[61]

---

[56] *CBCR* V: 265–7; and De Blaauw 1994: 530–9.   [57] Maskarinec 2018: 37–116.
[58] Manacorda 2001.   [59] Rovelli 1998; and Rovelli 2000.
[60] Ricci 1997. For a similar situation at Ravenna, where manufactured goods were eagerly sought by Lombard purchasers: Brown 1984: 41.
[61] Sagui 1998: 68–73.

A second deposit in the *esedra*, datable a few decades later in the first half of the eighth century, offered a stunning contrast: no imported *amphorae* or other large vessels used for the transport of oil and foodstuffs, no high-value coinage, and no evidence of manufacturing. Obviously this evidence must be used with some caution, as the previous activities may simply have shifted to another location, but the overall impression is one of dramatic discontinuity, at least at this one site. This led Riccardo Santangeli Valenzani to propose a shift to a more localized economy, based primarily on the exchange of goods rather than their sale, and a decline in specialized labour.[62] Contributing to this shrinking of Rome's Mediterranean connections were no doubt the final capture and destruction of Carthage by the forces of the Umayyad caliphate in 698 CE, and the loss of revenues and produce from the estates of the Roman church in southern Italy and Sicily, confiscated by the Byzantine emperor Leo III.[63] We shall return to this latter development, and its effect on Rome, in a subsequent chapter.

Perhaps not surprisingly, Rome in 700 was very much a bilingual city. It was not a case of Latin *or* Greek, of separate communities which may have had little or no interaction, but rather one of Latin *and* Greek, of a clergy and élite laity that was comfortable in both languages, although the communities of immigrant monks perhaps somewhat less so.[64] Even if Latin remained the official language of the Roman church, Greek was the common tongue employed by many members of the senior clergy, and the vast majority of the popes between 685 and 750. A telling insight into the nature of the papal court in the time of Pope John VI (701–5) is provided by Stephanus in his biography of Wilfrid, the Anglo-Saxon cleric and abbot of Hexham and Ripon. Wilfrid had journeyed to Rome in order to appeal the decision of the Council of Austerfield (702) to remove him as Bishop of York, and Stephanus comments that John and his clergy spoke Latin to the visitors but conversed among themselves in Greek: '*inter se graecizantes et subridentes*'.[65] Clearly the pope and his colleagues could function effectively in both languages, but, at least on this occasion, spoke Greek among themselves. It was this dual language proclivity with strong Greek roots that characterized Roman identity in 700. It permeated literary culture well into the early ninth century;[66] and, as we shall see, this is further reflected in the legacy of the city's material culture, for example, in the inscriptions, both painted and carved, which were placed in the church of Santa Maria Antiqua.[67] The Greek language also lies at the heart of the

---

[62] Santangeli Valenzani 2003; and Santangeli Valenzani 2004a. [63] Marazzi 1991.
[64] Sansterre 1983 I: 62–76. [65] *Vita Wilfridi*, cap. 53; ed. W. Levison, p. 247. [66] Noble 1985.
[67] Lucey 2007: 141–50.

formal development of papal ceremonial in the years around 700, with many of the words used in the *Ordo Romanus* I, the official protocol for papal processions and services during Easter week, constituting simple transliterations of Greek terms and phrases.[68] In their apparent obsession with the privileges accorded to various offices and ranks, the *Ordines Romani* also make extensive use of military terminology, indicating what John Romano has described as a blurring of the boundaries between the army and the church.[69]

But it was not only the use of the Greek language and terminology that linked the Roman church to its eastern counterparts. There was also a growing fusion of liturgical and other religious practices, for which the *Liber pontificalis* entry for Pope Sergius I (687–701) provides useful evidence. Sergius is an excellent example of the influx of hellenophones into the ranks of the senior Roman clergy in the second half of the seventh century. We are told that he was born in Sicily, to a father from the region of Antioch in Syria, and that he came to Rome in the time of Pope Adeodatus (672–6), where he became a distinguished chanter.[70] Sergius' pontificate was one of considerable activity in terms of papal efforts to restore and embellish Rome's churches: in addition to a new marble altar canopy and gifts of gold and silver liturgical implements to Santa Susanna (of which he had been titular priest prior to his election), he also provided new roof coverings for San Paolo fuori le mura, Sant'Euphemia, and Sant'Aurea at Ostia, arranging the acquisition of wooden beams from Calabria for this purpose (*LP* 86.12–13, ed. Duchesne I: 375–6). Pride of place in this regard went to Saint Peter's, where he repaired the leaking roof and the façade mosaic, installed new window coverings, and also provided an image of Peter and a censer, both made of gold, as well as six silver lighting fixtures, and various textiles for the high altar (*LP* 86.11, ed. Duchesne I: 374–5).

Pope Sergius' additions to the liturgy are perhaps even more interesting, however. Prompted by his discovery at Saint Peter's of a reliquary containing fragments of the wood of the True Cross, he revived its Roman celebration, but placed this on 14 September, the Feast of the Exaltation of the Cross developed earlier in the century at Constantinople.[71] But most

---

[68] Ekonomou 2007: 253–4. For the text, *OR* ed. Andrieu; English translation in Romano 2014: 329–48.
[69] Romano 2014: 77–86.
[70] *LP* 86.1, ed. Duchesne I: 371. It may be no coincidence that the reign of Adeodatus coincided with the first Arab invasions of Sicily, including the capture of Syracuse: see *LP* 79.3, ed. Duchesne I: 346. For the development of the papal *schola cantorum* at this time, see Page 2010: 243–59.
[71] *LP* 86.10; ed. Duchesne I: 374; see also Ó Carragáin 2013: 184–8.

significant in terms of what we shall see to be a growing Roman, and more specifically papal, emphasis on the cult of Mary, he is also credited with having promoted four major Marian feasts of eastern origin – the Annunciation (25 March), the Dormition (15 August), the Nativity of Mary (8 September), and the Presentation in the Temple (2 February) – by instituting litany processions on those days from Sant'Adriano in the Roman Forum to the principal Marian church, Santa Maria Maggiore (*LP* 86.14, ed. Duchesne I: 376, 381 note 43).[72] Devotion to the 'Mother of God' ('*theotokos*'), based largely on 'Byzantine' models of practice, would become one of the most defining characteristics of the eighth-century papacy,[73] but with the notable exception of Santa Maria Maggiore, all the numerous dedications of churches to Mary before 700 can be associated with non-papal donors, many of them related to the imperial administration or army, both of which regarded the '*theotokos*' as their special patron.[74]

Pope Sergius I is also important to this narrative for another reason. His defiance of the Emperor Justinian II, who requested papal subscription to the acts of the so-called Quinisext Council of 692,[75] containing several canons which went against actual Roman practice, and the subsequent Roman opposition to the imperial *spatharius* Zacharias who was sent to arrest him (*LP* 86.6–9, ed. Duchesne I: 372–4), marks the first significant step in a process which would lead ultimately to the permanent political rupture between the papacy and the 'Roman' emperors of Constantinople. This evolving separation will be one of the most significant threads in this study. But it will be my contention that, despite the political break between pope and emperor, exacerbated by increasing disputes over both economic revenues and religious doctrine, there was no immediate corresponding breach in cultural terms. The eighth century does not mark an indigenous 'Roman' revolution against all things 'Byzantine'. The popes of the first half of the eighth century, with one exception (Gregory II), remain of 'Eastern' background and culture, and overwhelming evidence for this is provided by the saints whose cults they promote, not to mention the churches and their decorations on which they spend their money. It is only in the middle of the century, when political events lead to a dramatic reinvention by the ruling and originally hellenophone élite of their constructed identity, that

---

[72] Although the *Liber pontificalis* states only that Sergius instituted processions on these feasts, there is no earlier evidence for the celebration of the Annunciation, Dormition and Nativity of Mary at Rome; see McKinnon 2000: 185–7.

[73] Ekonomou 2007: 257–64; and Dell'Acqua 2018: 32–3.   [74] Coates-Stephens 2006: 155–60.

[75] Also known as the Council in Trullo, *ODB*: 2126–7.

we encounter a new emphasis on the city of Rome as a physical entity of considerable antiquity, and a corresponding new focus on the historic origins of its Christian church. This will be manifested in the designation of Rome as the 'city of Romulus', in the promotion of the cults of specifically 'Roman' martyrs, and in the evolution of a new concept of temporal authority for the papacy based on the supposed 'Donation of Constantine'. We shall return to all these topics.

Central to an understanding of the transformation of Rome in the eighth century will be a grasp of the shifting notion of what constituted 'Roman' identity, a 'multi-layered and multifaceted concept' in the words of Clemens Gantner.[76] From the earliest days of the Empire, 'Romanness' was in many ways a political and legal construction, not based on any particular ethnicity or geographic origin. Already in the first century CE, for example, Roman citizenship could be claimed by a diasporic Jew from Tarsus named Saul/Paul. And this political understanding would survive through the course of the Middle Ages, uncluttered by cultural or linguistic 'baggage' apart from the weight of tradition. What we call today the 'Byzantine' Empire was always known officially in its own time as the 'Roman' Empire, and its emperors were similarly always styled as 'Roman'. In the eighth century, however, a new competing understanding of '*Romanitas*' arose, based geographically on the city of Rome, politically on the authority of the papacy, and theologically on the concept of Christian orthodoxy.[77] This new sense of 'Roman' identity appears mid-century, and is developed in the correspondence from popes Stephen II and Paul I to the Frankish king, Pippin III. And it is accompanied by a second and very much related transformation in nomenclature. If the term 'Roman' was no longer going to apply to the emperors in Constantinople, then how should they be referred to? The answer was 'Greeks', a concept also newly introduced into papal political discourse in the mid-eighth century.[78] Apparently it was not only the popes who embraced this new thinking: a similar understanding also infuses Paul the Deacon's *Historia Romana*, a continuation of Eutropius' *Breviarium* written at Benevento *circa* 770 for Adelperga, daughter of the Lombard king Desiderius and wife of Duke Arichis II. For Paul, the city of Rome, the papacy, and

---

[76] Gantner 2014b: 463. The various papers in McKitterick 2014 provide a useful introduction to the concept of 'being Roman after Rome'.
[77] Pohl 2014. See also the essays in Pohl *et al.* 2018.
[78] Gantner 2013b; and Gantner 2014a: 101–38. For a chart of the use of the term in papal correspondence with the Frankish kings, beginning with Stephen II but primarily under popes Paul I and Hadrian I, see Gantner 2014a: 122.

Christianity are fused together in a pre-ordained divine plan, with the emperors in Constantinople also now discredited as 'Greeks'.[79]

What it meant to be 'Roman' in the eighth century is a question to which as yet there is no complete answer. To some extent, of course, it depends on who is writing and using the term, and precisely when, although it seems likely that the inhabitants of both Rome and Constantinople would have self-identified in this fashion. In the context of the present study we shall focus on those who actually lived in Rome, regardless of bloodline.

Intriguingly, our sources provide us with the occasional tantalizing glimpse, for example, the passages in the *Liber pontificalis* which suggest there was a distinctive 'Roman' hairstyle and form of dress that could be used to distinguish 'Romans' from 'Lombards'. Hair and dress are among the most visible signs of claimed identity, particularly in instances where two different groups share a common physical space.[80] The first passage occurs in the *vita* of Pope Gregory III (731–41), although it is found only in manuscripts of the so-called Frankish recension, and thus is probably an interpolation added in or after the middle of the century for an audience north of the Alps. In describing the incursion into central Italy of the Lombard king, Liutprand, right up to the walls of the city of Rome, we are told that he 'shaved and clothed many noble Romans Lombard-fashion'.[81] What makes this notice of more than passing interest is that apparently this manifestation of identity could work in both directions, as demonstrated by a subsequent passage in the *vita* of Pope Hadrian I (772–95). When Charlemagne laid siege to Pavia in 774, the representatives of various other cities, including Rieti and Spoleto, the latter the seat of an important Lombard duchy, hastened to Rome to submit to the pope. We are told that they 'swore allegiance to the prince of the apostles and the holy pontiff, and were shaved Roman-fashion',[82] and the same phrase, 'Roman-fashion', is used in relation to hairstyle three more times in the following lines. What the specific difference might have been, and how one could move from one hairstyle to the other, in both instances apparently through an action of cutting or shaving, is nowhere documented and remains to be determined. For our purposes the important point is that there was an identifiable 'Roman' style of appearance, the adoption of which carried political

---

[79] Maskarinec 2013; and Costambeys 2018.   [80] Bartlett 1994: 45.
[81] LP 92.14, ed. Duchesne I: 420: '*multos nobiles de Romanis more Langobardorum totondit atque vestivit*'; English translation, Davis 2007: 27.
[82] LP 97.32, ed. Duchesne I: 495: '*in fide ipsius principis apostolorum atque praedicti sanctissimi pontifices iurantes, more Romanorum tonsorati sunt*'; English translation, Davis 2007: 137.

significance, although of course it may also have applied to the contemporary inhabitants of Constantinople. The evolving understanding of Roman identity will constitute an important theme of this study.

Most earlier treatments of the history of Rome in the eighth century have been constructed on the foundation of written documents, primarily but by no means exclusively the *Liber pontificalis* and papal correspondence, supplemented by snippets gleaned from non-Roman authors. These documents are exceptionally important and useful: the *Liber pontificalis*, for example, provides detailed summaries of the patronage activities of the various pontiffs,[83] particularly from Pope Hadrian I (772–95) onwards. But this record is far from complete. There are obvious omissions of some projects known to have had papal sponsors, for example, Pope Paul I's repainting of the church of Santa Maria Antiqua, not to mention the glaring absence in this document of activities undertaken by non-papal actors. It must always be remembered that these accounts were created for particular audiences at particular times and for specific purposes. The *Liber pontificalis* cannot be considered an impartial or comprehensive documentary record of people and events. It presents the official view of the Roman church, and contains distinct themes, including the role of the popes as the primary defenders of theological orthodoxy.[84]

In seeking to find a more holistic and balanced approach, my intention is not only to weave that thread with those of material culture and archaeology, in the process attempting to fashion a more accurate 'text', following the original etymology of that word, but in fact to organize the narrative around the latter, with a particular focus on buildings and their decoration: a 'history in art', with that last word obviously very loosely defined and taken to encompass the broad range of 'material culture' rather than any modern understanding of 'fine art'. It is often said that 'a picture is worth a thousand words', and an exploration of what those with money and power in Rome actually did with their assets may prove useful to our understanding of the age. This is not to suggest that buildings and images provide inherently less 'subjective' evidence than words, but simply that these do also constitute 'documents', and as such need to be brought into the conversation. Archaeological evidence is also useful, and in some ways perhaps more 'objective', at least in terms of its attempted interpretation, and thus it too must have a prominent place in the story. But the picture presented by any single class of document is inadequate on its own. If we had only the evidence of the Crypta Balbi excavation, for example, we

---

[83] Geertman 1975; and Barral i Altet 2016: 195–200.   [84] McKitterick 2016.

might conclude that civilized life in Rome virtually came to an end after 700, which is most certainly not the case. Churches such as Santa Maria Antiqua help to provide a more nuanced assessment.

The narrative that follows is mostly chronological and unabashedly 'hegemonic', given that primary 'agency' for the creation of material culture was in this period invested in the person of the pope and, on occasion, other members of his entourage, including both clergy and secular officials. The ordinary inhabitants of the city in the eighth century are conspicuous by their near total absence; indeed, archaeology has not yet even been able to identify the buildings in which they lived.[85] Thus the 'culture' being investigated is primarily that of the ecclesiastical and secular elite.

This was an inherently male collective, and as a consequence women are also missing from the story, their place in the ceremonial rituals set out in the *Ordines Romani* decidedly 'marginalized'.[86] To the best of my knowledge, and in contrast to the situation from the tenth century onwards, there is no evidence for 'matronage' in eighth-century Rome, perhaps because there is no apparent evidence for the active participation in the production of material culture by women patrons or even by female monastic communities, although presumably these must also have existed. Guy Ferrari found almost no secure evidence for female houses in the period between Pope Gregory I and the early ninth century, with the exception of the '*monasterium puellarum*' of Saint Eugenia, located outside the Porta Latina, built and endowed by Pope Hadrian I.[87] Most of the 'convents' included in his survey are first documented in the early ninth century, in the 807 donation list of Pope Leo III, and even then the gender of the community is not specified, but is adduced only from later sources. However, many of these institutions must have functioned for some length of time prior to receiving the pope's gifts and the general presence of nuns at Rome is attested, for example, by papal complaints to the Franks regarding the bad behaviour of the Lombards during the siege of Aistulf in 756.[88] And thus it could be the case that, as with domestic housing, evidence in the sphere of 'material culture' may exist but simply has not yet been found. Nor do we have much in the way of surviving images of eighth-century women, the exception that proves the rule being the figures of two unnamed members of the family of Theodotus in a chapel in the church of Santa Maria Antiqua. We shall encounter them later.[89]

---

[85] Coates-Stephens 1996; and Santangeli Valenzani 2004d. [86] Romano 2014: 100.
[87] Ferrari 1957: 132–3. *LP* 97.82; ed. Duchesne I: 510. [88] See Chapter 8.
[89] See Chapter 5. Very faint traces of two kneeling female figures have also been identified in the votive painting added to Sant'Adriano by the consul Constantine, dated by Giulia Bordi to the time of Pope Hadrian I; see Bordi 2011: 421 and fig. 10.

The sheer volume of evidence for eighth-century Rome in the realm of 'material culture' is remarkable, comprising work in a broad variety of media, from architecture and its decoration to sculpture, textiles, pottery, coins, and manuscripts. Some of it survives, mostly revealed through archaeological excavation, and much more is known through contemporary and post-medieval records. All will find some place in the 'text' that follows. The intention is to document a century of profound political change in the city, and also one of considerable activity and production, but nevertheless a remarkable element of continuity in the sphere of culture. It was certainly not a 'dark age'.

2 | Pope John VII *servus sanctae Mariae*

We are remarkably knowledgeable regarding the state of material culture in Rome at the dawn of the eighth century thanks to the excavations at the site of the Crypta Balbi, previously discussed, and the remains of two monuments for which the patronage of Pope John VII (705–7) is beyond any doubt. Together these produce a more complete picture for the years around 700 than we have for any other moment in the history of the early medieval city.

Although he served as pope for a scant '2 years, 7 months, 17 days', John VII, 'of Greek origin, son of Plato' (*'natione Grecus, de patre Platone'*) and 'a most learned man' (*'vir eruditissimus'*) in the words of his *Liber pontificalis* biographer, was responsible for a flurry of new papal building and artistic patronage. We are told that he constructed a new oratory inside Saint Peter's, repaired the church of Sant'Eugenia which needed a new roof, undertook work in two of the suburban cemeteries,[1] provided images to a variety of churches (names not specified), redecorated and provided church furnishings to the church of Santa Maria Antiqua in the Roman Forum, and built a new papal residence (*episcopium*) on the Palatine hill immediately above it. Nor does he seem to have been particularly modest about his involvement, for our author comments that anyone wanting to know what John looked like need only consider these images, and they 'will find his face depicted on them'.[2] It is difficult to know how to assess the tone of that remark, which is quite unprecedented. Was it intended as a mild criticism of papal hubris, or merely a statement of reality, reflecting a new interest in actual portrait likenesses?[3] As we shall see, John VII does seem to have been concerned with portrait images, and our two earliest Roman examples of the use of a so-called square halo to indicate such images both date to his pontificate.

---

[1] The *Liber pontificalis* names only the cemetery of Saints Marcellian and Mark, and that of Pope Damasus, neither of which has been identified. Although not mentioned here, it seems likely that the painted decorations in the entrance to the Catacomb of San Valentino on the Via Flaminia also date from his time: Osborne 1981a.

[2] *LP* 88.2, ed. Duchesne I: 385; trans. Davis 2010: 86.   [3] Ladner 1941a: 94.

Oratory in Saint Peter's

The oratory in Saint Peter's was located in the northeast corner of the basilica, set against the façade wall of the outer aisle, at the far right of those entering through the main portal from the atrium. We are told that it was dedicated to the holy mother of God,[4] that it was decorated with mosaics on which the pope 'expended ... a large amount of gold and silver', and that John was buried there on 18 October 707, in front of the altar. John's epitaph, the text of which is recorded in the Cambridge sylloge, affirms that the chapel was constructed with the specific intention that his body would lie 'at Mary's feet': '*Hic sibi constituit tumulum iussitque reponi/ Presul Iohannes sub pedibus domine*'.[5]

The enormous significance of his choice of location should not go unremarked. Saint Peter's was not a papal foundation, but rather a project of the Emperor Constantine (r. 306–37) and his family, and the basilica retained its imperial connections well into the early fifth century. About the year 400 the Emperor Honorius (r. 395–423) had established a dynastic mausoleum on its south flank, a structure which in the mid-eighth century would be converted into the Chapel of Santa Petronilla.[6] One of the first popes to have evinced an active interest in Saint Peter's was Leo I (440–61), and this has been linked to his energetic efforts to establish the authority of the bishops of Rome by emphasizing their direct line of descent from Peter, the 'rock' on which Jesus stated that he would establish his Church (Matthew 16:18).[7] Peter's relics must have constituted a potent locus of power and authority, but significant papal building activity in and around the basilica would have to wait until the time of Pope Symmachus (498–514) (*LP* 53.6–7, ed. Duchesne I: 261–2), no doubt, at least in part, because he was unable to reside at the Lateran during the period of the Laurentian schism. Whereas earlier pontiffs had chosen a variety of suburban cemeteries for their tombs, Leo I was also the first pope to be buried at Saint Peter's, ushering in 'une nouvelle époque' in the words of Jean-Charles Picard, that has continued with few exceptions through to the present day.[8] But the tombs of Leo and his successors were all situated outside

---

[4] An inscription, now lost, specified the dedication date as 21 March 706 (*LP* ed. Duchesne I: 386 note 2). In 706, March 21st was the Sunday preceding the Feast of the Annunciation (Ballardini 2011: 110 note 3).

[5] Silvagni 1943b: 111–12; van Dijk 1995: 115–16; and Ballardini 2011: 110.

[6] Johnson 1991; Johnson 2009: 167–74; Mackie 2003: 58–60; and McEvoy 2013. The conversion to the chapel of Santa Petronilla will be examined in Chapter 8.

[7] For Leo I's emphasis on Peter, and consequently on his shrine church: Ullmann 1960; Demacopoulos 2013: 39–72; Salzman 2013; and McKitterick 2013: 116–18.

[8] Picard 1969: 749. For the siting of early papal tombs, see also *LP*, ed. Duchesne I: clv–clix; Borgolte 1989: 49–126; De Blaauw 1994: 832–7; McKitterick 2013: 105–14; and De Blaauw 2016.

the church proper, in a *secretarium* located in the narthex, until the year 688 when Pope Sergius I (687–701) broke with precedent and moved Leo I's remains to a new resting place 'in a public part of the basilica as revealed to him', in the south transept.[9]

The precise rationale for this extraordinary action is not stated and remains unclear, but the relocation may have been related to the development of the south transept as the primary entrance into the basilica for pilgrims, who would have passed a series of monuments identified, accurately or otherwise, as the tombs of significant individuals associated with the history of the city of Rome (Hadrian, Romulus, Julius Caesar, the Honorian dynasty, and now also Pope Leo I) before descending into the semi-annular crypt to venerate the remains of the most famous 'Roman' of them all, Peter.[10] Pope Sergius I, and his immediate successor John VI (701–5), would also both be buried at Saint Peter's; and although the *Liber pontificalis* does not specify exactly where (*LP* 86.16, 87.3; ed. Duchesne I: 376, 383), there is nothing to suggest that these tombs were not in the usual place, in other words in the narthex or atrium, and not inside the basilica. Unfortunately, the texts of their epitaphs are not preserved. This leaves John VII as the first pontiff known with certainty to have elected burial inside the church, in a sumptuous oratory which he had constructed for that specific purpose. In doing so he established a new practice for the nature and location of papal tombs that a number of his eighth-century successors would emulate.[11] We shall meet them later.

John VII's funerary chapel was a lavish undertaking, and self-consciously so. His epitaph boasts: 'Previous squalor removed, he brought together splendour from all parts, so that posterity might be amazed by the lavishness, not with eagerness for ostentation . . . but with pious fervour for the Mother of God.'[12] Word of its 'most beautiful workmanship' even reached the ears of Bede in distant Northumbria, who includes mention of the 'chapel of the holy mother of God' ('*oratorium sanctae dei genetricis*') in his *De temporum ratione*.[13] The *Liber pontificalis* passage recording the dedication to the holy Mother of God is echoed in the surviving pieces of the original marble dedication inscription, where John is referred to as the '*servus*' (servant/

---

[9] *LP* 86.12, ed. Duchesne I: 375; trans. Davis 2010: 84.   [10] Osborne 2013.
[11] Herklotz 1985a: 85, 89.
[12] 'Hic decus omne loco, prisco squalore remoto,/ Contulit, ut stupeat prodiga posteritas,/ Non pompe studio . . . / Sed fervore pio pro genetricis Dei'; English translation from van Dijk 1995: 116.
[13] Bede, *De temporum ratione*, ed. Mommsen, 317; trans. Wallis: 234. This knowledge was most probably transmitted via a copy of the *Liber pontificalis*, a text from which Bede borrows liberally.

slave) of Mary.[14] The chapel would survive for some nine centuries, until its dismantling along with the demolition of the entrance wall itself in the year 1609, in order to make way for the new façade by Carlo Maderno that we see today; but much remains known about its nature and decoration, in large part from the detailed record made immediately prior to the demolition by the antiquarian and notary Giacomo Grimaldi, accompanied by drawings from the hand of Domenico Tasselli. Among the principal witnesses are a presentation copy made for Pope Paul V in 1620 (now Biblioteca Apostolica Vaticana [hereafter BAV], Barb. Lat. 2733) and an 'Album' preserved in the archive of the chapter of Saint Peter's (now BAV, Archivio del Capitolo di San Pietro A 64 ter).[15] But the *corpus* is extensive. The accuracy of the Grimaldi dossier can be verified from a handful of mosaic fragments that were carefully salvaged at the moment of the demolition, a number of which still survive.[16] The largest collection of these 'relics' is preserved in the Vatican grottoes, beneath the floor of the present church, but some have been dispersed much farther afield and can be found today in locations as diverse as the Roman church of Santa Maria in Cosmedin,[17] the Museo d'Arte Sacra at Orte,[18] the church of San Marco in Florence, and even the Pushkin Museum in Moscow.[19] In addition, there are six marble pilasters, carved with inhabited acanthus scrolls, whose original placement is recorded by Grimaldi: four on the north wall, and two on the east wall. Five of the six are classical *spolia* dating from the Severan period *circa* 200 CE,[20] and the last was newly carved in the early Middle Ages in imitation of the others.[21] All six survive and are again preserved today in the Vatican grottoes.

The techniques employed by John VII's mosaicists were first documented by Per Jonas Nordhagen,[22] based on a close examination of the surviving fragments, and his observations have been recently corroborated.[23]

---

[14] Silvagni 1943a I: pl. XII.6 a–b; Gray 1948: 49 no. 3; and Ballardini 2016c.

[15] For a complete survey of Grimaldi's prolific writings on a variety of topics, now widely dispersed among a number of libraries, see Grimaldi 1972: xvii–xviii; and for the accounts of the Oratory of John VII in particular, van Dijk 1995: 7–33; and van Dijk 2001: 306 note 9. The visual documentation is also catalogued by Waetzoldt (1964: 68–9).

[16] Principal bibliography: Nordhagen 1965; Tronzo 1987: 489–92; Andaloro 1989; De Blaauw 1994: 572–4; van Dijk 1995; van Dijk 2006; Ballardini 2011; Ballardini and Pogliani 2013; Ballardini 2016a; and Pogliani 2016a.

[17] Andaloro 2016b. [18] Andaloro, Anselmi, and D'Angelo 2017.

[19] Etinhof 1991: 29–30, and pl. IVa.

[20] Toynbee and Ward Perkins 1950: 21–2; and Kinney 2005: 30–1.

[21] Nordhagen 1969; van Dijk 1995: 97–103; Nobiloni 1999; Ballardini 2011: 95; and Ballardini and Pogliani 2013: 193–5.

[22] Nordhagen 1965: 145–53.

[23] Andaloro, Anselmi, and D'Angelo 2017. I am grateful to Carla D'Angelo for discussions regarding the fragment of the Adoration of the Magi in the course of a visit to Istituto Superiore

Tesserae of both marble and glass were employed, set deeply into plaster composed of lime and powdered marble. Perhaps as a result, losses have been few and, consequently, subsequent repairs and restorations minimal, mostly dating from the seventeenth century onwards. Marble tesserae in a variety of shades were used for flesh colours, with glass for more vibrant colours such as red, green and purple. A particular 'signature' of this workshop is the use of very small marble tesserae for hands and faces, a practice not previously encountered in mosaic decorations in Rome, while shading within the flesh areas is achieved through subtle variations in the colour of the marble. Another unprecedented aspect is the use of lines of transparent glass tesserae for the border outlines of those hands and faces, separating the areas composed of marble and glass tesserae. Gold tesserae are abundant, but there was no use of silver. Nordhagen noted the abrupt technical divergence from earlier seventh-century Roman mosaics – specifically those in Sant'Agnese fuori le mura, Santo Stefano Rotondo, and the San Venanzio chapel in the Lateran baptistery – all of which employed tesserae of a more uniform size, and lack the subtle modelling achieved by gradations of coloured marble.[24] By contrast, the characteristic features of John VII's mosaics have precise parallels in a number of contemporary or near-contemporary mosaics that pre-date the onset of Iconoclasm in the Byzantine heartland, including those in the church of Saint Demetrios at Thessaloniki, the church of the Dormition at Nicaea (Iznik), and a fragment preserved in the church of Saint Nicolaos in Istanbul.[25]

While it is known that the craft of mosaic continued to be practised throughout the course of the eighth century, and the *Liber pontificalis* records, for example, the commissions in that medium undertaken by Pope Paul I (757–67) in both San Silvestro in Capite and Saint Peter's (*LP* 95.5–6, ed. Duchesne I: 464–5), none of those works has survived. By the time we come to the mosaics commissioned by Leo III (795–816) and, especially, Paschal I (817–24), the techniques evident in the fragments from the Oratory in Saint Peter's have all but disappeared. Paschal's surviving apses in the churches of Santa Prassede, Santa Cecilia, and Santa Maria in Domnica, for example, use only large glass tesserae with

per la Conservazione e il Restauro on 17 May 2018, arranged by Claudia Bolgia. For an overview of the production of both raw glass and mosaic tesserae, as well as the craft of creating mosaics, see James 2017: 24–95.

[24] For a detailed analysis of the technique used in the Roman mosaics of the seventh century: Davis-Weyer 1989: 72–5. Both glass and stone tesserae had been employed at Sant'Agnese and Santo Stefano, a practice seen by Caecilia Davis-Weyer as 'nearly always an indication of byzantine craftsmanship or of some contact with it' (*ibid.*, 73). See also James 2017: 280–92.

[25] Nordhagen 1965: 158–62.

strong linear outlines.[26] The Oratory of John VII would thus appear to be a unique survival in Rome; and, given the similarities to contemporary mosaics from the eastern Mediterranean, Nordhagen concluded that 'the mosaics in the Oratory of John VII were executed by Byzantine artists'.[27] My only slight quibble with that statement is that this nomenclature may suggest that there existed a 'binary' construction of Rome-Byzantium at this time, something that this study will argue strongly against, at least for the early eighth century. Artists working in Rome in 700 were by definition 'Byzantine', in the sense that they worked within the traditions of the larger Mediterranean Christian world. Perhaps a clearer way of expressing it would be to say that John VII's mosaicists were trained in techniques not otherwise encountered in Roman examples, either earlier or later, and this probably suggests that they were not 'local' practitioners of the craft. And thus it comes as no surprise, as we are about to see, that strong similarities to the arts of the eastern Mediterranean may also be found in the subject matter.

The overall scheme of the decorations on the east wall of the chapel may be easily ascertained from the Grimaldi drawings (Fig. 2.1).[28] The central panel depicted the standing figure of Mary, richly dressed in the purple robes of a Byzantine empress, and wearing an imperial crown on her head, her hands raised and held outwards, palms forward, in the traditional position of prayer.[29] This specific iconography has no known precedents in Rome or Italy, and should probably be regarded as an import from Constantinople where special veneration was accorded to an icon of the Virgin *Blachernitissa*, who offered intercessory prayers on behalf of the Byzantine capital.[30] The growing interest in Marian iconography, documentable across the Empire in the late seventh century, has been linked to the ongoing theological debate concerning the nature of Christ, and most specifically with opposition to the theology of Monotheletism ('one will'), a concept that had been promoted as a compromise position between Chalcedonian

---

[26] *Ibid.*, 156.

[27] *Ibid.*, 165. James (2017: 290–1) argues for greater caution, given the lack of *comparanda* from contemporary Constantinople.

[28] Grimaldi 1972 comprises facsimile pages of a 'presentation copy' of his *Instrumenta autentica*, documenting parts of Old Saint Peter's, prepared in 1619–20 for Pope Paul V (now Vatican City, BAV, Barb. Lat. 2733), edited with transcriptions and annotations by Reto Niggl. Additional watercolour drawings by Domenico Tasselli are preserved in an 'Album' in the Vatican Library (Vatican City, BAV, Archivio del Capitolo di San Pietro A.64 ter), published by Waetzoldt 1964: 68–9 and figs 477–83. Pogliani (2006: 41, fig. 19; and 2016a, fig. 2) offers a useful integration of the surviving fragments into a Grimaldi drawing of the larger composition.

[29] van Dijk 1995: 44–7, 126–39.   [30] Nordhagen 2014.

Fig. 2.1. Saint Peter's, Rome: Oratory of John VII, as recorded by Giacomo Grimaldi, BAV, cod. Barb. Lat. 2732, fols 76v–77. © 2020 Biblioteca Apostolica Vaticana

'orthodoxy' (two natures) and Monophysitism (one nature) by the Emperor Heraclius in his *Ekthesis* of 638, but was then firmly opposed by the Lateran Council of 649 and the Sixth Ecumenical Council of 680–1. As the instrument of Christ's human incarnation, Mary was an obvious symbol of his two natures, simultaneously both human and divine.[31]

The person for whose soul Mary is praying, the donor, Pope John VII, stands at her right hand (the viewer's left), holding a model of a small building, presumably his chapel (Fig. 2.2).[32] His grave in the floor beneath would have been quite literally 'sub pedibus domin(a)e', in the words of his funerary epitaph. Of this composition the heads of both figures were salvaged in 1609 and have survived: Mary now functions as the altarpiece for the Ricci chapel in the church of San Marco in Florence, and the fragment

---

[31] Nordhagen 2018a; for Monotheletism, *ODB*: 1400–1.
[32] For the development of medieval donor portraits from classical antecedents, see Franses 2018: 47–62.

Fig. 2.2. Saint Peter's Rome: Oratory of John VII, mosaic fragment (heavily restored) depicting John VII, now in the Vatican grottoes.

with the head of the pope, unfortunately rather severely 'restored' in the modern period, is housed in the Vatican grottoes.[33] On the wall surrounding the central panel was an extensive narrative cycle of the life of Christ, organized in three horizontal registers, to be read from left to right and

---

[33] Pogliani 2016b. Nordhagen 1965: 127–9, cat. no. 2, notes that only the brow and the right eye are now original, and publishes a pre-restoration photograph of the head (pl. V).

top to bottom.[34] Here were depicted some fourteen scenes: the Annunciation to Mary, the Visitation, the Nativity (including the Annunciation to the Shepherds), the Adoration of the Magi, the Presentation in the Temple, Christ's Baptism, two miracle scenes (the healing of the man born blind, and of the paralytic), the Raising of Lazarus, the Entry into Jerusalem, the Last Supper, the Crucifixion, the Resurrection or Anastasis (Harrowing of Hell), and the Discovery of the Empty Tomb. Some scenes apparently included inscriptions in Latin, although unfortunately none are found in any of the surviving fragments. Grimaldi twice records captions identifying the figure of Joseph, as well as the words of the archangel Gabriel's salutation to Mary as stated in the New Testament, the latter constituting the earliest known example of this phenomenon in the Latin west, albeit with numerous Greek precedents.[35]

A number of other scenes also constitute iconographic 'firsts', but a discussion of those which have parallels in John VII's second surviving project will be postponed until that monument has been introduced. For the moment it will suffice to mention the episode of Christ's Nativity, located immediately above the figures of 'Maria *regina*' and the papal donor.[36] Here we find both the elements of a standard Nativity composition (Mary, Joseph, child lying in the manger) as well as the related story of the Annunciation to the Shepherds. But of considerable interest from an iconographical perspective are two additional details, not found in the canonical Biblical texts but deriving from more 'popular' or 'apocryphal' stories about the birth of Jesus. These are the bathing of the newly born infant by the two midwives, a fragment which is preserved today in the Vatican grottoes,[37] and the episode in which one of these women, Salome, extends her hand in hope of a cure.[38] She had refused to believe in Mary's virginity, and had suffered the withering of her hand as a punishment. The story of Salome, related in the apocryphal gospel known as the Protoevangelium of James 20:1-5,[39] was included in visual representations of the Nativity by at least the sixth century, when it may be found on a number of ivory plaques believed to have been carved in the eastern Mediterranean, including the throne of Archbishop Maximian in Ravenna.[40] However, its inclusion in Nativity scenes would not continue into the post-Iconoclastic period in Byzantium. By contrast, the detail of the Bathing of the Child, almost certainly derived from depictions in classical art of the births of gods and heroes, would become a standard

---

[34] van Dijk 1995: 47-77.   [35] van Dijk 1999.   [36] van Dijk 1995: 146-53.
[37] Pogliani 2016c.   [38] Nordhagen 1961.   [39] James 1924: 47.
[40] Nordhagen 1961: 335; for other examples, Weitzmann 1951: 55 note 57.

element of Nativity depictions in later Byzantine art. Nordhagen initially believed that the John VII mosaic constituted the first known instance of this latter motif, but it too can be documented as early as the mid-sixth century in the eastern Mediterranean, on a rock crystal in the Victoria and Albert Museum in London and a silver censer from the Sion treasure in Antalya.[41] Thus both details contribute to our understanding of the pervasive presence of Byzantine iconography in Rome immediately prior to the era of Iconoclasm. Perhaps even more intriguingly, the combination of the two episodes is paralleled in only two other known monuments. One of these is the Nativity scene in the entrance chamber of the Roman catacomb of San Valentino, which may also have been a project of Pope John VII;[42] and the second is a mural in the enigmatic church of Santa Maria *foris portas* at Castelseprio, situated in the foothills of the Alps northwest of Milan. The latter site also provides the only other known parallel for the conflation of the Nativity with the episode of the Annunciation to the Shepherds.[43] The date and patronage of the Castelseprio paintings still remain highly elusive, but one recent study has made a persuasive case for assigning them to the first half of the eighth century, in part due to strong similarities to the work commissioned by Pope John VII in Rome.[44] Although this combination is not known from any surviving examples in contemporary Byzantium, it should be noted that there are no surviving Nativity depictions known in the Greek East from this time, so it is an argument *ex silentio* and no conclusions may be drawn.

Perhaps the most astonishing aspect of the decorations is the central image in which the pope offers the model of the chapel to Mary, who responds in turn with her prayers for his salvation.[45] The device surrounding John's head is often misidentified as a 'square halo', based on its visual appearance, but in the early Middle Ages it was not intended to convey any indication of the pope's character or possible qualification for sanctity. Rather, it signifies that this head is a portrait,[46] and it is intended to represent a wooden portrait panel of the type commonly found in the eastern Mediterranean, particularly in funerary contexts: Egyptian 'mummy portraits', for example. And it is in the same geographical region that we find its first appearance in the sphere of monumental church

---

[41] For the rock crystal, Beckwith 1975; for the Sion treasure, Dodd 1980 and *ODB*: 1905–6.
[42] Osborne 1981a.   [43] Nordhagen 1972a.
[44] Rossi 2010; for a considerably later dating *circa* 900, based in part on dendrochronology, see Mitchell and Leal 2013.
[45] Ladner 1941a: 88–95; and Nordhagen 1965: 121–9.
[46] See de Jerphanion 1913; Ladner 1941b; and Osborne 1979.

decoration, in the mid-sixth-century apse mosaic of the Monastery of Saint Catherine at Mount Sinai, where the two patrons – Longinos *higoumenos* (abbot) and the deacon John – are shown with a similar device framing their heads.[47] There is no evidence for the use of this motif in Rome before the time of John VII, although it would be ubiquitous in portrait images in the city in the two centuries to follow.[48] We shall encounter it on numerous occasions.

This may be the first time that Mary had been depicted in the monumental decoration of a Roman church without her son also being present in some capacity, usually as an infant seated on her lap.[49] The closest precedent is the San Venanzio chapel in the Lateran baptistery, dating from the decade of the 640s, where an 'orant' Mary appears centrally in the apse,[50] but here the figure of Christ appears in the heavens directly above her, so the parallel is far from exact. And John VII's Oratory is certainly the first, and indeed perhaps only, occasion in Roman church decoration where she alone receives the donor's gift.[51]

This is also the first in a series of eighth-century representations of Mary in which she is shown dressed in the robes and crown of a Byzantine empress, and we shall encounter this iconography of Mary in her role as 'queen of heaven', or 'Maria *regina*', on a number of occasions. It can be documented, for example, in the churches of Santa Maria Antiqua (thrice, including the example from which the term 'Maria *regina*' is derived), Santa Maria in Trastevere, San Clemente, San Lorenzo fuori le mura, and Santa Susanna. Clearly it found favour among papal and other patrons of this time, many of whom, like John VII, professed a particular devotion to the 'Mother of God' or '*theotokos*' (in Greek).

The origins of this imagery have been the subject of considerable debate since an early study by Marion Lawrence made the case for its development in western Europe, while recognizing the influence of the portraits of empresses found on imperial coinage.[52] John VII's mosaic in Saint Peter's was not the first Roman instance of this Marian iconography.

---

[47] Forsyth and Weitzmann 1973: pls CXX, CXXI.   [48] Ladner 1984: 310–18.

[49] An early medieval icon of Mary, formerly in San Sisto Vecchio and now in Santa Maria del Rosario, and variously dated between the seventh and ninth centuries, also depicts her alone in an attitude of prayer, but facing sideways. Its origin remains unknown, although Roman tradition maintains that it came from Constantinople; and its presence in Rome is only attested much later. See Amato 1988: 41–9; Andaloro 2002: 723–4; and Wolf 2005: 39–41.

[50] Ladner 1941a: 81–5; Mackie 1996; and Mackie 2003: 212–30.

[51] For the imagery of donor presentations in Byzantine art: Brubaker 2010, and Franses 2018.

[52] Lawrence 1924–5. The subsequent literature on the 'Maria *regina*' iconography is extensive, but see especially Nilgen 1981; Osborne 1981b; Andaloro 1986; Stroll 1997; Osborne 2003: 138–42; Osborne 2008; Lidova 2016; and Lidova 2017.

Priority in that regard goes to an image in the church of Santa Maria Antiqua in the Roman Forum, where excavations undertaken by Giacomo Boni beginning in 1900 revealed an enormous quantity of early medieval painting, much of it fragmentary. We shall return to this church on multiple occasions, both later in this chapter and in those to follow. There, on the wall to the right of the apse, dubbed the 'palimpsest wall' because the same surface was repainted on numerous occasions, we find the remains of an enthroned Mary with the Christ child on her lap (Pl. 1 and Fig. 2.3).[53] Originally, the central figures were flanked by angels offering crowns, but only one now survives, on the viewer's right, its counterpart on the left having been destroyed when the apse was carved into the thickness of the structure's end wall. This suggests that the 'Maria *regina*' level must have been painted prior to the formal conversion of the existing imperial-era edifice into a basilica church, a process which is likely to have prompted the addition of the apse; and an approximate date for the image in the first half of the sixth century is now generally accepted, although there is still a lively debate about the specifics of the patronage. Does the mural pre- or post-date the reconquest of Italy by the armies of the Emperor Justinian from the Ostrogoths? Both regimes made use of the imperial palace on the Palatine hill, to which the church of Santa Maria Antiqua is connected by a ramp. We may never know the answer to that question, although a post-conquest date may make better contextual sense,[54] and the imagery exudes imperial resonances; but in either case the patronage is most unlikely to have been papal, and consequently the theme may not have originated in Rome. Indeed, external evidence strongly suggests an initial origin for this iconographic type in Constantinople, in association with the imperial court. The regalia of the empress became formalized in Byzantium over the course of the fifth and early sixth centuries,[55] and this is also the moment when the cult of Mary began to be formally promoted by the court at the Constantinopolitan shrine churches of Blachernai and Chalkoprateia.[56] At precisely the same time, the concept of Mary as queen of heaven made its first appearance in a wide variety of Byzantine texts, including both the famous *Akathistos* hymn and Corippus' panegyric poem celebrating the accession of the Emperor Justin II in 565 CE.[57]

---

[53] Rushforth 1902: 67; De Grüneisen 1911: 136–40; Tea 1937: 309–11; Nordhagen 1962: 56–7; Andaloro 2004; and Lidova 2017.
[54] Bordi 2014; for an opposing view, that it belongs to the earlier Ostrogothic period, see Lidova 2017.
[55] Angelova 2004.   [56] Mango 2000.   [57] Cameron 1978: 84–6.

Fig. 2.3. Santa Maria Antiqua, Rome: palimpsest wall detail of 'Maria *regina*'.

Contemporary with the architectural conversion of the building, or very shortly thereafter, the now reduced 'palimpsest' wall was repainted with a new subject, the Annunciation to Mary by the archangel Gabriel. Thus, while there is evidence for the early appearance of the 'Maria *regina*' theme in Rome, that specific example was probably not visible beyond the late sixth century, and hence could not have functioned as a model for subsequent Roman depictions of this theme. Despite his close association with Santa Maria Antiqua, John VII's inspiration must necessarily have come from elsewhere.[58]

Complicating the issue of a Roman or Constantinopolitan origin is a mosaic from a chapel inserted into a passageway of the amphitheatre at Durrës (ancient Dyrrachium) in Albania, site of the western terminus of the Via Egnatia, the Roman road which led from the Adriatic coast across the Balkans to Thessaloniki and then on to Constantinople. This chapel has two mosaic panels on the south wall: one depicting Saint Stephen (identified in Greek), and another depicting a central figure with imperial headgear, flanked by angels and two diminutive donors. Both the identity of the central figure and the date of the mosaics are problematic. Although published initially as an image of Christ, most subsequent observers have suggested that it depicts a 'Maria *regina*'; and have proposed dates ranging from the sixth to the eleventh centuries.[59]

On the issue of the dating we may now be on somewhat firmer ground, as a recent technical analysis of the mosaic tesserae provides much useful information.[60] This reveals a number of close similarities to the mosaic fragments from John VII's oratory in Saint Peter's: for example, the use of transparent green and brown glass for the gold tesserae, and the use of much smaller stone tesserae for areas of flesh, including coloured stone for the areas of shading.[61] But perhaps most interesting is the use of natron (soda) instead of plant ash as the fluxing agent in the manufacturing process. Natron (sodium carbonate decahydrate), for which the primary source was the Wadi el-Natrun between Cairo and Alexandria, from which the name derives, was used in Roman, Byzantine, and Islamic glass until the eighth century, at which point the supply seems to have been discontinued.[62] Thereafter, plant ash was employed. This demonstrates that the glass employed in the tesserae used at Durrës was made sometime prior to the start of the ninth century, and consequently a later date for the mosaic can be all but ruled out.[63] Clearly the

[58] The inherent irony of John VII not being aware that a 'Maria *regina*' already existed in his favourite church has been noted by Valentino Pace (2015: 481).
[59] Thierry 1968; Cormack 1985: 84–5; Andaloro 1986; Pace 2003: 96–110; Bowes and Mitchell 2009; and James 2017: 276–8.
[60] Neri 2017.
[61] For a similar technical analysis of the John VII fragment depicting the figure of Mary from the scene of the Nativity: Andaloro, Anselmi, and D'Angelo 2017.
[62] Whitehouse 2002; and James 2017: 25–6.
[63] Bowes and Mitchell (2009) proposed a probable date after the end of Byzantine Iconoclasm in 843. Supporting their view, Neri suggests that the mosaic tesserae could have been reused at that time, but there is no obvious physical evidence for this, and parallels to mosaics of the

theme was not exclusive to Rome, and its reappearance there in the time of John VII may well have been a reimportation from the eastern Mediterranean, as was so much else of the imagery in the monuments associated with his patronage.

And finally it should be noted that there were also mosaics on the north wall of John VII's oratory, depicting scenes from the lives and martyrdoms of Saints Peter and Paul, of which only a single heavily restored fragment, depicting Saint Peter from the episode in which he was shown preaching at Rome, remains today in the Vatican grottoes.[64] But opinion is mixed regarding their date. The traditional attribution to John VII was challenged by William Tronzo, although subsequently defended by Ann van Dijk.[65] While the issue is difficult to judge on the basis of seventeenth-century copies, the two cycles seem to have employed vastly different scales for their images, suggesting that they may not be contemporary.[66] It must also be said that the subject matter would have been quite unusual at such an early date, as would the crenellated towers used to divide the individual scenes. The most recent analysis proposes the late twelfth or early thirteenth century, perhaps in conjunction with the transformation of the Oratory of John VII to house the relic of the 'Veronica'.[67] But the question remains open.

Santa Maria Antiqua

John VII's intense devotion to the 'holy mother of God' ('*sancta Dei genetrix*') is also attested in his other important project which has partially survived. The pope's *Liber pontificalis* biographer relates that 'he adorned with painting the basilica of the holy mother of God which is called Antiqua, and there he built a new ambo, and above the same church an Episcopium which he wanted to build for his own use, and there his life and the time of his pontificate came to an end'.[68] The church of Santa Maria Antiqua is situated on the edge of the Roman Forum, between the Palatine hill and the Temple of Castor and Pollux. Prior to Gacomo Boni's 1900

---

seventh century in the church of Saint Demetrios at Thessaloniki are compelling; see Cormack 1985: 78–94.

[64] Nordhagen 1965: 141–2 cat. no. 8.   [65] Tronzo 1987: 489–92; and van Dijk 2001.
[66] Ballardini and Pogliani 2013: 206–8.   [67] Queijo 2012.
[68] 'Basilicam itaque sanctae Dei genetricis qui Antiqua vocatur pictura decoravit, illicque ambonem noviter fecit et super eandem ecclesiam episcopium quantum ad se construere maluit, illicque pontificati sui tempus vitam finivit.' (*LP* 88.2, ed. Duchesne I: 385); trans., Davis 2010: 86.

excavations in the Forum, it was known only by name, and in the late nineteenth century there had been a lively debate about its exact location, based on mentions in sources such as the *Liber pontificalis* and the Einsiedeln Itinerary.[69] Based on his analysis of the latter text, Rodolfo Lanciani hypothesized that it was set against the northwest slope of the Palatine hill, in the area then occupied by the much later church of Santa Maria Liberatrice, whereas Louis Duchesne insisted that it lay closer to Santa Maria Nova (now usually called Santa Francesca Romana).[70]

The discovery on 20 December 1900 of a painted inscription referring to 'the holy mother of God and ever virgin Mary called *Antiqua*' (to be discussed in Chapter 5), put that issue to rest once and for all.[71] On this matter, Lanciani had been right and Duchesne wrong.[72] And only a few days later (23 December) the excavators made a second remarkable discovery: the platform of the very *ambo* cited in John VII's *Liber pontificalis* entry.

This octagonal piece of white marble, 130 x 73 cm, has two parallel sides that are elongated, presumably the location of the access stairways, and three shorter sides at each end which bear inscriptions, one in Latin and one in Greek, proclaiming John to be the '*servus sanctae Mariae*' and '*doulou tes theotokou*' (Fig. 2.4).[73] The inscriptions are not quite identical, as the Greek is set in the genitive case, presumably implying that the pulpit is the gift '*of* John', whereas the Latin is in the nominative and refers to Mary by name. Slightly less care seems to have been taken with the latter: for example, the letters 'M' and 'R' of '*Mariae*' are run together, and the intervening 'A' is missing, although this may simply reflect the need to fit the expression into the space available. Both the phraseology employed and the technique of removing the stone around the letter forms, so that they appear in relief, raised from the base as opposed to being cut into its surface, are mirrored in the bilingual dedication inscription which has survived from the pope's

---

[69] The 'Einsiedeln Itinerary' comprises a series of descriptions of routes across the city of Rome, noting both ancient and contemporary monuments, and a sylloge of inscriptions. The text is preserved in a single ninth-century manuscript in Switzerland: Einsiedeln, Bibliotheca Monasterii Ordinis Sancti Benedicti, MS 326, fols 67v–86r (*CT* II: 155–207; Walser 1987: 14–63, 143–58; CCSL 175: 329–43). Internal evidence suggests a composition date at the end of the eighth century: for analysis, see Lanciani 1891; Walser 1987; Osborne 1996; Bauer 1997; Bellardini and Delogu 2002; and Del Lungo 2004.

[70] Lanciani 1891: 63–7; Duchesne 1897; Tea 1937: 3; and Osborne 1987: 187–8.

[71] Rushforth 1902: 3.

[72] For Boni's excavation and the intellectual fervour it stimulated, see Augenti 2000; Morganti 2004; Gasbarri 2015: 204–30; and Fortini and Bordi 2016.

[73] Rushforth 1902: 89–91; Silvagni 1943a I: pl. XII.4–5; Gray 1948: 48–49 no. 2; and Ballardini 2016b. For an attempt to reconstruct the original appearance: Bellini and Brunori 2016. For the larger context of early medieval pulpits in Rome: Rossi 1993.

Fig. 2.4. Santa Maria Antiqua, Rome: *ambo* of Pope John VII (705–7).

chapel in Old Saint Peter's,[74] but have no other parallels in early medieval Rome. Curiously, the Greek letters are more deeply cut than the Latin ones. This technique of carving inscriptions '*a sbalzo*' is, however, known from inscriptions in both Constantinople and Syria and on this basis Antonella Ballardini has suggested that the *ambo* is the work of Byzantine craftsmen ('*maestranze bizantine*').[75] Traces of pigment imply that the stone was originally painted, with the white letters set against a red background. Also found in the excavation were fragments of an arched structure (*ciborium*?), although its original placement in the church is uncertain.[76]

As noted previously, the church of Santa Maria Antiqua (Fig. 2.5) was inserted into an existing imperial building. This structure, whose precise original function is also unknown, was connected by means of a long ramp, still in existence, to the *Domus Tiberiana* palace on the Palatine hill above,[77] and is likely to have served some purpose related to that connection.[78] While the main administrative centre and the seat of the imperial exarch remained situated at Ravenna, Rome and its region were governed by a *dux*, and the main area of the imperial palace on the Palatine, the *Domus Augustana*, was maintained at least through to the end of the seventh century. It is thought to have been used by Emperor Constans II when he visited the city in 663, and is also the find-spot for a seal of the exarch Paul (723–6).[79] Indeed, John VII's

---

[74] Silvagni 1943a I: pl. XII.6 a–b; Gray 1948: 49 no. 3; and Ballardini 2016c.
[75] Ballardini 2016b: 230. [76] Severini 2015. [77] *LTUR* II: 189–97.
[78] For the theory that it functioned as a ceremonial entrance or 'vestibule' to the imperial palace: Knipp 2020.
[79] Bartoli 1947–9; Augenti 1996: 46–8; and Coates-Stephens 2017: 204–9.

Santa Maria Antiqua 39

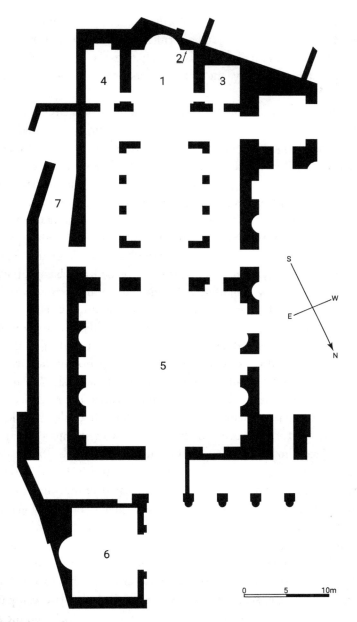

Santa Maria Antiqua, plan
(re-drawn by Michelle Duong)

1. presbytery
2. palimpsest wall
3. Chapel of the Holy Physicians
4. Theodotus chapel
5. atrium
6. Oratory of the Forty Martyrs
7. Palatine ramp

Fig. 2.5. Santa Maria Antiqua, Rome: ground plan (drawing by Michelle Duong).

father, Plato, '*vir illustris cura palatii urbis Romae*', had been its official caretaker, as we learn from his epitaph formerly located in the nearby church of Sant'Anastasia,[80] and this may possibly help to explain the pope's decision to leave the Lateran and move the papal residence to a new '*episcopium*' located here.[81]

Given the obvious political associations of a papal residence on the Palatine, home of the emperors for many centuries, it would be enormously useful to know more about the motives for John VII's undertaking in this regard. Was it a deliberate statement of claim to the mantle of the Caesars, or an effort instigated by the imperial authorities to bring the pope closer to their own seat of authority in the *Domus Augustana*, or simply a move to the area of the city that John knew best from his youth? Unfortunately, that question can probably never be answered fully, although it would be difficult to disagree with Andrea Augenti's contention that it was 'certainly a political choice'.[82] Gregor Kalas has proposed that John VII's activities should also be viewed within a tradition in Late Antiquity of the refurbishment and re-use of buildings in the city centre.[83]

Recent archaeology in the area of the Domus Tiberiana, at the upper end of the ramp, suggests that a period of abandonment starting in the second half of the fifth century was followed by a reoccupation in the early Middle Ages, including new structures built with reused materials.[84] Could this be the *episcopium* mentioned in the *Liber pontificalis*? The evidence is tantalizing, but ultimately inconclusive; and the same may also be said for the nineteenth-century discovery of two bricks, with stamps bearing John's name, adjacent to Santa Maria Antiqua in the area of the *Atrium Vestae*.[85] If the move were both unforced and deliberate, then it should be seen as an important early step on the road that would lead over the following decades to the emergence of the new papal state, given that the Palatine was virtually synonymous with the concept of political authority.

Both the nature and the date of the 'conversion' of the structure in the Roman Forum into the church of Santa Maria Antiqua remain the subject of considerable debate.[86] Clearly there was already some sort of Christian presence at the site, since there is evidence for at least two campaigns of painted decoration prior to the structural modifications,[87] and the second

---

[80] For the epitaphs of Plato, and John's mother, Blatta, see *LP*, ed. Duchesne I: 386, note 1; and De Rossi 1857–88 II: 442, nos. 152, 153. For English translations, Kalas 2018: 201–2.

[81] *LP* 88.2, ed. Duchesne I: 385; and Augenti 1996: 56–60.   [82] Augenti 1996: 58.

[83] Kalas 2018.   [84] Carboni 2016; and Spera 2016: 396–408.

[85] Lanciani 1883: 494–5; and Augenti 1996: 56–8, who reports that his search for the bricks in the collections of the Soprintendenza Archeologica di Roma was unsuccessful.

[86] For the most recent analysis: Morganti 2016.   [87] Bordi 2014.

of these included the image of the 'Maria *regina*' on the 'palimpsest wall' (Fig. 2.3), previously discussed. As we have seen, the image of Mary as empress, flanked by angels offering crowns, was partially destroyed when an apse was cut into the thickness of the end wall, necessitating a new campaign of decoration on the reduced section of wall that remained intact. Richard Krautheimer has also linked this transformation process with the replacement of the earlier brick piers by granite columns;[88] but the evidence of possible coins of Emperor Justin II (565–78), supposedly found under the base of one of the replacement columns in the course of Boni's excavation and later published by Eva Tea, used to date the moment of structural conversion, is highly problematic. Such coins may in fact have never existed, and even if they did, they may not have been from the reign of this emperor nor indeed related to the process of structural alteration.[89]

The architectural repurposing is nowhere mentioned in the *Liber pontificalis*, but this is hardly a surprise. That text was created to serve as a record of papal actions and aspirations, and naturally gives priority to their accomplishments; but a church connected to the imperial palace is unlikely to have been a papal project at a time when the popes exerted no authority over this space. On the other hand, as previously noted, churches dedicated to Mary were frequently sponsored by the Byzantine administration and imperial army, for whom she functioned as a special patron.[90] Already in the early seventh century, relics of her clothing (robe and girdle), paraded on the city walls of Constantinople, were credited with having saved the imperial capital when it was attacked by the Avars.[91]

There is also the question of whether the site of Santa Maria Antiqua could have functioned as a 'church' even before receiving any structural modifications.[92] In that regard it would be very helpful to know how the epithet '*antiqua*' was understood in early medieval Rome, but that too is an issue awaiting resolution.[93] One promising possibility would seem to be an early icon of Mary, referred to in the *Liber pontificalis* life of Pope Gregory III (731–41) as an 'ancient image of the holy mother of God' ('*imaginem sancte Dei genetricis antiquam*'), for which the pope provided a silver casing weighing 50 pounds (*LP* 92.10, ed. Duchesne I: 419), although the church which housed this image is not specified. Santa Maria Antiqua probably did possess an early icon of the Madonna and Child, transferred to Santa Maria Nova in the mid-ninth century when the interior of the older structure may have been at least partially abandoned. It remains on

---

[88] *CBCR* II: 254–5. [89] Paribeni 2011. [90] Coates-Stephens 2006: 155–60. [91] Baynes 1949.
[92] Pace 2004: 140–2. [93] For a preliminary exploration of the issue, see Rushforth 1902: 5–6.

display in the sacristy of the latter church today.[94] Was this the icon mentioned in the biography of Gregory III? Quite possibly,[95] but for the moment there is no definitive proof, and any possible link to the name of the church has been dismissed by Beat Brenk.[96]

What makes Santa Maria Antiqua so important is the vast quantity of wall painting which the site preserves, including fragments from numerous campaigns of decoration spanning multiple centuries. The director of the recent conservation campaign, Werner Schmid, has calculated that the painted surfaces totalled some 332 m^2.[97] This importance was recognized from the moment of the excavation in 1900, and it was not without reason that Gordon Rushforth described the find as 'the Sistine Chapel of the eighth century'.[98] Rather sadly, however, most of the painting survives today in much less than perfect condition. There are many areas where the plaster has simply fallen from the wall, and even where it does survive some of the murals have experienced significant damage due to water seepage, with the result that the subject matter is not always intelligible.[99] But enough remains to provide an enormous quantity of data about church decoration in early medieval Rome, including topics as varied as iconography, style, patronage, and function (both for the performance of the liturgy and private devotional practice); and these can be supplemented by a few fragments of painted plaster preserved in the deposit of the Soprintendenza Speciale per il Colosseo e l'area archeologica centrale,[100] and possibly one spectacular medallion depicting Saint Agatha now housed in a private collection.[101] The descriptions which follow will also make frequent reference to the watercoloured photographs published in 1916 by Joseph Wilpert, as these constitute a remarkable and unparalleled visual record of great accuracy.[102] We are fortunate to have such excellent documentation, for as Wilpert wrote on an earlier occasion: 'On Santa Maria Antiqua … much has already been written and discussed; nevertheless, there still remains much to say.'[103] Those words still ring true more than a century later.

---

[94] Cellini 1950; Ansaldi 1953; Andaloro 2016a; and Andaloro 2020. The most recent technical examination confirms an earlier analysis that only the heads of Mary and her infant son are original, painted in encaustic and incorporated into a late medieval reworking. The wooden support can be dated to the early fifteenth century: see Soavi *et al.* 2016.

[95] Curzi 2018: 10.   [96] Brenk 2010: 105–6; see also Wolf 2005: 27–8.   [97] Schmid 2020.

[98] In *The Times* of London, 9 January 1901, p. 13; see Wiseman 1985–6: 140.

[99] Schmid 2016 and Schmid 2020.   [100] Serlorenzi 2016; and Bordi 2016c.

[101] Bertelli 2016.   [102] Nordhagen 1985; Bordi 2009a; and Bordi 2009b: 458–60.

[103] 'Su S. Maria Antiqua … molto si è già scritto e discusso. Ciò non ostante resta ancora molto a dire' (Wilpert 1905: 578).

The scaffolding erected in the earlier years of the current century, to facilitate the conservation campaign directed by Werner Schmid, has also permitted a close observation of the paintings, facilitating new insights concerning workshop practices and the use of specific pigments.[104] For example, the plaster used in the decorative campaigns of the mid-seventh century and under John VII was found to contain significant amounts of organic material, including strands of straw in lengths of 4–5 cm, a practice commonly found in Byzantine painting and thought to have been intended to slow the process of drying and hardening. By contrast, no vegetal fibre was found in the plaster of the sixth-century 'Maria *regina*'.[105] For the most part, the painting is true *fresco*, and even retains the occasional imprints of the painters' fingers, embedded in the plaster before it dried.

The early phases of painting in Santa Maria Antiqua fall outside the chronological scope of this study, and thus need not concern us unduly. It shall suffice to mention that the process of architectural conversion to create something more closely resembling a basilica apparently included a new campaign of decoration in the area of the sanctuary, with evidence for scenes from the life of Christ and a stucco frieze,[106] and a repainting of the 'palimpsest wall' with an image of the Annunciation (Pl. 1).[107] Another major campaign of painting would occur in the middle of the seventh century, probably in the aftermath of the Lateran Council of 649, although the precise relationship remains a subject of continuing discussion.[108] This included the depiction of four theologians (Pope Leo I, Gregory of Nazianzus, Basil, and John Chrysostom), two on each side of the arch framing the apse, all holding scrolls bearing texts in Greek (Fig. 2.6).[109]

We are on much firmer ground with John VII's redecoration in the first decade of the eighth century, as recorded in the *Liber pontificalis* which now mentions Santa Maria Antiqua for the first time. The scope of John VII's project was substantial, and has been meticulously documented by Per Jonas

---

[104] Schmid and Valentini 2013; Schmid 2016; Schmid 2020; and Pogliani, Pelosi, and Agresti 2020.
[105] Schmid 2014: 439.
[106] Nordhagen 1978: 101–3. Nordhagen (1962: 61) dates the stucco to the mid-seventh century, but Knipp (2012) prefers to place it earlier, and presents close parallels for the design in sixth-century Coptic art.
[107] Tea 1937: 311; Nordhagen 1962: 57–8; and Nordhagen 1978: 93–5. Pigment analysis suggests that this Annunciation was painted by the same artist or workshop also responsible for the 'icon' of Saint Anne on the right wall of the sanctuary, spared in John VII's campaign of redecoration: see Pogliani, Pelosi and Agresti 2020.
[108] See comment of Catherine Cubitt in Price 2014: 81 note 55, and Price 2020, who make a persuasive case for the pontificate of Pope Vitalian (657–72).
[109] Rushforth 1902: 67–73; De Grüneisen 1911: 140; Wilpert 1916: 662–3 and pl. 142; Tea 1937: 311–13; Nordhagen 1962: 58–60; and Nordhagen 1978: 97–100.

Fig. 2.6. Santa Maria Antiqua, Rome: right side of apsidal arch wall with figures of Saints Basil and John Chrysostom.

Nordhagen.[110] It encompassed the sanctuary and apsidal arch, the small chapel to the right of the sanctuary (the so-called Chapel of the Holy Physicians), the low screens ('*transennae*') which organized the central space of the church for purposes of the liturgy, and numerous other walls and piers, in addition to parts of the atrium and the adjacent Chapel of the Forty Martyrs of Sebaste (see Fig. 2.5 for ground plan). In most instances the earlier murals were gouged with a pick in order to roughen their surfaces, presumably in an attempt to permit better adhesion of the new plaster; but in some instances, the earlier decorations appear to have been deliberately spared, for example, the figure of Saint Anne holding the infant Mary, on the right wall of the sanctuary (Pl. 2). Nordhagen makes a compelling case that this was done to allow these 'fresco-icons' to be incorporated into John VII's new programme.[111]

---

[110] Nordhagen 1968; and Nordhagen 2017. For a concise historiographical survey of thinking about the Santa Maria Antiqua murals from their discovery in 1900 through to the 1960s, see Nordhagen 1968: 3–12.

[111] Nordhagen 1968: 87–90; and Nordhagen 2018b.

In attempting to link the murals in various parts of the site to John VII's campaign, Nordhagen has employed a number of techniques. But his most important 'scholarly weapon'[112] has been the palaeography of the painted inscriptions; and fortunately in that regard the redecoration undertaken in the early eighth century is exceptionally 'letter heavy' in two languages. Both Latin and Greek inscriptions reveal solid squarish letters, a display script seemingly intended for easy legibility and unlike any others found in early medieval Rome. Many letter forms are embellished elegantly with hooks and serifs.[113] Guglielmo Cavallo's analysis of the Greek inscriptions led him to suggest the inspiration of Constantinopolitan, and more specifically imperial, models.[114] But that may be a stretch. What we can say with some certainty is that John VII's programme included a lot of words, and thus presumably assumed a literate audience.

We shall begin with the end wall of the sanctuary (Figs. 2.7, 2.8).[115] The large expanse situated above the apse was painted with an enormous Adoration of the Crucified Christ, first seen and recorded in May 1702 by Francesco Valesio in his *Diario di Roma* when the apse of the church was briefly exposed. Valesio records the excavation behind the later church of Santa Maria Liberatrice, intended to find reusable blocks of marble, and includes a watercolour view. Apparently the murals remained visible for almost three months, prompting considerable interest and throngs of curious visitors: '*Vi fu numeroso concorso di popolo per vederla.*'[116] At the same time, other watercolour copies and notes were made by Domenico Passionei, but these were never published and have only just recently come to scholarly attention.[117] Of this composition, only the right side now remains partially intact.

Rushforth was the first modern observer to note that 'The figure on the Cross was not draped',[118] a surprising departure from the standard *colobium*-clad Christ found, for example, in John VII's Oratory in Saint Peter's, and the accuracy of his observation has been confirmed by Nordhagen.[119] The way in which the head of Christ is depicted also marks a departure from customary practice, and we shall return to both of these aspects shortly. Standing beneath the cross on the right side is a male figure of

---

[112] Nordhagen 1983: 168.
[113] See Nordhagen 1968, pls. CVII–CXXV for his meticulous tracings of the letter forms.
[114] Cavallo 1988: 486–8; and De Rubeis 2001: 108.
[115] Rushforth 1902: 58–62; De Grüneisen 1911: 142–9; Wilpert 1916: 667–72 and pls. 151, 154–5; Tea 1937: 299–305; and Nordhagen 1968: 39–54.
[116] Valesio 1977–9 II: 169–70. See also De Grüneisen 1911: 34–7, and pl. IC III; and Tea 1937: 4.
[117] Mei 2020. The Passionei dossier is preserved in the Biblioteca Civica at Fossombrone.
[118] Rushforth 1902: 58.   [119] Nordhagen 1968: 44.

Fig. 2.7. Santa Maria Antiqua, Rome: sanctuary and apsidal arch wall.

whom only the head and halo remain, and Valesio and Passionei both record that a second figure once stood on the opposite side, now lost. In the standard formula for the depiction of the Crucifixion, these would have

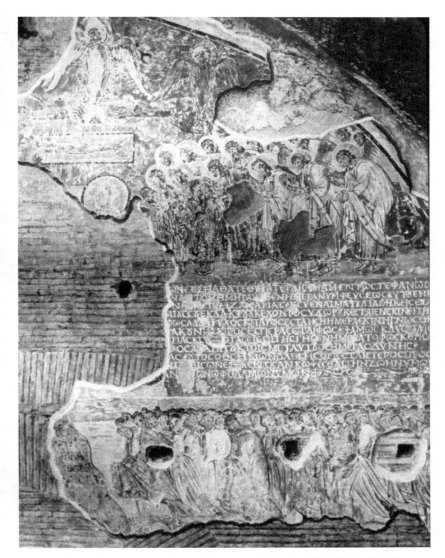

Fig. 2.8. Santa Maria Antiqua, Rome: Adoration of the Crucified Christ (J. Wilpert 1916, pl. 155).

been Saint John the Evangelist and Mary. Farther to the right stand a host of angels, all shown bowing towards the cross, while two seraphim hover in the sky above.[120] Both elements were formerly also present on the missing left side, balancing the composition.

---

[120] For the specific angelic ranks of cherubim and seraphim, see Peers 2001: 43–8.

Beneath the cross there are eleven lines of Greek text, painted in white letters against a red background, reminiscent of the original appearance of the words on John VII's *ambo*. Once again the script seems to have been intended for display: an elegant 'Biblical majuscule' recalling luxury manuscripts written on purple-stained vellum.[121] The inscription now survives only on the viewer's right, but presumably would originally have stretched across the entire wall. The remaining fragments provide evidence for a series of Old Testament passages, taken from the Septuagint (the Greek translation of the Jewish scriptures), all of which were interpreted exegetically as prefiguring the events of Christ's Passion. Sources include the Song of Solomon (3:11), Deuteronomy (28:66), and the prophecies of Zechariah (9:11, 14:6–7), Amos (8:9–10), and Baruch (3:36). This last author was excluded from Jerome's Latin Vulgate, and thus, like the language employed, presumably implies a hellenophone audience. In some instances, the verse begins with the name of the Old Testament author from whose book the passage is drawn.[122] As Rushforth noted, the quotations are not always precisely accurate, and occasionally omit some words found in the original, perhaps due to the limitations of space.[123] And beneath the inscription is another zone in which a crowd of standing figures worship the cross.[124]

The spandrels of the arch framing the apse depict four popes, two per side, all turned towards the centre and holding books in their covered hands.[125] Three have haloes, and two of these can be identified from their inscriptions as Leo I (440–61) and Martin I (649–53), the latter, at the far right, being the best preserved of the figures. The third of the haloed popes must remain unidentified, as the surviving letters of his inscription record only part of the papal title: [R]OMANU[S].[126] The fourth pope, at the far left, has a 'square halo' indicating a portrait, and although no trace of his inscription now survives he is universally assumed to be the patron, John VII. On the side walls beneath

---

[121] Nordhagen 1968: 47; De Rubeis 2001: 109; and Folgerø 2020.

[122] For the texts: Rushforth 1902: 59–61; and Nordhagen 1968: 48, 121–2 (transcription by E. Molland).

[123] Rushforth 1902: 59. They are also set almost 10 m above the floor of the church, and thus reading the texts in any detail would have required remarkable eyesight. Rushforth acknowledges his own difficulty in this regard. In 1702 the texts were transcribed and identified by Domenico Passionei: see Mei 2020.

[124] At the very bottom there may have been a band depicting the dead rising from their graves, a detail which later reappears in Carolingian and Ottonian Crucifixion scenes; see Folgerø 2009.

[125] Wilpert 1916: pl. 154.

[126] In 1702 the figures were in better condition, and Passionei identified him as Gregory I, without however providing a transcription of the painted inscription: see Mei 2020.

were a series of standing theologians: on the left Saint Augustine, identified by a Latin inscription, and another of whom nothing now remains; and on the right, on the last level on the famous 'palimpsest' wall, Saint Gregory of Nazianzus and Saint Basil, both with identifying captions in Greek. John's programme thus offers a balance of the two languages in daily use in the city. What that might mean for the community who worshipped in this space remains an open question, although the placement of the church on a major route between the Forum and the Palatine might suggest an audience drawn primarily from the imperial administration and the army. It should be remembered that John VII is the first pope known to have been associated with the site, and his patronage of the redecoration likely reflects some sort of transition in the administration of the building. There is no evidence that Santa Maria Antiqua was a monastery in the seventh or eighth centuries, and the presence of a pulpit may also imply the presence of a lay congregation.

The painting now visible in the apse itself belongs to a later campaign of the mid-eighth century, and includes the portrait of Pope Paul I (757–67). We shall return to it in due course. Gaps in that plaster reveal evidence for two earlier levels of decoration. It is generally considered that previously the apse would have depicted Mary in some form, given the dedication of the church, with the first level presumably dating from the moment when it was carved into the end wall. The *lacunae* reveal fragments of figures at the far left, and these have been identified provisionally as Peter and an angel;[127] but the main theme remains unknown. The apse was then repainted under John VII, but the only visible fragment depicts part of a fictive drapery (*vela*).[128] Nordhagen has recently reasserted his view that it would have shown Mary in the form of a 'Maria *regina*'.[129] This view is certainly plausible, but there is no evidence to either confirm or deny.

Both side walls of the sanctuary area were also completely repainted at this time.[130] The lower zone, rising approximately 2.10–2.14 m from the floor up to the earlier stucco frieze, was covered with a substantial design of fictive curtains (*vela*), themselves decorated with a series of birds in medallions, and complete with painted loops by which they are hung from painted nails (Fig. 2.9).[131] This marks a substantive change in decorative practice for Roman churches, as the earlier schemes had generally employed imitations of marble panels (*opus sectile*), for example, in Santa

---

[127] Tea 1937: 305–6; and Nordhagen 1978: 90–3.   [128] Nordhagen 1968: 54.
[129] Nordhagen 2018b: 239 note 8.
[130] Rushforth 1902: 55–8; De Grüneisen 1911: 151–62; Wilpert 1916: 673–5 and pls 152–3, 157–8, 161.2, 162; Tea 1937: 314–23; Nordhagen 1968: 15–39; and Viscontini 2014.
[131] Nordhagen 1968: 15–17; and Osborne 1992: 324–6.

Fig. 2.9. Santa Maria Antiqua, Rome: detail of fictive curtains (*vela*) on sanctuary wall.

Maria Antiqua itself in the seventh-century decorations of the walls framing the apse;[132] and it established a new custom which thereafter would be followed almost without exception.[133]

Above the frieze is a narrow band (65 cm in height) featuring medallions with the heads of Christ's twelve apostles, originally six on each side although a number have not survived, identified by Latin inscriptions. On the east (left wall) we can discern all or part of Saints Paul, Andrew (Fig. 2.10), John, and Bartholomew, and on the west (right) wall Peter, Thomas, and possibly Philip. And at the top of each wall were two registers of narrative scenes from the life of Christ. On the east side, the two scenes closest to the apse survive in comparatively decent condition: the Adoration of the Magi above, and below Christ carrying the Cross, with the figure of Simon of Cyrene identified by an inscription (Fig. 2.11). Further to the left are fragments of what may have been a Nativity,

---

[132] Nordhagen 1978: 98–9, 100.

[133] There do exist some possible earlier examples of fictive *vela* in the *corpus* of Roman mural painting, but none that are dated securely. One possible earlier example occurs in Santa Maria Antiqua in the 'vestibule' at the sanctuary end of the left aisle, beneath a depiction of the Forty Martyrs of Sebaste that Nordhagen assigns to the seventh century (Nordhagen 1978: 131–2). But his analysis of the plaster levels suggests that the '*vela*' in the dado zone may have been a later addition (Nordhagen 2018b: 244–5).

Fig. 2.10. Santa Maria Antiqua, Rome: medallion of Saint Andrew on sanctuary wall.

identifiable only from the figure of Joseph; a Last Supper; and the Betrayal by Judas. More paint survives on the west wall, including in the upper register the Presentation of Christ to the Temple and the Flight into Egypt, and in the lower zone various scenes which appear to depict post-Resurrection events. Nordhagen makes a case for Peter and John at the Tomb, the Incredulity of Thomas, the Appearance of Christ on the Lake of Tiberias, Christ adored by the Apostles, and the Disciples on the Road to Emmaus; but even those painted surfaces which survive are badly abraded, so many of the specific identifications must remain conjectural, even if probable. It is also interesting to note that the painters left intact and visible an earlier image on the west wall, a mural icon depicting Saint Anne holding the infant Mary, the earliest known example of this theme anywhere in Christian art.[134]

John VII's decorative programme in the sanctuary is unlike anything known earlier in Rome. Just to take one example, before his time there is no evidence in the city for any depiction of the Crucifixion, monumental or otherwise, apart from the small panel on the fifth-century wooden doors of Santa Sabina. It is a theme conspicuous by its almost complete absence in Early Christian Rome, and also elsewhere in the Latin west; for example, it is not found in the Roman catacombs, nor in the extensive sixth-century

---

[134] Wilpert 1916: pl. 159; Nordhagen 1978: 100–1; and Pogliani, Pelosi and Agresti 2020.

Fig. 2.11. Santa Maria Antiqua, Rome: Christological scenes on east wall of sanctuary.

mosaic cycle in the church of Sant'Apollinare Nuovo in Ravenna. But suddenly it appears not once but twice, in two iconographically very diverse instances: as part of a Christological cycle in John's funerary chapel in Saint Peter's, and as a more theologically inspired non-narrative composition on the apsidal arch of the Forum church. And if the murals in the entrance chamber of the Catacomb of San Valentino also date from this period, then there is even a third example from his pontificate.[135] At Saint Peter's and the Catacomb of San Valentino the iconographic formula for the scene is what we might expect in a 'Byzantine' context before Iconoclasm: Christ is depicted in a *colobium*, the long sleeveless garment which covers almost all of his body. We shall encounter this iconography again at Santa Maria Antiqua in the Theodotus Chapel, painted in the time of Pope Zacharias (741–52), and a discussion of its eastern Mediterranean origins will be postponed until that moment. But the mural on the apsidal arch, of monumental size and accompanied by a large amount of written text, is completely unparalleled, both earlier and later, and numerous scholars have attempted to understand what it signifies. In Nordhagen's words, 'it is a mystery and calls for an explanation',[136] although there is general agreement that it 'developed under an influence from the liturgy'.[137] Following that line of thought, Ursula Nilgen has proposed to view the arch decoration as a visualization of what took place on the altar beneath during the celebration of the eucharist.[138] Even more explicitly, as noted previously, the accompanying passages from the Greek version of the Old Testament were viewed exegetically as prefigurations of Christ's Passion, and the redemption of humankind which this sacrifice made possible. William Tronzo has observed that three of the texts were included in the liturgy for Good Friday in the church at Jerusalem, furthering a possible connection to the religious traditions of the eastern Mediterranean.[139]

Perhaps the most determined effort to explain the arch decorations has been made by Per Jonas Nordhagen,[140] who accepted the suggestion first made by Gordon Rushforth that 'the scene is a version of the worship of the Lamb by the redeemed',[141] based on passages in the Book of Revelation, and thus should be viewed in a tradition of Roman arch decorations

---

[135] Osborne 1981a. [136] Nordhagen 2002: 1754. [137] Nordhagen 1968: 50.
[138] Nilgen 2004.
[139] Tronzo 1985: 100; also Folgerø 2009: 214–16, and Folgerø 2020. The precise connection, however, remains uncertain.
[140] Nordhagen 1967; Nordhagen 1968: 50–4, 95–8; and Nordhagen 2000: 129–33.
[141] Rushforth 1902: 61.

extending back to San Paolo fuori le mura (mid-fifth century) and Santi Cosma e Damiano (early sixth century) which employ that same Biblical source for their visual components. The principal difference is that, at Santa Maria Antiqua, the Apocalyptic Lamb has been replaced by the figure of the Crucified Christ. Perhaps not coincidentally, the use of the image of the lamb to represent Christ had been specifically prohibited by canon 82 of the so-called Quinisext Council, convened by Emperor Justinian II in Constantinople in 692 to enact disciplinary legislation relating to the decisions of the Fifth and Sixth Ecumenical Councils, held in the years 553 and 680–1, respectively. It is sometimes also called the Council 'in Trullo' after the domed hall in the imperial palace where the 215 eastern bishops convened. Canon 82 reads: 'We ordain that from now on Christ our Lord, the Lamb who took upon himself the sins of the world, be portrayed in images in his human form, and no longer in the form of the lamb. Through his figure we perceive the depth of the humiliation of God the Word and are led to remember his life in the flesh, his suffering and his saving death, and the redemption which comes from it for the world.'[142] Given the usual exegesis of the Biblical passages painted beneath, the Santa Maria Antiqua arch mural could almost be regarded as a visual equivalent of canon 82.[143]

The acts of the Quinisext Council seem to have caused a stir when copies were sent to the pope for his signature, since a number of the canons appeared to contravene current Roman practice.[144] In addition to canon 82, which prohibited a usage popular in the decoration of the city's churches, the new legislation included authorization of lower ranks of the clergy to retain married status following ordination as sub-deacons (canon 13), and a prohibition of the Roman practice of fasting on Saturdays in Lent (canon 55). Pope Sergius I (687–701) refused to sign, in the words of his *Liber pontificalis* biographer 'choosing to die rather than consent to erroneous novelties'.[145] Furthermore, in what must surely have been an obvious repudiation of canon 82, he mandated that the words 'Lamb of God, who takes away the sins of the world, have mercy on us' ('*Agnus Dei, qui tollis peccata mundi, miserere nobis*') should be sung by the clergy and congregation at the moment of the breaking of the bread during the eucharist.[146] And die he almost did. Justinian II sent his chief

---

[142] Mansi 1759–98 XI: 977–80. See discussion in Cormack 1985: 99–101, whose English translation I have used here; Barber 1991: 58–9; and Corrigan 1998.
[143] Nordhagen 1968: 52.   [144] Laurent 1965: 32–3.
[145] LP 86.7, ed. Duchesne I: 373; trans. Davis 2010: 82.
[146] LP 86.14, ed. Duchesne I: 376; trans. Davis 2010: 84.

spatharius, Zacharias, to arrest the pope and convey him to Constantinople, but the Italian army rose to defend the pontiff and the imperial officer was lucky to escape with his life. We shall return to this pivotal historical moment in a later chapter.

The matter of Sergius' signature became moot after Justinian II was deposed, mutilated, and exiled by the usurper Leontios in 695, but resurfaced when Justinian regained his throne a decade later. Possibly in a more conciliatory frame of mind, he re-sent the documents to Rome inviting papal approval or emendation. This time the pope who received them was John VII, and in a *Liber pontificalis* passage which has engendered some puzzlement, we are told that 'he [John VII], terrified in his human weakness, sent them back to the prince ... without any emendations at all'.[147] Regardless of how we interpret this papal action, or rather inaction, there can be little doubt that the disciplinary rules developed at the Quinisext Council generated some controversy in the years after 705, making the mural in Santa Maria Antiqua even more fascinating.

But there is still more evidence to consider. Nordhagen's minute observation of the figure of Christ has also revealed that the face of Christ depicted in the mural departs from the traditional formula, and instead adopts a new and unusual format, a triangular head with short hair and a thin curly beard instead of the usual long-haired and full-bearded image. What makes this particularly interesting is that precisely this same new facial type for Christ was used by Justinian II on his coinage following his recovery of the imperial throne in 705.[148] Thus the replacement of the lamb with a figure of Christ, and the specific type of Christ employed, may suggest an attempt by John VII to be more conciliatory than Sergius when it came to imperial relations. On the other hand, the inclusion on the wall beneath of the figure of Pope Martin, the pope arrested and 'martyred' under the Emperor Constans II, 50 years earlier, initially suggested to Nordhagen that John was seeking some balance in the relationship, tempering his conciliatory approach with a clear reminder that the papacy had

---

[147] LP 88.5, ed. Duchesne I: 386; trans. Davis 2010: 86–7.
[148] Nordhagen 1967; and Nordhagen 1968: 52–4. See also Sansterre 1982, and Sansterre 1987. Justinian II was the first emperor to place an image of Christ on the obverse of his coinage (Cormack 1985: 96–8), and the issue of 692 CE in his first reign featured the standard facial type. The caption on the reverse identifies the emperor as '*servus Christi*' (Cormack 1985: 97–8 and fig. 32), making an interesting parallel to John VII's claim to be the '*servus sanctae Mariae*'. The new image of Christ employed on coins following Justinian II's restoration to the throne may have been a conscious attempt to implement canon 82, see Breckenridge 1959: 79–85, and especially Breckenridge 1972a. The practice of placing images of Christ on coins would be discarded in the early eighth century with the onset of Iconoclasm: Breckenridge 1972b.

Fig. 2.12. Santa Maria Antiqua, Rome: Chapel of the Holy Physicians (west wall).

not forgotten earlier wrongs. More recently, however, he has come to view all these elements as support for Justinian II's orthodoxy against continuing attempts to revive Monotheletism, the heresy fiercely opposed by Martin at the Lateran Council of 649.[149] This *rapprochement* between pope and emperor would be confirmed with the successful visit of Pope Constantine (708–15) to Constantinople in 710–11.[150]

The room to the right of the main sanctuary area has been dubbed the 'Chapel of Holy Physicians' due to the nature of its decorations.[151] It is a small rectangular space, with a shallow niche somewhat crudely excavated in its end (south) wall, rising from the floor level. As the name implies, the principal decoration comprises a series of standing male saints on the right and entrance walls (Fig. 2.12), all identified by Greek inscriptions, most of whom were popular for their ability to effect miraculous cures for diseases and other ailments without seeking payment. They were the '*anargyroi*': literally, 'those without silver'. The saints whose names have survived are Dometius, Panteleimon, Abbacyrus, John (of Edessa), Celsus, Cosmas, and Damian. Most carry what have been identified as

---

[149] Nordhagen 2002.
[150] *LP* 90.3–7, ed. Duchesne I: 389–91. See also Sansterre 1984a; and Brown 1995b: 31–3.
[151] Rushforth 1902: 76–81; De Grüneisen 1911: 163–5; Wilpert 1916: 675–7 and pls 145.1, 145.4, 165; Tea 1937: 337–43; Nordhagen 1962: 67; Nordhagen 1968: 55–66; Knipp 2002; and Bordino 2016.

surgeon's boxes, presumably containing scalpels and other instruments, as is common for this category of saint. The healing cult of Abbacyrus and John, for example, was deliberately initiated in the early fifth century in an attempt to replace the popularity of Isis *medica* at her shrine at Menouthis, outside Alexandria.[152] It seems to have been particularly popular among the hellenophone inhabitants of Rome, and additional images of Abbacyrus and John may be found in the atrium of Santa Maria Antiqua. We shall return to this pair in a later chapter. Beneath the saints on the west wall is an expanse of painted curtains,[153] which inexplicably begins some 1.25 m above the present floor. The lowermost zone seems not to have ever been painted, and Rushforth suggested that it might have been occupied by furniture for the storage of items such as books and vestments.[154] Similar fictive draperies decorate the north wall to the left of the entrance doorway from the aisle. In addition to the north and west walls, the niche in the south wall was also decorated with five standing figures, seemingly by a different artist or workshop, and mostly now lost apart from their identifying inscriptions, again in Greek: Cosmas, Abbacyrus, Stephen, Procopius, and Damian. Faint traces of painted plaster demonstrate that the east wall was also once decorated, but nothing now remains legible.

The precise original function of the space also remains unknown, and although it is invariably called a 'chapel' in the literature there is no evidence for the presence of an altar. David Knipp has proposed the ingenious theory that it functioned as a place for cures through the process of 'incubation', in which saints appeared to the afflicted in dreams, either providing a cure or informing them of what they needed to do in order to obtain one. The floor-level niche, containing a painted 'icon' of five saints, would thus have allowed someone seeking saintly intervention to sleep in immediate proximity to the agents being invoked in their prayers.[155] This practice of receiving 'dream oracles' was widespread in the ancient world, from the shrine of Asklepios at Epidaurus to that of Isis *medica* at Menouthis, and the custom carried over into early Christianity, for example, at the shrine of Saint Artemios in Constantinople, or those of Cosmas and Damian, and Abbacyrus and John.[156] The painted images created a virtual presence for the saints similar to that of the cult statues of Asklepios or Serapis. In this view, first posited by Eva Tea and substantially elaborated by Jaakko Aronen, Christian healing cults would have replaced similar pre-Christian practices located in this zone of the Roman Forum, centred on the adjacent Temple of Castor and Pollux

---

[152] Sinthern 1908; Delehaye 1911; Knipp 2002: 1; and Maskarinec 2017.
[153] Nordhagen 1968: 56; and Osborne 1992: 327–8.   [154] Rushforth 1902: 77.
[155] Knipp 2002.   [156] *ODB*: 992.

and the Fountain of Juturna.[157] Additional evidence may be found in the choice of Saints Cosmas and Damian for the dedication of the first Christian church to have been established in this area, inserted by Pope Felix IV (526–30) into an apsed hall that formed part of Vespasian's Forum of Peace (*LP* 56.2, ed. Duchesne I: 279). The notion is certainly *molto suggestivo*, but in the absence of additional evidence for the moment it must remain conjectural.

The low marble screens (*transennae*) used to delineate the space within the interior of the church that was reserved for the movement of the clergy were also the recipients of painted decorations.[158] The subject matter which survives is taken entirely from the Old Testament and includes narrative depictions of David and Goliath, the Sickness of King Hezekiah (Pl. 3), and Judith and Holofernes, in addition to other fragmentary scenes whose subjects remain unidentified. Their attribution to the time of John VII was proposed initially on the basis of the palaeography of the painted inscriptions,[159] but a recent technical analysis confirms that the painting of the sanctuary, the adjacent chapel, and the *transennae*, was all undertaken by the same workshop. Among its 'signatures' was the use of red guidelines created by snapping a painted cord into the wet plaster.[160]

The function of these murals, and the rationale for their individual selection, remain entirely unknown, although Ann van Dijk has suggested parallels to churches such as Saint Peter's, San Paolo fuori le mura, and Santa Maria Maggiore, all of which had Old Testament narrative cycles decorating parts of their naves.[161] But in Santa Maria Antiqua we have only a selection of scenes, and Rushforth and van Dijk are probably correct that the specific episodes chosen were intended to be interpreted as 'antetypes' for New Testament events or concepts. For example, David functions as a 'type' of Christ, and his defeat of the Philistine giant was interpreted as an allegory for the triumph of good over evil, of Christ over the devil, as stated explicitly by Augustine in his commentary on Psalm 33.[162] The killing of Holofernes by Judith evokes a similar theme. The practice of using the Old Testament as a source for prefigurations of this sort goes back as far as the authors of the New Testament gospels who, for example, likened Christ's death and subsequent resurrection to the story of Jonah, who spent three days and nights in the stomach of the 'whale' (Matthew 12:40). This

---

[157] Tea 1937: 48–54; and Aronen 1989.
[158] Rushforth 1902: 63, 86–8; De Grüneisen 1911: 162; Wilpert 1916: 694–8; Tea 1937: 295–9; Nordhagen 1962: 67–8; and Nordhagen 1968: 67–74.
[159] Nordhagen 1962: 68.   [160] Schmid and Valentini 2013: 416.   [161] van Dijk 2004.
[162] Rushforth 1902: 63; and van Dijk 2004: 121.

principle is ubiquitous in patristic literature as well as Early Christian art. Hezekiah's sickness, which also lasted three days (2 Kings 20:1–11), might be similarly interpreted as another 'type' of the same 'Resurrection' theme. But again, there is no absolute proof that this was the original intention.

In other parts of Santa Maria Antiqua, the redecoration campaign of John VII seems to have been somewhat less comprehensive. Some surfaces were repainted while others were left with their existing images untouched, paintings which Nordhagen has called 'fresco-icons'.[163] He detected a possible pattern in this regard, based on subject matter: the areas of intervention invariably involved images of Mary, perhaps not a great surprise given this pope's utter devotion to her cult. In one instance, on the southeast pillar, an existing image of the Annunciation was replaced by a new version of the same subject;[164] and in another, a small wall niche in the northwest pillar was decorated with the half-figures of Mary and her infant son (Pl. 4). This was presumably a place of special veneration and a close examination of the plaster suggests that it was also a site for the display of *ex voto* gifts.[165] The lay congregation in early medieval Roman churches was separated by gender, with the men on one side (the right-hand side of the celebrant) and the women on the other, and it perhaps no coincidence that this painted icon was located in the *pars mulierum* (women's side), as is also the case for another niche image of the Madonna and Child in the church of San Clemente.[166] It would be fascinating to know what devotional practices were actually performed in front of images of this sort. Of course, these can only be surmised, although here perhaps 'we see reflected the excesses which caused the Iconoclast reaction'.[167]

The singular exception to this apparent Marian fixation is the painting of the Anastasis (Greek for 'Resurrection', although the particular moment depicted is often rendered in English as the 'Harrowing of Hell') on the right wall of the doorway leading from the left aisle of the church to the Palatine ramp (Fig. 2.13).[168] This moment is not recorded in any Biblical account, but entered Christian theology at least in part as a response to the question of what happened to those just souls who lived before the 'era of grace'. Were they condemned to eternal life in hell? The answer was

---

[163] Nordhagen 1968: 75–89; and Nordhagen 2018b.
[164] Tea 1937: 287–9; and Nordhagen 1968: 78–9 and pl. XCVIII.
[165] Tea 1937: 292; and Nordhagen 1968: 75–7 and pls XCII, XCIII. For the practice of adding physical objects to icons: Nordhagen 1987.
[166] Osborne 2003: 141–4.   [167] Nordhagen 1968: 90.
[168] Wilpert 1916: 684, and pl. 168.2; Tea 1937: 262–3; and Nordhagen 1968: 81–2.

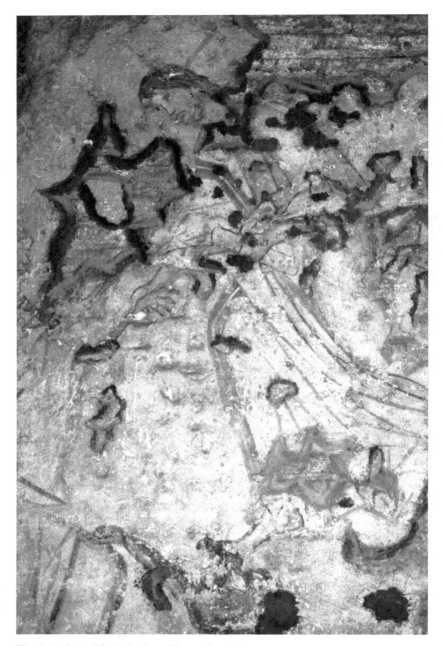

Fig. 2.13. Santa Maria Antiqua, Rome: Anastasis.

negative, and it was posited that Christ had descended into the underworld to raise up those who merited entry to heaven, usually represented visually by figures of Adam and Eve, along with the Old Testament kings David and

Solomon. This matter became particularly important in the Christological debates of the seventh century, and was invoked to support the Orthodox position that Christ had two natures, human and divine, and thus had experienced real death on the cross, and subsequent physical resurrection. A contemporary text, the *Hodegos* of Anastasius Sinaites, not only discussed this event but also argued for the importance of visual representations in the presentation of doctrinal issues, and this has led Anna Kartsonis to suggest that the iconography of the Anastasis was formulated in the last quarter of the seventh century.[169] In the Santa Maria Antiqua mural, Christ steps to the left to grasp Adam's wrist, while at the same time treading on a small figure beneath his feet, the personification of Hades. As we have seen, this event was also included among the mosaic decorations of John VII's Oratory in Saint Peter's; and together these constitute the first surviving instances of this theme anywhere in Christian art. And there is also third example from the time of John VII: a very fragmentary mural on the façade of the adjacent Oratory of the Forty Martyrs of Sebaste,[170] virtually identical in its composition to the mural inside the church.

In post-iconoclastic Byzantium, the Anastasis would become a standard component of church decoration, either as part of a larger narrative cycle reflecting important moments in the life of Christ, or else on its own, with examples in the latter category usually found in connection with funerary monuments. The appropriateness of such a subject for tomb decorations presumably requires no explanation, and it should be noted that there are two such examples known from Rome in the ninth century: a mosaic above the tomb of Theodora *episcopa*, mother of Pope Paschal I (817–24), in the San Zeno chapel in Santa Prassede, and a mural over what was almost certainly the tomb of the Byzantine missionary to the Slavs, Cyril (d. 868), in San Clemente.[171] But there is no suggestion that the Santa Maria Antiqua mural was associated with a grave, nor that it was part of a larger Christological cycle as had been the case for John VII's Oratory in Saint Peter's. So what was its purpose here? Once again there is no definitive answer; but Nordhagen, noting the mural's placement at the entry from the Palatine ramp, and recalling André Grabar's premise that the pictorial formula developed for the depiction of the Anastasis was adapted from imperial imagery, has suggested that it may have functioned as a special 'portal iconography' for palaces.[172] For the moment it shall suffice to note that it represents yet another example of a growing list of themes believed to

---

[169] Kartsonis 1986: 8; see also Nordhagen 2018a: 904–5.
[170] Wilpert 1916: 682, and pl. 167.1; and Nordhagen 1968: 86, and pl. CIII.
[171] Osborne 1981c. [172] Grabar 1936: 246–9; and Nordhagen 1982.

originate in the eastern Mediterranean which make their appearance at Rome for the first time under John VII. As Nordhagen has argued, 'The presence ... of this scene could serve, alone, to prove the closeness of the ties which existed between Rome and Constantinople in the pre-iconoclastic period.'[173]

Indeed, the importance of the John VII mosaics and wall-paintings for the history of art cannot easily be overstated, especially for our understanding of the development of Christian iconography. As we have seen, and as has been extensively documented by Nordhagen, the mosaics from John VII's chapel in Saint Peter's and the murals in Santa Maria Antiqua include the earliest surviving examples of subjects or iconographic types that would later become normative in Byzantine art. In addition to those already enumerated we can add post-Crucifixion events from the life of Christ, for example, the 'Apostles Peter and John at the Grave' and 'The Appearance of Christ on the Lake of Tiberias',[174] and the specific physiognomic attributes of saints such as Panteleimon.[175] Thus there is no reason to doubt Nordhagen's conclusion that 'the world of images seen in John [VII's] Roman works ... was essentially Byzantine'.[176]

Where did John VII find his painters and mosaicists?[177] Iconography, style, and technique may all suggest that they were newcomers to Italy who brought with them compositional formulae, decorative practices, and workshop techniques for which we have little or no earlier evidence in Rome, nor indeed anywhere else in western Europe. Taken individually, these elements may not appear to be significant; but when viewed collectively, the many new practices – the theme of the Anastasis and other previously unrecorded subjects, the new facial type of Christ on the apsidal arch, the inclusion of the bathing of the child in the Nativity, the 'Maria regina' and other 'types' of Mary, the 'square halo' to signify portraits, the replacement of fictive marbles with fictive textiles in the dado zone, the emphasis on the eastern 'anargyroi', the use of small multicoloured stone tesserae for the hands and faces of figures in mosaic, the addition of straw to the plaster, and so on – combine to create a powerful argument. Nor should it be a surprising one. At the dawn of the eighth century the city of Rome was still an integral part of the 'Roman' Empire, and the upper

---

[173] Nordhagen 2012: 188. See also Nordhagen 2015: 95–8.
[174] Nordhagen 1968: 31–2, 33–5; and Nordhagen 2000: 125.
[175] Nordhagen 2004; and Nordhagen 2015.   [176] Nordhagen 2018b: 245.
[177] For evidence that both the painters and mosaicists used the same figure templates: Pogliani 2014. For the possibility that the same workshop was also responsible for the murals depicting scenes from the life of Christ in the church of Santa Maria in Via Lata, see Bordi 2015: 401–2.

echelons of its secular and ecclesiastical administration continued to make frequent use of the Greek language, both spoken and written. It is entirely normal to expect that their patronage would reflect the cultural milieu of the eastern Mediterranean to which they belonged. While we have no data whatsoever on the composition and movement of artistic workshops in this period, given the extensive documentable travels of imperial officials, clerics, and monks, including the family of Pope John VII himself, there is no reason why artisans could not also have been equally mobile. Nordhagen's contention in the title of his 2012 article, that this matter is 'a puzzle solved', may be just slightly optimistic, but the evidence does appear to be overwhelming.

Icon from Santa Maria in Trastevere

There is a third possible surviving portrait of John VII which merits discussion, although in this instance the identification is far from certain. The Roman church of Santa Maria in Trastevere possesses a medieval icon, known popularly as the 'Madonna della Clemenza', depicting an enthroned 'Madonna and Child' flanked by two angels.[178] Mary is again depicted as '*regina*' with the imperial crown. Restoration undertaken by the Istituto Centrale del Restauro in 1953 revealed a much earlier image buried beneath various later levels of repainting, and the latter were removed. The original, painted on a linen fabric attached to boards of cypress wood, had been executed in encaustic, a technique developed in the ancient world in which the pigments are embedded in hot wax, usually beeswax, the latter serving as the binder. The process is described by Pliny in his *Natural History* (35.41). Encaustic was broadly used for painting on panel in the Roman era, particularly in the eastern Mediterranean where most early examples have survived. Best known in this regard are the 'mummy portraits' from Fayyum and elsewhere in Egypt, as well as the earliest Christian icons preserved in the collection of the Monastery of Saint Catherine at Mount Sinai; but from at least the mid-eighth century onwards, Byzantine icons were painted using a different technique: tempera.[179] Encaustic was also employed for some of the other earliest Marian icons to have survived in Rome, including those now in the churches of Santa Maria Nova and Santa Maria del Rosario.[180]

---

[178] Bertelli 1961; Amato 1988: 25–32; and Wolf 2005: 37–9.   [179] Weitzmann 1976: 8–9.
[180] Amato 1988: 17–24, 41–9.

The technique alone thus suggests a very early date, and the 'Madonna della Clemenza' has been associated with a passage in one of the earliest surviving 'guidebooks' for pilgrims visiting Rome, with the title 'Concerning the holy places of the martyrs which are outside the city of Rome' ('*De locis sanctis martyrum quae sunt foris civitatis Romae*'). Despite the suggestion in this name that it is concerned only with sites situated outside the city walls, the text also has an appendix, entitled '*Istae vero ecclesiae intus Romae habentur*', listing a series of churches located inside the circuit of the Aurelian walls.[181] Known from three manuscripts, two in Vienna and one in Würzburg, which range in date from the late eighth through to the tenth century, the composition of the *De locis sanctis martyrum* can be dated on the basis of internal evidence to approximately the year 640. Among the churches listed in the appendix is the 'Basilica of Santa Maria in Trastevere; there is the icon of Mary that made itself'.[182] In other words, the icon was believed to have been produced miraculously, and not painted by human hands. But is this a reference to our icon or some other? If it is the former, then the icon may already have been in place before the middle of the seventh century. Unfortunately, this line of reasoning presupposes that the appended list of churches inside the city walls dates from the same time as the *De locis sanctis martyrum*, and this may not be the case. In the earliest of the three manuscripts (Vienna, ÖstNB lat. 795), which has been associated with Arno, Archbishop of Salzburg, the appendix is written by a different hand. It may simply reflect the churches visited during that prelate's own sojourns in Rome, where he is known to have travelled on three occasions in the late 700s.[183]

The story has one other wrinkle. At the feet of the figure of Mary, on her right side (viewer's left) the restorers found traces of a donor figure in a posture of obeisance (*proskynesis*), including fragments of the head (enclosed in a 'square halo' and turned outwards towards the viewer), his clerical vestments, and two fingers near Mary's foot, which presumably he was moving to hold or to kiss. In the first major study devoted to the icon after its restoration, Carlo Bertelli presented a case for identifying the donor as another of the portrait images of Pope John VII, based principally on stylistic and iconographic similarities to the work executed under this

---

[181] CT II: 101–31; CCSL 175: 313–22.
[182] '*Basilica quae appellatur Sancta Maria Transtiberis; ibi est imago sanctae Mariae quae per se facta est*': CT II: 122.
[183] McKitterick 2006: 45–6; and McKitterick 2020a: notes 87 and 89. For this manuscript, see also Costambeys 2014: 259–61.

pontiff in Santa Maria Antiqua and Saint Peter's, as well as palaeographic comparisons for the letters in the very fragmentary inscription painted on the icon's frame.[184] And thus he dated the icon to the beginning of the eighth century, at the same time dismissing the *De locis sanctis martyrum* appendix phrase '*ibi est imago sanctae Mariae*' as a later gloss, added to the original text at some moment prior to the earliest extant manuscript. Bertelli's proposed dating is certainly not without merit, and dovetails rather nicely with both John VII's extreme devotion to the cult of Mary, and especially to the image of 'Maria *regina*', and the lack of any evidence for the use of the 'square halo' portrait panel motif in Rome before his time. Most subsequent scholarship has either followed Bertelli[185] or else opted for a much earlier date based on a presumed *terminus ante quem* provided by the reference in the aforementioned text.[186] Complicating matters from the point of view of a discussion of style, the two angels are represented in quite different fashions,[187] which may prove only that 'style' is not always a good indicator of date, especially when it can vary so dramatically within the confines of a single work.

It seems possible that both opinions regarding the date are at least partially correct, since the technical evidence suggests that at least parts of the donor figure at the bottom of the icon, including his 'square halo', were not painted in encaustic, and consequently we can surmise that some elements of the composition were not present in the original icon. They were later additions in tempera, although it cannot be determined how much later.[188] In addition to the images newly created in Saint Peter's and Santa Maria Antiqua, perhaps John VII also added his portrait to existing images of Mary, or at least altered the image to reflect his own features and added a 'square halo', prompting the unusual comment from his *Liber pontificalis* biographer. While it is unlikely that this question will ever be fully resolved, it is tempting to view the imposing 'Madonna della Clemenza' icon as an imported object which reintroduced the 'Maria *regina*' theme to Rome in the first decade of the eighth century.

We are indeed fortunate to have so much information about a pontiff whose reign was comparatively short, but evidently enormously active. The picture presented by the monuments which he commissioned does much to corroborate the notion that Rome in 700 was indeed a 'Constantinople on the Tiber', providing historians of Byzantium with a tantalizing glimpse

---

[184] Bertelli 1961; and Ladner 1984: 20–3. [185] Ladner 1984: 20–3; and Nordhagen 2014.
[186] Andaloro 1972–3; and Lidova 2016: 110–11. [187] Andaloro 2002: 740–4.
[188] Urbani 1964: 24; and Bertelli 1961: 72.

of what artistic production in the imperial capital might have looked like in the years immediately prior to the onset of Iconoclasm. The mosaics in Saint Peter's and murals in Santa Maria Antiqua also provide a base against which we can measure both continuity and change in the Roman artistic commissions which follow.

3 | Clerics, Monks and Pilgrims

In addition to buildings and decorations commissioned by Pope John VII, in the early decades of the eighth century we can identify three other substantial non-papal groups who were either 'patrons' or 'consumers' of artistic culture in early medieval Rome: clerics, monks, and pilgrims. This chapter will examine examples from each of those categories that can be dated to this period.

Santa Sabina

The fifth-century church of Santa Sabina, perched on the summit of the Aventine hill overlooking the Tiber, remains one of the best-preserved examples of an Early Christian basilica.[1] Its original architectural fabric has remained intact for almost sixteen centuries without experiencing substantial alteration, and most later accretions were removed in a restoration campaign undertaken by Antonio Muñoz between 1914 and 1919. It was not a papal commission, but rather is known to have been founded by a priest from Dalmatia, Peter, in the reign of Pope Celestine (422–32), as documented by a substantial mosaic inscription, using elegant gold letters set against a blue background, placed prominently on the inner wall of the façade; and the *Liber pontificalis* records that it was completed during the reign of Celestine's successor, Sixtus III (432–40), again crediting the priest Peter (*LP* 46.8, ed. Duchesne I: 235). This inscription, along with two flanking figures representing the two components of the Christian community, the Jews ('*ecclesia ex circumcisione*') and the Gentiles ('*ecclesia ex gentibus*'), is all that now remains of what must originally have been a substantial interior decorative programme. The church is today perhaps best known for its set of wooden doors, decorated with carved panels illustrating Christological and other scenes, including the earliest-known depiction in Christian art of the Crucifixion.

---

[1] *CBCR* IV: 72–98.

Restorations to the narthex porch in the year 2010 revealed a mural painting on the outer wall of the façade, hitherto concealed by layers of whitewash (Pl. 5).[2] Unfortunately the painted surface has been severely abraded, but enough remains that the general nature of the composition can be determined with certainty. The mural depicts an enthroned Madonna and Child flanked by four haloed saints, their heads set against a fictive architectural background comprising a colonnade. None of the saints are identified by inscription, but the two closest to the centre, both male and bearded, are presumably Peter and Paul, based on their facial types, while the outer pair, both apparently female, are plausibly identified as Sabina and her co-martyr Seraphia. But what makes the mural particularly interesting is the additional presence of no fewer than three contemporary figures, all sporting 'square haloes' signifying portrait likenesses. The two standing figures, at the extremities of the composition, are shown being presented by the two female saints. Both hold books in their veiled hands, and thus are presumably clerics. The figure at the left, who appears in almost every respect identical to the figure of John VII on the left side of the apsidal arch in Santa Maria Antiqua,[3] wears an ecclesiastical *pallium*, an ochre scarf clearly visible on both shoulders and descending across his chest. In a Roman context, this vestment identifies him as a pope. The third figure, also clutching a book, kneels at the feet of the central group, bowing forward in an act of *proskynesis* (obeisance) derived from imperial court ceremonial.[4]

Perhaps the most unusual features of the painting are the two painted Latin inscriptions, one running horizontally in the upper border and then descending on the right side, and the second placed vertically on the left side. Both are incomplete, in the sense that the surviving plaster breaks off before the terminations, but enough survives to identify the figures and allow a reasonably precise dating. At the top we read 'In the name of our Lord God and Saviour Jesus Christ in the time of our most blessed apostolic lord Constantine', and on the left 'Theodore the archpriest

---

[2] Gianandrea 2010; Gianandrea 2011; Gianandrea 2014; and Osborne 2014.
[3] Cf. Nordhagen 1968: pl. XLVII.
[4] McCormick 1991. Figures shown in *proskynesis* before a deity are not found in classical art, but become common in medieval Byzantium, see Franses 2018: 54–7. The earliest example known to Rico Franses is an icon from Sinai, depicting Saint Irene and a supplicant, and dated to the eighth or ninth century; but he seems unaware of both the Santa Sabina mural and the 'Madonna della Clemenza' icon in the church of Santa Maria in Trastevere. Needless to say, these two Roman examples of figures in the act of obeisance serve to solidify the view that painting in the city c. 700 CE needs to be viewed in the broader context of Byzantine art.

together with the priest George fulfill a vow.'⁵ Thus the pope in our composition is presumably Constantine I (708–15), and the figure kneeling beneath him, in the position of honour on the right hand of Mary and her infant son, is likely to be the archpriest Theodore. The third cleric is presumably the priest George. A dating to the years between 708 and 715 appears certain.⁶ The use of the letter 'B' for the initial letter of the word '*votum*', a phenomenon known as 'betacism', is characteristic of Roman inscriptions from the eighth century. We shall return to it shortly.

It may not be a coincidence that three of the four named members of the Roman clergy sent as papal legates to the Sixth Ecumenical Council convened in Constantinople in 680–1 were also Theodore, George, and Constantine (*LP* 81.3, ed. Duchesne, I: 350). All bear Greek names, and it may well have been an ability to function in that language that prompted their selection for this critical mission. The Council was an event of exceptional importance for the Roman church, as it healed the long-standing dispute between the emperor and the pope regarding the heresy of Monotheletism and its offshoots, and the *Liber pontificalis* devotes unprecedented attention to the activities of the papal delegation and their triumphant success in securing the adoption of Rome's position. The fourth Roman delegate who is named in our source, a deacon named John, was elected pope in 685 as John V, but he died the following year. Theodore clearly harboured the same ambition, but is recorded as the unsuccessful runner-up to Conon in the papal election of 686, when his candidacy was supported by the army, and again the following year when the choice fell ultimately to Sergius. Clearly the army did not always get its way. Between those two events, however, he became the most senior priest in the Roman church, with the title *archipresbyter* (*LP* 85.1, 86.2; ed. Duchesne I: 368, 371), and this seems to confirm his identification as the Theodore named in our mural.

Constantine, still only a sub-deacon in 681, apparently also went on to an illustrious ecclesiastical career, and may well be the cleric by this name elected pope in 708. Summoned to Constantinople by the Emperor Justinian II, he made what was probably his second lengthy journey to the imperial capital, leaving Rome in October 710 and returning in

---

[5] 'IN N(omine) D(omi)NI D(e)I SALVATORIS N(ostri) IH(s)U XP(ist)I TEMPORIBUS TER BEATISSIMI ET APOSTOLICI D(omi)NI N(ostri) CONSTANTI[ni] ...'; 'THEODORUS ARCHIP(res)B(iter) UNACUM GIORGIO P(res)B(itero) BOTUM So[lvit] ...'

[6] For an alternative suggestion, that the 'Constantine' in question is Constantine II who reigned briefly in 767–8, see McKitterick 2018. But there is no known 'archpriest' Theodore from his time.

October 711 (*LP* 90.3–7, ed. Duchesne I: 389–91). He would be the last of the medieval popes to travel to the eastern Mediterranean. The mission was apparently a success, and good relations were once again restored with the emperor, although this triumph was short-lived since Justinian II was assassinated very shortly thereafter (December 711). The *Liber pontificalis* is silent on the subsequent career of George, although he is possibly the priest named George who accompanied Pope Constantine from Rome in 710, but for some unspecified reason was left at Naples (*LP* 90.4, ed. Duchesne I: 390). Could the vow in question have been related somehow to this journey? Unfortunately, there is no way of knowing. The placement of the mural, well above eye level on the narthex wall, is also rather puzzling. What was significant about this church and specifically this rather odd location? Both format and location seem exceptionally anomalous.

There is no doubt that the pope's year-long journey was considered to have been important. Its success re-established the authority of the Roman church in matters of the faith, and also restored the good working relationship between pope and emperor. Both these goals had been achieved earlier at the Sixth Ecumenical Council, but three decades later were in considerable jeopardy, following Rome's rejection of the legislation approved by the Quinisext Council in 692. The *Liber pontificalis* makes much of the exceptional welcome accorded to Pope Constantine and his entourage by Justinian II. When the pope and emperor met at Nicomedia, it records that 'the Christian Augustus, crown on head, prostrated himself and kissed the feet of the pontiff', and then continues to stress the 'great joy of the people as everyone gazed at their good prince in his great humility'.[7]

Regardless of the specific circumstances which prompted the commission, the mural constitutes a document of considerable importance. For one thing, it is the first commission in a Roman church since the sixth century that we can associate with absolute certainty with a non-papal donor, clerical or otherwise. Clearly the patronage of such commissions was not restricted to the pope alone.[8] And in that regard it is perhaps worth noting a curious passage in the *Liber pontificalis*. The *vita* of Constantine is for the most part completely silent regarding papal gifts to Rome's churches, apart from one brief mention of a gold communion plate weighing 12 pounds ('*patenam auream pens. lib.*

---

[7] *LP* 90.6, ed. Duchesne I: 391; trans. Davis 2010: 88

[8] There is some evidence for non-papal donors in the catacombs, for example, the 'Gaudiosus' mentioned twice in painted inscriptions on murals in the catacomb of Pontianus; see Osborne 1985: 321. Giulia Bordi (2015: 401) has also suggested a lay patron for the seventh-century murals in the church of Santa Maria in Via Lata, although there is no specific evidence.

XII'), without however specifying the location or recipient (*LP* 90.8; ed. Duchesne I: 391). The one artistic commission it does mention comes in the aftermath of the pope's triumphal return from Constantinople and the subsequent usurpation of the imperial throne by Philippikos (r. 711–13), an advocate of Monotheletism who rejected the decisions of the Sixth Ecumenical Council.[9] But here agency is claimed unusually for the Roman people, not the pope: 'It was for this reason that the whole population of Rome, in their burning enthusiasm for the faith, erected in St Peter's the image which the Greeks call *Botarea*; it includes the six holy universal synods'.[10] Duchesne interpreted this action in Rome as a response to the destruction by Philippikos of a similar image in Constantinople,[11] and he may well have been correct.

More specifically, however, the Santa Sabina mural was a personal commission of the archpriest Theodore and the priest George; and it is likely not a coincidence that this expansion of ecclesiastical patronage of the arts comes at the very moment when the papal bureaucracy was itself being increased, with a wide variety of new administrative positions deemed necessary to administer the growing responsibilities of the bishops of Rome, along with the establishment of a more structured hierarchy.[12] It was at this same time, for example, that the papacy began to assume responsibility for the physical infrastructure of the city of Rome, beginning with its walls. We shall return to this topic when we examine the work of Pope Hadrian I (772–95), but it should be noted that the very first mention of papal interest in the upkeep of the walls occurs in the life of Pope Sisinnius (708). Although his reign lasted only a few weeks, Sisinnius is said to have 'ordered the burning of lime for the restoration of the walls';[13] and actual repairs are recorded under two of his successors, Gregory II (715–31) and Gregory III (731–41) (*LP* 91.2, 92.15; ed. Duchesne I: 396, 420). The spiritual welfare of their flock may still have been the primary concern of the vicars of Saint Peter, but it could no longer be their only concern.

In a related development, John Romano views the creation of a papal 'court' in the late years of the seventh century as being a primary catalyst for the development of more formalized rituals, known collectively as the 'Ordines Romani', of which the first, *Ordo Romanus* I, dated about the year 700, sets out the protocols for the activities to be undertaken during Easter week.[14] Probably deriving their structure from ceremonies undertaken by

---

[9] *ODB*: 1654.   [10] *LP* 90.8, ed. Duchesne I: 391; trans. Davis 2010: 89.   [11] *LP* I: 394 note 22.
[12] For the development of the various offices in the papal administration: Noble 1984: 218–27; and Noble 2015.
[13] *LP* 89.1, ed. Duchesne I: 388; trans. Davis 2010: 87.   [14] Romano 2014: 75–107.

the imperial court and the military, with an emphasis on the precise order of procession and the position of each individual in relation to the pope, this codification of ecclesiastical ceremony 'created an entire ballet of precedence regulated by strict rules'.[15] It both established and legitimized status, in precisely the same way as does the placement of contemporary individuals within the Santa Sabina mural.

Perhaps even more importantly, the Santa Sabina mural offers a substantial supplement to our knowledge of the artistic culture in Rome at the beginning of the eighth century, reinforcing the impression already created by the commissions of Pope John VII. For example, the depiction of a donor figure in the act of *proskynesis* has no earlier Roman precedents apart from the 'Maria *regina*' icon in Santa Maria in Trastevere; and the presence of three contemporary figures with 'square haloes' provides further evidence for the introduction of this motif to Rome from the eastern Mediterranean. At a less microscopic level, the painting suggests that the 'Byzantine' (i.e. eastern Mediterranean) elements present in the commissions of John VII were not unique to that specific patron, but were more generally characteristic of the cultural milieu of the church hierarchy.[16]

One final interesting aspect of the mural is the group of the Madonna and Child: not a 'Maria *regina*' on this occasion, but another iconographic 'type' with eastern roots. Mary holds her son on an oval shield. Other Italian examples of this theme are rare, and all are later, with the closest in time and place being the mural in a niche in the right aisle of Santa Maria Antiqua, generally ascribed to the pontificate of Paul I (757–67). We shall come back to it in a subsequent chapter. Earlier examples are known only from the eastern Mediterranean, including a mural at Bawît in Egypt, and an icon preserved in the monastery of Saint Catherine at Mount Sinai.[17] Manuela Gianandrea has linked the development of this image very convincingly to the Christological debates current in the seventh and early eighth centuries, and specifically to the reaffirmation of Christ's dual nature, human and divine, which took place at the Sixth Ecumenical Council to which Theodore, George, and Constantine had all served as members of the Roman delegation.[18] With the revival of the heresy of Monotheletism under the usurper Philippikos, this issue, and quite possibly this specific imagery, once again became important, prompting both the Roman refusal to acknowledge images of the new emperor (*LP* 90.10,

---

[15] *Ibid.*, 86.   [16] Osborne 2014.
[17] Grabar 1968: 609; and Weitzmann 1976: 51 (B 28) and pl. LXXVI.
[18] Gianandrea 2011; and Gianandrea 2014.

ed. Duchesne I: 392) and, as we have seen, the decision to paint the mural in Saint Peter's honouring the six ecumenical councils. There was no more cogent argument in favour of Christ's 'human' nature than his birth from a human mother, Mary; and at the same time the 'divine' nature was alluded to by portraying him on a shield, in the manner of classical depictions of gods and heroes.[19]

In terms of technique, the Santa Sabina mural bears a number of similarities to the near-contemporary decorations in Santa Maria Antiqua, including the addition of straw to the plaster.[20] Intriguingly, there is also evidence for the use for the colour blue of the mineral pigment lazurite (lapis lazuli), for which the only known pre-modern source was in north-eastern Afghanistan. If nothing else, this attests to the continuity of at least some international trade in the early eighth century. Once again, technique and iconography combine to suggest that the mural was probably executed by a workshop from the eastern Mediterranean: *'maestranze orientali'* in the words of Del Duca and Falcucci.[21]

San Saba

Santa Maria Antiqua was not the only early medieval site in Rome to have been brought to light by archaeology in January of 1900. In that same month, excavations were initiated by Mariano Cannizzaro beneath the twelfth-century church of San Saba on the 'little' Aventine hill, on the south side of the city near the Porta San Paolo, and these revealed the existence of an earlier apsed structure, some 10 m wide and 13.4 m long, at a depth of 1.4 m below the floor of the later medieval rebuilding. The early medieval church had itself been built into the remains of a late classical *domus*.[22] Only the lower portions of its walls survived, but, as at Santa Maria Antiqua, the wall surfaces had been completely decorated with mural paintings, and some evidence of this remained in place. Many more fragments of painted plaster had fallen to the floor, but some were recovered; and since 1955 most have been displayed in the corridor leading to the church's sacristy.[23]

---

[19] Independently, Richard Gem made the same suggestion for a similar image placed over the door of the Anglo-Saxon church of Saint Mary at Deerhurst in Gloucestershire: Gem and Howe 2008: 151–3. For the essential link between Mary and the Incarnation, leading to her growing prominence in Christian imagery, see also Kalavrezou 1990 and Dell'Acqua 2018: 33–5.
[20] Del Duca and Falcucci 2010.   [21] *Ibid.*, 39.
[22] *CBCR* IV: 51–71. See also Marucchi 1900; Cannizzaro 1901; Cannizzaro and Gavini 1902; Guidobaldi 1986: 203–5; and Bordi 2008: 13–41, 155–70.
[23] Wilpert 1906; Styger 1914; Lestocquoy 1929; Gandolfo 1989; and Bordi 2008.

A very plausible case has been made for identifying the original foundation with the '*xenodochium de via Nova*', a hospice for pilgrims and other visitors founded by Pope Gregory I (590–604) in a property belonging to his family.[24] But whatever its origins, in the middle of the seventh century the building was reassigned to a refugee community of monks who had fled the monastery of Mar Saba (Saint Sabas in the Kidron Valley outside Jerusalem in the aftermath of the Persian destruction in 614 CE, moving first to North Africa, and then onwards to Rome. The original Palestinian monastery of Mar Saba was named after its fifth-century founder, and still survives. It would become particularly prominent in the eighth century as the home of the principal defender of images and opponent of Iconoclasm, John of Damascus.[25] The Roman dependency was known initially as 'Cella Nova', and it played a prominent role in matters theological and political, beginning with the Lateran Council of 649 when two abbot-priests of the Sabaite houses in Palestine and Africa, John and Theodore, signed a document requesting permission to participate, and this was read into the council's acts.[26] John is in fact the first signatory (of some 36), perhaps implying that he was its principal author. While there is no firm date for the establishment of this Palestinian monastic community in Rome, a date *circa* 650 CE is generally accepted,[27] and the monastery quickly prospered.

In the eighth century, the hellenophone community at San Saba appears to have played a prominent role in international politics. In 772, following his election as pope, Hadrian I (772–95) appointed its abbot, Pardus, as one of two envoys dispatched to the Lombard king, Desiderius, and it is interesting to note that the *Liber pontificalis* uses the Greek word for abbot ('*higoumenos*') rather than the Latin '*abbas*' (*LP* 97.21, ed. Duchesne I: 493). A few years later Pardus, once again identified with his Greek title, played the same role in a mission to Charlemagne.[28] In 787 Hadrian sent another abbot of San Saba, Peter, to represent Rome at the Second Council of Nicaea, convened to restore the use of images in Byzantium (*LP* 97.88, ed. Duchesne, I: 511). This was highly appropriate and may have been a deliberate choice, given the role of the mother house at Jerusalem, and in particular its resident theologian, John of Damascus, in opposing the imperial policy when it had been first introduced. While there is no record of contacts being maintained between the Palestinian monastery and its Roman offshoot, such an eventuality is certainly not impossible. Under Pope Leo III (795–816), San Saba was the recipient of various gifts (*LP* 98.30, 76; ed. Duchesne, II: 9, 22), and in the latter passage,

---

[24] Coates-Stephens 2007. [25] *ODB*: 1063–4. [26] Price 2014: 154–5.
[27] Sansterre 1983 I: 22–9. [28] *Codex epistolaris carolinus* 51, 55, ed. Gundlach, pp. 572, 578.

the famous 'donation list of 807', it is named first in the survey of Roman monasteries. It would retain its 'Greek' character until at least the late tenth century, and among the few precisely datable 'documents' preserved at the site is the funerary epitaph of John, bishop of Nepi and the papal librarian, who died in the year 994.[29] At some point the community became mixed with Latin-speaking Benedictines, and in 1145 the monastery was assigned to Cluny by Pope Lucius II (1144–5). This transfer prompted the rebuilding.

The early medieval church was thus in use some five centuries, and over that period, as at Santa Maria Antiqua, it received numerous campaigns of decoration. In an expert stratigraphical analysis, Giulia Bordi has identified and described seven different stages.[30] The apse, for example, was painted at least twice. But our primary interest lies in the substantial decoration of the side walls with a well-organized scheme comprising three components: painted *vela* in the dado at the base of the wall, followed by a register of standing saints, and above that three registers of narrative scenes.[31] This tripartite formula is paralleled at a number of other early medieval sites in Rome,[32] including the left aisle wall of Santa Maria Antiqua (to be discussed in Chapter 8), but San Saba may represent its earliest documented appearance in the city.

The heads of various saints survive in fragmentary condition, and the only one whose facial type permits a certain identification is Sebastian.[33] Paul Styger identified some ten narrative scenes, many from remnants of their identifying inscriptions, all written in Greek, and beginning with the word '*entha*' ('where', equivalent to the Latin '*ubi*').[34] Bordi's reconstruction envisages the south (right) wall devoted to scenes from the life of Mary and Christ's infancy, and the north (left) wall to episodes from Christ's adult life and Passion, although she notes that none of the Passion scenes have survived, nor their inscriptions. Specific subjects that can be documented include Anna and Joachim (Mary's parents) in the Temple, the Betrothal of Mary and Joseph, the Presentation of Christ in the Temple, the Calling of James and John, the Calling of Peter and Andrew, the Healing of the Paralytic, the Storm on the Sea of Galilee, the Transfiguration, and the Entry into Jerusalem. The inclusion of moments from the early life of Mary draws once again on an apocryphal source, the Protoevangelium of James, constituting a second example of the influence of this text on the visual arts in early eighth-century Rome. San Saba represents the first documented instance of this Marian subject matter in any church in western Europe.

---

[29] Silvagni 1908.   [30] Bordi 2008: 67–78.   [31] *Ibid.*, 87–111.   [32] *Ibid.*, 151.
[33] Wilpert 1916: pl. 170.3; and Gandolfo 1989: pl. 29.   [34] Styger 1914: 60–78.

It is also worth noting that the Transfiguration was accorded much more space than the other scenes, occupying two registers. There are parallels for this practice elsewhere in medieval Roman church decoration, for example, the Crucifixion in the nave of Saint Peter's, but all are later.[35] While the rationale for this anomaly remains a matter of conjecture, it is possibly no coincidence that this Biblical episode, known in Greek as the *Metamorphosis*, was regarded as fundamental to the theological argument for the two natures of Christ, human and divine (Matthew 17:1–8, Mark 9:2–8, Luke 9:28–36). In the sixth century it was important in the campaign against the Monophysite (one nature) heresy, which may help to explain its choice for the apse mosaics in the monastery of Saint Catherine at Mount Sinai and at Sant'Apollinare in Classe, outside Ravenna. In the eighth century, it supported the argument of Christ's Incarnation as giving licence to portraying him in human form. While the Feast of the Transfiguration was broadly celebrated in eastern Christianity, it became official in the West only in 1456.[36]

The largest preserved fragment, roughly 166 x 124 cm, depicts Christ's miracle of 'The Healing of the Paralytic' at Capernaum (Fig. 3.1).[37] In keeping with the Biblical accounts (Mark 2:5–12, Luke 5:18–26), three men on the roof of the building are shown lowering the paralyzed man on his bed into the room beneath. Christ, his head enclosed in a three-rayed cruciform halo, raises his right arm to point towards the man, who in a second moment is shown walking away with his bed on his back.

From the time of the initial discovery, there has been a general consensus among scholars that this phase of the decoration should be dated to the eighth century.[38] There are a number of similarities to murals that we have already encountered: for example, the pattern of intersecting circles used in the borders between the narrative scenes finds an exact parallel at Santa Maria Antiqua in the decorations of Pope John VII, both on the *transennae* and in the Chapel of the Holy Physicians.[39] These designs did not convey specific iconographic meaning, and thus are likely to reflect the practices of specific workshops. Such border decorations are exceptionally rare in early medieval mural painting in Rome, and may again reflect an influence from the eastern Mediterranean. When this practice reappears in Roman church decoration in the second half of the ninth century, most notably at Santa Maria de Secundicerio, the closest parallels are all to be found in Byzantine painted churches in Cappadocia.[40] An eastern origin for the artists is

---

[35] Bordi 2008: 99. [36] *Ibid.*, 110–11. [37] Wilpert 1916: pl. 188.2; and Gandolfo 1989: pl. 32.
[38] For example, Styger 1914: 78; Kitzinger 1934: 31–2; and Belting 1968: 209.
[39] Nordhagen 1968: 64, 68–9. [40] Osborne 1997a: 31–3; and Bordi 2008: 95.

Fig. 3.1. San Saba, Rome: Healing of the Paralytic.

perhaps also suggested by a recent analysis of the pigments used. The blue is particularly interesting, revealing a combination of 'Egyptian blue' (a manufactured pigment combining copper and calcium silicate, used in Egypt at least as early as the Fourth Dynasty) and lapis lazuli from Afghanistan.[41] The murals at Santa Sabina and San Saba currently represent the earliest documented instances of the use of lapis lazuli in wall paintings in western Europe. Intriguingly, the presence of lapis lazuli has also been detected in the John VII murals at Santa Maria Antiqua. However, the uniform size of the particles suggests that it is a synthetic version, and thus probably to be associated with twentieth-century restorations.[42]

Is it possible to date the San Saba murals more precisely? Ernst Kitzinger, Anna Melograni and Giulia Bordi have made a compelling case for a dating to the pontificate of Pope Gregory III (731–41).[43] This is based principally on stylistic comparisons to the heads of saints in the 'lower church' of San Crisogono, attributable to the reign of that pontiff from a passage in his *Liber pontificalis* biography which records substantial work there, including the provision of '*picturas*' (*LP* 92.8, ed. Duchesne I: 418). The formula

[41] Gaetani, Santamaria and Seccaroni 2004.   [42] Amato *et al.* 2017: 1059.
[43] Kitzinger 1934: 32; Melograni 1990: 165–6; and Bordi 2008: 107–9.

for the decoration of the aisle wall at San Crisogono also follows the same overall pattern as San Saba. As Melograni noted, this is an exceptionally rare mention of wall-paintings in the *Liber pontificalis*, and may have been prompted by Gregory's strong opposition to the introduction of Iconoclasm in Byzantium. The prominence given to the scene of the Transfiguration at San Saba may suggest similar thinking by the Sabaite monastic community.

Catacomb of San Callisto

The largest single group of 'consumers' of visual culture in eighth-century Rome is likely to have been the pilgrims who flocked to venerate the tombs of Saint Peter and other martyrs in the hinterland of the city, prompting the compilation by at least the mid-seventh century of guidebooks such as the *Notitia ecclesiarum urbis Romae* and the *De locis sanctis martyrum*.[44] These visitors were primarily although not exclusively from western Europe, including many from Britain. As Bede noted, 'At this time many of the English, both nobles and commoners, men and women, leaders and people in private life, were wont to go from Britain to Rome, inspired by divine love.'[45] In addition to the establishment of hospices and *xenodochia* to physically house the new arrivals,[46] this traffic necessitated extensive renovations to existing ecclesiastical buildings, and in some instances the construction of new ones. For example, as previously noted, in an effort to physically separate the two primary activities in the church of Saint Peter's, namely the flow of pilgrims to the tomb and the performance of the liturgy at the altar, Pope Gregory I had restructured the sanctuary, raising the altar and constructing a passage beneath it to permit access to and from the actual shrine.[47] His predecessor, Pope Pelagius II (579–90), had constructed a new shrine-church for Saint Lawrence on the Via Tiburtina (*LP* 65.2; ed. Duchesne I; 309), and a few decades later Pope Honorius I (625–38) would do the same for Saint Agnes on the Via Nomentana (*LP* 72.3; ed. Duchesne I: 323). In both instances the new edifices were positioned in direct relation to the site of the saint's tomb.

---

[44] *CT* II: 67–95, 101–18; CCSL 175: 303–22; and Geertman 1975: 198–202. For the development of Rome as a 'city of pilgrims', focussed on relics, see Llewellyn 1993: 173–83; Osborne 1985: 284–6; Bauer 2004: 149–79; and Thacker 2007.

[45] Bede, *De temporum ratione*, trans. Wallis: 236. For *graffito* signatures of Anglo-Saxons in the Roman catacombs, see Izzi 2014.

[46] Noble 2013. [47] *CBCR* V: 265–7; and De Blaauw 1994: 530–9.

Other popes sponsored renovations to the catacombs, installing new staircases to provide direct access from the surface to popular tombs, and constructing walls to block off those regions of the underground cemeteries no longer in use. The identity of the saints whose presence ('*praesentia*') was to be venerated, and power ('*potentia*') invoked, was advertised by inscriptions and wall paintings. A typical example is provided by the Catacomb of Pontianus, on the hill of Monteverde above the Via Portuensis, an extensive cemetery first explored and documented by Antonio Bosio in 1618.[48] The *Notitia ecclesiarum* describes it in these words:

Next you proceed to the north, and you discover the church of St Candida, virgin and martyr, whose body lies there. You descend into a tomb chamber, and there you find a countless multitude of martyrs. The martyr Pumenius is there, and in another place the martyr Milix. The whole cavern is filled with the bones of martyrs. Then you come up to St Anastasius pope and martyr, and elsewhere lies the martyr Polion. Next you enter the big church, where saints Abdon and Sennen repose. Then you leave and enter where St Innocent pope and martyr lies.[49]

The site of veneration for Saint Polion, a martyr under Diocletian in 304 CE, was created by blocking off one of the catacomb galleries with a wall, on which a mural was painted depicting the saint holding a crown, flanked by Saints Peter and Marcellinus who hold scrolls. All three are named in inscriptions. On an adjacent wall, Saints Milix and Pumenius are shown flanking a jewelled cross. Both murals belong to the same campaign, as the plaster is contiguous, and may possibly date from the seventh century, more or less contemporary with the guidebooks. Here, and in other cemeteries, many pilgrims inscribed their *graffito* signatures.[50]

There are not a great many catacomb paintings which can be attributed to the early Middle Ages, in other words to the period after the catacombs had ceased to be used as places of burial. Precise datings are usually difficult to deduce, and hence rather rare, as the walls on which they are painted are not constructed, but rather excavated from the earth; but a site in the Catacomb of San Callisto on the Via Appia offers what is perhaps a promising possibility.[51] The tomb of Pope Cornelius (251–3), situated in the area of the cemetery known as the Crypt of Lucina, was rediscovered by Giovanni Battista De Rossi in 1852.[52] The *Liber pontificalis* credits Pope Leo I (440–61) with having established a cult shrine at this spot, and it was still being visited at the end of the eighth century, when Pope Leo III is

---

[48] Bosio 1632: 119–35.   [49] *CT* II: 61–2.   [50] Osborne 1985: 319; Carletti 2002; and Izzi 2014.
[51] Brandenburg 1968–9; and Osborne 1985: 305–10.   [52] De Rossi 1864: 274–305.

credited with its restoration.[53] The actual tomb is flanked by two large murals, each of which depicts two standing male figures with large ochre haloes. All four are tonsured clerics, vested with the pallium and holding books with elaborately decorated covers; and all four are identified by painted inscriptions written vertically beside their heads: to the left, Saint Sixtus II *'papa Romanus'* (257–8), and Saint Optatus *'episcopus'*, a fourth-century bishop from Numidia in North Africa whose relics may have been translated to Rome in the fifth century;[54] and to the right, Saint Cornelius *'papa Romanus'* and Saint Cyprian, a contemporary bishop of Carthage (Fig. 3.2). The cults of Cornelius and Cyprian were evidently closely intertwined. In the disputed papal election of 251, Cyprian had supported Cornelius against his rival Novatian, and the two also shared the same September feast day. Relics of Cyprian may also have been brought to Rome, since the text of the *De locis sanctis martyrum* places the bodies of both at this site: 'Close by in the cemetery of Calixtus, Cornelius and Cyprian lie in a chapel' (*'Inde haud procul in cimiterio Calisti Cornelius et Cyprianus in ecclesia dormiunt'*).[55] The *Notitia ecclesiarum urbis Romae* refers only to Cornelius: *'Cornelius papa et martir longe in antro altero requiescit'*.[56]

Various dates have been suggested for the two murals, covering a range of centuries. The first to tackle the question was Giovanni Battista De Rossi, who opted for a date *circa* 800, based on the documented restoration under Pope Leo III, despite his feeling that the quality of the painting was too good for such a late date.[57] By contrast, Joseph Wilpert initially suggested the mid-sixth century.[58] He believed that the compiler of the *De locis sanctis martyrum* had been misled by this very mural in making his claim that the site also housed the body of Saint Cyprian, and noted that Pope John III (561–74) was recorded as having a special affection for the adjacent cemetery of Praetextatus, where he apparently resided and even consecrated bishops (*LP* 63.5, ed. Duchesne I: 305–6). However, Wilpert would later change his mind, following the 1907 excavations beneath the twelfth-century church of San Crisogono. As previously mentioned, these

---

[53] *'Itemque renovavit ... cimiterium beati Xysti atque Cornelii, via Appia'*, *LP* 98.5, ed. Duchesne II: 2. Relics of Cornelius had been translated by Leo III's predecessor, Hadrian I (772–95), to a church on the papal agricultural estate of Capracorum (*LP* 97.69, ed. Duchesne I: 506) and more were at some point brought to the Roman church of Santa Maria in Trastevere, where a new crypt was later built to house them (as well as the bodies of two other saints, Pope Callixtus and the priest Calepodius) by Pope Gregory IV (827–44) (*LP* 103.32, ed. Duchesne II: 80).

[54] *CT* II: 149 note 1.   [55] *CT* II: 111.   [56] *CT* II: 88.   [57] De Rossi 1864: 298–304.
[58] Wilpert 1903: 459–63.

Fig. 3.2. Saints Cornelius and Cyprian, Catacomb of San Callisto, Rome: Tomb of Pope Cornelius.

revealed an earlier basilica, with mural paintings that have been attributed to the pontificate of Gregory III (731–41) on the basis of the *Liber pontificalis* notice that this pope had repaired the structure and repainted the walls (*LP* 92.8, ed. Duchesne I: 418). In Wilpert's view, the San Crisogono murals offered the closest stylistic parallels to the figures at the tomb of Cornelius, and he noted that Gregory III was also credited with an interest in maintaining liturgical celebrations at the suburban catacombs on the feast-days of the saints.[59] Subsequently, the only significant disagreement with this dating has come from Louis Reekmans, who argued that the best stylistic comparisons could be found in the mosaic decorations of the San Venanzio chapel in the Lateran baptistery, from the decade of the 640s.[60]

Wilpert's judgement in this instance seems astute, and his revised proposal finds strong support in an analysis of the palaeography. Just as manuscript scribes often have a unique and identifiable handwriting style, so too do those who carve or paint inscriptions, and these are often characteristic of a particular time and place. And it is not just the forms of individual letters that are useful: on occasion there are letter combinations, abbreviations, or even variant spellings that can offer valuable clues. The scholar who has demonstrated most effectively the importance of inscriptions for the dating of early medieval wall painting in Rome is Per Jonas Nordhagen, who devoted much of his career to an attempt to develop more objective 'tools' for dating the various campaigns of decoration in Santa Maria Antiqua, as opposed to a general reliance on stylistic analysis. This was vital because the two art historians who had undertaken the most comprehensive analyses of painting in the church before him, Joseph Wilpert (1857–1944) and Ernst Kitzinger (1912–2003), had sometimes disagreed significantly.[61] Wilpert, for example, considered that the redecoration undertaken in the mid-seventh century, in the aftermath of the Lateran Council of 649, was quite extensive, whereas Kitzinger believed it to have been less so, placing most of the first phase of the church's decoration earlier in the century. Nordhagen's examination of the actual plaster levels demonstrated that Wilpert had been right:

From these observations we may conclude that the Church Fathers of about A.D. 650 were no insertions. They are, on the contrary, elements belonging integrally to a large decoration that not only comprised the main wall of the presbytery but also ... had an extension further out in the room.... The best guide in this work of attribution is the *epigraphy*, as the Church Father inscriptions possess some very characteristic palaeographic features: somewhat thin, uneven letters with imprecisely placed seriphs.[62]

Nordhagen was not the first to look at the letter forms in the painted inscriptions. Wladimir De Grüneisen's 1911 monographic treatment of the

---

[59] *LP* 92.17; ed. Duchesne I: 421; and Wilpert 1916: 949–50. [60] Reekmans 1964: 174–84.
[61] Wilpert 1916; and Kitzinger 1934.   [62] Nordhagen 1962: 60.

church, for example, had included an extensive 'Album Epigraphique', and Wilpert had also given some consideration to this approach; but apparently both scholars believed that stylistic analysis offered much greater reliability as a dating tool. And thus the use of palaeography to associate murals from different parts of the church, or indeed beyond Santa Maria Antiqua from other early medieval sites in the city, was not at all a standard practice until Nordhagen demonstrated its utility, deeming it 'our most important instrument in the work of identifying... [the] decoration of the church'.[63]

Palaeography may also be usefully employed in dating the murals flanking the tomb of Pope Cornelius. Set above, beside, and beneath the figures are two substantial quotations from the Old Testament: on the left Psalms 58:17, and on the right Psalms 115:12;[64] and these painted inscriptions provide a large quantity of material which can facilitate an analysis of the letter forms.

Perhaps the most striking characteristic is the use of the letter 'B' to express the voiced 'U' (the sound made by the English letter 'V'), resulting in the spelling *'birtutem'* for the fourth word of the verse from Psalm 58. This is a common occurrence in the written culture of early medieval Rome, and may be found in a variety of media, including both formal contexts such as inscriptions and manuscripts and more informal contexts such as graffiti. We have already noted its occurrence in the painted inscription from the narthex of Santa Sabina. The most likely source of this odd spelling is confusion with the sound of the Greek letter β (*beta*), which had already undergone this linguistic shift, one that has continued in modern Greek; and the phenomenon has been dubbed 'betacism' as a result.[65] While confusion between 'B' and 'V' is not uncommon in manuscripts from western Europe in the early Middle Ages, and especially in Visigothic books, Lowe argued that when the confusion is primarily only in one direction, writing 'B' for a consonantal 'V' but rarely or never vice-versa, this likely implies that the individual responsible was a native Greek speaker, who when confronted with the need to express the sound of a Latin 'V' used the letter form which came most immediately to mind. This view is possibly strengthened by the presence of this shift in books assigned to early medieval Rome that appear to straddle the linguistic divide. Among the earliest examples is a manuscript containing parallel

---

[63] Nordhagen 1962: 66; see also Nordhagen 1983.
[64] Wilpert 1903: 460–1. Both generally follow the text of the Vulgate, except that the fourth word from Psalm 58 is here *'virtutem'*, not *'fortitudinem'*. Some letters are also transposed, for example, *'set'* for *'est'*.
[65] Lowe 1955: 184, 192–3.

Greek and Latin texts of the Acts of the Apostles (Oxford, Bodleian Library, Laud. gr. 35), for which Andrea Lai has recently proposed a date *c.* 600 and a possible origin in the Roman monastery of Sant'Andrea al Celio.[66] And approaching the other end of a dating range spanning roughly two centuries is a manuscript of Pope Zacharias's Greek translation of Pope Gregory I's *Dialogues* (Vatican City, BAV, cod. gr. 1666), a translation undertaken according to his *Liber pontificalis* biographer for the benefit of the 'many who do not know Latin' ('*plures qui Latinam ignorant*'),[67] and dated very precisely by a colophon to the year 800.[68] On folio 41v, someone has added a Latin invocation, '*Domine salvou conserva me*' ('Lord, keep me safe'), but written in Greek letters, using a *beta* for both 'V's. This phenomenon does continue beyond the end of the eighth century, for example, in the inscription on the carved ciborium from Portus, recording the gift of Bishop Stephen in the time of Pope Leo III (795–816), which begins with the word '*Salbo*';[69] but in the ninth century it is found only rarely, eventually disappearing completely from all media in Roman contexts. One of the last known examples in a monumental context occurs in the inscription naming Saint Mark '*ebangelista*' ('evangelist') in the apse of the Roman church of San Marco, undertaken by Pope Gregory IV (827–44) about the year 830.[70] And there is also the mid-ninth-century donor inscription of Sergius '*consol et tabellio*' in Sant'Adriano, which records work that he 'made it new' ('*nobiter fecit*').[71] While the interchangeability of 'B' and 'V' is not unknown in Early Christian epigraphy,[72] the vast majority of documented examples in which 'B' is used for 'V', but not the other way around, belong to the eighth century, at a time when many of those writing in the city may have had Greek as their principal tongue, although being functional orally in both languages.

A number of the individual letter forms are also rather unusual. These include the 'A' (with a horizontal stroke across the top, and the central bar sloping downwards to the left), the 'B' (in which the two loops are separated where they join the stem), the 'G' (with the right vertical post extending well below the rest of the letter), and the combination of 'T' and 'U', in which the second letter is indicated by a short stroke rising diagonally from the base of the 'T'. All these examples are paralleled exactly in the painted inscriptions in the Theodotus chapel in Santa Maria Antiqua, dated to the pontificate of Pope Zacharias (741–52), and the form of 'B' is also identical to the form of the *beta* in the Greek inscriptions

---

[66] Lai 2017. [67] *LP* I: 435; for the context Sansterre 1983 I: 75. [68] Osborne 1990: 77–80.
[69] Silvagni 1943a I: pl. XV.1; and Cardin 2008: pl. 50b. [70] See Bolgia 2006: 3.
[71] Bordi 2011: 477–8. [72] Testini 1980: 340.

from San Saba. These comparisons provide substantial support for a proposed date in the second quarter of the eighth century, and confirm the continued function of the catacombs as goals for pilgrimage. The murals served as 'posters' to identify which saints could be venerated, and where exactly their remains lay, providing a useful complement to the written guidebooks.

The Catacomb of San Callisto is named for Pope Callixtus I (218–22), who as a deacon prior to his election as bishop had been in charge of this Christian cemetery on the Via Appia. Callixtus was himself buried elsewhere, in the Catacomb of Calepodius on the Via Aurelia Antica, and the area of his grave also received mural decorations in the first half of the eighth century, quite possibly in the time of the same pontiff, Gregory III. Fragments of these murals were rediscovered in the decade of the 1960s by Aldo Nestori.[73] In contrast to the iconic images at the tomb of Pope Cornelius, here the decorations consist of narrative scenes, identified by painted inscriptions, illustrating the death of Callixtus, who suffered martyrdom by being thrown into a well, and his subsequent burial. Long after this space had ceased to be used as a cemetery, it continued to be visited by pilgrims; and in order to facilitate their access the galleries leading to other parts of the catacomb were blocked off, and two stairways installed for direct communication with the surface, presumably one functioning as an entrance and the other as an exit. Although their content was different, these murals also functioned as 'posters', educating visitors to the grave about the circumstances of the pope's martyrdom, and hence his claim on their attention. The proposed dating to the pontificate of Gregory III stems from a passage in the *Liber pontificalis* which mentions that he rebuilt the shrine of Saint Callixtus and decorated it with paintings (*LP* 92.11, ed. Duchesne I: 419).

Conclusion

The decoration of wall surfaces in the early Middle Ages was intimately linked to the function of the space in question. The selection of mural paintings examined in this chapter, recording a vow made by two senior members of the Roman clergy, decorating the walls of a Greek monastic church, and marking the grave of an early pope for the benefit of pilgrims visiting the shrines of the saints in the catacombs, all provide useful glimpses of different aspects of

---

[73] Nestori 1971; Osborne 1985: 313–6; Jessop 1999: 272–8; and Minasi 2009.

religious life in the city in the first half of the eighth century. These paintings all document activities or practices thought to be of sufficient importance to merit the creation of a permanent visual record, accompanied by inscriptions intended to assist the viewer in identifying the subject. The specific purposes varied: they might be commemorative, liturgical, or something akin to billboards; but all served some specific function.

Despite the apparent collapse of manufacturing revealed by archaeology at the Crypta Balbi, Rome was certainly not some form of abandoned 'wasteland', nor simply in John Romano's words 'an enormous farm ensconced amid gigantic ruins'.[74] The Crypta Balbi excavations present a 'snapshot' of urban life in and after 700, but not the full picture. The city had certainly experienced a precipitous decline in population, not to mention in its political fortunes; but from its apparent nadir in the mid-sixth century, in the calamitous aftermath of the Gothic wars, it would re-emerge with new purpose, and by the close of the seventh century had become a vibrant and enormously varied multilingual and multicultural community. Perhaps it is only in Rome that a Greek monk, Theodore from Tarsus in Cilicia, could find himself appointed archbishop of Canterbury and dispatched to distant Britain with a mandate to reform the English church.[75] Apart from imperial bureaucrats and army officers, most of the newcomers to the city in the first half of the seventh century are likely to have been refugees from the successive Persian and Arab conquests of the eastern littoral of the Mediterranean, as was likely the case with Theodore.

Following the successful campaigns to convert the Anglo-Saxons to Christianity, in the second half of the seventh century Rome would start to attract a second wave of visitors and pilgrims from across western Europe, and perhaps especially from Britain. Those visitors were both many and varied. A snapshot of their variety is perhaps provided by a single paragraph in the *Liber pontificalis* entry for Pope Constantine I (*LP* 90.9, ed. Duchesne I: 391–2), which records two Anglo-Saxon kings who journeyed to Rome in order to venerate the body of Saint Peter before they died,[76] and the archbishop of Milan who, like Wilfrid of York a decade earlier, came to have a jurisdictional dispute adjudicated at the papal court. This phenomenon would be further abetted by the development of close political ties with the Franks in the middle of the century, as well as the continued Christianization of central Europe by papally sponsored

---

[74] Romano 2014: 12.   [75] Lapidge 1995.
[76] The precedent had been set by Cædwalla, king of Wessex, who died in Rome on 20 April 689 and was buried in Saint Peter's. The text of his epitaph is preserved (Sharpe 2005; and Story 2010: 7).

missionaries such as Boniface. But despite its evolving development as a hub for contacts with western Europe north of the Alps, the city's ecclesiastical and monastic infrastructure remained firmly embedded in the artistic and religious culture of the broader Christian Mediterranean, as did the painting practices of the artists employed.

The popes in the early decades of the eighth century faced many challenges: the political vacuum resulting from the waning authority of the emperor of Byzantium and his exarch in Ravenna, the persistent doctrinal controversies, the growing physical threat posed by the Lombards, and the maintenance of infrastructure required to meet the daily needs of both residents and visitors. The *Liber pontificalis* passages are instructive, but the full flavour and deep cultural roots of early medieval Rome are perhaps best revealed in its functional spaces and their decorations.

4 | 'The City of the Church'

There is no single dramatic moment when the Roman 'republic' ('*res publica*'), as it would later style itself, came into being.[1] It was 'a process and not an event',[2] a gradual evolution, not a dramatic revolution; but it is not difficult to identify some important signposts along the path, nor the forces which caused it to happen.[3] The two most important catalysts were, firstly, a continuing struggle between the pope and the emperor for authority in matters of the faith and, secondly, the pressing need for Rome to defend itself militarily against the expansionist ambitions of the Lombard kingdom. In the first half of the eighth century both issues reached the tipping point.[4] But the underlying concept, that the Rome of Romulus and Remus and the Caesars was being replaced by the Rome of the popes, has much earlier origins, and had already been expressed, for example, in the poem declaimed by Arator in the church of San Pietro in Vincoli in 544.[5]

If this story were being made into a film, it would perhaps open in the reign of Pope Sergius I (687–701). Early in his pontificate, the Emperor Justinian II had convened a council in Constantinople with the aim of legislating various church practices, the so-called Quinisext Council of 692. As we have already seen, its disciplinary decrees, or 'canons', were sent to Sergius with a request that the pope add his signature, and this posed a problem since, as his *Liber pontificalis* biographer observed, 'certain chapters which were outside the usages of the church had been annexed to the acts'. No doubt mindful of the fate of Pope Martin, who a scant 40 years earlier had been arrested and sent to Constantinople, leading to his eventual death in exile at Cherson, Sergius nevertheless refused even to consider the document sent to him, in the words of his *Liber pontificalis* biographer, 'choosing to die sooner than consent to erroneous novelties'.[6]

---

[1] The phrase 'Roman republic' is first used by Pope Stephen II. For the understanding of this term, see Noble 1984: 94–8; Gantner 2014b: 467–9; Gantner 2015: 252–3; and Delogu 2015: 202–5.
[2] Noble 1984: 98.
[3] Useful surveys of this topic include Bertolini 1973 and, particularly, Noble 1984.
[4] Hallenbeck 1982; and Noble 1984: 15–60.   [5] de Nie 2014.
[6] *LP* 86.6–7, ed. Duchesne I: 373; trans. Davis 2010: 82.

In response, Justinian sent his 'ferocious chief *spatharius*' Zacharias to apprehend the pope; but in the opening salvo which presaged the changes to come, the army of Italy rose up to defend their pontiff, entering Rome and besieging the Lateran patriarchate where Zacharias had taken refuge. Our text conjures up a dramatic image of the imperial *spatharius* cowering under the pope's bed in abject fear for his life, and eventually he would escape unharmed only through Sergius's fervent intervention on his behalf.

One of the Quinisext canons, number 82, had prohibited the practice of depicting Christ symbolically in the form of a lamb, previously a common occurrence in the decoration of Roman churches; and in what has usually been interpreted as a direct challenge to that restriction, Sergius added the words '*Agnus Dei, qui tollis peccata mundi, miserere nobis*' to the text of the mass, to be sung at the moment of the *fractio panis*.[7] As Julius Caesar is said to have quipped many centuries earlier: '*Alea iacta est*'.

This was the first occasion on which the army of Italy had defied the emperor to protect the pope, but it would not be the last.[8] A few years afterwards, the '*militia totius Italiae*' rose again to protect Pope John VI (701–5) against the imperial exarch Theophylact (*LP* 87.1, ed. Duchesne I: 383). A brief *rapprochement* was achieved in the time of Pope Constantine I (708–15), who not only journeyed voluntarily to Constantinople, but also made it safely home again;[9] but when Justinian II was overthrown in 711 by Philippikos, and a new *dux*, Peter, was sent out to Rome, violence soon erupted on the Via Sacra, 'in front of the palace' ('*ante palatium*'), and again the pope had to intervene (*LP* 90.10, ed. Duchesne I: 392).

During the pontificate of Gregory II (715–31) and the reign of the Emperor Leo III (717–41), the situation deteriorated rapidly; but the pope managed to survive a series of plots against his life hatched by various imperial officials, and the army of Rome, supported by the neighbouring Lombard dukes, defended the city at the Milvian Bridge (*LP* 91.14–16, ed. Duchesne I: 403–4). Thomas Noble has viewed this as another defining moment: 'For all practical purposes imperial authority in the city and region of Rome had ceased to exist.'[10] But it was Leo's subsequent efforts to eradicate the use of religious images which seems to have tipped the balance irrevocably, leading to a broad revolt. We are told that 'throughout Italy . . . they all elected their own dukes'.[11] By the early 730s the duchy of

---

[7] *LP* 86.14, ed. Duchesne I: 376; trans. Davis 2010: 84. For an opposing view: Opie 2002: 1830–3.
[8] For an overview of the political situation in 'Byzantine Italy' between 680 and 751 CE, see Brown 1995a: 320–7.
[9] See Sansterre 1984a.   [10] Noble 1984: 29.
[11] *LP* 91.17, ed. Duchesne I: 404; trans. Davis 2007: 11.

Rome had become 'an autonomous region under the pope',[12] perhaps more by accident than any conscious design.

The origins of the new imperial policy of Iconoclasm, the prohibition of all figural religious imagery, have been sought in a wide variety of political, social and economic factors beyond the obvious Old Testament prohibition of idolatry (Exodus 20:4).[13] The Roman response was both clear and immediate: within six months of his March 731 election, Pope Gregory III (731–41) convened a synod at Saint Peter's, attended by almost 100 bishops in addition to other members of the clergy.[14] As the *Liber pontificalis* recounts in detail, this gathering anathematized anyone who 'should remove, destroy, profane and blaspheme against this veneration of the sacred images, viz. of our God and Lord Jesus Christ, of his mother the ever-virgin immaculate and glorious Mary, of the blessed apostles and of all the saints'.[15] This decree, and various papal letters, were despatched to Emperor Leo III in Constantinople, but the documents were either seized or refused, and their bearers dishonourably received. Neither party wished to give ground nor to recognize the other's authority.

In what must have served as a clear statement of the Roman position, Gregory added a series of images to the interior of Saint Peter's.[16] Six 'twisted onyx columns', the gift of the exarch Eutychius, were set up in front of the *confessio*. These supported wooden beams, sheathed with silver and bearing images in relief depicting Christ, Mary, and various saints;[17] and nearby he also constructed a new chapel, in the westernmost intercolumniation on the south side of the nave ('*iuxta arcum principalem, parte virorum*'), dedicated to Christ, Mary and all the saints (*LP* 92.6–7, ed. Duchesne I: 417–18).[18] In addition to making numerous other lavish gifts, here the pope also installed an icon of Mary, whose image was given a crown and necklace made of gold and decorated with precious gems, as well as jewelled earrings. Significantly, this space was apparently intended to serve as Gregory's funerary chapel. Inscribed stone panels not only recorded the dedication in April 732 but also the text of prayers for his soul.[19] Some fragments of these still survive in the Vatican grottoes.[20]

---

[12] Noble 1984: 40.

[13] Useful introductions to the topic include Brown 1973 and Mango 1976. For a more detailed survey of actual events in the eighth century, and the underlying theological debates, Noble 2009: 46–110.

[14] Noble 2009: 118–23.   [15] *LP* 92.3, ed. Duchesne I: 416; trans. Davis 2007: 20.

[16] McClendon 2013.   [17] *LP* 92.5, ed. Duchesne I: 417; trans. Davis 2007: 21–2.

[18] See also Maskarinec 2018: 124–30.   [19] *LP* ed. Duchesne I: 422–3 note 13.

[20] Gray 1948: 50–1, nos 6–7.

At the same time, as relations with Constantinople deteriorated, and probably in no small part because of this growing rift, the popes found themselves having to engage increasingly with the Lombards, who were quick to exploit the political situation, not only their ambitious king, Liutprand (r. 712–44), but also, in more immediate proximity to the city, the dukes of Spoleto and Benevento. In 717 the Lombards seized the *castrum* of Cumae, cutting the coastal road between the duchies of Rome and Naples, and it fell to Pope Gregory II to organize its recovery, and to pay 70 pounds of gold as a 'ransom'.[21] More seizures would follow, for example, Sutri, north of Rome, in 727/8, and again the pope had to pay for its return. It is probably significant that Liutprand couched the restitution as 'a donation to the blessed apostles Peter and Paul', in other words to the Roman church and not the Byzantine state.[22] The autonomous land of Saint Peter was slowly beginning to take shape.

Despite efforts by Popes Gregory III and Zacharias (741–52) to stem the Lombard tide through the judicious exercise of diplomacy, the writing was on the proverbial wall. Some solution to this growing threat needed to be found urgently, and no assistance was forthcoming from Constantinople. Gregory III was the first to make an approach to the Franks, communicating twice with Charles Martel, who as 'mayor of the palace' exercised actual authority in the Merovingian kingdom. Although the *Liber pontificalis* passage describing the dispatch by ship of the papal envoys Anastasius and Sergius is considered to be a slightly later interpolation and appears only in the so-called Frankish recension,[23] the texts of both letters are preserved in the *Codex epistolaris carolinus*.[24] Gregory's appeal was couched in the form of Christian duty, stressing what Charles needed to do if he hoped to gain eternal life; but the mayor of the Merovingian palace was on good terms with the Lombard king, and no intervention was forthcoming. Two decades later the situation had evolved further, and this time it was Charles Martel's son, Pippin, who approached Pope Zacharias, with his famous question whether those who wielded power *de facto* should also do so *de iure*.[25] He received the answer he

---

[21] *LP* 91.7, ed. Duchesne I: 400–1; trans. Davis 2007: 7.
[22] *LP* 91.21, ed. Duchesne I: 407; trans. Davis 2007: 14. See also Noble 1984: 31–2. An inscription formerly preserved in Liutprand's palace at Corteolona may suggest that the Lombard king joined the pope in opposing the iconoclastic policy of Emperor Leo III: see Dell'Acqua and Gantner 2019.
[23] *LP* 92.14, ed. Duchesne I: 420, and 424–5 note 34; and Davis 2007: 26–7.
[24] *Codex epistolaris carolinus* 1–2, ed. Grundlach, pp. 476–9. See also Noble 1984: 44–5.
[25] Noble 1984: 67–71. McKitterick (2004: 133–50) suggests that this story may have been fabricated by the Franks, in order to justify Childeric's deposition, as there is no record of it in the *Liber pontificalis* or other contemporary sources, including papal correspondence.

desired, and promptly proceeded to seize the throne from the last king of the Merovingian line, Childeric III. The door was thus open to a new political alliance between the papacy and the Franks, which would come to fruition with Pope Stephen II's historic meeting with Pippin at Ponthion in January 754.

The crisis faced by the papacy in the first half of the eighth century was not only political and theological; archaeological evidence suggests that it was also economic. Datable deposits from the site of the Crypta Balbi and the imperial *fora* demonstrate that manufacturing and trade continued to thrive in Rome through to at least the beginning of the eighth century, but then suffered a significant collapse, attested most dramatically by the sudden disappearance of transport amphorae and other ceramics imported from southern Italy and Africa, and also of the circulation of coinage, as well as an apparent end to the production of 'luxury' goods (*'artigianato specializzato'*, in the words of Riccardo Santangeli Valenzani) thought to have been intended for the export trade.[26] Finds of 'open' ceramics, which is to say plates and platters, which had constituted about 70 per cent of pottery finds prior to the year 700, drop to a scant 2 per cent by 750 and thereafter disappear entirely, suggesting that perhaps they had been replaced by objects made of wood or metal. And at the same time a new ceramic object makes its appearance: the bread mould (*'testa di pane'*), implying that the baking of bread was now a domestic activity undertaken by individual households, and no longer a larger-scale operation performed by commercial bakeries. The evidence for other trades suggests a similar pattern of simplification, as the city of Rome, and individual households, were increasingly constrained to become self-sufficient.[27]

This view has also been corroborated by archaeobotany. Soil from early medieval levels in the Forum of Caesar has revealed that this area was used for the cultivation of vegetables (cabbage, lettuce) and herbs and spices (coriander, mustard, mint, anise), to which would later be added grapevines and fruit trees;[28] and Daniele Manacorda has recently suggested that the development of intramural agriculture may well have been prompted by the 'devastations' experienced in the territory outside the walls in the eighth century.[29] As we shall see shortly, this issue was compounded by the

---

[26] Rovelli 1998; Rovelli 2000; Santangeli Valenzani 2003; and Santangeli Valenzani 2004a: 24–6.
[27] Santangeli Valenzani 2004a: 26–7.   [28] Santangeli Valenzani 2004b.
[29] Manacorda 2017: 293. Caroline Goodson's survey of the introduction of 'kitchen gardens' to urban spaces in early medieval Italy, although mostly based on evidence from the tenth century, takes a slightly different perspective, declining to see this practice as 'a barometer of decay' (Goodson 2018: 345).

imperial confiscation of revenues and produce from estates owned by the Roman church in southern Italy and Sicily. Rome could no longer depend on the importation of foodstuffs, and consequently needed to look closer to home for the necessities of life. This change may also have prompted Pope Gregory II's endowment of Saint Peter's with a series of olive groves, intended to ensure a sufficient supply of oil for the basilica's many lamps.[30] Survival would require new ideas, and a rethinking of the requisite infrastructure. Interestingly, the one area in which technical evidence points to the presence of 'non-Roman' specialists is church decoration, where the presence of new mortar techniques and new pigments suggests new exposure to practices otherwise associated with the eastern Mediterranean.

It is surely no coincidence that the first half of the eighth century also witnesses the first attempts by the papacy to issue its own coinage, at first in bronze and then also in silver, although this development may have been the result of the declining availability of imperial issues, coupled with the need for at least some coinage for daily use, rather than being a deliberate political statement.[31] Rome retained at least a partially monetized economy, even if a pale shadow of its former self, and there is anecdotal evidence for some continuation of its public markets (*LP* 93.22, ed. Duchesne I: 433), so some means of financial exchange was required. These first papal issues bore the monogram or initial of the reigning pontiff, for example, Gregory III (731–41) and Zacharias (741–52), although their unusual shape has raised some doubts as to whether they were truly 'coins'.[32] The issue of regular coinage would have to wait until the reign of Pope Hadrian I in the last quarter of the century, and would quickly change to follow Carolingian not Byzantine models, based on the silver *denarius*.[33]

In the years between 700 and 750 the papacy added political leadership to its already substantial hegemony in matters ecclesiastical and spiritual, with the result that rule of the city became more or less synonymous with occupation of the *cathedra* of Saint Peter. After four centuries in which ecclesiastical authority had remained subservient to political authority, Rome had finally evolved into a 'city of the church', to use Marazzi's

---

[30] Story 2018. The inscription, preserved at Saint Peter's, provides ample evidence of 'betacism' in the spelling of '*olibetum*'.

[31] For a general overview of early medieval papal coinage, Grierson and Blackburn 1986: 259–66.

[32] O'Hara 1985; Morrisson and Barrandon 1988; and Calabria and De Spirito 1995. As Noble observes (2001b: 72), 'Their intended use is hard to ascertain. And their political significance is impossible to interpret.'

[33] Noble 1984: 289–90; and Rovelli 2000: 95.

phrase.[34] With this new status came new papal duties, including responsibility for maintaining the physical infrastructure of the city as well as the welfare of its inhabitants. This necessitated in turn the creation of a variety of new institutions and the appointment of new administrators; and for the latter the papacy turned to an emerging nobility, the military officers and their families who had 'jumped ship', so to speak, to protect their bishop from his enemies in Ravenna and Constantinople. One of these men, Theodotus, has left a substantial footprint, along with his image, in the Roman church of Santa Maria Antiqua. We shall meet him next.

[34] Marazzi 2000: 35; and Noble 2001b: 49.

5 | The Chapel of Theodotus in Santa Maria Antiqua

The church of Santa Maria Antiqua in the Roman Forum preserves painting from a number of decorative campaigns undertaken between the sixth and eleventh centuries, many in a highly fragmentary condition, and some now all but illegible; but among the best preserved are the murals which adorn all four walls of the small chapel to the left of the main sanctuary, at the head of the eastern (left) aisle (Pl. 6; Fig. 2.5 for plan).[1] Gordon Rushforth called them 'perhaps the most interesting remains in the building'.[2] This space is known either as the Chapel of Saints Quiricus and Julitta, to whom it was evidently dedicated, or as the Theodotus chapel, from the name of its patron. And as it is the patron who will be of primary interest in the discussion which follows, we shall prefer the latter name here.

The Theodotus chapel is rectangular in shape, approximately 7 m long and 4 m wide, with a large square niche set into the south (altar) wall opposite the axial doorway.[3] A second point of entry may be found in the west (right) wall, immediately adjacent to the main entrance, providing direct access to and from the sanctuary. Originally, this entire space was covered with a marble revetment in *opus sectile*, probably of the fourth century, comprising a dado and three upper levels; and most of this decoration apparently remained intact until the middle of the eighth century, apart from some painted replacements to damaged areas adjacent to the niche. The coverings of the dado and first level were removed at some point, and then in the mid-eighth century replaced by murals. The upper walls probably retained much of their marble cladding until a later date, but this too was removed at some unknown point, perhaps at the moment of the structure's abandonment, or even as late as the sixteenth century, with the material presumably intended for reuse elsewhere. Only the preparatory levels survive, characterized by strips of terracotta taken from *amphorae* (*opus testaceum*).[4]

---

[1] Bordi 2016b. [2] Rushforth 1902: 38.
[3] For plans, see also Rushforth 1902: 18; Tea 1937: insert after p. 34; and *CBCR* II: pl. XVIII.
[4] Guiglia Guidobaldi 2004; Bordi and Guiglia Guidobaldi 2016; and Bordi 2016b: 261.

The interior of the chapel was divided in two by the addition of a marble screen, joining the two side walls; its footing may still be observed at floor level, and one fragment remains embedded in the west (right) wall. The screen presumably had a central opening, aligned with the altar, and the square base of the latter still survives, set out from the south wall. A cavity in its centre may have been intended as a space for relics.[5] Spanning the room above the screen was some form of transverse element, either an architrave supported on columns rising from the screen or perhaps simply a wooden beam, and this was in place, or at least planned, before the chapel was painted, since provision was made for it in laying out the borders of the decorative programme on the west (right) wall. The purpose of such sanctuary barriers was to separate the sacred space reserved for the clergy from that accessible to the laity, and the screen itself could also be decorated with images. Our knowledge of such objects is exceptionally scanty for the early Middle Ages. No early examples survive in Constantinople, and even the archaeological evidence is sparse.[6] In the west (right) wall beyond the screen and adjacent to the altar, a large cavity has been excavated into the thickness of the original wall. This likely functioned as a cupboard, presumably for the storage of vestments and utensils needed for the liturgy, and grooves on both sides of its interior suggest that there were formerly two shelves.

Before we turn to examine the decorations, it is probably useful to briefly consider the intended function of this space, about which rather little is actually known. It is tempting to see the two chapels flanking the main sanctuary as places for the preparation of the eucharist and storage of the liturgical books and vestments, in other words the *prothesis* and *diakonikon* of later Byzantine practice. But there is no evidence for such functions, nor even for the use of these terms, at this early a date.[7]

Another possibility is that it was intended for burials, and while there may be some evidence for at least one burial here,[8] it is again unlikely that

---

[5] Rushforth 1902: 39. The number of altars in the church is unknown, although a reference in the *Liber pontificalis* life of Pope Leo III (795–816) to his gift to Santa Maria Antiqua of a silver ciborium '*super altare maiore*' (*LP* 98.52, ed. Duchesne II: 14) implies that these were multiple. Part of another altar survives today in the church in the left aisle, see Tea 1937: 99–100. For the development of secondary altars in Roman churches, see Bauer 1999a: 398–417 (for Santa Maria Antiqua: 408–12). It has recently been suggested that the fragments of a marble altar canopy (*ciborium*) discovered in Boni's excavation may have belonged to this chapel (Severini 2015). But a date later in the eighth century may be preferable given the strong resemblance to the *ciborium* discovered in the excavations of Sant'Ippolito at Isola Sacra (Portus), which bears an inscription dating it to the pontificate of Leo III. For the latter object, see Pani Ermini 1976.

[6] Marinis 2014: 41–8.   [7] Ibid., 35–41.

[8] Rushforth 1902: 91, 106. However, there is no indication of its date.

this was the primary original intention. The presence of a sanctuary barrier and altar signify that it was a consecrated space, in use for the performance of the liturgy. This is confirmed to some extent by the cupboard, which must pre-date the addition of the murals as these were planned to take this reduced pictorial surface into account. At least in theory, the presence of an altar and the performance of the liturgy would have rendered the chapel inappropriate for burials. Subsidiary chapels flanking the main apse are certainly attested in Byzantium from at least the ninth century, for example, in Cappadocia and at Skripou in Greece. In the latter church the side chapels were dedicated to Saints Peter and Paul.[9] But their precise function remains murky. We shall return to the notion of a possible function as a funerary chapel later in this chapter.

Murals survive on all four walls, in two registers, in addition to the interior of the large niche; and their state of preservation, while far from complete, is nonetheless quite remarkable in comparison to other areas of the church. Rushforth noted that 'except where the plaster has fallen, they are as fresh as when they left the artist's hands'.[10] The paintings were executed for the most part in a true *fresco* technique,[11] in a single decorative campaign that, as we shall see, can be dated quite precisely to the middle of the eighth century. That they have survived so well is no doubt due at least in part to the fact that the barrel vault covering the chapel remained substantially intact, unlike the vaulting elsewhere in the structure; and consequently, while there are certainly areas of loss, these are comparatively few.

The lowest zone, or dado, of each wall is decorated with representations of fictive draperies (*vela*), imitating the real textiles which would have adorned many parts of an early medieval church (Fig. 5.1); and indeed the *Liber pontificalis* records the donation of some thousands of such draperies, for the most part silks imported from Byzantium or the Muslim world, on the part of eighth- and ninth-century pontiffs.[12] Prior to the eighth century the dadoes of Roman churches seem normally to have been decorated with marble, either real or fictive, and painted imitation of marble may be seen for example on the walls flanking the apse in Santa Maria Antiqua, dating from the seventh-century campaign of decorations.[13] But fictive curtains were also used for dadoes in the Roman era, and this practice appears to have survived through to Late Antiquity mostly in the

---

[9] Marinis 2014: 39.   [10] Rushforth 1902: 38.   [11] Valentini 2016.
[12] De Waal 1888; Croquison 1964; Petriaggi 1984; Osborne 1992: 314–19; Delogu 1998; Noble 2000: 73–6; Andaloro 2001–2; and Miller 2014.
[13] Nordhagen 1978: 98–100, and pl. VIII a–b.

Fig. 5.1. Santa Maria Antiqua, Rome: Theodotus chapel, detail of fictive curtains (*vela*).

eastern Mediterranean, where it may be found in ecclesiastical contexts in Egypt and, later in the Byzantine period, in churches in Cappadocia. As we have seen, its revival in Rome is first attested in the campaign of decorations in the sanctuary of Santa Maria Antiqua undertaken by Pope John VII in the first decade of the eighth century.[14] Given that pontiff's apparent predilection for artistic notions imported from the eastern Mediterranean, it is tempting to see this as a deliberate choice, overturning previous local custom, although the possibility cannot be ruled out that there were Roman examples of the sixth or seventh century that simply have not survived. Consciously intended or not, the concept immediately became the norm, and the use of such painted textiles would remain one of the standard forms of dado decoration in Roman churches from the eighth century onwards, well beyond the end of the Middle Ages. The particular design employed in the Theodotus chapel for the fictive fabric is similar to those found in other painted dadoes of the eighth century, and features a curtain decorated with 'spades' (possibly intended to represent stylized ivy leaves) and groups of four *orbiculi*, hanging from a simulated rod by *trompe l'oeil* rings.[15]

---

[14] Osborne 1992: 321–4.   [15] *Ibid.*, 328–30.

Moving upwards, we encounter a range of different types of subject matter, some hagiographic and some devotional. The east wall of the chapel, and southern half of the west wall (the part beyond the chancel barrier), is devoted to a narrative cycle depicting the passion of Saints Quiricus and Julitta, a mother and son who were martyrs at Tarsus, where they were judged and condemned by the *praeses* Alexander in the time of the emperor Diocletian.[16] Saints' lives provided tangible examples that humans were also capable of extreme acts of witness to their faith, *in imitatione Christi*, and by the eighth century, readings from their passions had been incorporated into the mass on their specific feast days;[17] but this one is particularly notable if only because no earlier hagiographic cycle of this sort has survived anywhere else in the world of Christian art.

There are eight scenes in all, to be read from left to right, beginning at the north (entrance) end. Originally, all were identified by Latin inscriptions beginning with the word '*ubi*' ('where'), although only portions of these survive.[18] On the left wall,[19] the episodes shown are (1) the arrest and arraignment of Julitta; (2) the arrest of her three-year-old son Quiricus; (3) Quiricus confesses his Christian faith (very poorly preserved); (4) the beating of Quiricus; (5) Quiricus addresses Alexander despite his tongue having been cut out: '+ UBI S(an)C(tu)S CUIRICUS LINGUA ISCISSA LOQUIT AT PRESIDEM' (quite well preserved) (Figs. 5.2, 5.3); and (6) Quiricus and Julitta in prison observe the preparations for their torture (Figs. 5.2, 5.4). Moving to the west wall for the two final scenes,[20] we see (7) Quiricus and Julitta, wearing only loincloths, tortured in a 'frying pan' ('*sartago*'), while Christ intervenes from the upper left to ease their torment (Fig. 5.5; and Pl. 7): '+UBI S(an)C(tu)S CUIRICUS CUM MATRE SUAM IN SARTAGINE MISSI SUNT' (a small panel, situated above the storage cupboard excavated into the thickness of the wall); and (8) a conflation of two scenes: the final torture of Quiricus, who is depicted having nails driven into his head while an angel descends from heaven to extract them, followed by his death when he is dashed against the ground in front of Alexander's throne (Fig. 5.6). Julitta's own death by decapitation is not shown, and, apart from the first scene in the cycle, the emphasis seems to be squarely on the boy, Quiricus, rather than his mother.[21]

---

[16] Rushforth 1902: 45–50; De Grüneisen 1911: 122–32; and Jessop 1999: 241–55.
[17] Jessop 1999: 253–4.
[18] For the early medieval Roman use of captions beginning with '*ubi*', or its Greek equivalent, '*entha*', Osborne 1982: 184.
[19] Wilpert 1916: pls 166.1, 186.   [20] Ibid., pl. 187.   [21] Jessop 1999: 251.

Fig. 5.2. Santa Maria Antiqua, Rome: Theodotus chapel, cycle of Quiricus and Julitta (east wall).

Little is known about the early cult of these two Tarsus martyrs, especially in Italy. Their *acta* may have reached Rome by the end of the fifth century, when Pope Gelasius I's synod of 495 supposedly condemned them as apocryphal,[22] but the text of the *De libris recipiendis et non recipiendis* is not attested before 700, and may actually have been written in Gaul.[23] More secure evidence is provided by a ninth-century Latin translation of their passion which survives in the Biblioteca Nazionale at Turin: MS Lat. Memb. D-V-3, fols 123r–133v.[24] In this account the scene of the torture in the *sartago* is placed at an earlier moment in the narrative, before Quiricus's tongue is removed, and the sequence in the chapel may well have been adjusted to accommodate the specifics of the pictorial space available. The 'frying pan' episode fits perfectly into the smaller space above the cupboard on the west wall, and is perhaps the only one which could have done so.[25] We may readily agree with Rushforth that 'the reason for the interest taken in the saints to whom the chapel is dedicated is not obvious'.[26] There can be little doubt that this particular devotion must have had some special meaning to the donor or his family, although the precise

[22] Rushforth 1902: 44; and Bordi 2016b: 261.   [23] McKitterick 1989: 202.
[24] Jessop 1999: 251.   [25] *Ibid.*, 245.   [26] Rushforth 1902: 44.

Fig. 5.3. Santa Maria Antiqua, Rome: Theodotus chapel, Quiricus speaks to the judge after his tongue has been removed (detail).

Fig. 5.4. Santa Maria Antiqua, Rome: Theodotus chapel, Quiricus and Julitta in prison (detail).

Fig. 5.5. Santa Maria Antiqua, Rome: Theodotus chapel, Quiricus and Julitta tortured in the *sartago*.

Fig. 5.6. Santa Maria Antiqua, Rome: Theodotus chapel, martyrdom of Quiricus.

nature of the relationship is one of the many mysteries of Santa Maria Antiqua that still remain unresolved.[27]

The murals on the south (altar) wall (Fig. 5.7) contain important details which allow us to identify the date of the chapel, and its patron, with considerable precision.[28] In 1947 this entire section was removed from the wall for conservation by the Istituto Centrale del Restauro,[29] and for many years it was stored in the offices of the Soprintendenza del Foro Romano (the former conventual buildings of Santa Maria Nova); but in March 2007 it was returned to the church and replaced in its original position.

The zone immediately below the niche depicts a variation on a standard Roman compositional formula, commonly used in the early Middle Ages, in which the donor is presented to the enthroned figures of, in this instance, Mary and the infant Christ, by their 'guarantor' saints: here the two principal patron

---

[27] There is also a Roman church dedicated to Saints Quiricus and Julitta, located just to the east of the Forum of Augustus and built into the remains of a fourth-century *domus* (Corbett 1970; Guidobaldi 2007); but its dedication to the two martyrs of Tarsus is not documented before the twelfth century (Hülsen 1927: 428–9). Pompeo Ugonio reported that the apse mosaic depicted saints Lawrence and Stephen (Guidobaldi 2007: 66).

[28] Wilpert 1916: pl. 179.   [29] Cagiano de Azevedo 1949.

Fig. 5.7. Santa Maria Antiqua, Rome: Theodotus chapel, altar wall.

saints of the Roman church, Peter and Paul, and the saints specific to the actual site, Quiricus and Julitta. In the earliest surviving examples of the use of this iconography in Rome, the sixth-century mosaics in the churches of Santi Cosma e Damiano (526–30) and San Lorenzo fuori le mura (579–90), the popes were placed at the viewer's extreme left, the position of honour at Christ's right hand, and were shown offering models of their churches, a sign of their patronage.[30] In the Theodotus chapel, however, the situation is somewhat different. The pope remains positioned at the left of the composition, identified by an inscription painted vertically beside his head as Zacharias ('+ZACCHARIAS PAPA') (741–52),[31] but here he holds a codex, signifying his status as a senior cleric, and not an architectural model. Thus he is apparently not the patron. That honour goes to his counterpart at the far right, who does hold a model of the chapel and is identified by inscription as

[30] For an overview of the 'formula', Thunø 2015: 13–29.
[31] Wilpert 1916: pl. 181; Ladner 1941a: 99–106; and Ladner 1984: 23–5.

Fig. 5.8. Santa Maria Antiqua, Rome: Theodotus chapel, Theodotus with model of chapel.

Theodotus (Fig. 5.8).[32] The iconography thus follows a variant on the Santi Cosma e Damiano formula that is first encountered in Rome in the narthex mural at Santa Sabina, where the pope (the figure wearing the pallium) is given the place of honour at the viewer's far left and is similarly shown holding a codex, although it is clear from the accompanying inscriptions that he is not

[32] Wilpert 1916: pl. 182.2.

the donor: the commissioners of the painting were the archpriest Theodore and the priest George. A similar arrangement may also be found at a later date in the lower church of San Clemente, where Pope Leo IV (847–55) is shown at the far left holding a jewelled codex, again with a non-papal donor, a priest who happens also to be named Leo. In this instance he is not shown, but only recorded in an accompanying dedication inscription.[33] Depicting a donor on the viewer's right is unusual, and seems to occur only in instances where the preferred space is already occupied by another figure, as at Santa Sabina, or where there is more than one donor, for example, the diminutive figures kneeling beside their saintly patrons in murals discovered in Sant'Adriano.[34] A parallel situation may be seen in the tenth-century mosaic in Saint Sophia in Istanbul, depicting the Madonna and Child flanked by two emperors: Justinian holding a model of the church and Constantine holding a model of the city.[35] The parallel to Santa Sabina is perhaps particularly relevant, as both place an image of Mary with the infant Jesus at the centre of their compositions, and both have non-papal donors. A discussion of the identity of Theodotus will follow, but for the moment it shall suffice to note that both his head and that of Pope Zacharias are enclosed in a 'square halo'. As we have seen, this is an indication that the heads were intended to be portrait likenesses, the framing device being another of the motifs from the eastern Mediterranean which may have been introduced to Rome in the time of Pope John VII.[36] The consequent implication is that the chapel was decorated during the pontificate of Zacharias, which is to say between the years 741 and 752.[37]

At the time of the discovery, the observation that the face of Zacharias was painted on an added level of plaster, coupled with the lack of any detail for the face of Theodotus, prompted considerable speculation about the nature of the two portraits and the manner of their execution; but more recent technical analyses have indicated that the underdrawing for both was included in the original campaign, while the finer details were added later in a subsequent application of plaster and paint... and for the head of Theodotus the additional layer has simply not survived.[38] Presumably it took longer to achieve a high-quality portrait image than working on a single batch of wet plaster permitted before it dried. To the right of Pope Zacharias are the standing figures of Saints Julitta and Paul, and to the left of Theodotus are Saints Quiricus and Peter. The boy saint, hands spread in the gesture of prayer, stands on a Byzantine *souppedion* or

[33] Ibid., pl. 210.   [34] Bordi 2011.   [35] Brubaker 2010: 43–55.
[36] Ladner 1941a: 99–106; Ladner 1941b; Osborne 1979; and Ladner 1984: 23–5.
[37] For a succinct summary of the political circumstances of his papacy: Delogu 2000.
[38] Valentini 2016: 273–6.

footstool, a mark of honour deriving from the ceremonial of the imperial court. It would be interesting, and indeed useful, to know if the same dignity was also accorded to his mother. Presumably it was, but the plaster bearing her feet has not survived. Almost nothing remains of the heads of the central group, but Peter and Paul may be identified from their painted inscriptions, written vertically, and Paul also from the fragment of his bald forehead. Only the lower half survives of the figure of Mary, but her richly decorated garments, including the lower portion of an imperial *loros*, as well as the traces of a sceptre held in the upraised right hand, strongly suggest that her head was originally crowned with an imperial diadem, following the iconography of the 'Maria *regina*'.

The niche above the donor panel is fully devoted to an image of the Crucifixion (Fig. 5.9),[39] and follows a well-known early Byzantine iconography in which Christ is dressed in a long sleeveless *colobium*. The cross is set in a rocky landscape, flanked by both Mary, who raises two covered hands towards her son, and Saint John the Evangelist ('SCS IOANNIS EUGAGELISTA'), his right hand making the gesture of speech/blessing. A soldier on the left, identified by inscription as Longinus, pierces Christ's side with his lance, while his unidentified counterpart on the right raises the vinegar sponge. Above the arms of the cross are depictions of the sun and moon. The inscription on the *tabula ansata* at the top of the cross is written in Greek; and it is also worth noting not only that the Greek spelling is used for the name of Saint John, but also that the misspelling of his epithet 'evangelist' may again reflect a Greek model, in which the sound 'NG' would have been rendered by means of a double letter 'gamma'.[40] That said, spelling errors are not uncommon in the early Middle Ages, and at the same time this 'NG' combination is rendered accurately in the inscription naming 'LONGINUS'. In July 1954 this mural was also removed for conservation.[41]

The remainder of the right wall, between the martyrdom of Quiricus and the opening through to the sanctuary, is occupied by another important and enigmatic panel in which four individuals, usually identified as the donor, Theodotus, and his family (wife and two children), are shown honouring the Virgin and Child (Fig. 5.10). In the centre, Mary is shown standing on a footstool and holding the infant Christ in her arms.[42] Sadly, only the lower half of the mural survives, and thus the precise Marian iconography cannot be determined. We see only the feet of Christ, and part of Mary's right hand holding a ceremonial cloth, or *mappa*. Similarly, both

---

[39] Wilpert 1916: pl. 180.   [40] As first suggested by Rushforth 1902: 40.   [41] Vlad Borelli 1954.
[42] Wilpert 1916: pl. 183.

Fig. 5.9. Santa Maria Antiqua, Rome: Theodotus chapel, Crucifixion.

the male figure at the left, shown holding a candle-lamp in each hand, and his female counterpart at the right, are only visible from the waist downwards. But we do have almost all of the two smaller figures who stand between their presumed parents and the central group: a boy on the left (Pl. 8), who extends both hands towards Mary and Jesus, and a girl on the right (Pl. 9), who holds a rose between the thumb and forefinger of her right hand and makes an open-palmed gesture with her left. She sports an

Fig. 5.10. Santa Maria Antiqua, Rome: Theodotus chapel, family of Theodotus.

elaborate jewelled necklace and earrings, reflecting contemporary Byzantine fashion.[43] The heads of both children are framed with 'square haloes', again indicating portraits.

The inner entrance wall of the chapel has murals in the upper register, above the fictive curtains, on both sides of the doorway. To the left a supplicant, presumably Theodotus, once again bearing candle-lamps in each hand, kneels before images of two saints, an adult woman and a young boy (Fig. 5.11).[44] Unfortunately, the heads of these two figures have not survived, and there are no inscriptions, but there can be little doubt that they represent the chapel's patrons, Quiricus and Julitta; and presumably this is a case of art imitating life, reflecting the actual devotional practice that would have occurred in this space. Lighting lamps before religious images was a popular practice, and the oil from such lamps was thought to have miraculous powers; for example, Venantius Fortunatus records that oil from a lamp burning before an image of Saint Martin at Ravenna cured his eye disease.[45] The kneeling worshipper is dressed in the same clothes as

---

[43] Teteriatnikov 1993: 39.   [44] Wilpert 1916: pl. 184.
[45] Venantius Fortunatus, *Vita Sancti Martini* IV, verses 680–712; ed. F. Leo: 369–70; see discussion by Sansterre 2002: 994–9.

Fig. 5.11. Santa Maria Antiqua, Rome: Theodotus chapel, Theodotus kneeling.

the standing donor in the family group, and again his head is framed by a 'square halo'. This time, however, the full face is preserved, and he looks out from the wall towards the viewer. Natalia Teteriatnikov believed that his gaze was directed at the Crucifixion on the opposite wall,[46] but this is not necessarily the case. Similar donor figures shown in a position of obeisance (*proskynesis*), either kneeling or prostrate, with their faces

[46] Teteriatnikov 1993: 43; see also Noble 2009: 134.

turned outwards in this fashion, may be observed in the 'Madonna della Clemenza' icon from Santa Maria in Trastevere and the Santa Sabina narthex mural, both discussed previously, and in the apse mosaic in the Roman church of Santa Maria in Domnica from the pontificate of Pope Paschal I (817–24).[47] The precise meaning of the outward-turned head remains obscure, but the explanation could be as simple as requiring a frontal position in order to render an accurate and recognizable portrait within the frame of the 'square halo', something that would be impossible to achieve if the head were viewed in profile.

The decorative programme concludes with a painting to the right of the entrance doorway,[48] depicting four standing saints 'whose names God knows', according to the inscription written above the upper border (Fig. 5.12). One figure, the male saint who stands second from the right, is however identified by a painted caption: SCS ARMENTISE.[49] The other three appear to be female, and all hold crowns and crosses identifying them as martyrs. The same formula for saints whose identities were unknown may also be found a decade later in an inscription from the pontificate of Paul I (757–67), recording a translation from the catacombs to the church of San Silvestro in Capite.[50] And finally, it should also be noted that stylized palm trees decorate the jambs of the main entrance doorway, as well as the sides of the niche depicting the Crucifixion.

The images of Theodotus and other members of his family are documents of enormous importance for the history of early medieval Rome, and consequently merit a detailed examination. On the end wall, as we have seen, Pope Zacharias occupies the place of honour at the far left (Christ's right), but he was not the person responsible for the decoration of the chapel. Rather, the patron was the pope's counterpart at the other extremity, who holds what must be regarded as a remarkably accurate model of the barrel-vaulted space. These paintings constitute the earliest instance of actual images of 'non-clerics', including children, to have survived in Rome since Late Antiquity, presaging a practice that would become reasonably commonplace in subsequent centuries; for example, Giulia Bordi has found parallels in the votive images added by various secular donors to the walls of another *diaconia*, Sant'Adriano in the Roman Forum.[51] Very

---

[47] Ladner 1941a: 136–9 and pl. XIVb.   [48] Wilpert 1916: pl. 185.
[49] The identification of the saint remains obscure, for as Rushforth (1902: 53) accurately observes: 'There appears to be no trace of such a saint in any of the Martyrologies.' For the seemingly unlikely suggestion that it refers to Saint Artemius, martyred by decapitation in mid-fourth-century Egypt, see De Grüneisen 1911: 510.
[50] Silvagni 1943a I: pl. XXXVII.1.   [51] Bordi 2011; and Bordi 2016d.

Fig. 5.12. Santa Maria Antiqua, Rome: Theodotus chapel, four saints 'whose names God knows'.

little is known about the subject of lay patronage in Rome in the early Middle Ages.[52] In fact, there are seemingly rather few parallels to be found anywhere in the Mediterranean world, apart from some sixth- and seventh-century mosaics in the church of Saint Demetrios in Thessaloniki, which depict a number of non-ecclesiastics, including children,[53] and an icon from Mount Sinai which depicts Saint Theodore and the *dekanos* Leo, the latter dressed in what Kurt Weitzmann calls 'a stylish secular costume', and also with a 'square halo' framing his head.[54] In all of these examples the context appears to be votive, with the donor figures either beseeching or perhaps thanking Christ, Mary, or the saint in question for their favour. A niche in the atrium of Santa Maria Antiqua depicted something very similar: two diminutive figures, shown holding lamps or candles in both hands, flanking a large central image, probably of Mary; but not enough survives to make any identification certain nor to permit a reasonable dating. What perhaps makes this last example unusual is that the figure on the viewer's left, in the position of honour, is very clearly a woman.[55]

Who was Theodotus? Fortunately, the inscription painted in white letters, flanking the square nimbus framing his head, provides some useful information in this regard, and additional details may be gleaned from other sources, specifically a carved inscription in another Roman *diaconia* and two passages in the *Liber pontificalis*, although only one of the latter names him directly.

The painted inscription, uncovered on 20 December 1900,[56] and with only a few very small areas of plaster loss, is now badly eroded but was more clearly seen, transcribed, and photographed at the time of the excavation. It reads:

+ [... T]heodotus prim(iceri)o defensorum et d[isp]ensatore s(an)c(ta)e D(e)i genetr[ic]is senperque birgo Maria qui appellatur antiq(u)a'[57]

Translation: Theodotus, *primicerius* of the *defensores* and *dispensator* of the holy mother of God and ever-virgin Mary who is called *antiqua*.

That the inscription was added last may be surmised from the fact that the painter had difficulty fitting it into the available space, and thus the final 'R'

---

[52] For the much debated topic of lay patronage of Rome's 'titular' churches in the fourth and fifth centuries: Hillner 2006 and Hillner 2007.
[53] Hennessy 2003.   [54] Weitzmann 1976: 37–8 cat. B 14, pls. XVI, LX, and fig. 17.
[55] Osborne 1987: 197–8 and pl. XVIa.   [56] Rushforth 1902: 3.
[57] Rushforth 1902: 43; Wilpert 1905: 580; De Grüneisen 1911: 120, and pl. IC XXXVIII; Wilpert1916: pl. 182.2; Tea 1937: 328; and Silvagni 1943a I: pl. XXXIV.3.

in the word 'appellatur' was set outside the vertical border of the panel. While this detail is no longer visible, it is readily apparent in the early photographs. As noted previously, possibly the most important element of the inscription is the very last word, '*antiqua*', as this confirmed the identity of the church, the location of which had previously been unknown and the subject of considerable debate.

The elegant and rather ornate letter forms of the painted inscriptions to be found throughout the Theodotus chapel are unlike those in any other part of the church, and function as a form of 'signature' for the painter or workshop responsible. Particular characteristics include the combination of the letters 'T' and 'U', in which the 'U' is designated by a diagonal line rising upwards and to the right from the base of the stem of the 'T' (here in 'Theodotus'), the 'B' in which the two loops do not join in the centre (also employed in the *beta* beginning '*basileus*' (king) in the Greek inscription on the *titulus* in the Crucifixion), and the 'A' with a horizontal bar across the top and a central bar descending to the left. As we have seen, all of these forms were also present in the painted inscriptions from the tomb of Pope Cornelius in the Catacomb of San Callisto, lending weight to Wilpert's suggested eighth-century dating for the catacomb murals.

The name Theodotus appears again a few years later in a carved inscription preserved today on the inner façade wall of an early medieval church built into the remains of the Porticus of Octavia, initially dedicated to Saint Paul but now known as Sant'Angelo in Pescheria.[58] After a lengthy list of saints whose relics had been deposited in the church, ranging from archangels to apostles and other Biblical figures, and both Roman and non-Roman martyrs,[59] we are given various particulars about the patron, the dedication, and the date:

> + EST ENIM DEDICATIO ECCLESIE ISTIUS
> AT NOMEN BEATI PAULI APOSTOLI CALEN(DAS)
> IUNIAS PER INDICTIONE OCTABA ANNO
> AB INITIO MUNDI SEX MILIA DUCENTOS
> SEXXAGINTA TRES TEMPORIBUS DOMNI
> STEPHANI IUNIORIS PAPAE THEODOTU(S)
> HOLIM DUX NUNC PRIMICERIUS S(AN)C(T)AE SEDI(S)

---

[58] For the structure, *CBCR*: 64–74; *LTUR* IV: 141–5; Meneghini 1997; Coates-Stephens 1997: 198–200; and Claussen 2002: I, 78–82.

[59] 'Roman' male saints include Silvester, Lawrence, Peter and Marcellinus, Valentine and Pancras, but Petronilla and Aurea (of Ostia) are the only arguably 'Roman' names in the female list. We shall return to Petronilla in a subsequent chapter.

APOSTOLICAE ET PATER UIUS BEN(ERABILIS) DIAC(ONIAE)
A SOLO
EDIFICAVIT PRO INTERCESSIONEM ANIMAE SUA
ET REMEDIUM OMNIUM PECCATORUM[60]

Translation: This church is dedicated to the name of blessed Paul the apostle on the kalends of June, in the 8th indiction, in the year 6263 from the beginning of the world, in the time of the lord pope Stephen the younger. Theodotus, formerly duke and now *primicerius* of the holy apostolic see and *pater* of this venerable *diaconia*, built it on his own, for the intercession of his soul and release from all sins.

As the inscription indicates, the initial dedication of this church was to Saint Paul, but the prominence given to relics of Michael, who is named immediately after Mary in the list of saints, may have been responsible for the subsequent shift.[61] Another possibility, that the inscription has been moved from some unknown church dedicated to Paul, seems very much less likely. No such dedication of a *diaconia* is anywhere else attested, whereas there are numerous references to one dedicated to Michael.[62] Not that it matters for our purposes. What is important here is the valuable information provided about Theodotus.

It is interesting to note that in both inscriptions, one painted and one carved, we are once again confronted with the curious phenomenon of 'betacism': the Latin letter 'B' has been used for the sound of the modern letter 'V' ('U' voiced as a consonant) in the words '*birgo*' (for *virgo*), '*octaba*', and '*benerabilis*', as well as for Saint '*Balentinus*' in the relic list. A similar situation may also be found in one of the graffiti scratched by 'John the servant of St Mary' into the plaster on the end wall of the Theodotus chapel, where the language is Latin, but the alphabet employed to write the words is primarily Greek, again using a 'beta' for the 'v' in '*servus*'.[63]

The date of the San Paolo/Sant'Angelo in Pescheria inscription has been the subject of considerable discussion, as the year can possibly be construed as either 755 or 770, depending on whether one uses the Byzantine/Constantinopolitan or Alexandrian system of reckoning the *annus mundi*.[64] Both years fell in the eighth year of the Byzantine fifteen-year

---

[60] For the full text: Silvagni 1943a I: pl. XIV.3; De Rubeis 2001: 111 (fig. 80), 118–9, no. 10; Cardin 2008: 68–9 and pl. 47; and Maskarinec 2018: 180–1 and fig. 3.
[61] Maskarinec 2018: 22.   [62] Sanfilippo 1994: 233–4.
[63] De Grüneisen 1911: 427, 439 no. 169, pl. XII.14; and Sansterre 1983: II, 126 note 158.
[64] For the development of *annus mundi* dating systems, the classic study remains Grumel 1958: 52–128. For the conversion formulas, see *ibid.*, 97 (Alexandrian) and 128 (Constantinopolitan).

indiction cycle,[65] and in both the pontifical see was occupied by a pope named Stephen.[66] But the earlier possibility is much more likely, and now seems generally accepted,[67] albeit with the odd exception.[68] In the year 755, June 1 fell on a Sunday, a more likely day for a church dedication, whereas in 770 it was a Friday; and while second popes of a name were frequently referred to as *iunior*, the normal designation for a third was *secundus iunior*. Moreover, the *primicerius* of the Roman church in June 770 is known to have been Christopher.[69] This may be the earliest recorded instance of a Roman inscription employing the Byzantine 'year of the world' ('*annus mundi*') in a dating formula,[70] and that in itself is worthy of consideration. The name of the reigning emperor is conspicuous by its complete absence.

The titles of '*dispensator*' and '*pater*' both occur in other contemporary sources, and belong to the very specific context of *diaconiae*, charitable institutions whose nature and origins have been the subject of considerable scholarly investigation and some disagreement.[71] The term *diaconia*, used explicitly in the Sant'Angelo in Pescheria inscription, is likely to have originated in fourth-century Egypt,[72] although it is not known when or by what means the concept spread to the Latin west. It had certainly done so by the beginning of the seventh century, when *diaconiae* in the Italian cities of Pesaro and Naples are attested in the correspondence of Pope Gregory I (590–604).[73] The primary function of these welfare centres was to provide the necessities of life and hygiene to the urban populace, specifically food and opportunities for bathing, but it remains unclear whether they were intended from the outset as ecclesiastical replacements for the previous Roman system of grain distribution (the *annona*); and the two welfare institutions, one associated with the state and the other administered ultimately by the church, appear to have overlapped chronologically for some time. Indeed, the papacy is attested to have been involved in feeding the populace of Rome since at least the late fifth century, when

---

[65] For the history of indictional dating, see Handley 2003: 126–9.
[66] See Duchesne in *LP* I: 514, note 2; Halphen 1907: 91–2; Grossi-Gondi (1920): 524–32; *CBCR* I: 73; Bertolini 1947: 25–8; Osborne 1979: 59–60; Sanfilippo 1994: 232–4; and Pugliesi 2008: 380.
[67] For example, Coates-Stephens 1997: 198; and Toubert 2001: 73.
[68] For example, Claussen 2002: I, 80, who provides no justification for the choice.
[69] Bertolini 1947: 25–8; *LP* ed. Duchesne III: 105; and Osborne 1979: 59–60.
[70] Von Falkenhausen 2015: 50–1.
[71] See Lestocquoy 1930; Bertolini 1947; D'Amico 1976; Noble 1984: 231–3; Sternberg 1988; Durliat 1990; Hermes 1996; Saxer 2001: 584–90; Dey 2008; and De Francesco 2017: 22–32. Like Ferrari (1957: xviii), I shall avoid translating '*diaconia*' by the misleading English word 'deaconry', as there is no specific connection to the ecclesiastical rank of 'deacon'.
[72] Marrou 1940. [73] Bertolini 1947: 2–14, 91–7; and Hermes 1996: 17–20.

Pope Gelasius I (492–6) 'delivered the city of Rome from danger of famine'.[74]

The first known appearance of the term *diaconia* in a Roman context, in the *Liber pontificalis* life of Pope Benedict II (684–5), certainly occurs after the disappearance of all references to the *annona* and following a period in which the city and its inhabitants were frequently the victims of natural disasters and severe food shortages; but Durliat argues that they had existed since at least the time of Pope Gregory I (590–604), and until the end of the seventh century were simply of a modest scale that flew beneath the radar of our limited sources. The need to feed the populace continued long after the previous civic distribution system had ceased to function, and this may explain the concentration of *diaconiae* in the areas of densest population, in and around the Forum and the adjacent Tiber port, including a number that, like San Teodoro and Santa Maria Antiqua itself, were situated in the immediate vicinity of a major grain warehouse, the *Horrea Agrippiana*.[75] And of course this was also where grain supplies from southern Italy and Sicily would have arrived in the city until at least the 730s. Many *diaconiae* seem to have reused existing public buildings which had previously been abandoned.[76] In addition to the Porticus of Octavia, the *diaconia* of Sant'Angelo in Pescheria also extended to two adjoining classical temples.[77]

Jean Lestocquoy believed that, at least initially, the *diaconiae* were not connected directly to the papacy, but this view was challenged by Ottorino Bertolini. The earliest Roman references involve bequests of money following the deaths of Popes Benedict II, John V (685–6), and Conon (686–7) (*LP* 83.5, 84.5, 85.5; ed. Duchesne I: 364, 367, 369), although it is not stated that these were given to specific institutions; and as the individual Roman *diaconiae* mentioned in subsequent papal biographies were all associated with churches, the absence of earlier testimony may suggest that, at least initially, they did not come under formal ecclesiastical jurisdiction. Regardless of their origins, the *diaconiae* became very prominent in Rome in the second quarter of the eighth century, by which time they had certainly passed into papal control. Pope Gregory III (731–41) rebuilt two of them on a much larger scale: Santa Maria in Aquiro and Santi Sergio e Bacco (*LP* 92.12, 92.13; ed. Duchesne I: 419, 420). Maya Maskarinec has observed astutely that all the earliest attested *diaconiae* in Rome were dedicated to saints who either came from the eastern Mediterranean or

---

[74] *LP* 51.2, ed. Duchesne I: 255: '*Hic liberavit a periculo famis civitatem Romanam*'; trans. Davis 2010: 41.
[75] Milella 2004; and Bertolini 1947: 61–9.   [76] Saxer 2001: 589–90.   [77] Meneghini 1997.

were popular there, a possible reflection of the origin of this specific type of 'welfare station'.[78]

It is surely no coincidence that the dramatic increase in their documented activity, and also the frequency of their mention in the *Liber pontificalis*, occurs at the precise moment when the centuries-old practice of feeding the Roman population from estates in southern Italy and Sicily comes to what must have been an unexpected and rather abrupt end, as part of the efforts of the Emperor Leo III to rein in the papacy, and in particular its opposition to both his fiscal reforms and his attempts to eliminate the use of images in religious practice. Popes such as Gregory II (715–31) and Gregory III (731–41) had every reason to feel beleaguered. Not only did they have to cope with an enemy close at hand, the Lombards, not to mention frequent attempts by imperial troops under the command of the exarch of Ravenna to plot their arrest or even murder, but now the theological unity of the Church was once again in a state of complete disarray.[79] Papal opposition to the imposition of increased taxes and staunch defence of the role of images in opposition to the introduction of iconoclasm was met with a fiery response: the revenue from papal patrimonies in Sicily and Calabria was reassigned to the imperial treasury, and ecclesiastical jurisdiction over these areas and Illyricum transferred to the jurisdiction of the patriarch of Constantinople.[80] The date of the confiscation and jurisdictional reassignment is not known with certainty and, somewhat curiously, is nowhere mentioned in the *Liber pontificalis*. The primary witness is the Byzantine historian Theophanes, writing a century later. Although most scholars place the event in the early 730s, Vivien Prigent has made a case for the following decade, early in the reign of Zacharias.[81] Whatever its precise moment, this fiscal 'earthquake', in the words of Federico Marazzi,[82] made necessary a complete rethinking of how the population of Rome was to be fed, prompting not only the reorganization and expansion of the *diaconiae* but also the concurrent development of a series of new papal agricultural estates, known as *domuscultae*, in order to establish a new and reliable source of food supplies. Previously it was not uncommon for churches to have been endowed with properties,[83] but the *domuscultae* raised this process to a much higher level, and their primary function was to provide food, not income. First attested in the time of Pope Zacharias, these were situated in the immediate environs of the city.[84]

---

[78] Maskarinec 2018: 77. [79] Richards 1979: 216–32.
[80] Noble 1984: 39–40; and Marazzi 1991. [81] Prigent 2004. [82] Marazzi 1991: 255.
[83] De Francesco 2017: 34–44.
[84] Marazzi 1998: 235–61; Marazzi 2001–2; Davis 2007: 30–3; and De Francesco 2017: 44–9.

Later in the century, Pope Hadrian I (772–95) presented each of the *diaconiae* with six silk hangings (*LP* 97.61; ed. Duchesne I: 504), totalling 96 as we are helpfully informed by the author of his biography, from which we can readily deduce that by his time they were sixteen in number. Later we are additionally told that Hadrian added two more, both at existing churches in the Roman Forum: Santi Cosma e Damiano and Sant'Adriano, granting them fields, vineyards, olive groves, and workmen, so that they could provide for the needs of 'Christ's poor' (*'pauperes Christi'*; *LP* 97.81, ed. Duchesne I: 509–10). This brought the final total of urban *diaconiae* to eighteen, in addition to four situated outside the walls in the vicinity of Saint Peter's, and clearly they were all under ecclesiastical control by Hadrian's time, if not earlier.[85] It is not known when Santa Maria Antiqua became a *diaconia*, and the painted inscription in the Theodotus chapel is our earliest evidence for it having exercised this function. The only other such reference occurs half a century later in the *Liber pontificalis* life of Pope Leo III (795–816), recording papal gifts on no fewer than four occasions (*LP* 98.45, 98.52, 98.70, 98.83; ed. Duchesne II: 12, 14, 19, 26), with the last three all using precisely the same formula of '*diaconia . . . Dei genetricis quae appellatur Antiqua*'. But it should be noted that there are no other references to the church in the *Liber pontificalis* until the middle of the ninth century.

While the status of the '*diaconitae*' who served at these welfare stations also remains uncertain,[86] there is no disagreement that there were two administrative officers responsible for overseeing the activities of the *diaconiae* and ensuring adequate supplies: the *dispensator* and the *pater*. That the two offices were separate is demonstrated by a lengthy inscription preserved in the porch of the church of Santa Maria in Cosmedin, immediately adjacent to the famous Roman drain cover known popularly as the '*Bocca della verità*'.[87] This records a substantial donation, with a list of properties, made by the *dispensator* Eustathius, identified as a *dux*, and two other members of the landed aristocracy, George *gloriosissimus* and his brother David, 'for the sustenance of Christ's poor' ('*pro sustentatione Chr(ist)i pauper(um)*'), with the proviso that the *pater* pay a priest to say a daily mass. Gray dates this inscription to the mid-eighth century on

---

[85] For a complete catalogue, see Lestocquoy 1930: 296–8; Hermes 1996: 48–72; and Saxer 2001: 587.

[86] Durliat (1990: 168) challenged the previously accepted view (Ferrari 1957: 355–61) that the *diaconiae* were served by monks, but the monastic nature of Rome's charitable institutions is reaffirmed by Dey (2008).

[87] Lestocquoy 1930: 277–9; Silvagni 1943a I: pl. XXXVII.4–5; Bertolini 1947: 142–5; De Rubeis 2001: 112 (figs 81–2), 119–20, no. 11; De Francesco 2004: 197–202; and Cardin 2008: pl. 45.

stylistic grounds,[88] but it appears that we can be even more precise. In a letter written by Pope Hadrian I to Charlemagne, Duke Eustathius is listed among a group of officials who had been sent by Pope Stephen II (752–7) on the 756 mission to Ravenna, intended to replace the previous Lombard administration,[89] and this serves to confirm Gray's hypothesis.

Although we should be careful to avoid the assumption that painted and carved inscriptions should necessarily resemble one another, given the very different technical skills required in each medium, it is perhaps worth noting that a number of the letter forms in the Santa Maria in Cosmedin panel (specifically: the 'A' with central bar descending sharply to the left, the 'B', and the 'G') closely resemble those painted in the Theodotus chapel. The 'B' and 'G', but not the 'A', also have parallels in Theodotus' carved inscription of 755 in Sant'Angelo in Pescheria, although the lettering in the latter is characterized by much greater internal consistency and is much more refined. Luca Cardin contends that the epigraphy of Theodotus' Sant'Angelo inscription fails to meet the high standards of what he calls 'papal capital' script ('*capitale dei papi*'), and implies that only the senior clergy might have access to the latter, and not the laity;[90] but there is little evidence of 'papal' inscriptions from the 750s to which we can make comparisons, so this conclusion may not be warranted. While it is tempting to link scripts to social status, there is simply not enough known about either subject to establish a reliable pattern of practice.

The role of the *dispensator*, as the name itself presumably implies, was probably intended to ensure that the *diaconia* had adequate supplies of food to 'dispense', apparently at least in part by donating privately owned agricultural lands, or at least the produce thereof, for this purpose; and thus members of the landed nobility were ideally suited to the role. It is not known how long the title remained in use, although the *Liber pontificalis* life of Hadrian I relates an amusing anecdote regarding the unnamed *dispensator* of the *diaconia* of Santi Sergio e Bacco, also situated in the Roman Forum. Fearing that part of the adjacent Temple of Concord might collapse and damage the church, he attempted to forestall such an event by pulling the ancient structure down. But in doing so his worst fears were realized, and he 'obliterated the basilica to its foundations'. Fortunately, Pope Hadrian stepped in and 'restored and enlarged it to a state of great beauty'.[91]

---

[88] Gray 1948: 55, no. 15.
[89] *Codex epistolaris carolinus* 49, ed. Grundlach, p. 569, line 5; see also Bavant 1979: 86.
[90] Cardin 2008: 84. [91] *LP* 97.90, ed. Duchesne I: 512; English trans., Davis 2007: 166.

The role of the *pater*, by contrast, seems to have been intended to provide administrative oversight and oversee day-to-day operations. In the earliest surviving document to provide a set of 'stage directions' for papal ceremonial, the *Ordo Romanus* I, thought to have been compiled at the end of the seventh century, this official is also given a formal ceremonial role in welcoming the pontiff when the stational liturgy brought the pope and his clergy to a *diaconia* church.[92]

There are a few other titles provided in the two inscriptions that require some comment. In Santa Maria Antiqua, Theodotus is identified as the *primicerius defensorum*. The *defensores* constituted a sort of papal 'legal department', one representing each of the city's seven regions, charged with defending those who could not defend themselves, and especially widows, orphans, and the poor generally, as well ensuring that church properties were not alienated. In the time of Pope Gregory I, these officials were organized into a *schola*, under the leadership of a *primus* or *primicerius*, and while technically 'clergy', they were usually in minor orders and thus could be married.[93] A holder of this office named John was among the entourage accompanying Pope Constantine I to Constantinople in 710 (*LP* 90.3, ed. Duchesne I: 389).

The *primicerius defensorum* should not be confused with the *primicerius notariorum*, or as it is often called, the *primicerius sanctae sedis apostolicae*, the title ascribed to Theodotus at Sant'Angelo in Pescheria. That the two were quite distinct is made explicitly clear by the *Ordo Romanus* I, in which both offices play a prominent role.[94] For example, *Ordo Romanus* 1.69 stipulated that when the pope descended from the altar to the *senatorium*, in order to receive the gifts of the nobility, his left hand would be taken by the *primicerius defensorum* and his right hand by the *primicerius notariorum*.[95] The notaries constituted the papal administrative secretariat, responsible for the chancery and archive, and their senior member, again bearing the title *primicerius*, often served as a papal envoy.[96] The *primicerius notariorum* Ambrose, for example, first appears in 742/743 when he was sent by Pope Zacharias on a mission to the Lombard king, Liutprand (*LP* 93.12, ed. Duchesne I: 429). Ambrose apparently occupied the position for a full decade, since he is known to have died in December 753, at the monastery of Saint Maurice d'Agaune, in the course of Pope Stephen II's historic mission to the Frankish court (*LP* 94.24, ed. Duchesne I: 447). His body would be returned to Rome some six years

---

[92] *OR* 1.26, Andrieu II: 46–8, 75; and Romano 2014: 233.
[93] Noble 1984: 222–3; Noble 2003: 247–8; and Noble 2015: 247–8.   [94] Romano 2014: 93.
[95] *OR* II: 91; Romano 2014: 240.   [96] Galletti 1776; and Noble 1984: 218–22.

later, in September 759, for burial in the south transept of Saint Peter's, and copies survive of his epitaph.[97]

The next holder of this office of whom we have mention in the *Liber pontificalis* is Christopher, the *primicerius* who would play a pivotal role in the election of Pope Stephen III in 768, who would lead the defence of the Roman church against various court intrigues and the machinations of the Lombard king Desiderius and his agent Paul Afiarta, and who would eventually lose his eyes and then his life.[98] Hadrian I (772–95) would later arrange for his burial, and that of his son Sergius, in Saint Peter's (*LP* 97.14, ed. Duchesne I: 490). It is not known when Christopher was appointed to this office. He first appears at the end of the life of Stephen II (752–7), but then only with the title of *consiliarius*, when he accompanied the pope's brother, Paul, and Abbot Fulrad of Saint-Denis, on a mission to support the duke of Tuscany, Desiderius, in his claim to the Lombard throne (*LP* 94.49, ed. Duchesne I: 455). The same Paul would become pope himself following Stephen's death in 757, and it is presumably during his reign that Christopher acquired his new title. This would place Theodotus' elevation to this office sometime after December 753, and continuing until, at the earliest, 757, lending further credence, should it be required, to the 755 date of the Sant'Angelo in Pescheria inscription.

The Sant'Angelo inscription also refers to Theodotus as a former duke ('*holim dux*'). The duchy of Rome was one of the many subdivisions of Byzantine Italy, under the overall governance of the exarch based at Ravenna, and the title of 'duke' ('*dux*'), held by the chief military officer, seems to have replaced that of 'master of the soldiers' ('*magister militum*') at some point, probably in the seventh century. The first known holder is George, mentioned in an inscription preserved at Terracina.[99] The first reference to a duchy of Rome in the *Liber pontificalis* occurs in the life of Pope Constantine I (708–15). When Rome rebelled against the imperial usurper Philippikos, Duke Christopher sided with the pope in his refusal to accept the imperial images or to include the emperor in official prayers during the mass, and led the armed opposition to the arrival of the newly appointed Duke Peter (*LP* 90.10, ed. Duchesne I: 394). Thereafter, the title occurs with some frequency. The *patricius et dux* at the end of the reign of Gregory III (731–41) was named Stephen (*LP* 93.2, ed. Duchesne I: 426), and Pope Zacharias left him in charge of the city when he went to meet the

---

[97] Galletti 1776: 39–42; and *LP* ed. Duchesne I: 457–8 note 27.
[98] *LP* 96.5, 96.7–8; 96.11, 96.15; 96.28–32; ed. Duchesne I: 469, 470, 471, 472, 478–80. See also Noble 1984: 126–30.
[99] Bavant 1979: 70.

Lombard king, Liutprand (*LP* 93.12, ed. Duchesne I: 429). Precisely the same title, written in Greek and thus perhaps indicative of the working language of the military administration well into the second quarter of the eighth century, appears on Stephen's seal, an example of which was found at Blera in 1882. Bernard Bavant proposes to place Theodotus with this title somewhere in the period between 728 and 739.[100]

Our two inscriptions thus combine to suggest that the donor of the chapel, Theodotus, formerly the commanding officer of the troops defending the duchy of Rome, had by the decade of the 740s transferred into papal service, where he first exercised the function of *primicerius defensorum* under Pope Zacharias, before being 'promoted' in the time of Pope Stephen II to the more senior role of *primicerius sanctae sedis apostolicae*. At the same time, he was involved in the church's efforts to feed Rome's populace, through an active engagement with at least two of the *diaconiae*.

But there is still more grist for our mill. Further particulars regarding Theodotus are provided by the *Liber pontificalis* biographer of Pope Hadrian I (772–95). Hadrian, we are told, was

of Roman origin, son of Theodore, from the region Via Lata .... A very distinguished man, sprung from noble ancestry[101] and born to influential Roman parents .... On his father's death, the blessed man was left as a child with his noble mother; after his mother's death he was brought up and educated carefully by his uncle Theodotus, formerly consul and duke, later *primicerius* of our holy church.[102]

There can be no doubt whatsoever that the Theodotus of the Sant'Angelo in Pescheria inscription is the same as the homonymous uncle of Pope Hadrian I, since both were former dukes who subsequently would hold the title of *primicerius sanctae sedis apostolicae*, although some scholars have questioned whether this is the same person as the Theodotus of Santa Maria Antiqua. And while there is no conclusive proof, neither are there any obvious objections. This Greek name is most unusual in early medieval Italy, and the only other instance noted in Brown's prosopographical survey is a Sardinian *hypatos* from

---

[100] Ibid., 77.
[101] This is the first use of the word 'noble' in the *Liber pontificalis*; see Delogu 2015: 211.
[102] Davis 2007:120; *LP* 97.1–2, ed. Duchesne I: 486: 'natione Romanus, ex patre Theodoro, de regione Via Lata .... Vir valide praeclarus et nobilissimi generis prosapia ortus atque potentissimis romanis parentibus editus .... His namque beastissmus vir, defuncto eius genitore atque parvulus suae nobilissimae genetrici relictus, studiose a proprio thio Theodoto, dudum consule et duce, postmodum vero primicerio sanctae nostrae ecclesiae, post antedicate suae genetricis obitum nutritus atque educatus est.'

the previous century.[103] The odds against two members of the new Roman aristocracy with this name having such close connections to the civil administration and the administration of *diaconiae* in precisely the same span of years would seem rather long, although of course the possibility cannot be excluded entirely.[104]

There is one final passage in the *Liber pontificalis* that may prove useful to this discussion, as it relates both to the death of Hadrian's father, Theodore, and to the foundation by Pope Zacharias of a *domusculta* on estates which this family had donated to the Roman church:

> In his time the late Theodore, elder son of Megistus Cataxanthus, to gain the pardon of his sins, bequeathed to St Peter the estate he enjoyed from his father's legacy; it is at the 5th mile from this city of Rome on the Via Tiburtina, and an oratory of St Caecilia is reckoned to be in it. The blessed pope adorned it with the large buildings he constructed and with paintings. He enlarged its territory on every side; by paying fair compensation to those who held properties in the neighbourhood of this place, with no compulsion but rather as befits a father, he bought in an amicable contract all the estates alongside the place, and laid down that the place should remain to St Peter in perpetual ownership as a domusculta; even to the present day it is called St Caecilia's domusculta. He also constructed in it an oratory of St Abbacyrus in which he deposited many saints' relics.[105]

The *domusculta* of Santa Cecilia has been identified with the estate of Pratolongo, located some 11.5 km from Rome on the Via Tiburtina, on the left side of the road after Ponte Mammolo.[106] It followed the pattern for the formation of the new papal estates: a core property received by donation or bequest, to which the popes then added adjacent properties acquired through gift or purchase. Interestingly, in those instances where the property donor is named, these individuals appear to belong to Greek

---

[103] Brown 1984: 278.

[104] Bordi 2016b: 260–1. For example, Halphen 1907: 91–2, 124, treats them separately, and caution is also expressed by Bertolini (1947: 28). More recently, however, Hartmann (2006: 40) has considered it 'unquestionable' that there was only one single individual by this name.

[105] Davis 2007: 47–48; *LP* 93.25, ed. Duchesne I: 434: Huius temporibus defunctus Theodorus maior filius Megisti cata Xanthi, ob veniam suorum delictorum, praedium quod ex hereditate fruebatur paterna, situm quinto ab hac Romana urbe miliario, via Tiburtina, in quo et oratorium sanctae Cecilie esse dinoscitur, beato Petro dereliquid. Quod ipse beatissmus papa magne constructionis fabricis atque picturis decoravit; ampliavitque in eo fines ex omni parte; data enim digna reconpensatione his qui in vicino eiusdem loci possessions tenere videbantur, nemini vim inferens, sed magis, ut condecet patri, cuncta secus eundem locum amica pactione emit, praedia et domum cultam beato Petro eundem locum iure perpetuo statuit permanendum; quae et domus culta sanctae Caeciliae usque in hodiernum diem vocatur. Construxit quippe in ea et oratorium sancti abba Cyri ubi et multas sanctorum condidit reliquias.

[106] Coste 1984: 734–8; and Marazzi 1998: 248–9.

families in military or administrative service,[107] as is the case with the next *domusculta* to be mentioned, partly comprising properties left by Anna, widow of a *primicerius* named Agatho (*LP* 93.26, ed. Duchesne I: 434–5).

Once again there is no certain proof that this Theodore is the same as the father of Hadrian I, but the date of his death would be almost exactly right, and the connection between both Theodores and the new system for meeting the physical needs of the city's inhabitants is exceptionally close.[108] There is one other detail which may further bind them: devotion to a particular Alexandrian saint: Abbacyrus.[109] The cult of (Abba)Cyrus and John, centred on their shrine at Menouthis, was propagated in the early seventh century by the theologian Sophronius, who may himself have brought it to Rome during the course of his visit to the city.[110] Parts of his hagiographic 'dossier' are known to have been translated into Latin at Rome around or before the year 700, by a certain Boniface *consiliarius*; and Maya Maskarinec has made a persuasive case for devotion to these healing saints, and apparently especially to Saint Abbacyrus, by the city's Greek-speaking elite, while making the important point that this cult was not seen as specifically 'eastern', and hence 'other', but simply as an inherent part of the Mediterranean environment in which Rome then existed. In addition to the oratory established at the *domusculta* on the Via Tiburtina, relics of both Abbacyrus and John, were also included in the dedication list of Theodotus's *diaconia* of San Paolo.[111] The San Paolo/Sant'Angelo relics of Abbacyrus may have been considered of some special importance, since the *Liber pontificalis* life of Pope Leo III (795–816) singles out for mention an altar in the church with this particular dedication (*LP* 98.108; ed. Duchesne II: 32); and in the tenth century, the altar of Abbacyrus and John is again mentioned in the *Chronicon* of Benedict of Monte Soratte.[112]

---

[107] De Francesco 2004: 251.

[108] The only scholar to have previously linked this passage to the brother of Theodotus is apparently Rettner 1995: 40. For Megistus Cataxanthus, see also Cosentino 1996–2000 I: 384.

[109] It is interesting to speculate that the interest in Saints Quiricus and Julitta may have stemmed from the similarity of the names of Cyrus and Quiricus, which are close in Greek, and actually identical in modern French (Cyr). For the popularity in Rome of variants on the name Cyriacus, including Quiricus, see Solin 2003: 39. It may also be worth noting that in the inscription from Sant'Angelo in Pescheria the name of Abbacyrus is spelled 'Abbaquiri' (in the genitive case), in other words similarly employing the Latin letter 'q' for a Greek *kappa*.

[110] Sinthern 1908; Sansterre 1983 I: 148–9; and Maskarinec 2017.

[111] Maskarinec (2017: 355) notes that the relic list also includes the names of the three females who were martyred with them: Athanasia, Theoctiste, and Eudoxia.

[112] *Chronicon*, ed. G. Zucchetti, 165; see also Sanfilippo 1994: 236.

Another reference to their relics may possibly bring us back to the family of Theodore, and specifically to his son, Pope Hadrian I, although the evidence is weak. When the façade of the old basilica of Saint Peter's was demolished in the early seventeenth century, relics were discovered in the chapel of Pope John VII, identified by a papyrus as being those of Saints Cyrus, John, Blaise and Nicholas. Giacomo Grimaldi associated these chronologically with an inscription in 'the most inept characters' embedded in the chapel's north wall, recording a donation of relics by Pope Hadrian I in the year 783.[113] This inscription is now preserved in the Vatican grottoes, but the connection is exceptionally tenuous. Relics of Saint Blaise are rather unlikely in Rome at this early date, although Nicholas is included in the 755 relic list in Sant'Angelo in Pescheria. Grimaldi's opinion was shared by Nicolette Gray: 'The inscription represents the lowest depth to which epigraphy sinks in our period. Some of the letters are so shapeless that they seem a reversion to senseless marks, as if the mason were illiterate.'[114] Antonella Ballardini is much less critical of the carver, but argues persuasively for a relic related to Mary.[115]

Abbacyrus also features prominently among the painted decorations of Santa Maria Antiqua, although not in the Theodotus chapel itself. His image appears on no fewer than four occasions: twice in the Chapel of the Holy Physicians, from the time of John VII (705–7), once in the company of his companion John and once on his own;[116] and twice more in the atrium, including a mid-eighth-century iconic image in a niche (Fig. 5.13), and later in a tenth-century mural in which he and John flank the enthroned figure of Christ.[117] In the later Middle Ages, their cult would be centred on the church of Santa Passera on the Via Portuense, but this dedication is not attested before the thirteenth century.[118]

Theodore is, of course, not an uncommon name in 'Byzantine' Italy, although Brown's prosopographical survey lists only three examples in the context of eighth-century Rome: the two individuals discussed here, and a third who appears near the end of the century and is identified as the nephew of Pope Hadrian.[119] So it may have been a preferred name in this particular family.

In addition to the donor portrait on the end wall, two other murals in the chapel also depict Theodotus, or at least this identification has generally

---

[113] '*inscriptio ineptissimis caracteribus*'; Grimaldi 1972: 106–7.   [114] Gray 1948: 53–4 no. 12.
[115] Ballardini 2011: 104–9, and fig. 33.
[116] Rushforth 1902: 78–9; Nordhagen 1968: 62, 65; and Knipp 2002.
[117] Osborne 1987: 199, 205–9; and Maskarinec 2017: 349–57.   [118] Maskarinec 2017: 360–2.
[119] Brown 1984: 277–8.

Fig. 5.13. Santa Maria Antiqua, Rome: atrium niche, Saint Abbacyrus.

been assumed... until fairly recently. The panel on the right wall, depicting the group of two adults and two children, flanking a standing image of the Madonna and Child, has traditionally been interpreted as depicting the *dispensator* and his family.[120] But there are no identifying inscriptions, and the heads of the two adults do not survive. By contrast, the image on the inner side of the entrance wall, to the right as one enters through the doorway from the left aisle, is more complete, and depicts a male figure offering lighted candles or lamps to Saints Quiricus and Julitta. Once again there is no identifying inscription. Hans Belting believed that all three adult

---

[120] Rushforth 1902: 50–2; and Tea 1937: 89.

males in the programme were images of Theodotus, but in each instance representing a different aspect of his intentions in commissioning the decorations: an official dedication image ('*offiziellen Dedikationsbild*'), a family votive image ('*Votivbild der Familie*'), and a personal votive image ('*persönlichen Votivbild*').[121] But the traditional identifications of the individuals depicted have more recently been called into question in studies by Natalia Teteriatnikov and Arno Rettner.[122]

Teteriatnikov observes that the feet of the girl do not stand on the ground line, but seem to float in space above it, something which may have been both deliberate and significant, and she also holds a rose, a symbol of paradise. Taken together, these details may have been intended to indicate that she was deceased, although Rushforth, followed by Tea, offered an alternative non-funerary interpretation of the rose, noting a close similarity to the early fifth-century depiction of Serena, wife of the *magister militum* Stilicho, on an ivory diptych preserved in the treasury at Monza.[123] And Nordhagen has suggested that the figures of the two children were possibly added to the composition as an 'afterthought'.[124] Teteriatnikov then makes a similar case for the woman assumed to be Theodotus's wife, noting the evidence for a veil hanging from her left arm, and comparing this to the image of the widow Turtura in her funerary portrait from the Catacomb of Commodilla, dated *c.* 525–30 CE.[125] But her most interesting suggestion is that the boy is not in fact the son of Theodotus, but rather his nephew and adopted son, the future Pope Hadrian I.[126]

Arno Rettner takes the argument a step further, proposing that the adult male in the second and third images is not Theodotus, but rather his deceased brother, Theodore, Hadrian's father. In the view of both scholars, the chapel functioned as a funerary space for this important aristocratic family, and Rettner accords considerable significance to the report by Rushforth that a grave had been found, just inside the side entrance from the sanctuary, of a size and form that implied suitability for multiple burials.[127] Unfortunately, Rushforth did not provide any information about its contents, and apart from one passing reference it is not included in Tea's discussion of the tombs found in the excavation of the church.[128] Both Teteriatnikov and Rettner, and subsequently also Lesley Jessop, have

---

[121] Belting 1987: 56–7. [122] Teteriatnikov 1993; and Rettner 1995.
[123] Rushforth 1902: 52; and Tea 1937: 90–1, [124] Nordhagen 1996: 183.
[125] For the Turtura mural, see Osborne 1985: 300–2; and Deckers, Mietke and Weiland 1994: 61–5 and pl. 8.
[126] Teteriatnikov 1993: 41. [127] Rushforth 1902: 91, 105–6. [128] Tea 1937: 89, 115–17.

looked for some link between the family group and the choice of saints shown in the hagiographic cycle, and in particular the panel immediately adjacent which curiously depicts the death of Quiricus, but not that of his mother Julitta. Was this apparent focus on the child martyr 'precipitated by the death of either one, or both, of Theodotus' two children'?[129] The thought is certainly not implausible, but in the absence of any incontrovertible evidence, the jury must remain out. It would be rather interesting to know if Quiricus was alone in being honoured with a *souppedion* in the mural on the end wall. There he is shown praying, although in this instance the prayers are presumably offered on behalf of Theodotus, who stands beside him, and not another family member. A mixture of individuals within a single panel, some of whom were living and some dead, would seem unprecedented in funerary portraiture, at least as it is known from the Roman catacombs... but many aspects of the decoration of the Theodotus chapel constitute unique survivals from the early Middle Ages, and this serves only to underline its importance as a fundamental document for the study of early medieval Rome.

On one other matter, however, Teteriatnikov seems clearly to have been mistaken. She observed that the location of the funerary chapel is appropriate for the burial of the two female members of the family, because the space immediately outside, at the head of the left aisle would have functioned as a *matroneum*, reserved for women of elevated social status, balancing the *senatorium* on the opposite side.[130] But in Rome, where churches were usually 'occidented' not 'oriented', the *matroneum* was in fact on the north side of the church, and thus at the head of the *right* aisle. The chapel installed by Gregory III in Saint Peter's, in the first intercolumniation on the south (left) side of the nave, is explicitly described in the *Liber pontificalis* as being in the '*parte virorum*' (LP 92.6, ed. Duchesne I: 417). This is also implicit in the directions in the *Ordo Romanus* I, and again explicit in the *Liber pontificalis* account of the construction of a stone *matroneum* in the church of Santa Maria in Trastevere by Pope Gregory IV (827–44) (LP 101.32, ed. Duchesne II: 80), which may explain the predominance of images of female saints, and of Mary, on the right side of Santa Maria Antiqua and other Roman churches, and the phalanx of male saints who occupy the left aisle wall.[131] Ultimately, these suggestions are impossible to prove or disprove, and thus must remain in the realm of hypothetical speculation ... much as it would be interesting to have

---

[129] Jessop 1999: 251.   [130] Teteriatnikov 1993: 44.
[131] Osborne 2003: 142; for the *senatorium* and *matroneum*, see De Benedictis 1981.

a portrait of the young Hadrian, balancing his later image as pope from the atrium of the church.[132] We shall return to that other image in a later chapter.

The question was posed earlier whether the Theodotus chapel could have ever been intended as a funerary chapel. Both imperial legislation and ecclesiastical practice prohibited burials within the interior space of churches, at least in theory. While archaeological evidence suggests that such legislation was often ignored in practice, most early medieval burials associated with churches, whether in Rome or the larger world of the Byzantine Mediterranean, are normally found in outer areas, for example, the atrium or the narthex, and not in the nave or sanctuary.[133] As we have seen, however, by the beginning of the eighth century this custom had begun to shift somewhat in Rome, at least in the case of popes like John VII; but even John's tomb in Saint Peter's was set against the façade wall, as far from the sacred space around the altar as one could get and still be inside the basilica. The Theodotus chapel, by contrast, is situated in immediate proximity to the sanctuary; and moreover, its patron was a layman at the time, not even a cleric let alone a pope. If it were intended to function as a funerary space for a family, then once again this would have broken with all known existing precedent. That said, if anyone had the ability to disrupt the established practice, then Theodotus might well have been that person. This family clearly enjoyed substantial wealth and privilege.

Thomas Brown, Thomas Noble, Federico Marazzi, Paolo Delogu, and others have examined the new social situation which emerged in Italy following the Byzantine reconquest of the peninsula in the mid-sixth century, and the elimination of the Ostrogothic kingdom.[134] As we have seen, the Gothic wars had all but eliminated the former Roman senatorial class of landowning nobility, who had either perished in the conflict or fled to safety in Constantinople, and none of the families who previously wielded power can be traced beyond the seventh century.[135] The last mention of a meeting of the Roman Senate occurs in the year 603, convened to acclaim the images of the new emperor and empress, Phocas and Leontia; and, probably significantly, it was held in the papal residence at the Lateran, not the Senate House in the Roman Forum.[136] The latter building was presumably no longer in regular use, and a few decades

---

[132] Wilpert 1916: pl. 195; and Osborne 1987: 195–6.
[133] Marinis 2009: 150–3; and Marinis 2014: 60–2, 73–6. For a general introduction to the theme of Christian burial in Late Antiquity: Rebillard 2003; and Mackie 2003: 11–52.
[134] Brown 1984: 101–8; Noble 1984; Noble 2001b; Marazzi 2001; Noble 2003; and Delogu 2015.
[135] Wickham 2005: 236.   [136] Burgarella 2001: 169.

later it would be converted by Pope Honorius I (625–38) into a church, Sant'Adriano (*LP* 72.6, ed. Duchesne I: 324). The period 550–700 was one of dramatic demographic change, as the old order passed away and a new one slowly began to replace it.[137]

The new aristocracy would develop from a new group of landowners: bureaucrats and army officers, primarily of hellenophone backgrounds, who were granted, or had the means to rent or purchase, agricultural lands. Once the initial shock waves from the Lombard invasion had abated, military activities shifted from offence to defence, resulting in less mobile garrisons who became permanently attached to specific locations, and this led in turn to a new process of settlement and, eventually, the development of family estates.[138] Initially, the allegiance of the military élite was to the emperor in Constantinople through his appointed representative in Italy, the exarch based in Ravenna. But when imperial power in Italy declined in the early eighth century – due in part to an inability to respond effectively to the growing strength and ambition of the Lombards, and in part to the realization that local bishops, and above all the bishop of Rome, were more effective leaders in terms of maintaining stability and protecting the populace, who increasingly rewarded them with their loyalty – their allegiance shifted, and many sought or were given positions of authority in the new administrative structures that were rapidly developing, linked now to the Church. Brown and Noble both view this as a deliberate strategy, intended to maintain their political dominance, and 'military' influence on the development of papal ceremonial has been suggested by Romano.[139] This 'new nobility' would survive until the beginning of the eleventh century, when it would be replaced in a subsequent wave of social change.[140]

From our inscriptions and *Liber pontificalis* passages a picture emerges of a powerful Roman family, comprising important landowners who held senior military commands, almost certainly of 'Eastern' origin, descended from an otherwise unknown Xanthus.[141] If our assessment is accurate, in the second quarter of the eighth century two brothers, Theodore and Theodotus, sons of Megistus, at some point both held the military title of *dux*. When Theodore died in the early 740s, he bequeathed to the Roman church some of the family holdings at the fifth mile on the road to Tivoli; and, adding to these through the purchase of adjacent properties, Pope Zacharias created the *domusculta* of Santa Cecilia. Taking up the cause that

---

[137] Brown 1984: 61–81.   [138] *Ibid.*, 101–8.
[139] Brown 1984: 185–7; Noble 1984: 187–8; and Romano 2014: 77–8.
[140] Wickham 2015: 182.
[141] The Greek prefix '*kata*' indicates parentage; see von Falkenhausen 2015: 55.

presumably had also been championed by his deceased brother, Theodotus became more directly engaged in the welfare of the city's population, taking on roles in the administration of at least two of the *diaconiae*: Santa Maria Antiqua, where he served as *dispensator*, and San Paolo (Sant'Angelo in Pescheria), where at a slightly later date he served as *pater*. Additionally, he moved from a senior position in the military hierarchy to a formal role in the administration of the church, becoming the leader of the regional *defensores* before rising, presumably after the death of Ambrose in 753, to the more exalted and influential role of *primicerius sanctae sedis apostolicae*. His nephew and adopted son, Hadrian, who became pope in 772 – 'a powerful nobleman and a Lateran careerist all wrapped up in one'[142] – belonged to the first generation of the family known to have been given a Latin name, and that choice may well have been deliberate on the part of his father.[143] But other family members continued to receive Greek names, including Hadrian's nephew.

'Identity' in the early Middle Ages was largely constructed. It reflected political and cultural choices and aspirations. And for the family of Xanthus this meant rebranding themselves as 'Roman', an action in which they were presumably far from alone at this time. Furthermore, the strategy appears to have been entirely successful: in a single generation authority in the city passed from the military duke (Theodore) to the office of the pope (his son, Hadrian), now proudly declared by the *Liber pontificalis* to be '*natione Romanus*'.[144] And Hadrian would continue the tradition initiated by his father and uncle by donating even more family lands to the church, establishing additional *domuscultae*, including that of Capracorum. Is it a coincidence, one wonders, that the only *Liber pontificalis* biographies to use the term *domusculta* are those of Zacharias and Hadrian? But the church on the Capracorum estate received the relics of four early Roman pontiffs – Cornelius, Lucius, Felix, and Innocent – presumably translated from the catacombs (*LP* 97.54, 97.69; ed. Duchesne I: 501–2, 506). By the last quarter of the century the prevailing culture of saint veneration had clearly shifted.

In order to flesh out the cultural 'baggage' of Theodotus and his family, we need look no further than the decorations of his chapel; and given his

---

[142] Noble 1984: 198.
[143] Gantner (2014a: 118–9) views Theodotus' Greek name as a red herring ('*trug*'), believing him to be part of the city's emerging Latin-speaking élite, but the cultural context of his chapel suggests otherwise.
[144] For this family, see also Hartmann 2006: 37–62. For a similar situation in Naples, where Duke Stephen himself transitions to become the city's bishop, see Brown 1984: 185.

background, and the prevailing climate in Rome in the first half of the eighth century, it should not come as any surprise to discover that the cultural milieu evinced by the murals is overwhelmingly 'Byzantine' or, perhaps more properly and less anachronistically, 'eastern Mediterranean' in nature. A number of these elements have already been discussed, including the elaborate narrative cycle of the titular saints from Tarsus, Quiricus and Julitta; decorative features such as the use of the 'square halo' for portraits, or the decoration of the dado with fictive *vela*, both of which are first attested in Rome in the time of Pope John VII; and the possible influence of Greek on the Latin spellings of words such as '*virgo*' and '*evangelista*'. But perhaps the most dramatic evidence may be found in the niche on the end wall.

As documented by Wladimir De Grüneisen,[145] the iconography of the Crucifixion is entirely dependent on contemporary eastern Mediterranean models, and this borrowing encompasses a great deal more than the use of Greek in the inscription on the *tabula ansata*. Images of the crucified figure of Christ are exceptionally rare in Early Christian art, and the episode is conspicuous by its complete absence, for example, from the funerary decorations of the Roman catacombs or the Christological mosaic cycle on the nave wall of Sant'Apollinare Nuovo in Ravenna. The few examples which do survive, including a panel on the fifth-century wooden doors of the church of Santa Sabina, depict Christ dressed in a *perizoma* (loin-cloth), and that iconographic type will reappear in Rome in the Carolingian era, for example, in a mural in the lower church of San Clemente from the era of Pope Leo IV (847–55), as well as becoming the standard in post-iconoclastic Byzantium.[146] By contrast, the more modest *colobium* Crucifixion is characteristic of the art of Byzantium before the mid-ninth century, with prominent examples including the Rabbula Gospels (Florence, Biblioteca Medicea Laurentiana cod. Plut. 1.56, fol. 13a);[147] the painted panel from the Sancta Sanctorum reliquary box, now in the Vatican Museum;[148] and an icon from the monastery of Saint Catherine at Mount Sinai.[149] The similarity to the Sinai panel is particularly striking, and Kurt Weitzmann has dated the icon to the eighth century primarily on this basis. In Rome, in addition to the Theodotus chapel, the *colobium* Crucifixion

---

[145] De Grüneisen 1911: 325–35. [146] Osborne 1984a: 54–61.
[147] Bernabò 2008: 105–8, and pl. XXV. Although the miniatures can no longer be linked to the scribe Rabbula, writing at the Beth Zagba monastery near Apamea in the year 586, there is no question of their sixth-century dating: Bernabò 2014.
[148] Morey 1926. As the box contains relics from the sites associated with the life of Christ, an origin in Jerusalem and a sixth-century date are usually suggested.
[149] Weitzmann 1976: 61–4, cat. B 36, pl. XXV; and Brubaker and Haldon 2001: 60–1.

occurs in three other documented instances, all either dated or attributed to the eighth century: (1) the lost mosaic from the Oratory of John VII in Old Saint Peter's;[150] (2) a mural, now mostly destroyed, in the entrance chamber of the Catacomb of San Valentino on the Via Flaminia, also possibly from the time of Pope John VII;[151] and (3) a mural in the substructures beneath the church of Santi Giovanni e Paolo, loosely dated to the eighth century.[152] The San Valentino mural is particularly close to the Theodotus chapel Crucifixion, and both share a highly unusual iconographic detail: the indications of the sun and moon flanking the top of the cross, something also recorded by Grimaldi for the funerary chapel of Pope John VII in Old Saint Peter's.[153] This addition first appears in the Rabbula Gospels miniature, and a possible link has been suggested to the hymns on the Crucifixion written by Ephrem the Syrian.[154]

That the liturgy performed in the chapel was undertaken by priests, about half of whom used Greek as their primary tongue, is demonstrated by the graffiti which survive on the end wall. Of the eight examples documented by De Grüneisen, four use Latin letters, three Greek, and one contains a mixture of alphabets (primarily Greek, but using Latin for the name of Mary), presumably reflecting the bilingual character of Rome's clergy at this time.[155] The overwhelming dominance of Greek clergy has also been suggested by Andrew Ekonomou, who notes that of the 31 clerics who subscribed to Gregory III's Roman synod of April 732, only two have Latin names.[156] Even taking into account Thomas Brown's warning about names reflecting fashion and not ethnicity,[157] this figure is surely

---

[150] Although the mosaic no longer survives, at the beginning of the seventeenth century it was seen and published by Angelo Rocca (1609: 43), whose woodcut is reproduced by De Grüneisen 1911: 331, fig. 273, and Nordhagen 1965: 143, cat. no. 12, and pl. XXI(e). For the larger composition, Grimaldi (1972): 120–1.

[151] The *colobium* is documented in copies made by Ciacconio and Bosio, see Osborne 1981a: 85, 87–8.

[152] Germano di S. Stanislao 1894: 425–33, fig. 74; and Curzi 1999, fig. 1.

[153] Grimaldi 1972: 120–1.   [154] Krueger 2015: 115–16.

[155] De Grüneisen 1911: pl. XII. Although the sample is small, the language mix stands in stark contrast to that found in the Roman catacombs, primarily the names of early medieval pilgrims, where a sample size of approximately 400 reveals that 92 per cent were written in Latin; see Carletti 2002: 344. It is interesting to note that the signature of 'Christopher presbyter peccator' (De Grüneisen 1911: 439 no. 166, pl. XII.11) is paralleled exactly, in the same script but minus the epithet 'peccator' ('sinner'), on murals in both the Catacomb of Commodilla and the Catacomb of Pamphilus (Iosi 1924: 79–81; Osborne 1985: 303). Could this, one wonders, be the powerful *primicerius sanctae sedis apostolicae* who played a prominent role in papal politics under Paul I and Stephen III?

[156] Ekonomou 2007: 246. Gantner (2013b: 314 note 55) suggests that this figure is exaggerated, but agrees nonetheless that 'Easterners' comprised the majority of the Roman clergy.

[157] Brown 1984: 67–8.

significant. And if it were merely 'fashionable' for priests to appear 'Greek' in the early eighth century, then presumably it was for a reason.

The historiography of the Santa Maria Antiqua paintings in the years since their rediscovery in 1900 has tended to focus almost exclusively on the analysis of style, and the question of Byzantine influence. Indeed, it was largely due to the problems posed by the levels on the so-called palimpsest wall that Ernst Kitzinger developed his theory of 'perennial hellenism', emanating in waves from the city of Constantinople where he believed that a classicizing style had been preserved.[158] The Theodotus chapel has been almost entirely absent from that debate, and hence from the literature, for as Leslie Brubaker has noted, it is 'never called "Byzantinising"'.[159] But style is only one part of the equation, and a comparatively minor one at that, particularly given our almost total lack of understanding regarding the factors that determined style in the Mediterranean world in the centuries before and during the period of Byzantine iconoclasm (726–843). To put it bluntly, we have little idea whether the murals in the Theodotus chapel resembled murals in Constantinople or not, as there are no surviving examples in the imperial capital to use for comparison. What we can say is that the subject matter, the iconographic formulae deployed for the depiction of that subject matter (where these can be assessed), and the overall patterns of decoration all suggest that the chapel belongs to the cultural milieu of the Christian Mediterranean, as opposed to the context of western or north-western Europe. And so too does its patron. The saints whose relics Theodotus deposited in his foundation of San Paolo/Sant'Angelo in Pescheria were primarily non-Romans,[160] including most of the 'Byzantine' healing saints who had been depicted a half century earlier in the Chapel of the Holy Physicians in Santa Maria Antiqua (Abbacyrus and John, Cosmas and Damian, Dometius, Panteleimon, and Procopius).

In sum, the Theodotus chapel may be seen as painting a broad canvas illustrating the religious and cultural background of at least one prominent member of the newly emerged Roman aristocracy. In fact, it may well constitute our most important 'document' in this regard. Their wealth and social position stemmed primarily from their military heritage, which in

---

[158] First presented in a paper presented at the Eleventh International Byzantine Congress in Munich (Kitzinger 1958), and subsequently elaborated in a book (Kitzinger 1977). See also the discussions by Nordhagen (1972b; 2007).

[159] Brubaker 2004: 44. See also the comments by Brenk (2004: 67) on this 'historiographical blind alley'.

[160] Maskarinec 2018: 94.

turn had opened the door to the acquisition of substantial rural landholdings. They were 'gentlemen and officers', to use Thomas Brown's phrase, with their family homes located in the centre of the city, adjacent to the ancient Forum in the region of the Via Lata. And while they may have been 'blue-blooded Romans', in the words of Thomas Noble,[161] their roots were solidly grounded in the hellenophone Mediterranean world that encompassed Tarsus and Alexandria in addition to Rome, providing a useful foil to Brown's assessment of the situation in other parts of the Italian peninsula, and primarily Ravenna.[162] Noble's comment that the Roman clergy 'were Romanized in a political sense well before they were Romanized in an ethnic sense'[163] seems to grasp the situation with perfect accuracy, and appears to be equally valid for the city's secular magnates. Like many immigrant families who prosper in new surroundings, they adopted their new home and status with great enthusiasm; but as time progressed, and divisions began to arise along a more sharply defined divide between 'Greek East' and 'Latin West',[164] they sought to forge new and specifically 'Roman' identities for their families, and perhaps especially for their children. And at a larger level this new sense of 'Romanness' also applied to their city and its dependent territory, the 'Republic of Saint Peter', which would become the Papal State.

Stephen Lucey has viewed the increasing use of Latin in Santa Maria Antiqua as indicative of 'a process of acculturation and/or the introduction of an indigenous Roman audience', noting that this might represent 'a microcosm of broader change in the city as a whole'.[165] Rome was indeed changing, but I would like to suggest a slightly different view. It was not the audience that had changed: the population which produced the social élite and the clergy had not experienced any fundamental demographic alteration since the beginning of the century. Their DNA remained unchanged. What had changed was how they undertook to present themselves, how they were redefining their identity as 'Roman' in a context of 'Byzantine' indifference and the new *volte face* in favour of the Franks. The use of Latin became more privileged, even if most other artistic and cultural practices remained unaffected, including the community of saints to whom one prayed. But that too would start to shift significantly in the next decade.

[161] Noble 2001b: 60.
[162] Brown 1984: 64–9. Noble (2003: 22) has correctly urged caution in extending Brown's assessment of Ravenna and the Pentapolis to the situation in Rome.
[163] Noble 1984: 192. [164] Gantner 2013b. [165] Lucey 2007: 147.

6 | Pope Zacharias and the Lateran Palace

Although Pope Zacharias (741–52) was not the donor of the Theodotus chapel, his deep engagement with the city and its inhabitants, as demonstrated by his efforts to establish the earliest documented *domuscultae*, was also manifested in an interest in material culture. Much of his attention was devoted necessarily to political matters, and primarily to external relations with the Lombards, the Franks, and the Byzantine emperor in Constantinople;[1] and at the same time he aided and abetted the Anglo-Saxon missionary, Boniface, in his undertaking to convert the Saxons. Zacharias' biography in the *Liber pontificalis* focusses almost exclusively on the Lombards, and in particular the pope's relationship with King Liutprand, whom he twice journeyed to meet, first at Terni and then later at Pavia. Considerably less attention is given to the political events at the end of his reign, prompting the suggestion that the account may not have been finished.[2]

Like many pontiffs, Zacharias made a number of rich donations to the city's churches, and above all to Saint Peter's, which received 'veils of silk material to hang between the columns', 'a gold-worked altarcloth … decorated with precious jewels' depicting Christ's Nativity, '4 crimson silk veils, which he decorated with wheels and various gold-worked adornments', and 'a crown of fine silver with dolphins, weighing 120 lb.'[3] His biographer, who begins the entry with an effusive tribute to the pope's saintly character, is here quick to point out that the silver crown was a personal gift, made 'at his own expense', possibly implying that the others were acquired with church funds. Other buildings received necessary repairs, including Sant'Eusebio, whose roof had collapsed (*LP* 93.27; ed. Duchesne I: 435), and a number of unspecified saints' shrines, presumably primarily in the suburban cemeteries since the massive translations of the bones of the martyrs to churches inside the city walls would only commence a decade later. Saints and their relics were clearly an interest, and we have already encountered the chapel of Saint Abbacyrus at the *domusculta*

---

[1] Bartolini 1879; and Delogu 2000. [2] Davis 2007: 29.
[3] *LP* 93.19; ed. Duchesne I: 432; trans. Davis 2007: 44.

of Santa Cecilia 'in which he deposited many saints' relics'.[4] Zacharias is also credited with having discovered a 'great treasure' ('*magnum thesaurum*') in the Lateran Palace: the head of the Palestinian martyr Saint George, enclosed in a casket with an identifying document 'in Greek letters', which he then bestowed with great ceremony on the *diaconia* of San Giorgio in Velabro where it was credited with working numerous miracles.[5] Maya Maskarinec has suggested that this donation might have been part of a campaign to gain greater papal control over the existing *diaconiae*.[6]

Two aspects of Zacharias's patronage merit special attention: his keen personal interest in book culture, and his efforts to restore the papal residence at the Lateran, the action which presumably occasioned the dramatic rediscovery of the head of Saint George. The *Liber pontificalis* rarely pays much attention to the subject of books, so this *vita* stands out in that regard. We are informed that Zacharias established a book collection at Saint Peter's, using 'all the codices he owned in his own house', in order to facilitate the matins readings over the course of the ecclesiastical year.[7] What can we learn from this? Perhaps most importantly, we can ascertain that at least some members of the Roman clergy owned books, and it would be interesting to know whether these were acquired by Zacharias before or after his election as pope. The *Liber pontificalis* is curiously silent regarding his early career, apart from noting his Greek background ('*natione Grecus*') and that his father's name was Polychronius, although it has been very plausibly surmised that he is the deacon by this name who subscribed to the acts of the Roman council of 732.[8]

Books must certainly have been available in early medieval Rome, and there are frequent references in early medieval sources to visitors from elsewhere looking to Rome to meet their librarial needs,[9] among them Benedict Biscop, founder of the Northumbrian monasteries of Wearmouth and Jarrow, who made numerous shopping trips to Rome. In the mid-eighth century Ælberht, the master of the cathedral school at York in England and later the city's archbishop (767–80), made a number of European journeys at least one of which took him to Rome, as recorded by his pupil, Alcuin. These were undertaken

---

[4] *LP* 93.25, ed. Duchesne I: 434; trans. Davis 2007: 48.
[5] *LP* 93.24, ed. Duchesne I: 434; trans. Davis 2007: 47.   [6] Maskarinec 2018: 117.
[7] *LP* 93.19, ed. Duchesne I: 432; trans. Davis 2007: 43–4.
[8] Delogu 2000: 656. For the rather implausible notion recorded in tenth-century Constantinople that Zacharias was 'Athenian', Bulgarella 2002: 943–51.
[9] Petrucci 1972; Bullough 1977; Dumville 1995; and Ganz 2002.

with joy, led by love of holy wisdom and hope
of finding new books and studies there
to bring back with him[10]

And a letter preserved in the *Codex epistolaris carolinus* records Pope Paul I's gift of books to Pippin III including texts on grammar, geometry, and Aristotelian philosophy.[11] So there can be no doubt that a wide range of texts could be found in the city.

Later we are told that Pope Zacharias personally translated the four books of Pope Gregory I's *Dialogues*, a text which relates miracle and other stories concerning various Italian saints (and notably Saint Benedict), from Latin into Greek, so that it might be more accessible to the 'many who do not know Latin'.[12] The earliest surviving manuscript copy of this translation is now housed in the Vatican Library (Vatican City, BAV, cod. gr. 1666). Dated by a colophon to the year 800 and generally ascribed to a Roman scriptorium, it begins with an acrostic prologue naming the pope.[13] The translation seems to have enjoyed a wide circulation, and a century later it would be included in the *Bibliotheka* of the great Byzantine scholar and bibliophile, Photios;[14] but the apparent need for such a translation in mid-eighth-century Rome conveys a potent message regarding the nature of readership for books in the city. Once again we are presented with evidence for a literate audience who preferred to read Greek. Nor is this the only such instance. Other Greek texts produced in Rome in the second quarter of the eighth century included a life of Pope Martin I (649–655), the anti-Monothelite martyr; and Rome would remain a centre for Greek learning well into the ninth century.[15] It is perhaps worth noting that even Pope Gregory II, the only pontiff in the first half of the eighth century to be identified in the *Liber pontificalis* as '*natione Romanus*', wrote to Emperor Leo III in Greek, not Latin.[16] As a useful example of the many hellenophones who occupied administrative and clerical positions in early medieval Italy, Filippo Burgarella has suggested a family, recorded in a Greek inscription later reused in a church at Orbetello north of Rome, which emigrated from Syria probably in the second half of the seventh century.

---

[10] Alcuin, *De pontificibus et sanctis ecclesiae Eboracensis*, ed. J.-P. Migne, 841; trans., Godman, verses 1455–7.

[11] *Codex epistolaris carolinus* 24, ed. Gundlach, p. 529.

[12] '*plures qui latinam ignorant*': *LP* 93.29; ed. Duchesne I: 435; trans. Davis 2007: 49. For an overview of early medieval Rome as a place for the production of translations between Greek and Latin, in both directions, see Chiesa 2002.

[13] For Vat. gr. 1666: Battifol 1888; Mercati 1919; Grabar 1972: 30–31; Osborne 1990: 77–79; and Bulgarella 2002: 953.

[14] Photios, *Bibliothèque* VII: 209.   [15] Noble 1985.   [16] Grotz 1980.

Over multiple generations it included Sergius *consiliarius*, Anastasius *scrinarius*, Mamalos *scrinarius*, and an archdeacon, Moschos.[17]

Zacharias's example may also have prompted a similar interest in books among other members of the Roman clergy, a unique testament to which survives in the Roman church of San Clemente. When the high altar was dismantled in 1725 at the behest of Cardinal Alessandro Albani, one of the marble slabs was found to have a substantial inscription carved on its underside, presumably salvaged from the early medieval church and reused when the standing church was rebuilt at a much higher level at the beginning of the twelfth century. The inscription, now set into the wall to the left of the doorway as one enters from the atrium, records a gift of Biblical manuscripts to the church made by Gregory, '*infelix . . . primus p(res)b(yter) almae sedis apostolicae, huiusque tituli gerens curam*', for the remission of his sins and to secure entry into eternal life, in the time of Pope Zacharias ('*temporibus S(an)c(t) iss(imi) Zacchariae presulis summi*').[18] Presumably this is the same Gregory who signed the acts of two Roman councils convened by Zacharias in the years 743 and 745, in the latter instance styling himself '*humilis presbyter sanctae Romanae ecclesiae tituli S. Clementis*'.[19] Rather intriguingly, the Old Testament books are listed by name – the Octateuch, the Books of Kings, the Psalms, the Books of the Prophets, Solomon (presumably Proverbs, Ecclesiastes, and the Song of Solomon), and Ezra – which may imply separate codices as opposed to a single large Bible, and the latter would in any case have been extremely rare at this time. In its original form, the inscription may have continued onto a second panel, where the New Testament and possibly patristic texts would have been similarly enumerated.[20]

The Lateran Palace

The building project for which Zacharias is best known is the refurbishment of the Lateran *patriarchium*[21] which he had found 'in great penury'

---

[17] Burgarella 2002: 951–2. The Orbetello inscription is examined by Cosentino (1996–2000 I: 507–16), who suggests that the archdeacon Moschos may be the same one who subscribed to the acts of Pope Gregory III's 731 synod defending images (*LP* ed. Duchesne: I: 422–3 note 13). See also von Falkenhausen 2015: 55–6.
[18] Silvagni 1943a I: pl. XIV.2; Gray 1948: 45, 51 no. 8; and Cardin 2008: pl. 44. For analysis: Smiraglia 1989.
[19] Mansi 1759–98, XII: 368, 380.
[20] Smiraglia 1989: 359–60. For a general survey of literacy in the papal administration in the early Middle Ages: Noble 1990.
[21] *LTUR* II: 62–6.

('*in magnam ... penuriam*'; *LP* 93.18; ed. Duchesne I: 432). Named for the Roman senator Titus Sextius Magius Lateranus, consul in 197 CE, this site resonated with memories of the Emperor Constantine I (r. 306–37), who had reputedly given the palace to the bishops of Rome for their use, and had constructed and endowed the adjoining cathedral, at first known after him simply as the 'basilica Constantiniana' (*LP* 34.9–15). As we have seen, at the beginning of the eighth century Pope John VII had moved the papal residence to an *episcopium* on the Palatine hill, above the church of Santa Maria Antiqua, and there is no firm evidence to suggest that his immediate successors had moved it back. Indeed, this is the first subsequent explicit reference we have to the Lateran Palace in our eighth-century sources. Both versions of the *Liber pontificalis* life of Gregory II (715–31) mention that he built and decorated a chapel of Saint Peter '*in patriarchio*' (*LP* 91.9; ed. Duchesne I: 402), but it is not clear what building or location is meant; and the fact that this chapel is never mentioned again might support an argument in favour of locating it on the Palatine. It is perhaps also significant that Pope Gregory III's 731 synod to condemn iconoclasm was held at Saint Peter's, the first Roman council not to have been held at the Lateran (*LP* 92.3, ed. Duchesne I: 416). On the other hand, the *vitae* of both Stephen II (752–7) and Paul I (757–67), the two orphaned brothers who would succeed Zacharias on the papal throne, both state that they had been raised 'in the Lateran patriarchate' (*LP* 94.1, 95.1; Duchesne I: 440, 463). But even if Zacharias was not the one who made the decision to move the papal residence back from the Palatine, he certainly initiated the process of transforming the aging palace into a residence worthy of the growing political status of the popes,[22] an undertaking that would be continued later in the century by his successors Hadrian I (772–95) and Leo III (795–816).

The description of Pope Zacharias's repairs and additions to the Lateran is lengthy and full of intriguing details, thus meriting a full transcription:

In the Lateran patriarchate in front of the basilica of pope Theodore of blessed memory, he newly built a triclinium and adorned it with varieties of marble, glass, metal, mosaic and painting. He adorned both St Silvester's oratory and the portico with sacred images; and he gave orders that all his wealth should be brought inside it by the hands of Ambrose the *primicerius notariorum*. He built from the ground up in front of the Lateran office a portico and a tower, where he installed bronze doors and railings, and in front of the doors he adorned it with a figure of the Saviour; making use of the stairs which went upwards to the top of that tower he

---

[22] Spera 2016: 408–10.

constructed there a triclinium and bronze railings, and there he painted a representation of the world and decorated it with various verses. He restored the whole patriarchate almost like new – he had found the place very poverty-stricken.[23]

A number of scholars have attempted to reconcile the many references to the Lateran patriarchate and its various chapels in the *Liber pontificalis* and other sources, no easy matter given that very little of the complex has survived.[24] When the popes returned to Rome from Avignon in the early fifteenth century, they chose to live elsewhere, at the Vatican, and the older residence was all but demolished in the time of Pope Sixtus V (1585–90). It had comprised two principal groups of structures: one to the northeast of the narthex of the church, and the other north of the transept, and these were joined by a covered passageway known as the '*macrona*' (*LP* 98.92; Duchesne II: 28). The only parts of the building which have been preserved are the Sancta Sanctorum, the private papal chapel situated on the upper floor,[25] and the main entrance staircase known as the Scala Santa, which by later tradition was thought to have been the staircase of Pontius Pilate's *praetorium* in Jerusalem. In 1589, the Sancta Sanctorum was embedded in a new building constructed by Sixtus V's chief architect, Domenico Fontana, and the Scala Santa moved to provide access to it.[26]

The 'basilica of Theodore' is mentioned on a number of occasions in the *Liber pontificalis*, and was apparently located in the vicinity of the pope's private apartment.[27] It was a place where pontiffs such as Sergius I and Stephen III made public appearances (*LP* 86.9, 96.29; ed. Duchesne I: 374, 479), and was presumably named for Pope Theodore (642–9), who is otherwise recorded as having built an oratory dedicated to Saint Sebastian '*intro episcopio Lateranense*'.[28] But it is not clear that the two names should be regarded as applying to the same space. The chapel of

---

[23] Hic in Lateranense patriarchio ante basilicam beate memorie Theodori papae a novo fecit triclinium quem diversis marmorum et vitro metallis atque musibo et pictura ornavit; sed et sacris imaginibus tam oratorium beati Silvestri quamque et porticum decoravit; ubi etiam et suam substantiam omnem per manus Ambrosii primicerii notariorum introduci mandavit. Fecit autem a fundamentis ante scrinium Lateranensem porticum atque turrem ubi et portas ereas atque cancellos instituit et per figuram Salvatoris ante fores ornavit; et per ascendentes scalas in superioribus super eandem turrem triclinium et cancellos aereos construxit, ubi et orbis terrarum descriptione depinxit atque diversis versiculis ornavit, Et omnem patriarchium paene a novo restauravit: in magnam enim penuriam eundem locum invenerat (*LP* 93.18; ed. Duchesne I: 432; trans. Davis 2007: 43).

[24] Recent studies include Liverani 1999; Massimo 2003; Liverani 2012; and Ballardini 2015.

[25] Righetti Tosti-Croce 1991; and Tomei 1991.   [26] Delle Rose 1991; and Ippoliti 1991.

[27] Liverani 1999: 540–1; Massimo 2003: 18–22; *LTUR* I: 189.

[28] *LP* 75.5; ed. Duchesne I: 333; see also *LTUR* IV: 261.

Saint Silvester, by contrast, seems to have been situated in an outer area.[29] In the contested papal election of 687 it was held by the archdeacon Paschal and his supporters, while the inner areas of the patriarchate were occupied by the faction of the archpriest Theodore.[30] Giacomo Grimaldi's early-seventeenth-century sketch of the western end of the Lateran complex identifies a chapel of Saint Silvester at the north-western corner.[31]

The overall impression created by the *Liber pontificalis* account of Zacharias's actions is of a rather substantial and impressive refurbishment: the new rooms and porticoes were lavishly adorned and decorated, with the subject matter encompassing a world map and verses in addition to religious figures. It would be both interesting and useful to have a sense of the eighth-century papacy's conception of the world as expressed in the map, but sadly no other record of it has survived.[32] It may possibly have resembled the late-eighth-century map preserved in a manuscript in the Vatican Library,[33] which 'superimposes Christian topography onto a classical representation of the world'.[34] This map covers the known world from Britain to India, with a focus on the Mediterranean, placing the city of Jerusalem at the centre.

The overall intent of the Lateran rebuilding seems readily apparent, and perhaps more than any specific detail the importance of the *Liber pontificalis* description lies in its evocation of an 'architecture of power' and the new papal exercise of temporal sovereignty. Zacharias created a residence appropriate to the new status of the bishops of Rome as political leaders and diplomats on a world stage, complete with a *triclinium* (dining hall) in which to host ceremonial meals. When the Emperor Constans II visited Pope Vitalian at the Lateran in 663, dinner was served in the 'basilica of Vigilius' (*LP* 78.3; ed. Duchesne I: 343), which may imply that there was no formal *triclinium* then in place. The mention of a tower is also notable, perhaps suggesting that the new structure was envisaged as including a defensive function.[35] It is interesting to track the changing nomenclature used to refer to the building in the *Liber pontificalis*. As the papal residence grew in importance it evolved from a bishop's residence ('*episcopium*') to a patriarchate ('*patriarchium*') and finally to a palace (*palatium*'), this last term being first used

---

[29] Massimo 2003: 22; and *LTUR* IV: 325.
[30] *LP* 86.2; ed. Duchesne I: 371; see also Ballardini 2015: 901–2.   [31] Grimaldi 1972: 350–1.
[32] Kupfer 1994: 267–8. For the association of maps with political power, McKitterick 2008: 372–7.
[33] BAV, cod. lat. 6018, fols 63v–64r; CCSL 175: 455–66.   [34] McKitterick 2008: 376.
[35] For the addition of defensive towers to medieval bishops' palaces, Miller 2000: 60–1.

in the life of Pope Valentine, who reigned very briefly in the year 827 (*LP* 102.3 and 6; ed. Duchesne II: 71, 72).[36]

The space beneath the Sancta Sanctorum chapel is occupied in part by a vaulted hall, still accessible, where various fragments of medieval painting, assignable on stylistic grounds to the first half of the twelfth century, remain visible,[37] and in part by a fill of tufa blocks and rubble thought to have been put in place in the time of Pope Nicholas III (1277–80) when he rebuilt and redecorated the chapel above.[38] These substructures constitute the one part of the early medieval palace to have survived, and it is tempting to relate the hall, which includes the remains of a colonnade, to one of the porticoes in the *Liber pontificalis* description.[39] But the palace was large, and the description is vague, making it difficult to draw any firm conclusions. No trace remains of Zacharias's mural decorations ... with one possible exception. In the spring of the year 1900, at the same moment that the church of Santa Maria Antiqua was returning to light in the Roman Forum, Philippe Lauer, then a young scholar in residence at the École Française, was granted permission to tunnel into the area of rubble fill, where he discovered two sections of wall, both bearing mural decorations from a much earlier date.[40] The narrow space was too restricted to permit photography, but Wilpert's publication of drawings and watercolour copies provide a very accurate record (Fig. 6.1), now verifiable through comparison to more recent photographs, taken when the first mural was removed in sections in April 1961 for restoration at the Vatican Museums.[41] That painting depicts a male figure, seated in front of a lectern on which there is an open book. On the wall beneath is a painted inscription, comprising three lines of metrical verse, almost fully complete, and missing only a few letters at the end of each line. It reads:

> \+ diversi diversa patres s[ed his]
> omnia dixit Romano eloqu[io]
> mystica sensa tonans [...]

Lauer associated these verses with the seated reader, shown in the act of making a gesture of speech, although the actual text is not otherwise found

---

[36] For the evolving terminology, see Liverani 1999: 542–7; Noble 2015: 237–9; and Ballardini 2015: 43.
[37] Pennesi 2006; and Croisier 2006a. [38] Lauer 1900: 286; and Pennesi 2006: 231.
[39] D'Onofrio 2002: 224.
[40] Lauer 1900: 276–85; Lauer 1911: fig. 36; Wilpert 1916: 148–53, and pls 140.2 and 141.4; and Pennesi 2006: figs 20–27.
[41] Redig de Campos 1963.

Fig. 6.1. Lateran Palace, Rome: substructures below the Sancta Sanctorum, drawing of figure of Saint Augustine (?) (J. Wilpert 1916, pl. 141.2).

in any known source. Presumably this was an author who wrote about many subjects in 'Roman' (in other words, Latin), stressing their allegorical interpretations; and his suggested identification of the figure as Augustine of Hippo, author of *The City of God* and other works, has subsequently been broadly accepted. But there are also other possibilities, and it is interesting to note that the same phrase '*Romano eloquio*' is applied to Jerome by the ninth-century Carolingian monk, Wandelbert of Prüm.[42]

Many scholars have also followed Lauer in believing that this space formed part of a papal library; and two separate libraries, presumably one for Greek and one for Latin books, are known to have been established in the mid-fifth century by Pope Hilarus (461–8). Unfortunately, the *Liber pontificalis* passage in question is rather vague regarding their exact location,[43] although the Lateran would have been an appropriate place for such a project, and a good part of Hilarus' biography is devoted to work undertaken there, including the three chapels which he added to the baptistery. It was also a common practice in the ancient world for libraries to be decorated with images of authors, although these were usually portrait busts and not paintings, as attested by Pliny in his *Natural History* (35.2.9–11). But all of this is pure conjecture, and the precise function of the space remains undetermined.

The second painting, on the adjacent wall, features the lower part of an imitation marble roundel set above a dado adorned with a fictive hanging textile. The roundel also bore an inscription, unfortunately too eroded to be intelligible apart from a few scattered letters.[44]

The dating of the two murals remains something of an open question. Most previous studies have placed them in an arc between the late fifth and early seventh centuries, with recent scholarship settling on the sixth.[45] This determination is based primarily on stylistic analysis, although there is very little painting surviving in Rome that can be assigned to the sixth century with any certainty, and hence there is not much of a larger context in which to place them. But a date in the mid-eighth century may also be possible, and two factors lend support to such a suggestion.[46] The first is the presence of the painted drapery on the dado of the second wall, a phenomenon for which we have no secure evidence in Rome until the apparent revival of this practice by Pope John VII in Santa Maria Antiqua at the beginning of the eighth century. Furthermore, the apparent attention to detail with regard to the curtain rod and rings, as well as the actual

---

[42] *PL* 121: 583. I am grateful to Maria Laura Marchiori for drawing this text to my attention.
[43] *LP* 48.12; ed. Duchesne I: 245; see also Massimo 2003: 22.   [44] Lauer 1900: 277.
[45] Bisconti 2004; Pennesi 2006: 231.   [46] Osborne 2011b.

designs on the fictive fabric – a diamond or 'diaper' pattern of alternating rosettes and stylized 'spades' – have their closest parallels in Roman dadoes of the first half of that century in Santa Maria Antiqua, including the Theodotus chapel. The second indication is provided by palaeography, and especially the letters in the first verse inscription, which was the better preserved. To judge from Wilpert's copies, the elongated letter forms, height exceeding width, are notable for the decorative serifs attached to the bases of the vertical stems, once again with strong parallels to the painted inscriptions in the Theodotus chapel. The similarity also extends to the actual letter forms, in particular the 'signature' A, with a square or flat top and a transverse bar that slopes downwards to the left. We have already encountered an almost identical script in the Catacomb of San Callisto and the Theodotus chapel in Santa Maria Antiqua; and this particular form of 'A' was viewed by Nicolette Gray as characteristic of carved inscriptions from the same period.[47] Could these paintings, one wonders, have been part of Zacharias's campaign of restoration and redecoration, and the inscriptions among the verses ('*versiculi*') mentioned by his biographer? Again the question must be left open, but it is an intriguing possibility, as Lauer himself admitted.[48]

The explicit references to bronze doors and railings, and the mention of 'a figure of the Saviour' in front of the doors, invites an obvious comparison to the famous entrance vestibule of the imperial palace in Constantinople, the '*Chalke*' (Greek for 'bronze'), rebuilt by the Emperor Justinian I following the Nika riots of the year 532, and named either for its bronze doors or its bronze roof tiles. Here, in one of the first acts ushering in the new era of iconoclasm, a famous icon of Christ (*Christos Chalkites*) had been taken down in 726 or 730 by soldiers acting on behalf of the Emperor Leo III (r. 717–41)[49] ... and the parallel would not have been lost on contemporary audiences in Rome, where the popes were vehement in their opposition to the new imperial policy.[50] This is but one of a number of similarities between the Lateran, considered to have been an imperial palace which Constantine had gifted to the bishops of Rome, and the

---

[47] Gray 1948: 46.
[48] Lauer 1900: 285. In a recent discussion, Antonella Ballardini has discounted the possibility of an eighth-century date on stylistic grounds: Ballardini 2015: 893 note 13.
[49] Mango 1959: 108–42, 170–4.
[50] Marie-France Auzépy has argued that the action of Leo III was invented at the end of the eighth century, when an icon of Christ was 'restored' to the *Chalke* by Empress Irene (Auzépy 1990). But she doesn't consider the Roman evidence which, although circumstantial, lends considerable credence to the story: see Haldon and Ward-Perkins 1999. Noble (2009: 52–61, 126) reserves judgement.

imperial palace in Constantinople, whose construction had been initiated by the same emperor as his new residence at the time of his transfer of the capital in the year 330 CE. Paolo Verzone has argued that these parallels were deliberate, intended to assert the importance of the Lateran through a process of association, although his focus was on the further renovations and additions made by Pope Leo III at the end of the century.[51] But there is no reason why this same thinking could not already have been present some five decades earlier, when the papal court first began to undertake substantial political and administrative activities over and above its previous ecclesiastical functions. Pope Zacharias's construction of an entrance portico with bronze doors, associated with an icon of Christ, does much to bolster such a hypothesis.

The Lateran Bronzes

The emphasis on the medium of bronze prompts speculation that Zacharias may also have been responsible for initiating the remarkable collection of ancient bronze statues which is known to have stood outside the entrance to the Lateran Palace throughout the Middle Ages, where they were seen and recorded by numerous visitors. The main pieces were the she-wolf, the equestrian statue of Marcus Aurelius, the head and hand from a colossal imperial statue, a tablet bearing the so-called law of Vespasian ('*lex Vespasiani*'), and the *Spinario* or 'thorn plucker', all now in the collection of Rome's Capitoline Museum.[52] Our discussion will include a brief account of each of these pieces.

In Rome's foundation myth a she-wolf suckled the twins Romulus and Remus in a cave at the foot of the Palatine hill, and this became the site of the Lupercal festival held annually in mid-February. The wolf subsequently became a potent symbol of the city, often used on coinage, and in the modern era it has served as the emblem of the A.S. Roma football club. Various ancient authors, including both Livy and Pliny the Elder, mention a bronze statue of the she-wolf erected in the Roman Forum, and it was long thought that this was the statue formerly on display outside the Lateran Palace, and generally considered to date from the early fifth century BCE, which was transferred to the Capitoline hill in 1471 by Pope Sixtus IV (Fig. 6.2).[53] The figures of the twins were added only in

---

[51] Verzone 1976. [52] Heckscher 1955; Erler 1972; Liverani 1991; and Herklotz 2000: 57–87.
[53] Erler 1972: 8–16; Buddensieg 1983; Herklotz 2000: 57–61; and Parisi Presicce 2000.

Fig. 6.2. Capitoline Museum, Rome: *Lupa*.

the late fifteenth century, following the transfer. More recently, following a restoration undertaken between 1997 and 2000, some doubts have been raised regarding the presumed antiquity of the *Lupa Capitolina*.[54] A detailed technical examination revealed that the bronze statue had been cast as a single entity, using a 'lost wax' technique;[55] and this process would have been unusual in antiquity, when statues were generally cast in separate pieces and then assembled. These doubts were further amplified when a thermoluminescence test suggested a date in the eleventh or twelfth centuries CE. Could the 'Etruscan' wolf be medieval?

The first secure reference to the presence of the statue at the Lateran occurs in a description of the marvels of Rome dating probably from the early thirteenth century: the *De mirabilibus urbis Romae* written by an otherwise unknown author, identified in the text as 'Magister Gregorius'. Gregorius was probably English, as the only extant manuscript of his composition is preserved in the library of Saint Catharine's College, Cambridge (E IV 96), and the only known subsequent use of the text is by the fourteenth-century English chronicler, Ranulph Higden. But his

---

[54] Carruba 2006; and Bartoloni 2010. [55] Parisi Presicce 2000: 75–8.

account of ancient buildings and statues that were still visible in medieval Rome reveals a familiarity that could only have come from direct personal observation. Regarding the wolf, Gregorius writes: 'In the portico in front of the winter palace of the lord pope there is a bronze statue of the she-wolf which is supposed to have suckled Romulus and Remus. ... Water for handwashing used to run from the wolf's teats, but now its feet are broken and it has been removed from its original place.'[56]

Two slightly less direct references would appear to push the statue's presence at the Lateran back to at least the second half of the tenth century. The *Chronicon* of Benedict of Monte Soratte and the anonymous anti-papal *Libellus de imperatoria potestate in urbe Roma*, both identify the 'place of the wolf' outside the Lateran Palace as a location where judicial sentences were pronounced and punishments inflicted.[57] This tradition seems to have continued through to the end of the Middle Ages. In 1438, three men who had been caught stealing gems from Urban V's Lateran reliquaries of the heads of Saints Peter and Paul had their hands severed following their execution, and these were nailed up beside the wolf. The event was also documented in a painting inside the Lateran basilica, presumably intended as a warning to future malefactors. That mural has not survived, but is known from a drawing.[58]

These records are important for the light they cast on both chronology and function. The 'place of the wolf' was clearly associated with the judicial authority of the papacy; and while the two tenth-century texts, Benedict's *Chronicon* and the anonymous *Libellus*, do not explicitly mention a statue, that connection is undoubtedly implicit in the choice of name. At the moment there is no consensus regarding the evidence for a revised dating,[59] but if the *Lupa Capitolina* is indeed a work of the central Middle Ages, then it must have replaced an earlier statue, now lost. Also, it should be noted that the historical contexts being referenced in the two tenth-century texts are not contemporary; both occur in discussions of

---

[56] Magister Gregorius, *Narracio de mirabilibus urbis Romae*, ed. Huygens, cap. 32; *The Marvels of Rome*, trans. Osborne: 36.

[57] Benedict, *Chronicon*, ed. Zucchetti, 145: '*locus qui dicitur a Lupa, quod est mater Romanorum*'; and Anon., *Libellus de imperatoria potestate in urbe Roma*, ed. Zucchetti, 199: '*in iudiciali loco ad Lateranis, ubi quidam locus dicitur ad Lupam, quae mater vocabatur Romanorum*'.

[58] von Duhn 1928; and Erler 1972: 12–13.

[59] Most contributors to the 28 February 2008 conference on this topic (Bartoloni 2010) supported the early dating and believed the statue to be Etruscan in origin. It should be noted that the thermoluminescence tests produced a variety of results, and could easily have been affected by repairs undertaken in the late fifteenth century. Intriguingly, the lead in the bronze can be identified with certainty as having come from the mine at Calabona on Sardinia, a site not known to have been worked between antiquity and the twentieth century.

events which had taken place in the early ninth century. So the link between the statue, the location, and the administration of justice was presumably not a new concept at their time of composition.

This apparent judicial function of the space outside the palace portico is also attested by the most imposing and most frequently mentioned piece in the collection: the equestrian statue of Marcus Aurelius (r. 161–180 CE).[60] In 1538, under Pope Paul III, the statue was moved to the Capitoline, where for almost five centuries it formed the centrepiece of Michelangelo's Piazza del Campidoglio. Following damage to the *piazza* by a terrorist bomb in April 1979, the statue was examined carefully and discovered to be suffering from significant corrosion, due probably to air pollution. In January 1981 it was removed for restoration, and it is now housed in the Capitoline Museum with its place on the plinth outside occupied by a replica. A somewhat similar arrangement may also have occurred in the Middle Ages at the Lateran, with the statue set on an elevated base supported by columns.[61]

The identification of the emperor as Marcus Aurelius dates only from the fifteenth century.[62] In the Middle Ages, various names were suggested;[63] Magister Gregorius, for example, offers three different possibilities: 'There is another bronze statue in front of the papal palace: an immense horse, with a rider whom the pilgrims call Theoderic, although the Roman people say he is Constantine, and the cardinals and clerks of the Roman curia call him Marcus or Quintus Quirinus.'[64] The preponderance of opinion seemed to have favoured the second possibility, namely Constantine, based presumably on his associations with the Lateran Palace.

Once again there is no secure information regarding the circumstances which brought the statue to the Lateran Palace, nor concerning its original location. Philippe Lauer suggested that it may have come from the Antonine emperor's family home on the adjacent Celian hill, although Paolo Liverani has preferred a possible origin in the Campo Marzio, perhaps from the vicinity of the Antonine column.[65] The earliest documentation of the statue's presence at the Lateran, and of its identification as the 'horse of Constantine' ('*caballum Constantini*'), occurs in two tenth-century passages in the *Liber pontificalis*, in the lives of Popes John XIII (965–72) and John XIV (983–4) (*LP* ed. Duchesne II: 252, 259). In the former, the prefect Peter is punished by being hanged by his hair from the statue 'as an example for all'; and two decades later it is again

---

[60] de Lachenal 1990; and Herklotz 2000: 63–5.   [61] Fehl 1974.   [62] Zucchetti 1953.
[63] Kinney 2002.
[64] Magister Gregorius, *Narracio de mirabilibus urbis Romae*, ed. Huygens, cap. 4; *The Marvels of Rome*, trans. Osborne: 19.
[65] Lauer 1911: 22–3; and Liverani 1991: 107.

Fig. 6.3. Capitoline Museum, Rome: bronze head and hand from an imperial statue.

recorded as the place for the display of the naked body of Pope Boniface VII, which had been dragged through the streets by an outraged mob.

Also bearing obvious 'political' connotations were the two fragments of a colossal statue of an emperor (Fig. 6.3): the head and left hand, the latter holding an orb 'representing the world', in the words of Magister Gregorius who notes that they 'make a wonderful sight for onlookers, elevated on two marble columns in front of the papal palace'.[66] Gregorius identifies the statue as the Colossus originally set up by the Emperor Nero in a vestibule of the Domus Aurea, which would later lend its name to the great Flavian amphitheatre constructed by Vespasian and Titus, the Colosseum. He then goes on to report that it had been destroyed by his papal namesake, Gregory I. Other medieval sources also link the fragments to Nero's statue, for example, the twelfth-century *Graphia aureae urbis*, which speaks of the Colossus 'whose head and hand are now in front of the Lateran'.[67] However, most attribute its destruction

---

[66] Magister Gregorius, *Narracio de mirabilibus urbis Romae*, ed. Huygens, cap. 6; *The Marvels of Rome*, trans. Osborne: 23.
[67] CT III: 90 '*cuius caput et manus nunc sunt ante Lateranum*'.

to Pope Sylvester, the pope who by tradition had received the Lateran Palace from Constantine.[68] Another medieval viewer, Rabbi Benjamin of Tudela who visited Rome in the year 1166, identified the head as that of Samson, perhaps because the deep eye cavities suggested blindness.[69] Curiously, the orb also came to be known as the 'ball of Samson' ('*palla Sansonis*'), although the compiler of a late medieval version of the *Mirabilia urbis Romae* notes this identification but then goes on to state that it is erroneous.[70] The fragments are likely to have belonged to a statue of the fourth-century emperor Constans I, son of Constantine, and the hand and orb are now separated.[71] They were probably still together in the mid-fifteenth century, as suggested by a drawing, improbably attributed by Christian Hülsen to Cyriac of Ancona, included in a 1465 miscellany of Giovanni Marcanova, *Quaedam antiquitatum fragmenta* (Modena, Biblioteca Estense, Lat. 992 [formerly XI.G.2], fol. 31v).[72] This shows both the hand with orb and the head, as well as the adjacent equestrian monument, albeit in fanciful architectural settings. The head and hand, along with the equestrian statue of Marcus Aurelius, are also depicted at the Lateran in one of the earliest maps of the city of Rome, created by Fra Paolino in the early fourteenth century (Vatican City, BAV, cod. lat. 1960, fol. 270v, and Venice, Bib. Marciana, MS Lat. Zan. 399, fol. 98).[73]

The '*lex de imperio Vespasiani*', the bronze tablet recording the powers extended to the Emperor Vespasian by the Senate and People of Rome in December of the year 69 CE,[74] was also understood in the Middle Ages as an important political and legal document recording the transmission of authority, even if many observers were rather uncertain about what precisely it meant.[75] Magister Gregorius, for example, confesses that 'On this tablet, I read much but understood little'.[76] Richard Krautheimer has suggested that it formed the missing link in the papal claims to temporal sovereignty: the *lex de imperio* recorded the transfer of power from the Senate and People to the Roman emperor, and another document, the so-called Donation of Constantine, to be discussed below, completed the picture by documenting the subsequent transfer from Christian emperor to pope.[77] In the later Middle Ages the tablet was located in the north

---

[68] For example, *CT* III: 196, and IV: 132. For the medieval view that Pope Gregory I had played a prominent role in the general destruction of pagan culture, see Buddensieg 1965.
[69] Borchardt 1936: 70.   [70] *CT* III: 196.   [71] Jones 1926: 173–4.
[72] Hülsen 1907: 28–9 and pl. VII.
[73] Buddensieg 1983: figs 19, 20; and Michalsky 2015: 55 fig. 6.
[74] Cantarelli 1890; and Erler 1972: 16–20.   [75] Collins 1998; Beneš 1999; and Calvelli 2012.
[76] Magister Gregorius, *Narracio de mirabilibus urbis Romae*, ed. Huygens, cap. 33; *The Marvels of Rome*, trans. Osborne: 36.
[77] Krautheimer 1980: 193.

transept of the Lateran basilica, whence it was brought to the Capitoline by Pope Gregory XIII about the year 1576. But previously it was outside, and Magister Gregorius locates it 'in front of' the wolf.

The last of the surviving statues known to have formed part of the papal collection of bronzes, the boy pulling a thorn from his foot, or *Spinario* (Fig. 6.4), has fewer records in medieval sources, and there is much less certainty about how it was understood by medieval audiences. It was

Fig. 6.4. Capitoline Museum, Rome: *Spinario*.

observed and recorded by both Benjamin of Tudela and Magister Gregorius, but they offer completely different interpretations. The Spanish rabbi identifies the figure as Absalom, son of King David, perhaps based on the Old Testament text of II Samuel 14.25: 'Now in all Israel there was no one so much to be praised for his beauty as Absalom; from the sole of his foot to the crown of his head there was no blemish in him'.[78] Gregorius, by contrast, seems to be focussed on the boy's nudity: 'There is another bronze statue, a rather laughable one, which they call Priapus. He looks as though he's in severe pain, with his head bent down as if to remove from his foot a thorn that he had stepped on. If you lean forward and look up to see what he's doing, you discover genitals of extraordinary size.'[79]

There is no obvious link to the other bronzes, other than the material, and it may simply have been added to the group for that reason, although Joanne Snow-Smith has made the intriguing suggestion that the theme of the thorn-plucker, widely copied by artists in the Middle Ages and Renaissance, was interpreted as representing the redemption of sin, and in particular the sin of heresy.[80] Once again the suggestion is that the piece was set atop a column, and thus intended for display. Magister Gregorius also mentions a bronze ram, adjacent to the wolf, and in his time this was apparently still in use as a fountain, providing water to visitors and pilgrims for ablutions. But his *Narracio* is the only text to mention it, and the statue seems not to have survived.[81]

There can be little doubt that, individually and certainly collectively, these bronze statues functioned as symbols of imperial power and authority, now transferred to the pope.[82] As noted previously, they were in some ways a visible manifestation of the famous 'Donation of Constantine', which purported to document the grant by the first Christian emperor to his contemporary, Pope Sylvester I (314–35), of temporal jurisdiction over all of western Europe. It also explicitly identified the Lateran as an 'imperial' palace: '*palatium imperii nostri Lateranensis*'.[83] This document is of course an early medieval forgery and was recognized as such by Lorenzo Valla in the fifteenth century,[84] but it would be useful for our purposes to ascertain when

---

[78] Borchardt 1936: 70.
[79] Magister Gregorius, *Narracio de mirabilibus urbis Romae*, ed. Huygens, cap. 7; *The Marvels of Rome*, trans. Osborne: 23.
[80] Snow-Smith 1989.
[81] Magister Gregorius, *Narracio de mirabilibus urbis Romae*, ed. Huygens, cap. 32; *The Marvels of Rome*, trans. Osborne: 36.
[82] Boholm 1997: 262.   [83] *Constitutum Constantini*, ed. Fuhrmann: 87, line 219.
[84] Coleman 1922.

and where it was concocted, and the most likely possibility remains the papal court in the middle or second half of the eighth century.[85] The concept also finds an echo in a letter sent in May 778 by Pope Hadrian I to Charlemagne, where Constantine's transfer to the papacy of '*potestas*' is mentioned in a passage that also refers to the Frankish king as the 'new Emperor Constantine' ('*novus ... Constantinus imperator*').[86] We shall return to the 'Donation' and its political implications in a subsequent chapter.

The descriptions of Rome which mention the bronze statues are mostly from the twelfth century or later, but can we be more precise about their date of collection at the Lateran? Most of those who have contemplated this question have cited the construction of Charlemagne's imperial palace at Aachen as a probable *terminus ante quem*. The Carolingians were hugely impressed with the buildings and objects which they encountered in Italy in the aftermath of their annexation of the Lombard kingdom, and the impact was both immediate and profound on production north of the Alps, including monumental architecture.[87] Italy was not merely a source of models, but also of actual materials, including mosaics, marble, and other materials ('*mosivo atque marmores ceterisque exemplis*') taken from buildings in Ravenna with explicit papal permission.[88] Even before his coronation as *imperator* in the year 800, Charlemagne had broken with previous Frankish royal practice to construct a more permanent residence at Aquisgranus (Aachen). The great palace complex, of which the chapel still stands, was clearly modelled on Italian and possibly also Byzantine buildings, including the Lateran Palace of the popes. Quite apart from the numerous similarities in the nature and arrangement of the spaces in the complex, a significant clue to the Frankish thinking may be found in the name which the Aachen palace was accorded by contemporary writers: the 'Lateran' ('*domus Aquisgrani palatii quae Laterani dicitur*').[89] Presumably this was largely due to the Lateran's associations with the legacy of the Emperor Constantine I, whom Charlemagne was being encouraged to regard as a role model. As Rutger Kramer and Clemens Gantner have demonstrated, it was an ideological concept, and in a later chapter we shall see how this political parallel spanning five centuries was displayed visually in the decorations of the Roman Lateran in the time of Pope Leo III, the pope who would crown Charlemagne with the imperial title in 800. But what is of primary

---

[85] Huyghebaert 1979; Goodson and Nelson 2010, in response to the heterodox view of Fried 2007; and Delogu 2015: 210 and note 55.
[86] *Codex epistolaris carolinus* 60, ed. Gundlach, p. 587.   [87] Krautheimer 1942.
[88] *Codex epistolaris carolinus* 81, ed. Gundlach, p. 614.
[89] Falkenstein 1966; Kramer and Gantner 2016.

importance for the discussion at hand is the effort made by Charlemagne to amass a collection of bronze statuary at his 'Lateran', clearly emulating what must have already been in place outside the papal palace in Rome by the decade of the 790s. Pride of place went to a bronze equestrian statue, probably representing the Ostrogothic ruler Theoderic, shipped north across the Alps in 801 from Ravenna, where its loss was recorded by the ninth-century chronicler Agnellus.[90] A few decades later it would also be the subject of a poem by Walahfrid Strabo.[91] This figure has not survived, but visitors to Aachen today can still admire the bronze statue of a bear or wolf, of unknown provenance, but presumably intended to parallel the Roman *Lupa*.[92]

On the basis of the evidence at hand, it is not possible to determine the precise date for the development of the Lateran collection of bronzes, but we can at least identify a probable 'window of opportunity'. Robert Coates-Stephens has argued that the stripping of bronze statuary and other materials from the city in 663 by the Emperor Constans II, what he calls 'the Byzantine sack of Rome', probably served as a 'catalyst', and hence can be regarded as a probable *terminus post quem*.[93] The assembly of the group is unlikely to have happened before Rome and Constantinople parted company in the second quarter of the eighth century, not only because the obvious political implications inherent in the choice of statues would not have been relevant until that time, but also because until that moment the Roman church could not claim ownership of public monuments. They belonged to the emperor. Nor is it likely to have happened before the decision by Pope Zacharias to re-establish the papal court at the Lateran, and his efforts to begin the process of converting the palace structure into a residence suitable for a temporal ruler. And at the other end of the chronological spectrum, it must have taken place before its imitation at Charlemagne's 'Lateran' at Aachen. Consequently, we are looking almost certainly at a date in the middle or second half of the eighth century.[94] Zacharias is a plausible candidate for having initiated this process, given his documented penchant for bronze, but if not him then it is likely to have been one of his immediate successors, perhaps Paul I (757–67) or Hadrian I (772–95). We shall look at both those pontiffs in subsequent chapters.

---

[90] Agnellus, *Liber pontificalis ecclesiae Ravennatis* 94, ed. Deliyannis: 258–60. English translation in Agnellus of Ravenna, *Book of Pontiffs*, trans. Deliyannis: 206–7. For its meaning in a Frankish context: Thürlemann 1977.
[91] Walahfrid Strabo, *Carmina* XXIII, ed. Dümmler, 370–8.   [92] Mende 1999.
[93] Coates-Stephens 2017.   [94] Herklotz 2000: 75–87.

And one final postscript. Robert Coates-Stephens has recently offered the intriguing suggestion that an early medieval inscription containing verses 274–8 of Book One of Virgil's *Aeneid*, a prophecy regarding the future of Rome that refers to both the she-wolf and Romulus, may have been connected somehow to the *Lupa* statue.[95] This inscription was found in the sub-structures of the Sancta Sanctorum, where it remains on display. No details are apparently recorded about the circumstances of its discovery, nor even when this occurred, although it was presumably at some point after 1911 since it is not mentioned by Lauer. First published by Silvio Panciera as 'fifth or sixth century, or even later',[96] Coates-Stephens has presented a convincing argument for dating the carved slab to the mid eighth century, noting various characteristic features of this age including the 'ivy leaf' dividers and examples of 'betacism'. The closest parallel for the epigraphy may be found in the inscription in the porch of Santa Maria in Cosmedin, recording the gifts of Duke Eustathius. Could this have been another of the '*versiculi*' posted by Pope Zacharias? What makes the suggestion compelling is the link made by Virgil between the wolf and the eternal greatness of the city of Rome, transcending time and space, a view perfectly matched to the papal *zeitgeist* of this era. The importance of Rome was being re-established, as Virgil had predicted, and the *Lupa* provided an important visual symbol of that thinking. It is probably no coincidence that the eighth century is also the moment when Paul the Deacon and other authors begin to refer to Rome as the city of Romulus.[97]

---

[95] Coates-Stephens 2018.   [96] Panciera 1986: 196.
[97] Costambeys 2018: 52–7. See also Alcuin, *De pontificibus et sanctis ecclesiae Eboracensis*, ed. Migne, 841.

7 | Rome and the Franks

In the second half of the eighth century the political situation in Italy would eventually become more settled, bringing to fruition various initiatives and directions previously set in motion; and after some initial turmoil the duchy of Rome would enjoy an extended period of peace.[1] The prime catalyst was once again the threat posed by the Lombards, whose King Aistulf (r. 749–56) besieged Rome for three months early in 756, followed by a second move against the city under King Desiderius (r. 756–74) in 773.[2] In both instances the popes appealed to the Franks for assistance, and on both occasions the Franks responded. Encouraged to fulfil the duties of his new role as *patricius Romanorum*, Pippin III invaded Italy, and for the moment brought the Lombards to heel. Eighteen years later his son, Charles (Charlemagne), would take an additional step. After receiving the surrender in 774 of both the capital, Pavia, and its ruler, he annexed the Lombard kingdom entirely and assumed its crown. Desiderius would finish his years in enforced exile at the monastery of Corbie. Protected by the new Frankish 'security umbrella', the city of Rome would, with a single exception in 846, enjoy almost a century free from external attack. In the short term, however, conflict in the city's streets persisted, as various local factions and their external allies now vied to control the papal throne.

The papal election of Stephen II (752–7), followed by that of his brother Paul I (757–67), appear to have been fairly orderly, at least in comparison to what would follow. Both popes were members of the new landowning aristocracy, the sons of an otherwise unknown Constantine, but had been orphaned at an early age in the time of Gregory III; and both were subsequently educated at the papal court, where they were ordained as deacons in the time of Pope Zacharias (*LP* 94.1, 95.1; ed. Duchesne I: 440, 463). Like the family of Theodotus, their home was in the Via Lata district, and after his brother's death Paul would convert this residence into a monastery dedicated to two papal saints, Stephen I (254–7) and

---

[1] For a concise overview of the political situation after 750, see Brown 1995a: 328–33.
[2] For the siege of Aistulf, see Hallenbeck 1978; for relations with the Lombards under King Desiderius: Hallenbeck 1989, and Motta 2015.

Silvester (314–55), now the church of San Silvestro in Capite (*LP* 95.5, ed. Duchesne I: 464). The two families were clearly acquainted and apparently on good terms, as it was under Stephen II that Theodotus was elevated to the role of *primicerius sanctae sedis apostolicae*; and Paul I would bring Theodotus's nephew and adopted son, Hadrian, into the papal service, appointing him as one of the regional notaries and simultaneously ordaining him as a sub-deacon (*LP* 97.3, ed. Duchesne I: 486). It was at Paul's death in 767 that the succession was contested, leading to a period of considerable turmoil in the city, with many acts of shockingly brutal violence. The entire biography of Stephen III is devoted to narrating this sorry tale.[3]

The problems began even as Paul I lay dying, when Duke Toto of Nepi raised a military force, invaded the city, seized the Lateran, and installed his brother Constantine (II) on the papal throne. This was opposed by the church administration, and presumably also the urban magnates, whose leader, the *primicerius notariorum* Christopher, was forced into exile along with his son, the *sacellarius* Sergius. They in turn sought military assistance from the Lombards. The following summer (768), in the skirmish which followed Sergius' return to Rome, Toto was killed and Constantine arrested and deposed, confined to a monastery, and later blinded.[4] Following a brief interlude in which the Lombard priest Waldipert attempted to place a priest named Philip on the papal throne, Christopher eventually prevailed. He then presided over yet another papal election, which this time chose the priest of Santa Cecilia, a Sicilian named Stephen who was elected as Pope Stephen III (768–72). But the anarchy in the streets continued, with Christopher's party having fallen out with their erstwhile Lombard allies, and numerous protagonists are reported to have been killed or severely mutilated. Among them was Waldipert, and we are offered a vivid picture of him being dragged forcibly out of the church of Santa Maria *ad Martyres* (the Pantheon), where he had attempted to seek sanctuary, still clutching its Marian icon (*LP* 96.15, ed. Duchesne I: 472–3). He too was blinded and had his tongue cut out, dying soon afterwards. At first, Christopher's faction appeared to have emerged victorious, but the papal chamberlain, Paul Afiarta, conspired with the Lombard king, Desiderius, to oppose him, and in yet another dramatic turn of events Christopher and Sergius, the latter now promoted to the rank of *secundicerius*, were seized by the Lombards and themselves blinded. The *primicerius* soon succumbed

---

[3] *LP* 96, ed. Duchesne I: 468–85; Noble 1984: 112–27; and Llewellyn 1993: 221–8.
[4] McKitterick 2018.

to his wounds, and afterwards his son was murdered.[5] Complicating the picture even further, Pope Stephen then died.

The next pope was Hadrian I (772–95), son of Theodore and nephew of Theodotus, whom we have previously encountered. Curiously, although his lengthy *vita* in the *Liber pontificalis* devotes considerable attention to political matters, we are not provided with many details concerning the circumstances of his actual election (*LP* 97, ed. Duchesne I: 486–523). Presumably Hadrian was the candidate preferred by both the church administration and the Roman military aristocracy, a 'genuine clerical-noble symbiosis' in the words of Thomas Noble,[6] and he would have been no friend of the Lombards. We are told that on the day of his consecration he recalled or released those who had been previously exiled or imprisoned, and shortly thereafter launched an inquiry into the circumstances surrounding the death of Sergius, whose tortured body was eventually discovered.[7] This led to the arrest of Paul Afiarta at Rimini, and he was subsequently tried and executed at Ravenna, apparently against the wishes and without the knowledge of Hadrian, who had determined that he should be sent to the emperor in Constantinople (*LP* 97.4–17, ed. Duchesne I: 486–91). Desiderius subsequently launched an assault on Rome, prompting the papal appeal to Charlemagne for urgent assistance; and once again the Franks came to the rescue. By the end of 774, following the surrender of Pavia, the Lombard threat had been permanently removed;[8] and no subsequent internal opposition to Hadrian is recorded, resulting in two decades of comparative peace within Rome that left the pope free to attend to other urgent matters, including the city's infrastructure. We shall examine that activity in a subsequent chapter.

The final papal election of the eighth century, at the very end of December 795, chose Leo III (795–816), a distinguished cleric who was serving as priest of the church of Santa Susanna. The *Liber pontificalis* makes no mention of any opposing candidates (*LP* 98.2, ed. Duchesne II: 1), but it either passes over this matter in silence or else the opposition developed in the following years. On 25 April 799, as Leo was making his way from the Lateran to San Lorenzo in Lucina, the starting point for the annual procession known as the Major Litany, he was attacked in the street near the monastery of San Silvestro in Capite by a mob who attempted, unsuccessfully as it turned out, to put out his eyes and cut out his tongue. Interestingly, the named ringleaders were the *primicerius* Paschal and the

---

[5] Noble 1984: 125–6. [6] *Ibid.*, 198. [7] McKitterick 2020b.
[8] Noble 1984: 127–32; and Llewellyn 1993: 231–5.

sacellarius Campulus, senior members of the church administration who are known from other documents to have been members of the family of Pope Hadrian,[9] and it may be no coincidence that the attack took place in the region of Rome, the Via Lata, where this family is known to have lived. In the end, however, the plot was unsuccessful: Leo eventually escaped from custody, finding refuge first at Spoleto, and then he travelled north to meet Charlemagne at Paderborn. By the end of November, he was back in Rome with Frankish military support, and the following year Charlemagne came to Italy himself to put an end to the dispute. This set up the dramatic moment at Saint Peter's on Christmas Day 800 when the king of the Franks and Lombards was crowned additionally by the pope as emperor of the Romans (*LP* 98.11–23, ed. Duchesne II: 4–7).

The issue which has most engaged historians is the level of conscious political intent inherent in Pope Leo's action; indeed, as Richard Krautheimer once observed, 'whole libraries have been written about the question'.[10] What exactly was it intended to signify? This is neither the time nor the place to attempt an answer to a problem that lies outside the scope of this study, but in the context of attempting to understand the broader cultural forces at play in eighth-century Rome it may be appropriate to suggest that the break with Constantinople was anything but 'final' at this point. Indeed, there is evidence pointing in both directions. On the one hand we have suggestions that the emperor of Byzantium was still accorded some measure of legal authority. How else, for example, should we interpret Pope Hadrian's decision, at the conclusion of his inquiry into the murder of the *secundicerius* Sergius, to send the group of guilty 'Campanians' into exile at Constantinople (*LP* 97.13, ed. Duchesne I: 490)? A similar fate was planned for Paul Afiarta, the chief conspirator, with a plea that the emperors Constantine V and Leo IV would spare his life, but Paul was executed at Ravenna before this could happen.[11] Was the pope still thinking in terms of renewing the links to Byzantium? Noble discounts any political overtones, arguing that no other place of exile was available, but he possibly overstates the case.[12] And on the other hand we have the cessation under Hadrian of the time-honoured formula for dating documents by the imperial regnal year, albeit not in the first years of his reign but only after the crushing defeat of the Lombards by Charlemagne. A papal privilege for the abbey of Farfa, issued on 22 April 772 some two months after his election, still follows the customary practice and names the emperors Constantine and Leo; but by

---

[9] Noble 1984: 199–200; and Marazzi 2001: 49. [10] Krautheimer 1942: 13 note 97.
[11] Noble 1984: 130. [12] *Ibid.*, 133.

781 documents are being dated using the years of his own pontificate.[13] At approximately the same time Hadrian began to exercise his *ius moneta*, issuing coins bearing his name and image, and now aligned with the new Frankish standard.[14]

These changes coincide almost exactly with the new characterization of the 'Romans' of Constantinople as '*Greci*' ('Greeks').[15] Byzantium was now being viewed as the 'other', the foil to a newly redefined 'Roman' identity that was in the process of emerging; and Clemens Gantner, who has meticulously documented this shift in terminology in papal correspondence, views it as 'a deliberate decision by the papacy to vilify its Byzantine enemies'.[16] Presumably Hadrian was emboldened by his growing relationship with Charlemagne, especially after the Frankish annexation of the Lombard kingdom. He no longer needed to fear retribution from an irate emperor or exarch. At the same time, it is interesting to speculate what might have happened if the Second Council of Nicaea, which restored the use of icons in Byzantium, had taken place in, say, 767 and not 787. Like his predecessors, Pope Hadrian was a passionate defender of religious images, and he later worked to counter Frankish opposition expressed in the *Opus Caroli Regis* (also known as the *Libri Carolini*), thought to have been penned by Theodulph of Orléans.[17]

It is tempting to see the faction of Christopher and Sergius as representing the interests of the Roman nobility, one which I contend had strong 'Byzantine' cultural roots, who by this time had become more or less synonymous with the city's clerical and administrative hierarchy; and this may also explain why Hadrian did so much after his election to avenge their deaths.

Although his own family may not have been affected directly, as they seem not to be mentioned in the *Liber pontificalis* 'life' of Stephen III, it had nonetheless been an attack on his larger affiliative group by a faction based outside the city. While recognizing the dangers inherent in placing any special emphasis on the social construction of names, it is perhaps worth noting that both 'Christopher' and 'Sergius' are Greek, not Latin, suggesting perhaps at least a hellenophile context if not hellenophone origins. And what, one wonders, prompted members of Hadrian's family to launch the failed 799 *coup* against Pope Leo III?

---

[13] *Ibid.*, 133–4; and Noble 2001b: 75–83.
[14] Ladner 1941a: 111–12 and pl. XXVa; Noble 1984: 289–90; and Rovelli 2000: 95. For Charlemagne's attempt to standardize coinage in western Europe, see Coupland 2018.
[15] Delogu 2001: 75–6; Gantner 2013b; and Gantner 2014a: 101–38. [16] Gantner 2013b: 340.
[17] Freeman 1985; and Noble 2009: 149–56, 158–206.

Central to any understanding of the political situation is the document known as the 'Donation of Constantine', which we first encountered in our look at Zacharias' rebuilding of the Lateran Palace. This represents a seismic shift in political understanding, establishing the legal basis for the primacy of the see of Rome and papal assumption of secular authority ('*potestas*') over Rome and the former western Empire, specifically centred at the Lateran, stemming from the supposed transfer of the imperial insignia from Constantine to Pope Silvester I following the emperor's conversion and baptism. Such a vision presupposed a Rome that was politically independent from Constantinople, and for the first time in the history of the two cities this separation was becoming a reality. Thomas Noble has deemed it 'one of the most famous of all historical documents',[18] and the circumstances of its production are inevitably discussed by all those who treat the eighth century and its aftermath. Nicolas Huyghebaert viewed it as a move by the Lateran clergy to oppose the growing importance of Saint Peter's.[19]

It would be very useful to know the precise date for the creation of the 'Donation', and this issue has been the subject of considerable controversy. A *terminus ante quem* is provided by the earliest surviving manuscript (Paris, BNFr, cod. lat. 2777), thought to have been written at Saint-Denis early in the ninth century.[20] Most scholars prefer a composition date for the *Constitutum Constantini* in the second half of the eighth century,[21] if not specifically in the reign of Pope Hadrian.[22] The outlier is Johann Fried, who argued for a ninth-century Carolingian origin, possibly at Corbie; but its non-Roman production seems entirely implausible, and Fried's proposal has been effectively countered by Caroline Goodson and Janet Nelson.[23] We shall meet the 'Donation of Constantine' yet again when we look at the mosaic decorations of Leo III's Lateran Palace triclinium, which constitute a form of visual equivalent. Pope Hadrian I seems to have employed the thinking implicit in this document in his correspondence with both Charlemagne[24] and the Byzantine court, using it as justification not only

---

[18] Noble 1984: 134. [19] Huyghebaert 1979; Noble 1984: 134–7; and Delogu 2015: 210.
[20] *Constitutum Constantini*, ed. Fuhrmann: 20–1. Bischoff 1998–2017, III: 81, no. 4229.
[21] Goodson and Nelson 2010: 467; and Gantner 2015: 251. Delogu (2001: 76) suggests the pontificate of Paul I.
[22] Hartmann 2006: 182–93; and Barral i Altet 2016: 184.
[23] Fried 2007; and Goodson and Nelson 2010.
[24] *Codex epistolaris carolinus* 60, ed. Gundlach, pp. 585–7. The letter, dated May 778, refers to Constantine's gift to Pope Silvester of '*potestatem in his Hesperiae partibus*' (p. 587). See discussion by Emerick 2017: 133–4.

for jurisdiction over the 'patrimony of St Peter' but also for the primacy of the Roman see.[25]

The second half of the eighth century is also characterized by an apparent blossoming in the production of sumptuous 'material culture', or at least we have better evidence for such production, mostly in the form of donations to Roman churches, and these are increasingly the focus of the biographies in the *Liber pontificalis*. This implies the acquisition of enormous wealth by the Roman church. Some of the numerous papal projects offer interesting perspectives on the political situation, in particular those associated with Leo III (see Chapter 10).

The improving economic situation in Rome is also attested by the results of recent archaeology, and ceramics provide one instructive example. As we have seen, the excavations at the Crypta Balbi revealed the dramatic collapse of imports of African red-slip ware *c.* 700, probably related to the Arab conquest of Carthage in 698, with the result that only poorer local wares were found in the deposit dated to the early eighth century. But from the middle of the century we have evidence of a substantial revival of commercial ceramic production in Rome, both for local use and also for export to ports like Marseilles. This took the form of a new type of pottery, primarily jugs with a distinctive green or greenish-brown glaze, perhaps reflecting the influence of contemporary Byzantium where glazed pottery of this sort had become prominent by the eighth century: *ceramica a vetrina pesante*, better known as 'Forum Ware' from the initial find spot of some 1500 fragments in the fill of the Lacus Juturnae in the Roman Forum.[26]

The years after 750 are also notable for what seems to have been an intense revival of monumental building activity, encompassing not only churches but also walls, aqueducts, other civic structures, and even houses.[27] We shall encounter a number of these in subsequent chapters. The primary building material was reused blocks of *tufa*, a technique first encountered at Sant'Angelo in Pescheria (755) and then subsequently in churches such as San Silvestro in Capite (Paul I) and Santa Maria in Cosmedin (Hadrian I), as well as in Hadrian's other infrastructure projects.[28] In this regard it would be useful to know something about the

---

[25] Patlagean 2002: 41–4.
[26] Whitehouse 1982: 327–30; Bonifay, Paroli and Picon 1986; Christie 1987; Paroli 1990; Mazzucato 1993; and Romei 2004: 285–6.
[27] Noble (2000: 58–70) surveys some 263 papal building projects, of which 147 were undertaken by Hadrian I and Leo III.
[28] Santangeli Valenzani 2004c.

construction materials used in Pope Zacharias' additions to the Lateran Palace, but unfortunately no secure evidence for his building work there has survived.

Franz Alto Bauer has noted that a dramatic sense of physical 'recovery' can also be detected in the actual language employed in the *Liber pontificalis* biography of Hadrian I.[29] Rome before his pontificate is evoked with words such as *'vetustas'* and *'desolatio'*, and we are told, for example, that cattle and horses had been grazing in the overgrown atrium of San Paolo fuori le mura until the pope paved it with marble (*LP* 97.47, ed. Duchesne I: 499). By contrast, Hadrian's building activities are accompanied by verbs such as *'renovavit'*, *'restauravit'*, and *'noviter fecit'*. As we shall see, this theme of renovation and renewal of the city and its buildings runs throughout the account of Hadrian's pontificate, and the political overtones were presumably not lost on medieval readers. Nor have they escaped modern scholarship. As Richard Krautheimer observed long ago: 'The goal of these currents within the later eighth century was clearly a return to a period in Roman history which preceded the Byzantine domination. The idea was to renew the "great Roman" tradition of the Church, to create a *renovatio* of Rome as of old.'[30]

The last quarter of the eighth century is also characterized by a dramatic revival of marble sculpture, almost exclusively in the form of church furnishings, including choir screens, pulpits, altar canopies (*ciboria*), *fastigia*, and one spectacular episcopal throne,[31] all of which assisted in facilitating the performance of the liturgy. Copious quantities of material have survived from churches in and around Rome, and we shall come back to a few specific examples in our discussion of the patronage of Pope Hadrian I. This phenomenon continues into the first half of the ninth century, and includes the substantial remains which are still visible in the churches of Santa Prassede (Paschal I, 817–24) and Santa Sabina (Eugenius II, 824–7). The 'language' of the carved designs is distinctive: primarily abstract or vegetal, featuring geometric and ribbon interlace, and patterns of interlocking circles and lozenges, in addition to stylized lilies and rosettes, but also incorporating crosses, and with some animal forms, particularly where these were imbued with theological significance (peacocks and lambs, for example).[32] So too was the technique, using both pointed and bladed chisels.[33]

---

[29] Bauer 1999b: 514–5; and Bauer 2001–2: 191. [30] Krautheimer 1942: 15. [31] Aimone 2019.
[32] Macchiarella 1976a. [33] Macchiarella 1976b; and Aimone 2019: 31–3.

Lidia Paroli believed that the Roman examples depended directly on contemporary or earlier Lombard models,[34] but a more nuanced view may perhaps be preferred.[35] The apparent reappearance of stone liturgical furnishings, perhaps replacing earlier objects made of wood, should also be viewed in the context of a larger efflorescence of sculpture at this time that has left its traces across a very broad geographic swath encompassing the entire northern littoral of the Mediterranean from southern France to Anatolia. The so-called Lombard sculpture, known principally from north Italian sites such as Pavia, Brescia and Cividale, is more likely to have been one element of this larger phenomenon, rather than its ultimate source.[36] That said, the immediate models for Roman production, as well as the actual craftsmen, may well have come from nearby Lombard territories. Complicating matters, we know rather little about sculptural production in Rome in the decades after Pope John VII. It may well have continued to flourish, and Eugenio Russo has proposed that various fragments of a stone screen now in the Vatican grottoes belong to the renovations made to the area around the main altar of Saint Peter's undertaken under Pope Gregory III.[37] Pope Zacharias' documented refurbishing of the Lateran Palace may also perhaps lend support for such a view. But if so, the evidence has mostly not survived, the Vatican fragments excepted, apart from a few examples of epigraphy.

The *Liber pontificalis* is rather silent on the issue of objects in stone, perhaps because this material lacked intrinsic value in comparison to silk textiles or metalwork in gold and silver. By contrast, page after page of the *vitae* of Hadrian I and Leo III are devoted to examples of the latter categories, and there can be no doubt that Rome's churches were the recipients of a veritable explosion of donations in the last quarter of the eighth and first decades of the ninth century. For example, the last 53 chapters of the *vita* of Hadrian are devoted to his repairs and gifts, listed in more or less chronological sequence, as argued persuasively by Herman Geertman.[38] Luxury textiles were divided into three basic categories: *cortinae*, or large curtains to hang in entranceways; *vela*, small curtains or drapes to hang on walls and between columns; and *vestes*, to decorate altars. These are not merely enumerated, but often described in considerable detail, including information on both their material and

---

[34] Paroli 1998.　　[35] Melucco Vaccaro 2001; and Aimone 2019: 44–7.
[36] Osborne 1997b: 7–8. Melucco Vaccaro 1999 suggests that Rome was the source of the sculptural revival, but this doesn't explain the diffusion of similar motifs to places like Venice, Dalmatia and Byzantium.
[37] Russo 1985.　　[38] Geertman 1975; and Davis 2007: 116–18.

their design.[39] Most were silks, undoubtedly imported from the eastern Mediterranean as there is no evidence of a silk industry in Rome itself, although some bore additional embroidered designs with specific relevance to Rome, and these are most likely to have been added locally. Jean Croquison has calculated that Hadrian I's gifts of textiles totalled some 1343.[40] The *vestes* often bore figural scenes, either woven or embroidered, with the subject matter ranging broadly across Biblical narrative as well as being drawn from apocryphal and hagiographical texts.[41] Sadly, little trace of these textiles remains today apart from two fragments, preserved over the centuries in the altar of the Sancta Sanctorum chapel in the Lateran Palace, and today in the Vatican Museum. These depict scenes of the Annunciation to Mary and the Nativity.[42] For the gifts of objects made of precious metals, the weight is usually recorded, and these total almost 4,500 pounds of gold and 46,000 pounds of silver.[43]

The first two chapters of the *vita* of Hadrian I which deal with non-political matters (*LP* 97.45–46) are devoted to gifts made by the pope to Saint Peter's in the immediate aftermath of his election. This entry both covers a broad range of typical categories of object and also sets the stage for what will follow:

At St Peter's this angelic man provided a cloth of wondrous beauty with gold and jewels, representing St Peter's release from chains by the angel. In the same basilica he coated the pavement from the entrance of the railings to the confession with fine silver weighing 150 lb. Close to the great silver doors in St Peter's he provided a curtain of wondrous size, its material cross-adorned and fourfold-woven silk. For all the arches of the same basilica of the prince of the apostles he provided 65 veils of tyrian material with interwoven gold. Then in the same church His Beatitude provided the great cross-shaped light with 1365 candles, hanging over the *presbyterium*, and arranged for this light to be lit four times a year, at Christmas, Easter, the feast of the Apostles, and the pontiff's anniversary. In the same basilica the holy prelate provided a gold-rimmed silver chalice weighing 5 lb … In St Andrew the apostle's church close to St Peter's this thrice-blessed pontiff provided afresh a pure silver canopy weighing 135 lb.[44]

---

[39] Croquison 1964; Petriaggi 1984; Osborne 1992: 312–21; Delogu 1998; Martiniani-Reber 1999; and Noble 2000: 73–6.
[40] Croquison 1964: 603–4. The number rises to well in excess of 5,000 when the gifts of his papal successors are included in the tally; see Noble 2001b: 54.
[41] Croquison 1964, 581–97; and Osborne 1992: 315–16.   [42] Martiniani-Reber 1986.
[43] Delogu 1988b; and Noble 2001b: 54–5.
[44] *LP* 97.45–46; ed. Duchesne I: 499; trans. Davis 2007: 140.

The 65 veils of purple silk interwoven with gold thread constitute evidence for a technique well-known from Byzantium ('*chrysoclavum*'), and a similar eastern origin for many of the fabrics enumerated elsewhere in the *Liber pontificalis* is revealed by the vocabulary used to describe them: Greek words such as '*alithinum*', '*periclysin*', or '*holosiricum*', which have been transliterated directly into Latin.[45] If Mediterranean trade had collapsed in the early decades of the century, there can be no doubt that it was now substantially restored. And as an aside, it is perhaps worth noting that the growing status of the pope now permitted the anniversary of his election to be celebrated in a fashion more normally associated with secular rulers, in this instance by the lighting of the great candelabrum which Hadrian had presented to Saint Peter's, one of only four times in the year that this was done, as we are informed.

Clearly there was no shortage of funding for patronage of the arts, although there has been little agreement on its source. Paolo Delogu has proposed a combination of rents derived from the formerly imperial and Lombard territories now being administered by the papacy, and gifts made to the shrine of Saint Peter by increasingly wealthy pilgrims and the Frankish rulers, with a probable emphasis on the latter.[46] Thomas Noble, by contrast, has preferred to credit the burgeoning economic activity, and hence wealth, of central Italy, with perhaps a special role being played by the emerging Roman nobility, in other words the class of major landowning families to which Hadrian I himself belonged.[47] But perhaps the most intriguing suggestion has been made by Michael McCormick. Noting the substantial evidence for the importation into western Europe of luxury goods (especially silks) and other commodities from Byzantium and the Muslim world, he wonders aloud what might have been sent in the other direction by way of payment; and his answer is: slaves.[48]

There is no question that slaves were being bought and sold in Rome in the mid-eighth century. The *Liber pontificalis* makes specific reference to Venetian slave traders in the city in the *vita* of Pope Zacharias, although expressing papal concern at their presence (*LP* 93.22; ed. Duchesne, I: 433); and later in the century a similar reservation is expressed by Charlemagne in a letter to Pope Hadrian. In both instances the issue was not the practice

---

[45] Petriaggi 1984: 43–4. For the broader use of Greek vocabulary in the *Liber pontificalis*: Mosino 1983.
[46] Delogu 1988a: 37–8; Delogu 2017. See also Costambeys 2014: 266–7.
[47] Noble 2000: 79–82.
[48] McCormick 2001: 618–27; and McCormick 2002: 41–4. For slavery in early medieval Italy, see also Brown 1984: 202–4.

of slavery *per se*, but rather the possibility that Christian slaves were being sold to non-Christians, and in this instance specifically Muslims.[49] The papacy itself certainly made use of indentured labour, and slaves are given specific mention in the endowments accorded to new religious institutions established by Paul I and Hadrian I.[50]

For the moment this question, like so many others, must remain open, but there can be no question that popes Hadrian I and Leo III enjoyed unprecedented levels of disposable wealth. The visual appearance of the city and its churches in 800 must have been quite spectacular, especially if compared to the situation a century earlier. Although undoubtedly intended in a metaphoric sense, and as a description of Charlemagne's palace at Aachen, the words of the Carolingian poet, Moduin of Autun, seem particularly appropriate: 'Our times are transformed into the civilisation of Antiquity. Golden Rome is reborn and restored anew to the world.'[51]

---

[49] The pope's response is preserved: *Codex epistolaris carolinus* 59, ed. Gundlach, pp. 584–5; see also Noble 1984: 282; and Rio 2017: 35–6.

[50] Federici 1899: 258 (Paul I); and *LP* 97.81; ed. Duchesne I: 509–10 (Hadrian I). It may be important to distinguish between two different words for those who did not enjoy legal freedom: *mancipia* and *servi*.

[51] 'Rursus in antiquos mutataque secula mores/Aurea Roma iterum renovata renascitur orbi', *Ecloga*, ed. Dümmler, 385; trans. Godman, 193.

8 | Paul I

The pontificate of Paul I (757–67) marks a significant change in direction for the *Liber pontificalis*. Whereas previous papal *vitae* had focussed primarily on politics, and Rome's delicate and often fraught relations with both the emperors in Constantinople and the Lombard kings closer at hand, with the result that the patronage of building projects was generally consigned to the proverbial 'back burner', now the emphasis is switched and political matters are conspicuous by their almost total absence. Perhaps this reflects the success of the new papal policy of engaging the Franks against the Lombards, initiated by Paul's two predecessors. This new relationship not only provided Rome with a decade comparatively free from armed conflict, despite continuing tensions over the failure of the Lombards to honour earlier promises, but also allowed the pontiff to focus attention on other matters; and it is worth noting that one of Paul's first acts, even before his formal consecration, was to write to Pippin, informing him of his brother's passing and his own election, and seeking to reaffirm the papal-Frankish alliance.[1] A second letter sent subsequently to the Frankish king is also interesting, as Paul writes in the name of '*Omnis Senatus atque Universa Populi Generalitas ... Romanae Urbis*', possibly the first occasion on which the pope claimed to speak for all of Rome, and not only its church.[2] Raymond Davis comments that the *Liber pontificalis* entry for Paul is 'disappointing in its brevity and single-minded selectivity'.[3] It is certainly brief, but the information presented is of enormous significance. The life is probably also incomplete, and at least one of Paul's known projects, a major redecoration of the church of Santa Maria Antiqua, finds no mention.

---

[1] *Codex epistolaris carolinus* 12, ed. Gundlach, pp. 507–8; see also Noble 1984: 103–4. For the growing break with Byzantium, see Miller 1974 and Miller 1975.
[2] *Codex epistolaris carolinus* 13, ed. Gundlach, pp. 508–10. See comments by Noble 1984: 104; and Gantner 2014b: 473–4.
[3] Davis 2007: 76.

San Silvestro in Capite

Paul succeeded his brother, Stephen II, the first time that the papacy is known to have passed directly from one family member to another. Both had been orphaned at an early age, both were subsequently raised by and in the Roman church, and both had entered the clergy as deacons in the time of Pope Zacharias (*LP* 94.1, 95.1; ed. Duchesne I: 440, 463). They may have lacked parents, but they seem not to have lacked wealth, and a large part of Paul's biography is devoted to the monastery which he founded on family property located in the aristocratic neighbourhood of the Via Lata: the site of the church known today as San Silvestro in Capite. A few fragments still survive of the eighth-century structure, including the reused tufa blocks employed in the foundation.[4]

In addition to the notice in the *Liber pontificalis* (*LP* 95.5, ed. Duchesne I: 464–5), the circumstances of the foundation are reported in a letter from Paul to Abbot Leontius, a sort of foundation charter subscribed by a large number of Italian bishops in addition to the priests of Rome's titular churches. Its text has survived,[5] and it is interesting to note that the dating formula still employs primarily the names of the emperors of Byzantium, Constantine V and his son Leo IV, while also mentioning Pippin. This echoes Paul's *vita* in the *Liber pontificalis*, which similarly defines his reign chronologically by reference to Constantinople: '*Fuit autem temporibus Constantini et Leonis imperatorum*' (*LP* 95.2, ed. Duchesne I: 463). So at least some of the traditional ties to the old order were still being maintained. The foundation document also records a lavish endowment made in perpetuity, intended to provide for the daily needs of the monks: both urban and rural properties, including a wide variety of agricultural estates ('*massas, fundos, casales, colonias*'), vineyards, gardens, olive groves, salt pans, water mills, and fishponds, along with the servants or slaves who staffed them.[6]

While the *Liber pontificalis* describes both brothers as '*natione Romanus, ex patre Constantino*', it would be useful to know more about this family and its origins. Was their father, Constantine, like Megistus Cataxanthus

---

[4] *CBCR* IV: 148–62.   [5] Federici 1899: 254–63.

[6] *Ibid.*, 258. It is open to debate whether the expression 'servorum famulantium ... peculia' refers to 'slaves' in the traditional sense, although the institution of slavery was certainly still alive and well in eighth-century Rome. Davis does use the word 'slave' to translate a rather similarly worded record of the endowment accorded a few decades later by Pope Hadrian I to the diaconates of Sant'Adriano and Santi Cosma e Damiano (*LP* 97.81, ed. Duchesne I: 509–10; trans. Davis 2007: 162).

Plate 1. Santa Maria Antiqua, Rome: right side of apsidal arch (palimpsest wall).

Plate 2. Santa Maria Antiqua, Rome, right wall of the sanctuary: Saint Anne with the infant Mary.

Plate 3. Santa Maria Antiqua, Rome: Sickness of King Hezekiah.

Plate 4. Santa Maria Antiqua, Rome: niche with Madonna and Child.

Plate 5. Santa Sabina, Rome: narthex mural of Madonna and Child with saints and donors.

Plate 6. Santa Maria Antiqua, Rome: Theodotus chapel, view from entrance.

Plate 7. Santa Maria Antiqua, Rome: Theodotus chapel, Quiricus and Julitta tortured in the *sartago*.

Plate 8. Santa Maria Antiqua, Rome: Theodotus chapel, family of Theodotus on right wall, detail of boy.

Plate 9. Santa Maria Antiqua, Rome: Theodotus chapel, family of Theodotus on right wall, detail of girl.

Plate 10. Santa Maria Antiqua, Rome: right aisle, painted niche with the three 'holy mothers'.

Plate 11. Santa Maria Antiqua, Rome: atrium, Pope Hadrian I and his 'guarantor'.

Plate 12. San Clemente, Rome: Madonna and Child in a niche, right aisle of the lower church.

and his sons Theodore and Theodotus, someone who had acquired lands and wealth through military service? And was his family now attempting to construct a 'Roman' identity in keeping with the new ambitions of the city's emerging aristocratic élite? Probably we shall never know, although a few possible clues may emerge.

The monastery was dedicated to two early popes, the martyr Stephen I (254–7) and Silvester (314–35), whose remains were brought from the Roman catacombs and placed in an oratory built on the upper floor. Both translations, and their precise dates in the summer of 761, are recorded as postscripts to the letter to Leontius, and that of Silvester is also mentioned in one of Paul's letters to Pippin.[7] The dedication of the monastery's main church is not recorded until much later, but appears to have been to another early pope, Dionysius (260–7), whose relics, like those of Stephen, had previously been located in the Catacomb of San Callisto on the Via Appia.[8] The body of Silvester presumably came from his burial site in the Catacomb of Priscilla. The *Liber pontificalis* tells us that the main church was decorated in mosaic, and lavishly adorned with gold, silver, and marble, including a silver altar canopy weighing some 720 pounds. No trace of those decorations has survived.

In addition to the remains of Stephen I and Silvester, the charter letter to Abbot Leontius also mentions the relics of other innumerable martyrs and confessors of God (*'aliorum innumerabilium martyrum et confessorum Dei'*) which for some time had languished neglected in the ancient cemeteries outside the walls of Rome (*'diversa ... foras muros huius Romanae urbis sita antiquitus coemeteria neglecta'*) until these sites had been destroyed by the impious Lombards (*'ab impia Longobardorum gentium ... demolita'*), who had even taken away some of the bodies (*' ... secum deportaverunt corpora'*);[9] and a similar although much more abbreviated statement appears in the *Liber pontificalis* (LP 95.5, ed. Duchesne I: 464–5).

At least some of these saints were also recorded by name in two inscriptions, one listing men and the other women, organized by the calendar of their feast days; and parts of both inscriptions survive today in the atrium of the standing church.[10] Pope Dionysius is included in the

---

[7] Federici 1899: 263; *Codex epistolaris carolinus* 42, ed. Gundlach, p. 556.
[8] *CT* II: 87; *CBCR* IV: 160–1.   [9] Federici 1899: 255–6, 257.
[10] Silvagni 1943a I: pl. XXXVII.1–2; Gray 1948: 52–3 no. 10; Cardin 2008: pls 48–9; and Goodson 2010: 208–11. Another inscription naming the same saints, preserved at Saint Peter's, suggests that some of the relics also went to the Vatican, but its dating is uncertain; see Gray 1948: 53 no. 11; and Bauer 2004: 129–32.

list. Curiously, and possibly significantly, the feast days of at least two of the saints, Chrysanthus and Daria, follow the Byzantine rather than the Roman calendar.[11] But most striking is the new and overwhelming emphasis on 'Roman' saints, now brought in great numbers from the suburban cemeteries. Almost every saint listed can be identified with one or another of the catacomb sites;[12] and the list of early popes includes, in addition to Dionysus, Zephyrinus (199–217), Anteros (235–6), Lucius (253–4), Gaius (282–95), and Miltiades (310–14).

These translations to a church inside Rome's Aurelian walls are highly significant, for they mark an abrupt change from previous practice. Already in the fourth century, cities such as Milan and Constantinople, neither of which was blessed with an abundance of Early Christian martyrs, had attempted to rectify this deficiency through the importation of relics.[13] Rome, by contrast, had no shortage of native saints whose remains were venerated in the suburban cemeteries, at the actual sites of their initial burial; and in the fourth century a number of such shrines had been adorned with verse inscriptions by Pope Damasus (366–84).[14] Even after the practice of extramural burial faded away in the first half of the sixth century, the suburban cemeteries lived on as places of pilgrimage for the devout arriving from near and far, and their upkeep and decoration was an activity undertaken by numerous pontiffs, with their efforts now focussed on isolating the most important sites and facilitating access.[15] The earliest surviving pilgrim guidebooks to the city, the *Notitia ecclesiarum urbis Romae*[16] and the *De locis sanctis martyrum quae sunt foris civitatis Romae*,[17] thought to have been compiled about the year 640 CE,[18] provide detailed lists enumerating which saints could be found in which cemeteries, organized by the roads that led out from the city. The *Notitia ecclesiarum*, for example, begins with the Via Flaminia and then proceeds clockwise around the perimeter. Its entry for the Via Salaria lists Silvester, and that for the Via Appia lists Dionysius, although no mention is made of Pope Stephen.[19] It seems possible that Stephen's tomb was not previously identified, or was not popular with pilgrims, but that it became important to Paul I because his brother had shared the same papal name. The *De locis sanctis martyrum* begins with the Via Cornelia and circles in the opposite

---

[11] Sansterre 1983 I: 160. [12] Goodson 2010: 213.
[13] For Milan, see Mackie 2003: 18–22; for Constantinople, see Mango 1990, and Klein 2006: 82–8.
[14] Trout 2015. [15] Osborne 1984b, and Osborne 1985: 284–6.
[16] *CT* II: 67–99; CCSL 175: 303–11. [17] *CT* II: 101–31; CCSL 175: 313–22.
[18] Geertman 1975: 198–202. [19] *CT* II: 76–7, 87.

direction. It too mentions Silvester but omits both Dionysius and Stephen.[20]

As we have seen, the existence of intramural burials can be documented from at least the sixth century. At first such graves were sporadic, perhaps the result of moments when access to the cemeteries outside the walls was impossible due to siege warfare,[21] but soon they became the norm, and eventually were associated with the peripheral zones around churches: for example, the excavation of the atrium of Santa Maria Antiqua revealed a large number of early medieval burials, some of which reused older sarcophagi.[22] But there is no direct connection between the change of burial practice and the movement of saintly relics. Although by at least the mid-sixth century the Roman church seems to have been willing to accept corporeal relics brought from the eastern Mediterranean, for example, the Maccabee brothers venerated at San Pietro in Vincoli,[23] there was apparently much greater reluctance to disturb the bodies of their local saints and bring them inside the Aurelian walls, perhaps in part because this would have disrupted a flourishing pilgrimage industry.

The *Notitia ecclesiarum urbis Romae* lists but a single site of veneration inside the walls: the church of Santi Giovanni e Paolo on the Celian hill, where the remains of the two titular saints 'repose in a large church' ('*quiescunt in basilica magna*'), and this same information is also provided by the *De locis sanctis martyrum* in its appendix listing churches situated inside the city.[24] But it is not certain when their relics came to be associated with this location, and the earliest reference to the church by this designation occurs only *circa* 500 (*LP* 53.9, ed. Duchesne I: 262).

It appears that a number of special circumstances in the middle of the seventh century began to disrupt the previous pattern, invariably involving translations to Rome from beyond the immediate environs of the city.[25] Three such instances can be documented securely. In or about the year 640, Pope John IV (640–2), a native of Dalmatia, sent an expedition to the cities of the north-eastern Adriatic following their devastation by Avar attacks, intended both to purchase the freedom of those who had been enslaved and also to recover the relics of various saints and martyrs whose shrines had been ransacked and destroyed (*LP* 74.1, ed. Duchesne I: 330). These relics

---

[20] *CT* II: 116.
[21] Osborne 1985: 281–3; Rea 1993; Meneghini and Santangeli Valenzani 1993; and Costambeys 2002.
[22] Rushforth 1902: 104–7; and Augenti 1996: 163–8.
[23] Goodson 2007: 63–5; and Goodson 2010: 202–4.   [24] *CT* II: 72, 124.
[25] Osborne 1985: 286–7.

were placed in a new oratory attached to the Lateran baptistery, dedicated to Saint Venantius of Salona, the name saint of the pope's father; and a number of Dalmatian and Istrian saints were depicted in the chapel's mosaic decorations.[26] John IV's successor, Pope Theodore (642–9) is recorded as having brought the relics of Saints Primus and Felicianus from a sandpit ('*arenarium*') on the Via Nomentana to his new chapel in the church of Santo Stefano Rotondo, intended to serve as the burial chapel of his father (*LP* 75.4; ed. Duchesne I: 332).[27] And finally, Pope Leo II (682–3) is recorded as having built a church adjacent to Santa Bibiana 'where he deposited the bodies of Saints Simplicius, Faustinus, Beatrice, and other martyrs'.[28] Their relics came from the Cemetery of Generosa on the Via Portuense, again at some distance from the city. But these examples remain the exceptions which prove the rule. In the year 750 most of Rome's saintly guardians still reposed in their original extramural catacomb graves, as attested by the guidebooks, the painted decorations marking the tombs for the benefit of visitors, and the large number of graffiti left by pious pilgrims.[29]

In addition to the legislation which prohibited burial inside the city, evidently largely ignored from at least the first half of the sixth century, various sources attest that the Roman church was probably opposed in theory to any unnecessary displacement of bodies, which also explains their predilection for contact relics over actual body parts. This reluctance is perhaps best documented in the response made by Pope Gregory I to the Empress Constantina, wife of the Emperor Maurice, who wrote from Constantinople to request the head of Saint Paul. The pope responded in June 594 that he did not dare to accede to the imperial request, as Roman custom did not permit anyone to touch corporeal remains. This would be a sacrilege, and he offered her instead a '*brandeum*' (contact relic) and some filings from the saint's chains.[30] Of course we may well ask how much of this response accurately reflects Roman attitudes, and how much was invented by Gregory in order to justify his refusal to part with an object of considerable importance for the authority of the Roman church.

---

[26] Mackie 1996; Mackie 2003: 212–30; and Goodson 2007: 69–70.

[27] For the chapel and its mosaic, Davis-Weyer 1989, Mackie 2003: 75–7, and Goodson 2007: 70–1. The original site of their burial on the Via Nomentana has been identified some 22 km from Rome: *LP* ed. Duchesne, p. 334 note 9.

[28] *LP* 82.5, ed. Duchesne I: 360: '*ubi et corpora sanctorum Simplici, Faustini, Beatricis atque aliorum martyrum recondidit*'. English trans. Davis 2010: 77.

[29] Carletti 1986; and Carletti 2002.

[30] Gregory I, *Registrum Epistolarum* IV, 30 (ed. Ewald and Hartmann, 263–6). See also McCulloh 1976: 147–50; Leyser 2000: 302; Goodson 2007: 66–7; and Smith 2014: 184–7.

With the pontificate of Paul I, however, any general aversion to relic translation disappears more or less overnight, at least for those made to churches inside the city of Rome itself. The following century is characterized by a series of campaigns to empty the catacombs of saintly remains, reaching their maximum extent in the pontificate of Pope Paschal I (817–24), who translated some 2,300 bodies to his new church of Santa Prassede alone.[31] And the way was also opened to permit a substantial flow of relics to religious foundations north of the Alps, both in the years around 760 and then again in the early ninth century.[32] What prompted this complete reversal of earlier custom? The correspondence of Pope Paul is absolutely explicit in this regard: it was a response to the experience of the three-month siege of Rome in 756, undertaken by the Lombard King Aistulf.

The first suggestion of Lombard devastation of the city's hinterland, including incursions into the suburban cemeteries, appears in the *Liber pontificalis* biography of Stephen II: 'Everything outside the city this pestilential Aistulf devastated with fire and sword, and thoroughly wrecked and consumed it, pressing mightily on so that he could capture this city of Rome. He even dug up the sacred cemeteries of the saints and stole many of their bodies, which was greatly to his own soul's detriment.'[33] The language of Pope Stephen's letter to Pippin, imploring his urgent assistance, is even more vivid, accusing the Lombards not only of the profanation and destruction of rural churches, but also the destruction of papal agricultural estates, the torturing and killing of monks, and the raping of nuns.[34] But unlike the *Liber pontificalis* entry, no specific mention is made of the catacombs.

The link between the Lombard siege and the subsequent translations is, however, stated explicitly in Paul I's 'charter letter' to Abbot Leontius. Apart from a general state of neglect, to the point that some cemeteries were now being used to house animals, the pope states specifically that the suburban shrines had been profaned, and some bodies of the saints had been removed, by the 'impious' Lombards.[35]

---

[31] Goodson 2010: 228–44.   [32] Smith 2000.
[33] LP 94.41, ed. Duchesne I: 451–2: '*Omnia extra urbem ferro et igne devastans atque funditus demoliens consumit, imminens vehementius hisdem pestifer Aistulf ut hanc Romanam capere potuisset urbem. Nam et multa corpora sanctorum, effodiens eorum sacra cymiteria, ad magnum anime sue detrimentum abstulit.*' English trans. Davis 2007: 68.
[34] *Codex epistolaris carolinus* 8, ed. Gundlach, pp. 494–8. See also Llewellyn 1993: 213–14.
[35] Federici 1899: 257: '*Qui etiam, et aliquanta ipsorum effodientes martyrum sepulchra et impie devastantes, quorumdam sanctorum depraedati auferentes, secum deportaverunt corpora.*' See also Llewellyn 1993: 219–20; and Osborne 1985: 290.

This belief seems to have lingered in the Roman consciousness for some time. The *Liber pontificalis* biography of Paschal I recounts an anecdote concerning his attempt to translate the relics of the martyr Cecilia to her newly rebuilt shrine church in Trastevere. Having sought to find her body in the catacombs, without success, he concludes that it must have been stolen by Aistulf and the Lombards. But one night, while celebrating a vigil in Saint Peter's, Paschal falls asleep, and Cecilia appears to him in a dream. She tells him that the Lombards had indeed sought to take away her remains, but had not been able to discover their location. She urges him to renew the search, which he does – and this time he is successful.[36]

It is important to recognize that these papal reports of Lombard atrocities were intended to spur the Franks into action, and are likely to have been significantly exaggerated in order to achieve that end. And in this goal Pope Stephen II was completely successful. No doubt some element of truth lies at their core, however. The city certainly incurred damages, including an interruption to its water supply which would need to be repaired in subsequent decades, and it is certainly possible that some relics of Roman saints were taken away; but the Lombards were generally not impious desecrators of religious institutions. Indeed, to the contrary, despite being on the receiving end of a 'bad press' in this regard. As first noted by Louis Duchesne,[37] their interest in acquiring relics was undoubtedly genuine, and in the Middle Ages the 'theft' of relics was only regarded as illegitimate if the saint intervened to oppose it.[38] Saints were widely believed to function as protectors of the cities or institutions which housed their remains, and this view was certainly prevalent in the Lombard kingdom: for example, a poem written about the year 740, the *Laudes mediolanensis civitatis*, celebrates the many '*sanctos defensores*' who acted collectively to defend the city of Milan.[39] Many Lombard kings and queens were notable founders of monasteries, and also avid collectors of relics in a tradition going back at least as far as Queen Theodelinda (570–628), wife of the successive kings Authari and Agilulf, who assembled a substantial collection now preserved in the cathedral treasury at Monza.[40]

Relics were often sought outside the Lombard kingdom itself. In the early eighth century for example, when the island of Sardinia was

---

[36] *LP* 100.15–16, ed. Duchesne II: 56. See also Osborne 1985: 290; and Goodson 2010: 1–2. For the Lombard claim that the relics of Cecilia had indeed been taken by Aistulf to Pavia, see Tomea 2001: 43.

[37] *LP* I: 459–60 note 44.   [38] Geary 1978: 132–43.

[39] MGH *Poetae Latini aevi Carolini*, ed. Dümmler I: 24–6.

[40] These were 'contact' relics: *ampullae* containing oil from lamps burning at the saints' shrines, all identified by papyrus labels: *CT* II: 29–47. See also Leyser 2000: 298–9.

threatened by Arab raiders, King Liutprand (r. 712–44) is known to have sent a mission to 'rescue' the relics of Saint Augustine of Hippo,[41] an action that even reached the ears of Bede in distant Northumbria.[42] Augustine's body was brought to the Lombard capital, Pavia, and installed in the church of San Pietro in Ciel d'Oro, where it remains today; and Liutprand would subsequently select this church for his own burial. Another king, Desiderius (r. 756–74), Aistulf's successor, was both an avid founder of monasteries and an avid collector of saintly remains with which to endow them.[43] Relics of Saint Benedict (from Montecassino) and of Saints Vitalis and Martial (from Rome) were donated to the monastery which he founded at Leno, south of Brescia.[44] Of particular interest is the foundation by Desiderius and his wife, Queen Ansa, of San Salvatore at Brescia, a monastery for women of which their daughter, Anselperga, became the first abbess. In addition to the remains of Saint Giulia of Corsica, said to have been brought by Ansa from the island of Gorgona in the Tuscan archipelago, the church also received relics of at least six Roman saints: Pumenius, Hippolytus, and Sophia, along with her daughters Agape, Elpis and Pistis.[45] Were these gifts from Pope Paul, perhaps on the occasion of Desiderius' visit to Rome in 759, or had they been 'stolen' by the Lombards during the siege of 756? Complicating matters, the same six saints all appear in the inscribed lists at San Silvestro in Capite.[46] It is unlikely that we shall ever know, but it is certainly possible that Paul's *inventio* was an attempt to 'save face' following the loss. Another tradition maintains that the pope presided personally at the dedication of San Salvatore on 29 October 763,[47] in which case the Roman relics may have been gifts presented on that occasion. We can certainly lament the silence of the *Liber pontificalis* on the political events of these years in the early 760s.

Nevertheless, the overall picture seems reasonably clear. From the perspective of Pope Stephen II, Aistulf was 'a follower of the Devil, a devourer of Christian blood, and a destroyer of the churches of God',[48] but from another he was a good Christian who wished to bolster the sanctity of the

---

[41] Paul the Deacon, *Historia Langobardorum* VI.48, ed. Bethmann and Waitz p. 181; see also Tomea 2001: 34–6.

[42] Bede, *De temporum ratione*, ed. Mommsen, p. 321.   [43] D'Acunto 2015; and Succurro 2015.

[44] It remains uncertain whether the Roman relics were a papal gift or booty from 756; see Tomea 2001: 46–7; Brogiolo 2014: 23; and Succurro 2015: 612.

[45] Tomea 2001: 48; and Brogiolo 2014: 23.   [46] Tomea 2001: 52–6; and Brogiolo 2014: 23.

[47] Brogiolo 1999: 25.

[48] '*sequax diaboli ... devorator sanguinem christianorum, ecclesiarum Dei destructor*': *Codex epistolaris carolinus* 11, ed. Gundlach, p. 505.

cities and religious institutions in the Lombard kingdom by increasing their holdings of sacred relics. Although the question of Paul I's motives remains open, the realization that the catacombs were unprotected, rendering their relics vulnerable to easy plunder, is likely to have been the primary catalyst for his actions. Caroline Goodson has linked the extramural burial sites of the specific saints brought to San Silvestro with areas known to have been the locations of Lombard encampments.[49]

Pope Paul I's selection of saintly patrons for his new monastery also merits a brief comment, although again we are firmly in the realm of speculation. The choice of Pope Stephen can be explained as honouring the name of his brother and papal predecessor, recently deceased; but Silvester represents a significant revival of interest in the fourth-century pope who was the supposed recipient of the infamous 'Donation of Constantine'. And is it a coincidence that Dionysius bore the same name as the principal saintly patron of the Frankish monarchy, whose burials were located at the royal monastery of Saint-Denis outside Paris? One suspects not.[50]

The monastery of Saints Stephen and Silvester was not the only recipient of relics from the catacombs at this time. The *Liber pontificalis* devotes an entire, albeit short, chapter to this topic, noting the pope's concern that many of the cemeteries had been 'nearly reduced to ruin'. With considerable pomp and ceremony Paul brought the saintly remains 'inside the city of Rome, and he took care to have some of them buried with fitting honour around the *tituli*, deaconries, monasteries and other churches.'[51] No trace now remains of that distribution, with the possible exception of a fragmentary inscription preserved in Saint Peter's;[52] but the lettering is, in the words of Nicolette Gray, 'particularly unpleasant', and a dating to Paul's pontificate is far from certain.

There is one final fascinating detail which the *Liber pontificalis* provides to its readers regarding Pope Paul's new foundation: 'There he established a community of monks and decreed it should be a monastery for chanting the psalms in the Greek manner.'[53] Some scholars have interpreted this as the pope offering a home in exile for iconophile monks who had fled the persecutions of Emperor Constantine V (r. 741–75), and that may well be the case.[54] Given that the iconoclast emperors were also accused of seeking to suppress the cult of the saints,[55] the combination of relic transfer and

---

[49] Goodson 2010: 213. [50] *Ibid.*, 214. [51] *LP* 95.4, ed. Duchesne I: 464; trans. Davis 2007: 81.
[52] Silvagni 1943a I: pl. XXXVII.3; and Gray 1948: 53 no. 11.
[53] *LP* 95.5, ed. Duchesne I: 465; trans. Davis 2007: 82. [54] Sansterre 1983 I: 47.
[55] Wortley 1982.

eastern monasticism appears highly suggestive. But the choice might also simply reflect the hellenophone roots of the family of Constantine, and the language spoken in the home of Stephen and Paul's youth. Regardless of the motivation, the Greek language and Greek liturgy were alive and well in mid-eighth-century Rome.

While the immediate impetus for Paul's translations may have been to safeguard the bones of Rome's native saints and martyrs, increasingly regarded as valuable commodities, the clear emphasis on earlier pontiffs also signals an apparent shift in thinking about the choice of specific saints who were regarded as important. As we have seen, before 760 the most 'popular' saints among Rome's ruling élite hailed primarily from the eastern Mediterranean, their cults presumably arriving in the seventh century in the baggage of the wave of hellenophone monks, bureaucrats and military officers. But in a city now becoming refocussed on its own history, on the legacy of Constantine and Silvester, on *papal* power and authority, a new emphasis on 'Roman' saints was not only desirable but also politically expedient. Rome's hegemonic claims did not, and could not, depend on Abbacyrus and John, or George or the Maccabees. Rather, they rested on Peter and his episcopal successors, as well as others from the city, male and female, who had sanctified this physical space with the blood of their martyrdoms.[56] Viewers contemplating Paschal I's ninth-century mosaics on the triumphal arch of Santa Prassede gazed at the walls of the 'heavenly' Jerusalem, inhabited at the end of time by the congregation of the saints; but they were no doubt also meant to think of the Aurelian walls of Rome, now the abode of many of those same individuals until the day of the Last Judgment. In the words of Hendrik Dey, the walls of Rome had become 'the world's largest reliquary'.[57]

Saint Peter's

The other major site of Paul's activities mentioned in the *Liber pontificalis* was the church of Saint Peter's, where his name is associated with no fewer than three projects, all involving the installation of new chapels. It is difficult to know how much significance should be read into this, and into the comparative total lack of attention to the Lateran. Did it reflect a renewed emphasis on Peter and the papal claims to succession, including the thinking that underlies the 'Donation of Constantine'? Or was it simply

[56] Krautheimer 1942: 14.   [57] Dey 2011: 235–40.

that the Lateran patriarchate, recently rebuilt by Pope Zacharias, was not thought to require further immediate attention? It would certainly be interesting to know, but Paul's *Liber pontificalis* biography is by far the shortest for all the eighth-century pontiffs after Constantine and thus it is difficult to get any sense of his intentions. If anything, he seems to have had some special interest in his saintly namesake, Paul, and we are told not only that he was living at San Paolo fuori le mura when he died, but also that he was initially buried there (*LP* 95.7, ed. Duchesne I: 465), although that had not been his intention.

His first undertaking at Saint Peter's was the conversion of the former imperial mausoleum situated adjacent to the south flank of the church into the chapel of Santa Petronilla.[58] This project had been commenced by his brother, Pope Stephen II, following a promise made to the Frankish king, Pippin, but remained unfinished at Stephen's death (*LP* 94.52, ed. Duchesne I: 455). The transformation was completed by Paul, who also brought Petronilla's remains from a cemetery '*foris porta Appia*' (*LP* 95.3, ed. Duchesne I: 464).[59] The entire undertaking was imbued with explicit political significance, as the cult of Petronilla, by tradition the daughter of Saint Peter and herself also a martyr, was developed for special veneration by the new Frankish royal family; and the development and promotion of her cult in Rome by both Stephen II and Paul has been viewed convincingly as sending an important signal regarding the importance to Rome of the new papal-Frankish alliance. Furthermore, the space in question was associated with imperial rulers, and one can presume that popes of an earlier age would not have dared take such liberties without explicit permission. But times had changed. The chapel was chosen for the display of the baptismal shawl of Pippin's daughter, Gisela; and it can be no coincidence that Petronilla's feast day was established as 9 October, the same as Saint Denis.[60] This may also explain why the two *Liber pontificalis* passages which mention Petronilla are found only in manuscripts of the so-called Frankish recension (group B) of the text.[61] Independently, however,

---

[58] For the mausoleum of the Honorian dynasty: Johnson 1991; Johnson 2009: 167–74; Mackie 2003: 58–60; and McEvoy 2013.

[59] The seventh-century *De locis sanctis martyrum* places the tomb of Petronilla with those of Saints Nereus and Achilleus on the Via Ardeatina, in the cemetery now known as the Catacomb of Domitilla; *CT* II: 110. It is worth noting that relics of Petronilla also featured in the 755 CE inscription of Theodotus in Sant'Angelo in Pescheria, where she is the only Roman female martyr to be named apart from Saint Aurea of Ostia. Clearly her cult became of interest at this time.

[60] Schieffer 2000: 287; McKitterick 2004: 146–8; Goodson 2015; and Emerick 2017: 134.

[61] For the three versions of the *vita* of Stephen II, see Gantner 2013a: 70–3; for the manuscripts in 'group B', Davis 2007: xvii–xviii.

the chapel's location and dedication are recorded in the eighth-century description of Saint Peter's appended to the earlier *Notitia ecclesiarum urbis Romae*,[62] and this mention is an important factor in determining a *terminus post quem* for the compilation of that additional text.

The *Liber pontificalis* reports that Petronilla's relics were found inside a marble sarcophagus bearing the identifying inscription '*Aureae Petronillae filiae dulcissimae*'; but when this object was actually rediscovered during renovations to the chapel's altar in 1474, the first word was deciphered more accurately as '*Aureliae*'.[63] There is no early evidence to suggest any factual basis for the tradition of a filial relationship to Saint Peter, and the supposed association was probably derived from the similarity of names.

We are also told that Paul had the chapel decorated with 'wondrously beautiful pictures',[64] and scenes from the story of the Emperor Constantine were recorded here in the fifteenth century, presumably taking their inspiration from the text of the *Actus Silvestri*.[65] Assuming that these were original to the mid eighth century, or at least reflected the original subject matter, they would constitute important additional evidence for the new emphasis now being accorded to the story of Constantine's conversion,[66] and thus might support the proposed dating of the 'Donation of Constantine' document to this time. Unfortunately, these murals did not survive the later rebuilding of Saint Peter's, and seem not to have been recorded when the Early Christian basilica was demolished.

Pope Paul I's second project in Saint Peter's was his own funerary chapel, dedicated to Mary, *sancta Dei genetrix*, and situated in the south transept, between the entrance into the church from the chapel of Santa Petronilla and the funerary chapel of Pope Leo I. The *Liber pontificalis* describes it as decorated with mosaics and a gilded silver image of the Virgin weighing 150 pounds (*LP* 95.6, Duchesne I: 465). The choice of location is enormously significant.

As we have seen, until the end of the seventh century the tombs of the popes were clustered outside the church in the atrium and narthex. This pattern was broken in June 688 when Pope Sergius I moved the body of Pope Leo I inside the building to a new chapel in the south transept,

---

[62] CT II: 96. [63] *LP* ed. Duchesne I: 466 note 5.
[64] *LP* 95.3, ed. Duchesne I: 464, '*picturis miro decore*'; trans. Davis 2007: 80.
[65] Davis 2007: 80 note 6; and Emerick 2017: 134–5. For the *Actus Silvestri*, which related the story of Silvester's cure of Constantine's leprosy and the emperor's subsequent conversion to Christianity, see Liverani 2008: 165–70.
[66] Goodson 2010: 215.

apparently considered to be a more 'public' location,[67] perhaps because it was also the place where early medieval pilgrims approaching the shrine of Peter entered the basilica.[68] Leo thus joined a number of other illustrious Romans whose tombs lined the '*via sacra* for the cult of Saint Peter', in the words of Joanna Story.[69] John VII was the first pope to actually prearrange his burial inside the basilica, but only just inside: against the façade wall. In this he was followed by Gregory III (731–41), who moved much closer to the altar (*LP* 92.6–7, ed. Duchesne I: 417–18);[70] but Paul was the first to join Leo in the south transept – on the main thoroughfare as it were.

Again, it would be fascinating to have a better sense both of his intentions and of how this choice was interpreted by his contemporaries. Paul would die at San Paolo fuori le mura, where we are told he had gone in an attempt to escape the summer heat, and initially he was buried there. It would take some three months before his remains were brought to Saint Peter's for burial; and rather intriguingly, apparently this action was undertaken by the people of Rome and foreigners, presumably pilgrims,[71] who employed boats on the Tiber rather than processing through the streets. Was there some initial reluctance on the part of the clergy to bury the pope in such a prominent location; or, perhaps more plausibly, does it simply reflect the general chaos which pervaded the Roman church following his death, when the papal throne was seized for a year by Constantine, the brother of Duke Toto of Nepi (*LP* 96.3–4, ed. Duchesne I: 468–9)? Regardless of the precise circumstances, Paul's construction of a funerary oratory in the south transept, and his eventual burial there, mark an important step in the evolving self-image of the vicars of Saint Peter, and his choice of location would be emulated in the following decades by other pontiffs, including Popes Hadrian I (772–95) and Paschal I (817–24).

Another noteworthy detail of the very brief mention of Paul's funerary chapel in the *Liber pontificalis* is the gilded silver statue of Mary: '*ubi et effigiem sancte Dei genetricis in statu ex argento deaurato*' (*LP* 95.6, ed. Duchesne I: 465). Both the description and recorded weight (150 pounds) suggest that this may have been an actual statue, rather than an icon.[72] If so, this reference is apparently unique for eighth-century Rome. Three-dimensional figural

---

[67] '*in denominata basilica publico loco*': *LP* 86.12, ed. Duchesne I: 375.
[68] *CT* II: 95. See also Story 2013: 261–3.   [69] Story 2013: 264.   [70] Mackie 2003: 78–9.
[71] '*omnes Romani cives et alie nationes*': *LP* 95.7, ed. Duchesne I: 465.
[72] For the term '*effigia*', see Andaloro 1976: 71–2. It is normally used in the *Liber pontificalis* to describe figures within '*imagines*' (icons), for example, in describing the three silver panels given by Hadrian I to San Paolo fuori le mura (*LP* 97.60, ed. Duchesne I: 504), two of which bore images of angels ('*effigies angelorum*'). By way of comparison to Paul I's statue of Mary, it is worth noting that their collective weight was a mere 24 pounds.

sculpture was exceptionally rare in the early Middle Ages, presumably reflecting the widespread suspicion of possible idolatry. It would be difficult not to interpret this commission as a deliberate challenge to the Byzantine policy of Iconoclasm, still in full force.

Paul's third project at Saint Peter's was also a chapel dedicated to the 'holy mother of God, Mary', later to be known either as Santa Maria ad Grada or Santa Maria in Turri. This was constructed in the gatehouse leading to the atrium, and decorated 'magnificently' (*LP* 95.6, Duchesne I: 465). Once again it is mentioned only in the 'Frankish recension' (manuscript group B) of the *Liber pontificalis*, although in this instance there are no obvious political implications; and once again the location and dedication are attested independently in the eighth-century description of Saint Peter's appended to the text of the *Notitia ecclesiarum* guidebook, where the dedication is given as Santa Maria Nova.[73] In the early seventeenth century, Giacomo Grimaldi would witness its demolition. Grimaldi also records the mosaic placed on the façade of the chapel, depicting the figure of Christ enclosed in a *mandorla* (aureole) supported by angels, with four standing figures beneath.[74] Only part of a dedication inscription survived in his time, and the name of the papal patron was illegible, but a generation earlier it had been read by Pompeo Ugonio as naming Paul.[75]

Santa Maria Antiqua

Of all Paul I's numerous projects and commissions, the only one for which we have any substantial surviving evidence may be found, yet again, in the church of Santa Maria Antiqua in the Roman Forum. Although the *Liber pontificalis* makes no mention of any activity here, his intervention was apparently substantial, and included the complete repainting of the conch of the apse, while apparently leaving untouched the arch which framed it.[76] Fortunately for modern historians, Paul included his own image in the composition, along with an identifying inscription. Above a substantial dado, the apse was painted with a monumental figure of Christ,[77] seated on a throne, holding a book in his left hand and blessing with his right, and flanked by two angelic tetramorphs. These were creatures with four heads,

---

[73] *CT* II: 99, and note 3.
[74] BAV, Barb. Lat. 2733, fols. 152v–155r; Grimaldi 1972: 188–91. See also Belting 1961; and Bauer 2004 164–6.
[75] *LP* ed. Duchesne I: 467 note 13. [76] Wilpert 1916: pl. 151.
[77] Rushforth, De Grüneisen and Tea all use the same adjective: 'colossal'.

representing the symbols of the four Evangelists (man, lion, ox, eagle – based on texts from both the Old and New Testaments),[78] and six wings. At the time of the excavation, only the tetramorph on the right was sufficiently preserved to be identifiable.

To the left (at Christ's right hand) we find the pontiff, holding a jewelled *codex*, being presented by his saintly patron, Mary, who places her hand on his shoulder. His head is enclosed in a 'square halo' signifying a portrait, and was originally identified by an inscription written vertically to the left, except for the last word which was placed horizontally above: +SANCTISSIMUS PAULUS P(A)P(A) ROMAN(US).[79] Some two centuries before Giacomo Boni's excavation, the inscription was recorded both by Francesco Valesio in his diary entry for 24 May 1702, when the apse and sanctuary of the church were briefly uncovered,[80] and also by Domenico Passionei.[81] The letters were still fully discernible in the early 1900s, and thus while little now survives of the figure of the pope, there can be no doubt whatsoever regarding his identity. The general state of preservation of the mural is poor, and its fragmentary state can't have been helped by Joseph Wilpert's effort in December 1909 to remove plaster belonging to this level, in an unsuccessful attempt to ascertain what had been painted beneath.[82]

Despite its condition, the apse constitutes a document of some considerable importance, for it marks a significant departure from the usual Roman iconography in which the papal donor is presented to Christ by Peter and Paul and other saints. Here Paul's sponsor is Mary, and she is depicted alone, in keeping with the dedication of the church and echoing the devotion to the *sancta dei genetrix* which we observed a half century earlier on the part of John VII.[83] Paul I was clearly not averse to the cults of Peter and Paul, and the *Liber pontificalis* records his foundation of a church with that twin dedication, in the centre of the city on the Via Sacra, where legend maintained that the two saints had knelt to pray and where a stone preserved their resulting knee-prints (*LP* 95.6, ed. Duchesne I: 465).[84] But perhaps more telling is the dedication chosen for both Santa Maria in Turri and his funerary chapel in Saint Peter's.

---

[78] See Rubery 2009: 188–9.
[79] Rushforth 1902: 73–4; De Grüneisen 1911: 150–1; Wilpert 1916: 701–2 and pl. 151; Tea 1937: 306–9; Ladner 1941a: 107–8; and Rubery 2009: 187–8.
[80] Valesio 1977–9 II: 169–70. [81] Mei 2020. [82] Wilpert 1916: 668.
[83] Lucey (2007: 152) suggests that it was his particular devotion to Mary that may have prompted Paul I's interest in Santa Maria Antiqua.
[84] *LTUR* IV: 83–4. For a recent attempt to identify this site, see Spera 2016: 406.

Also unusual is the presence of the tetramorphs, and this marks the first documented appearance of this specific form of angel in the decoration of a Roman church.[85] In a detailed study of this iconography, Eileen Rubery has linked the tetramorphs both to the world of eastern Christianity (citing examples from Georgia, Armenia, Syria, Egypt, Constantinople, and Thessaloniki) and more specifically to the Roman church's spirited defence of images against the imperial policy of Iconoclasm. In 754 that policy had been given both an official endorsement and a theological underpinning at the Council of Hiereia, convened by Emperor Constantine V, and images of Christ and the angels were considered particularly problematic since they attempted to contain the 'uncontainable'.

The new apse mural can thus be interpreted as a defiant statement of perceived orthodoxy in the face of persistent Byzantine diplomatic attempts to bring its troublesome duchy of Rome to heel, and would likely have been interpreted as such at the time.[86] The imagery would also appear to depict the vision of the Old Testament prophet Isaiah (Isaiah 6:1–3), and Gaetano Curzi has astutely observed that this Biblical passage may well have been regarded as 'an argument for legitimizing the depiction of Christ and the angels'.[87]

While Paul I's name and image do not appear elsewhere in Santa Maria Antiqua, a large amount of painting in the church has been plausibly assigned to his pontificate, including both aisle walls.

The vast expanse of the outer wall of the left aisle, approximately 12 × 5 m, was decorated with four registers of murals: a dado with fictive textiles,[88] a phalanx of standing saints flanking the enthroned figure of Christ (Fig. 8.1),[89] and then two registers of eight framed narrative scenes depicting events from the Old Testament Book of Genesis.[90] This campaign also included the short stretch of wall immediately adjacent to the façade, to the left of the doorway giving access to the Palatine ramp. The uppermost register is significantly truncated, but enough survives that we can identify at least two scenes from the story of Noah: the animals entering the ark, and the Flood. Most of the register beneath is devoted to the lives of Jacob and Joseph and, as was the case in the Theodotus chapel, the individual episodes were identified with

---

[85] Wilpert (1916: 668) interpreted two figures from the earlier level in the apse as representing an angel and Saint Peter, identifications corroborated by Nordhagen (1978: 90–3). But the earlier angel, like those on the 'palimpsest wall', was of the more usual type.

[86] Miller 1975; and Rubery 2009: 209–10.   [87] Curzi 2018: 10.   [88] Osborne 1992: 331–2.

[89] Maskarinec 2018: 130–3; and Grafova 2020.

[90] Rushforth 1902: 25–36; De Grüneisen 1911: 106–15 and pl. IC XXI-A; Wilpert 1916: 703–9 and pl. 192; Tea 1937: 263–80; and Vileisis 1979.

Fig. 8.1. Santa Maria Antiqua, Rome: left aisle, Christ and saints.

Latin inscriptions beginning with the word *'ubi'* ('where'). Best preserved are the scenes at the right depicting Joseph being sold by his brothers (Genesis 37:28), the episode with Potiphar's wife (Genesis 39:11–12), Joseph led to prison ('UBI IOSEPH DUCITUR IN CARCERE') (Genesis 39:20), and pharaoh's banquet (Genesis 40:20–22). The row of standing saints comprises some 22 haloed figures in addition to Christ, each identified by name in inscriptions written vertically in Greek. The two in the space beyond the doorway have not survived in legible condition, but the remainder are rather well preserved. From left to right they are Saints Bacchus, Gregory (presumably Pope Gregory I), Sergius, Sabas, Euthymius, Abbondius, Valentine, Alexander, Leo, Silvester, Clement (holding a small anchor in his right hand, the symbol of his martyrdom), Christ (enthroned, holding a book, and blessing with his right hand), John Chrysostom, Gregory (presumably Gregory of Nazianzus), Basil, Peter of Alexandria, Cyril, Epiphanius, Athanasius, Nicholas, and Erasmus. Examples of 'betacism' may be found in the inscriptions identifying both Valentine and Silvester.

The dress of each figure is appropriate to his status. The martyrs, for example, carry crowns and small crosses; the popes wear the episcopal pallium over their chasuble; and the eastern bishops wear an *omophorion*, very similar to a pallium except with crosses on the shoulders in addition to the one at the front.[91] Only Clement holds an identifying attribute: the anchor of his martyrdom. A recent study by Serena La Mantia has demonstrated that the workshop responsible for their execution adhered meticulously to a standard of proportion both within and between the figures that is recorded later in Byzantine painting manuals, based on a module of the size of the nose (6 cm), and using templates to ensure that all the figures were of similar size and shape.[92] The slightly elongated and 'pinched' faces of the Greek church fathers recall the standard facial types which had developed in Byzantine art, perhaps most clearly paralleled in the Sinai icons and surviving manuscripts such as the ninth-century *Sacra Parallela* (Paris, BNFr, cod. gr. 923).[93]

The choice of saints seems slightly odd, and includes important theologians from both the Greek and Latin churches, but with a clear emphasis on the former. It is probably not a coincidence that the three figures immediately to Christ's right (viewer's left) are popes intimately connected to the role of the Roman see as agent for the physical and spiritual safety of the city's inhabitants.[94] Maria Grafova has argued that the selection reflects

---

[91] For the history of these vestments, Osborne 1984a: 165–6. This distinction, and the different shapes of the crosses in question, has been noted by Maskarinec 2018: 131.
[92] La Mantia 2010.
[93] For example, the head of Saint Basil, see Weitzmann 1979: 219. Kurt Weitzmann believed that this manuscript of the *Sacra Parallela*, a *florilegium* of patristic texts supposedly compiled by John of Damascus, the principal theologian to oppose iconoclasm in the early eighth century, had been written in Palestine; but an origin in Constantinople seems more likely. For the recent suggestion that it was produced for the Byzantine emperor Basil I (r. 867–86), see Declerck 2017.
[94] Maskarinec 2018: 132.

the defenders of 'Orthodoxy' against heresy, and thus should be viewed against the continuing dispute with the emperor of Byzantium over the issue of iconoclasm;[95] but a number of the individuals included can with difficulty be considered as prominent in this regard, among them Alexander, Valentine, Abbondius, Sabas, Nicholas and Erasmus, and thus the rationale for the specific selection remains elusive. The absence of significant Latin authors such as Jerome and Augustine, not to mention the two most important Roman saints, Peter and Paul, is also puzzling: one more little mystery that awaits resolution.

An extensive analysis of the iconography of the Genesis scenes has been undertaken by Birute Vileisis, who concluded that the Roman murals bore almost no resemblance to scenes depicting the same subjects in some of the earliest illuminated Genesis manuscripts to have survived, including the Vienna Genesis (Vienna, ÖstNB, cod. theol. gr. 31) and the fragmentary Cotton Genesis (London, British Library, cod. Cotton Otho B. VI). Close parallels for the Joseph scenes were, however, found in a Byzantine manuscript of the Homilies of Gregory of Nazianzus (Paris, BNFr, cod. gr. 510), produced in Constantinople for the Emperor Basil I (r. 867–86), and thus dating a century after the aisle paintings in Santa Maria Antiqua. The nature of their connection, presumably a common Genesis recension that has not otherwise survived, has never been determined; and Vileisis's contention that 'the model likely originated in the eastern artistic milieu of Syria-Palestine' remains highly conjectural and unproven.[96] Once again, however, we do find the patron and decorators of Santa Maria Antiqua firmly positioned in the cultural orbit of the eastern Mediterranean.

A small altar is situated immediately beneath the enthroned figure of Christ, set against the wall, but this was clearly added afterwards as there is no break in the *vela* of the painted dado.[97]

The corresponding wall of the right aisle was also decorated with narrative scenes, organized in four horizontal registers, the lowermost of which is interrupted by a small niche. At the time of the excavation these murals were already in exceptionally poor condition, prompting Rushforth to observe that 'the merest scraps remain'.[98] The subject matter included the story of Anne and Joachim, Mary's parents, followed by scenes from the

---

[95] Grafova 2020. [96] Vileisis 1979: 149.
[97] Bauer 1999a: 412–13 and fig. 14. By contrast, when a chapel was constructed in the church of San Clemente in the time of Pope Leo IV (847–55), the space for the altar was clearly planned from the outset: Osborne 1984a: 29; and Tronzo 1987: 479.
[98] Rushforth 1902: 81.

infancy of Christ.[99] The best preserved depicted the Nativity, including the figure of the midwife Salome who holds out her withered hand towards Mary for a cure, a detail which we encountered earlier in the mosaic decorations of the oratory of John VII in Saint Peter's. Immediately adjacent on the right was the Adoration of the Magi, with an identifying caption written in Greek. The one bit of painting which has survived in comparatively good condition may be found in the niche, where we see the figures of the three 'holy mothers' holding their infant children: Anne with Mary, Mary with Jesus, and Elizabeth with John (the future Baptist) (Pl. 10). Mary alone is seated on a throne. Her mother and cousin are both identified by Latin inscriptions. Unusually, the infant Christ is not shown in Mary's arms, but enclosed in an oval *clipeus* or shield. Once again we have already encountered this comparatively rare iconography of 'Byzantine' origin, painted a half century earlier in the narthex of Santa Sabina.

Manuela Gianandrea has made a compelling case for linking the emphasis on the Nativity, the principal argument used to support Christ's 'human' nature, and hence for the permissibility of showing him in human form (the 'word made flesh'), to the mid-eighth-century debate regarding Iconoclasm.[100] The inclusion of Anne and Elizabeth in the niche composition extends this emphasis on humanity to Mary and John the Baptist, the two other primary intercessors for the souls of humankind who flank Christ in Byzantine depictions of the *Deësis* (intercession).

Stephen Lucey has suggested that the low position of the niche may indicate that it was a focus for the devotion of kneeling worshippers.[101] With the clear emphasis on Mary and the theme of motherhood, the subject matter was perhaps considered particularly appropriate for the 'women's side' ('*pars mulierum*'), although there is no evidence of a corresponding line of female saints (as was the case in the sixth-century mosaic decoration of the nave in the church of Sant'Apollinare Nuovo at Ravenna).[102]

While the dating of the apse mural to the pontificate of Paul I is beyond question, given his presence in the composition, that of the aisle walls depends largely on stylistic judgments, and it is perhaps no surprise to discover that on this question there has been some considerable

---

[99] Rushforth 1902: 81–3; Wilpert 1905: 581–3; De Grüneisen 1911: 103–5 and fig. 83; Wilpert 1916: 710–12 and pl. 194; Tea 1937: 282–5; and Gianandrea 2020.
[100] Gianandrea 2020.   [101] Lucey 2007: 156.
[102] For the relationship between church decoration and gendered space in other Roman churches, including Santa Maria Maggiore and Santa Prassede: Neuman de Vegvar 2007.

disagreement. Much of the discussion has stemmed from a perception that these murals are 'linear', as opposed to 'painterly', and thus they don't fit well into Ernst Kitzinger's notion of 'perennial hellenism'. Consequently, they are seen as belonging to a trend away from the style of the John VII workshop that surpasses the murals of the Theodotus chapel in an emphasis on strong outlines; and most scholars have concluded that they must therefore be later in date, believing this stylistic trend to have increased over time. Rushforth, the first to offer an opinion, suggested that they were 'probably not earlier than the middle of the eighth century'.[103] Tea divided them into two groups, assigning the narrative scenes to Paul I and the standing saints to the pontificate of Hadrian I (772–95),[104] and De Grüneisen had earlier pushed them into the mid-ninth-century pontificate of Nicholas I (858–67).[105] But in recent years a consensus seems to have formed around the suggestion first made somewhat hesitantly by Wilpert, and subsequently supported by Romanelli and Nordhagen, linking the aisle murals to the mid-eighth-century repainting of the apse.[106] While that date cannot be proven definitively, it can and will be adopted as a working hypothesis until such time as better evidence emerges. However, it should be noted firmly that this remains conjecture, and the argument is fraught with various perils. For one thing, it is based primarily on what the murals are not, yet we have almost no sense of the nature of painting in Byzantium in the eighth century, nor indeed much in the way of *comparanda* even closer to home. And on the other hand, as we have seen, in terms of iconography there can be no doubt that the aisle campaigns both belong squarely in the context of 'Byzantine' art from the eastern Mediterranean, whether for the Genesis and Nativity scenes, the specific type of Mary holding Christ on a shield, or the facial features of the standing 'eastern' saints. Leslie Brubaker has commented on this problematic issue in previous scholarship, which has tended to privilege 'style' over other forms of analysis, and she observes astutely that 'style and iconography do not necessarily travel together'.[107] Two non-stylistic factors which support a mid-eighth-century date are the plaster and the palette of colours, both of which are similar to the datable mural in the apse.[108] To these may be added the palaeography of the inscriptions, which reveal some affinities to those in the Theodotus chapel, and the patterns on

---

[103] Rushforth 1902: 28.   [104] Tea 1937: 135.   [105] De Grüneisen 1911: 106.
[106] Wilpert 1910: 96–7; Wilpert 1916: 702; Romanelli and Nordhagen 1964: 62; Vileisis 1979: 141–4; Andaloro and Matthiae 1987: 285; La Mantia 2010; Bordi 2016a: 51; and Gianandrea 2020.
[107] Brubaker 2004: 43.   [108] Gianandrea 2020.

the fictive draperies (*vela*), which employ the same decorative designs found on numerous other Roman dadoes of this period.

Paul I's apse provides solid evidence that, in artistic terms, Rome still remained in the cultural orbit of the Christian Mediterranean into the third quarter of the eighth century. And if the aisle walls also date from his time, then the evidence in support of that statement becomes overwhelming. Political and theological disputes came and went, but it would take many centuries for Rome to make a definitive break with 'Byzantium' in terms of its visual culture.[109]

---

[109] Artistic and cultural ties between Rome and Constantinople would in fact be strongly renewed in the mid-ninth century, following the end of Iconoclasm: see Osborne 2011a.

9 | Hadrian I *dux Dei*

Hadrian I (772–95) is the last of four eighth-century popes whose portraits were placed in the Forum church of Santa Maria Antiqua (Fig. 9.1 and Pl. 11), and indeed the last pope whose connection to the site in some capacity can be documented securely. And once again the precise rationale for the creation of this mural seems elusive, with the painting in many ways raising more questions than it answers. To begin with, it was placed outside the church proper, on the west wall of the atrium, but in 1956, to better ensure its preservation, the painting was detached from that wall and mounted on a support currently housed inside the church in the right aisle. Why it was painted in the atrium and what purpose it was intended to serve are both quite unknown, although Wilpert suggested that it recorded papal patronage at the church and needed to be placed in the atrium because the interior was now fully decorated.[1] But such a trifling detail had not troubled earlier patrons, witness the many levels of decoration on the palimpsest wall. We must also ask: what might have prompted Hadrian's interest in this building? Was it perhaps the family connection, given the administrative role of his uncle and adoptive father, Theodotus, in the *diaconia* established at this site?[2]

The formula for the composition is one that we have encountered elsewhere: a central image of Mary with the infant Jesus on her lap, flanked by saints, and at the far left the pope, his head framed by a 'square halo' and identified by inscription (already fragmentary at the time of the excavation, and now all but entirely illegible), holding a book.[3] The inscription read '[Sanct]ISSIMUS [Hadr]IANUS [Pa]PA [Romanus]', and Rushforth observed that Hadrian was the only pope from this era whose name ends in these five letters.[4] No subsequent scholar has challenged that statement.

Taking a different view, Franz Alto Bauer has discounted the possibility of direct papal involvement, seeing Hadrian's presence as indicative of the date of execution and also as an expression of loyalty on the part of the

---

[1] Wilpert 1916: 714.   [2] Lucey 2007: 153.
[3] Rushforth 1902: 102–4; De Grüneisen 1911: 93–4, 492–3; Wilpert 1916: 713–14 and pl. 195; Tea 1937: 135, 258–60; Ladner 1941a: 109–10; and Osborne 1987: 194–6.
[4] Rushforth 1902: 102.

Fig. 9.1. Santa Maria Antiqua, Rome: atrium, 'Maria *regina*' with Pope Hadrian I (J. Wilpert 1916, pl. 195).

unknown patron.[5] If this were the case, then the figure of the pope would function in a manner similar to the image of Pope Zacharias in the Theodotus chapel. But given that parallel, we might then have anticipated seeing a donor figure at the far right, offering a model of their gift; but unfortunately the plaster has been lost on this side, and thus we cannot be certain how far it continued. De Grüneisen believed that one additional figure could be discerned, a pope, but there is no evidence for this in the earliest photographs, and there are faint traces at the far right of what might have been a vertical border. Rushforth noted that Hadrian does not hold his book upright, but rather as angled forward: 'and therefore it is clear that he is presenting the volume to the church … for use in its services, and the picture is a commemoration of the fact'.[6] But the same could also be said elsewhere in the church of the figures of Pope John VII on the apsidal arch and Pope Zacharias in the Theodotus chapel, where their *codices* are similarly shown at an angle. A parallel situation can also be found in the mosaics of the San Venanzio chapel in the Lateran baptistery, where the unidentified pope at the far right, usually identified as Theodore

[5] Bauer 2001–2: 193.   [6] Rushforth 1902: 104.

(642–9), holds a jewelled book in this fashion. Clearly he was not the donor, since that honour goes to the pope at the left who holds a model of the chapel, presumably John IV (640–2).[7] So, while the precise meaning of the angled *codex* remains unknown, this specific conclusion does not seem warranted.

Only one of the four attending saints can be identified by inscription: Saint Silvester, who stands immediately at Mary's left hand. The inscription reads 'S(an)C(tu)S SILBESTRUS', yet another example of eighth-century 'betacism'. Curiously, his episcopal 'pallium' is decorated with shoulder crosses, unlike other contemporary examples of this vestment. Perhaps the painter was confused, and has given the pope an *omophorion*, an almost identical scarf worn by bishops in the Greek church. Otherwise this would be by far the earliest example of an episcopal *pallium* with shoulder crosses, something not otherwise found in the depictions of popes before the second half of the ninth century.[8] The presence of Silvester may itself perhaps be regarded as a dating clue. The memory of this early-fourth-century pontiff became quite important in the latter half of the eighth century, as his reign corresponded to the time of the Emperor Constantine, whom the new Frankish allies were encouraged to emulate, and of course it had been to Silvester that Constantine had made his famous 'donation'. This parallel will be seen again in the mosaic decorations of the Triclinium of Pope Leo III, to be discussed in Chapter 10.

Beyond Silvester are two male saints holding crowns and crosses, and consequently to be identified as martyrs. They are not ecclesiastics, but rather are dressed in imperial court costume (*chlamys* with *tablia*), as first noted by Rushforth.[9] He suggested Saints Sergius and Bacchus, given the presence of a gold ring around Sergius's neck: a torque, his usual attribute. As earlier recounted, Pope Hadrian is known to have 'restored and enlarged' the *diaconia* in the Roman Forum dedicated to these two healing saints after its *dispensator* had accidentally damaged the structure while dismantling part of the adjacent Temple of Concord.[10] The saint to Mary's immediate right (viewer's left) was also a pope, given the presence of a *pallium* (again with traces of shoulder crosses), but the only parts of the inscription visible in 1900 were the last letters of 'PP ROMANUS'. Joseph David suggested Pope Mark, in whose church Hadrian had prayed and fasted as a youth (*LP*

---

[7] Ladner 1941a: 81–5.
[8] See Osborne 1985: 311. Wilpert also commented on this apparent anomaly (Wilpert 1916: 713 note 4).
[9] Rushforth 1902: 102.   [10] *LP* 97.90, ed. Duchesne I: 512; trans. Davis 2007: 166.

97.2, ed. Duchesne I: 486);[11] and more recently Marios Costambeys has proposed Gregory I.[12] Both suggestions are entirely plausible, but neither can be proven. The saint to his left, introducing the pope (Fig. 9.1), is again dressed in a *chlamys*, so once again is not a cleric, and Rushforth very plausibly suggested that it could be Hadrian's name saint,[13] to whom the Curia Senatus building had been dedicated at the time of its conversion into a church by Pope Honorius I (625–38) (*LP* 72.6, ed. Duchesne I: 324). Pope Hadrian had restored this structure and installed a new *diaconia* (*LP* 97.81, Duchesne I: 509). We shall return to that building shortly.

Mary and her infant son both gesture towards their right, presumably accepting the intercessory prayers of Pope Hadrian's patron saints and welcoming him to heaven. This may constitute an additional clue that no additional contemporary figure was ever present at the other extremity, and consequently that Hadrian was the mural's patron.

One final detail should be noted, as it is of considerable importance. Immediately to the right of Mary's halo is an inscription, written vertically: 'MARIA REGINA'. Unfortunately, only a few of the letters now remain visible, but all were noted at the time of the excavation and appear clearly in Wilpert's photograph. This is the only known instance of this particular Marian iconography to be labelled explicitly in this fashion, and it is from this mural that the terminology derives. Beneath the figures to the left of the throne are traces of the dado zone, bearing painted *vela*, but unfortunately not enough survives of the design to allow useful comment.[14]

The depiction of Mary wearing the robes and jewelled crown of the Byzantine empress is an image found frequently in the arts of medieval Rome, prompting Marion Lawrence, the first to consider the iconography in any detail, to consider it a specifically Roman invention.[15] And even though written texts, the imperial images from which the iconography derives, and perhaps also the mosaic from Dyrrachium in Albania, combine to suggest that Rome may not have been the place of origin, pointing instead to Constantinople and the Byzantine court,[16] there is no doubt that it became particularly popular in Rome, and that popularity would persist throughout the Middle Ages. Four centuries later, for example, it would be the central image in the important papal chapel of Saint Nicholas in the

---

[11] David in De Grüneisen 1911: 493.
[12] Costambeys 2020. Perhaps understandably, there is better evidence for the cult of Pope Gregory I in Anglo-Saxon England than in Rome; see Thacker 1998.
[13] Rushforth 1902: 103–4.   [14] Osborne 1992: 332.   [15] Lawrence 1924–25.
[16] Osborne 2008.

Lateran Palace, constructed by Pope Callixtus II (1119–24), marking the papal triumph over secular powers in terms of authority for ecclesiastical investiture, encapsulated in the Concordat of Worms (1122);[17] and it is perhaps worth noting that one of the flanking figures was again Pope Silvester.

The cult of Mary was espoused by a number of medieval pontiffs, especially in the eighth and early ninth centuries,[18] and it is likely not a coincidence that John VII styled himself as the 'servant of the Holy Mother of God', in both Latin and Greek, in the two monuments that he is known to have commissioned.[19] Whether the pope intended this as a deliberate response to the motto '*servus Christi*', which the Emperor Justinian II had placed on his coinage in 692, remains an unanswerable question, but from that moment onwards images of Mary in the form of the 'Maria *regina*' are found frequently in Roman churches. The very earliest such image, on the 'palimpsest wall' at Santa Maria Antiqua, is most unlikely to have been a papal commission given its location and proposed dating in the first half of the sixth century, and it was covered by a later level of painting, and hence invisible and unknown, by the early seventh century. Thus it stands apart from the subsequent sequence, and there is a certain irony in the thought that Pope John VII, who reinvigorated the popularity of this theme, would not have known of its existence some three levels of plaster below his own campaign of decorations in that church.[20] We have already encountered 'Maria *regina*' images in John VII's funerary chapel in Saint Peter's and on the icon which he installed in Santa Maria in Trastevere, on the icon which Gregory III placed in his funerary chapel in Saint Peter's, and in the murals of the Theodotus chapel. There are at least three additional examples in Rome which may also date from the second half of the eighth century, and thus possibly also from the time of Pope Hadrian I, in the churches of San Clemente, San Lorenzo fuori le mura, and Santa Susanna.

Of these, the only one to survive *in situ* is the painting in a niche inserted into the thickness of the right-aisle wall of the so-called lower church of San Clemente, the name given to the Early Christian basilica (*c*. 400 CE) which lies beneath the standing church of the twelfth century, revealed by

---

[17] Osborne and Claridge 1996–8, I: 108–11; and Croisier 2006b. [18] Themelly 2008.

[19] Earlier popes had styled themselves as the '*servus servorum Dei*', for example, Sergius I, in a fragmentary inscription recording donations to the church of Santa Susanna: see Gray 1948: 48, no. 1. That same phrase is used by Paul I in his foundation letter for San Silvestro in Capite (Federici 1899: 255), so clearly it had not gone entirely out of fashion.

[20] Pace 2015: 481.

excavations which began in the autumn of 1857 and are still ongoing. This wall and niche were among the first areas of the earlier basilica to be discovered.

Given the absence of any contemporary formal record of the excavation, an account of the discovery in a contemporary newspaper report is exceptionally useful. In the *Giornale di Roma* for 8 January 1859, Felice Profili, the secretary of the recently founded Commission for Sacred Archaeology, records that, when first unearthed, there were two levels of plaster in the niche, and that the upper level almost immediately fell away, revealing the mural visible today. Both levels had apparently depicted a similar theme. Mary is depicted enthroned, and dressed elaborately in the robes and diadem of an empress; she holds the infant Jesus on her lap (Pl. 12).[21] Given the central cross and hanging *prependoulia*, there can be no doubt that an imperial crown was intended, and it is in many respects reminiscent of that worn by the Empress Theodora in the famous sixth-century mosaic panel in San Vitale at Ravenna. Indeed, the similarity is so close that the suggestion has even been made that the painting began its life as an image of Theodora, later converted into a figure of Mary.[22] However, an analysis of the plaster reveals that the mural was painted in a single operation, and thus the figure can never have represented the consort of the Emperor Justinian. Two female saints, also richly attired and bejewelled, occupied the side walls of the niche. Only their heads now remain, along with fragments of their identifying inscriptions. The name of one began with the letters 'EU'. 'Euphemia' is normally suggested, but 'Eugenia' may possibly be preferred.

Two highly unusual aspects of these inscriptions – the uncharacteristic forms of the letters 'A' and 'U', and the placement of the abbreviation 'S(an)C(t)A' to the right of the head of the saint on the niche's left wall (as opposed to the usual position to the left of the head, with the actual name on the right side) – find exact parallels in another Roman mural from approximately this same period, decorating one of three painted niches set in the eastern wall of what was originally the narthex of the sixth-century shrine church of San Lorenzo fuori le mura.[23] The niche's rear wall was painted with an almost identical 'Maria *regina*' and child, flanked by

---

[21] Osborne 1981b; Osborne 1984a: 112–35; and Bordi 2006a: 188. The mural is also recorded in a photograph from the 1860s preserved in the J.H. Parker collection (The British School at Rome), no. 1267.

[22] Theory of Dominic Darsy, OP, reported in a letter by Enrico Josi in *L'Osservatore Romano*, 23 November 1959.

[23] Osborne 1981b: 303, 307–8; and Osborne 1984a: 132–5.

images of saints identified by inscriptions as Agatha and Lawrence; and the side walls featured four female saints on the left side and four male saints on the right. Brought to light in restorations undertaken in the church by Virginio Vespignani in the early 1860s, and documented in both photographs and watercolour copies, this niche was once thought to have been destroyed, perhaps at the end of the nineteenth century when the eastern end of San Lorenzo was remodelled to serve as the funerary chapel of Pope Pius IX (d. 1878). However, fragments of the mural decorations have recently been rediscovered.[24] The remarkable similarities in minor details between the two murals, and especially the palaeography and format of the painted inscriptions, are sufficient to support the hypothesis that both were painted at approximately the same time and by the same workshop. Additionally, the identification by inscription of one of the female saints as Eugenia offers a suggestive possibility for the figure on the right side of the San Clemente niche.[25]

Neither mural can be precisely dated, but the second half of the eighth century is generally suggested on the basis of both iconography and style; and it may not be a coincidence that Pope Hadrian is known to have undertaken important structural repairs to both buildings. He restored the roof of San Clemente, which has been '*in ruinis*' (*LP* 97.64; ed. Duchesne I: 505); and San Lorenzo benefitted from various alterations (*LP* 97.75; ed. Duchesne, I: 508) in addition to multiple gifts of silk textiles (*LP* 97.49, 97.60; ed. Duchesne I: 500, 504) and objects made of precious metals (*LP* 97.87, 97.90; ed. Duchesne I: 511, 512). Those of an iconoclast persuasion would no doubt have been horrified to learn of the golden image of Saint Lawrence, presumably an icon, weighing some fifteen pounds!

Also with apparent links to these pictorial campaigns in San Lorenzo and San Clemente is the remarkable discovery made in September 1991 beneath the floor of the church of Santa Susanna.[26] Inside a second-century sarcophagus, itself reused in the early Middle Ages for a privileged male burial, were some 7,000 fragments of painted plaster. When reconstructed like pieces of a jigsaw puzzle, these were found to comprise the almost complete decoration of a painted niche, representing an enthroned 'Maria *regina*' with child, flanked by two female saints, in most respects identical to the images in the two churches previously discussed, right down to small details such as

[24] Acconci 2002; and Bordi 2006b: 81, 91.
[25] Acconci 2002 notes that Hadrian '*noviter restauravit*' her church on the Via Latina, and built and endowed an adjacent convent (*LP* 97.78, 97.82; ed. Duchesne I: 509, 510). See also Ferrari 1957: 132–3.
[26] Andaloro 2001; Nilgen 2002; Andaloro 2003; and Cecchelli *et al.* 2004.

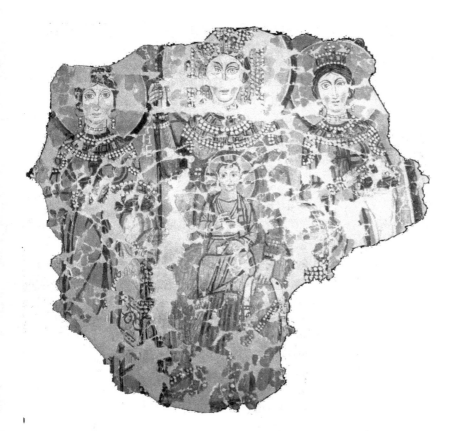

Fig. 9.2. Santa Susanna, Rome: reconstructed mural with 'Maria *regina*'.

the depiction of the gemstones in the saints' necklaces (Fig. 9.2). Apart from the obvious but unanswerable question of why someone would have gone to such an extraordinary effort to dismantle the niche decoration and carefully preserve the pieces for posterity in this unparalleled fashion, what makes the discovery interesting is that the archaeology provides a secure *terminus ante quem* for the dating: the space housing the sarcophagus was sealed beneath the floor of the left aisle of the medieval rebuilding of Santa Susanna, undertaken early in the reign of Pope Leo III (795–816), whose *vita* in the *Liber pontificalis* describes the project in extraordinary detail (*LP* 98.9, ed. Duchesne II: 3). We shall return to it in the next chapter.

In addition to the 'Maria *regina*', the sarcophagus also contained the fragments of the murals which framed the arch: at the top, a medallion depicting Christ in the form of a lamb (*agnus Dei*), flanked by figures of the two saints John, John the Baptist and John the Evangelist, who point upwards towards the medallion. Each saint is accompanied by an appropriate text. To the left, John the Baptist speaks the words he is recorded as having uttered when he saw first encountered Jesus: 'Behold the lamb of God, who bears the sins of the world' (compare John 1:29, '*Ecce agnus Dei qui tollit peccatum mundi*'). The painted inscription departs from the Vulgate text in making the 'sins' ('*peccata*') plural, and in altering the verb '*tollit*' (third person singular) to '*tollis*' (second person singular). In both instances this mirrors the words added to the liturgy of the Roman church by Pope Sergius I, to be said at the time of the fraction of the host (*LP* 86.14, ed. Duchesne I: 376), possibly as a response to canon 82 of the Quinisext Council. Understandably, the words of the mass would have been more familiar than the scriptural text on which they are based. And to the right, John the Evangelist's text comprises the opening words of his Gospel: 'In the beginning was the word, and the word was with God' (John 1:1; '*In principio erat verbum et verbum erat apud Deum*'), with the spelling of both instances of the word '*verbum*' again constituting examples of betacism: '*berbum*'. This particular iconography – the apocalyptic lamb flanked by the two saints John – was also enormously popular in early medieval Rome, and has a number of known parallels including the murals formerly in the narthex of San Lorenzo fuori le mura.[27] The burial of the Santa Susanna murals must have taken place either before or contemporary with the complete rebuilding of the church by Pope Leo III, which may indeed have been the occasion that prompted it. In terms of their original dating, Maria Andaloro has argued convincingly for the pontificate of Hadrian I, noting that he is again credited with repairing the roof of the basilica (*LP* 97.70, ed. Duchesne I: 507).

The stylistic and iconographic similarities shared by the murals in San Clemente, San Lorenzo fuori le mura and Santa Susanna are compelling, and attest both to the importance of the theme of the 'Maria *regina*' in the last quarter of the eighth century and its ubiquity in the contemporary decoration of Roman churches.[28] What conclusions can be drawn from this emphasis on the queen of heaven? As we have seen, the ardent promotion in Rome of this aspect of the cult of Mary seems to have its origins at the end of the seventh century, and can be readily documented in the pontificates of Sergius I and John VII, thus clearly predating the formal introduction of Iconoclasm in Byzantium. But the theological debates regarding the nature of Christ, with the Incarnation seen as signalling

---

[27] Bordi 2006b: 89, fig. 32. Other examples of this lamb iconography in late-eighth-century Rome are surveyed by Andaloro 2005.
[28] Noble 2001b: 61–8.

that the 'word became flesh', as well as the official designation of Mary as *theotokos* (mother of God), continued to be relevant in the eighth century, prompting Thomas Noble to view Gregory III's installation of a 'Maria regina' icon in Saint Peter's as a 'denial of imperial iconoclasm'.[29] It may also be relevant that two new Roman churches founded in the second quarter of the eighth century were dedicated to Mary: Santa Maria in Sassia and Santa Maria in Aquiro.[30]

Images did not exist in a vacuum, and need to be seen and interpreted within the context of their production. Jean-Marie Sansterre has made the interesting suggestion that depictions of Mary became particularly important in Roman churches primarily because the city did not possess any significant physical relics associated with her cult.[31] There can be little doubt that the cult of Mary was intimately linked to the theological issues that captured contemporary attention throughout the Christian world,[32] but the evidence of material culture suggests an interest in Rome that far surpasses anything found elsewhere, and specifically a particular fascination with the concept of Mary as 'regina'. Did Mary fill some sort of psychological void created by the absence of a female consort for the emerging papal rulership? There is no conclusive documentation to support such an assertion, but a considerable quantity of circumstantial evidence certainly makes it an interesting possibility.

The *vita* of Hadrian I was by far the longest of all the *Liber pontificalis* biographies to date, and would be surpassed only by that of his immediate successor, Leo III. The first 44 chapters are devoted to an exceptionally detailed account of political events in the years 772–4, culminating in Charlemagne's defeat of the last Lombard king, Desiderius, and the Frankish annexation of northern Italy; and most of the final 53 chapters are devoted to the pope's subsequent building and patronage activities, made possible by the absence of an external threat, the resulting revival of commerce, and also, no doubt, lavish gifts from the city's new political patron. The only exceptions are a mention of the Second Council of Nicaea, held in 787 to overturn the policy of Iconoclasm and restore the use of images in Byzantium; the severe Tiber flood of 791; and an exceptionally brief notice of the pope's death on 26 December 795 and subsequent burial in Saint Peter's (*LP* 97.88, 94–95, 97). The absence from this otherwise extensive record of any discussion of political events during the last two decades of Hadrian's pontificate is both striking and rather

---

[29] Noble 2009: 125–6. [30] Coates-Stephens 1997: 190–2. [31] Sansterre 2002: 1030.
[32] Themelly 2008.

puzzling. Franz Alto Bauer notes, for example, that no mention is made of Charlemagne's visits to Rome in 781 and 787, moments that must certainly have been of considerable significance, not to mention pomp and ceremony, but concludes that this mystery must remain for the moment unresolved.[33] Instead, the focus is clearly on Hadrian as a patron of art and architecture, and above all as a builder.[34]

The biographer begins the documentation of patronage by noting that Hadrian 'was a lover of God's churches and took increasing care to carry out the adornment and restoration of them all'.[35] The pope also undertook the restoration of numerous suburban cemeteries.[36] As we have already seen for the churches of San Clemente, San Lorenzo fuori le mura, and Santa Susanna, much of the papal building activity comprised repairs to existing buildings, whose fabrics had deteriorated over time. The extramural shrine church of San Paolo fuori le mura, for example, was among the many in dire need of a new roof, requiring some 35 large beams ('*trabes maiores XXXV*'), a project entrusted to the *vestiarius* Januarius, although we are told that Hadrian assisted in the work personally (*LP* 97.67, ed. Duchesne I: 506). Only fourteen beams were needed to repair the roof of Saint Peter's, a project once again supervised by Januarius, but Santa Maria Maggiore required twenty (*LP* 97.64, 74; ed. Duchesne I: 505, 508). The language used to describe the scope of some activities may have been exaggerated in an effort to promote Hadrian as the restorer of the city's buildings: for example, Franz Alto Bauer notes that little evidence of a Hadrianic restoration has been found at Santa Pudenziana, despite the fact that the *vita* claims it to have been '*in ruinis*'.[37] On the other hand, Hadrian does appear to have restarted the production of bricks in the city, and his correspondence with Charlemagne reveals his need not only for materials but also for construction expertise.[38]

One substantial new structure was the church of Santa Maria in Cosmedin, located in the Forum Boarium, adjacent to the Tiber at the foot of the Aventine hill. In the early Middle Ages this region became identified with the 'Greek' community in the city, and the epithet 'Cosmedin' presumably bears some relation to the 'Kosmidion' quarter on the outskirts of Constantinople, where an important healing shrine of

---

[33] Bauer 2001–2: 189–90.
[34] Noble 2000: 62–6. The most extensive monographic treatment of Hadrian's reign is Hartmann 2006, although his focus is primarily political.
[35] *LP* 97.45, ed. Duchesne I: 499; trans. Davis 2007: 139.
[36] Spera 1997, who documents some 134 'interventions'.
[37] *LP* 97.76, ed. Duchesne I: 508; Bauer 2001–2: 191.   [38] Bauer 2001–2: 192–3.

Saints Cosmas and Damian was located. Similar church dedications are attested in Ravenna and Naples.[39] By the time of the Einsiedeln Itinerary, the area adjacent to the Roman Santa Maria in Cosmedin was also being identified as the '*schola Graecorum*',[40] although this term appears to have developed only after the political shift of the mid eighth century and the subsequent construction of a distinction between 'Greeks' and 'Romans'.[41] We are told that the existing and homonymous *diaconia*, 'a small building, was in ruins, as a huge monument of Tiburtine tufa was tilting over it'.[42] The pope first demolished the overhanging structure that posed the threat, removed the rubble and cleared the site, and then built a substantial new church, using the tufa blocks characteristic of constructions of this era. Much of this edifice has survived despite subsequent modifications in both the twelfth and eighteenth centuries, and a late nineteenth-century restoration.[43] The new building comprised a central nave and two side aisles, all three terminating in apses, and incorporated portions of two earlier structures: a loggia facing the Forum Boarium, perhaps the site of the existing *diaconia* and before that possibly the location of the *statio annonae* for food distribution;[44] and the podium of an earlier construction which it abutted.[45] The loggia was altered to form the western half of the new church, reusing parts of an existing colonnade, and the podium formed the base for the eastern (sanctuary) end. The building was also provided with a substantial crypt.[46] This was excavated into the temple podium, and comprised a rectangular hall, its ceiling supported by six columns. The side walls housed sixteen niches, each with a horizontal shelf, presumably intended for the placement of relics.

The inclusion of three apses, terminating the side aisles in addition to the nave, is an unusual architectural feature in early medieval Rome, which may also explain why this detail is singled out for mention in the *Liber pontificalis* entry. Most earlier precedents are to be found in the eastern Mediterranean; and it is certainly tempting to relate this feature to the use

---

[39] *CBCR* II: 305; Davis 2007: 157, note 146; Taddei 2014b.   [40] *CT* II: 171.
[41] For the term '*schola Graecorum*', see Sansterre 1983 I: 47 and II: 102–4 note 388. The other Roman *scholae*, associated with the Franks, the Frisians, the Saxons and the Lombards, and thought to have been intended primarily for the support of pilgrims coming from those regions, were unsurprisingly all located in the vicinity of Saint Peter's: see Santangeli Valenzani 2014: 79–85.
[42] *LP* 97.72; ed. Duchesne I: 507; trans. Davis 2007: 156–7.
[43] *CBCR* II: 277–307; Fusciello 2011: 79–105.   [44] *CBCR* II: 288.
[45] Hülsen 1927: 328, identified it as the Temple of Hercules, but more recent scholarship is much less certain and prefers to leave the question open, see Richardson 1992: 186–7; and Claridge 1998: 256–8.
[46] *CBCR* II: 298–9; Bauer 1997–8; Bauer 2004: 132–7; and Fusciello 2011: 82–3.

of the structure by a Greek-speaking community, although Richard Krautheimer cautioned against reading too much significance into this one aspect.[47] Nevertheless, it is anomalous, and the only secure Roman precedent is another *diaconia* church already encountered, Sant'Angelo in Pescheria, constructed about 25 years earlier and for a similar purpose. Is it a coincidence, one wonders, that this is known to have been a project of Hadrian's uncle and guardian, Theodotus? Or is the alteration in design somehow related to the specific function of these buildings as 'welfare stations'?

Another of his architectural projects for which some evidence has survived is Sant'Adriano in the Roman Forum, the former Senate House which had been converted into a church in the time of Pope Honorius I (625–38), one of two Forum churches in which Hadrian installed a *diaconia* (*LP* 97.81, ed. Duchesne I: 509). In order to provide continuing revenue to support the 'regular refreshment for Christ's poor',[48] the pope endowed the two *diaconiae* with agricultural lands, including vineyards and olive groves, as well as the labourers needed to operate them. Sant'Adriano also received various silver objects, including a chalice, totalling some 67 pounds.

In the years 1932–7 the Baroque alterations of Sant'Adriano were stripped away by Alfonso Bartoli, revealing the original late classical brick structure that we see today.[49] Attached to the exterior of the building, to the right of the apse, was a small chapel containing a reliquary altar, and on one of its walls were some comparatively well-preserved mural paintings, arranged in three horizontal registers and following a pattern previously observed at Santa Maria Antiqua: narrative scenes at the top, standing saints in the middle, and fictive curtains beneath (Fig. 9.3).[50] To facilitate preservation, these murals were removed from the site to the Antiquarium Forense, and then in the year 2000 they were installed in the newly created museum of early medieval Rome at the Crypta Balbi. The painted *vela* bear designs incorporating small *orbiculi* and 'spade' motifs, placing them firmly in the context of eighth-century churches.[51]

The construction of the chapel and its campaign of decoration are thought to have formed part of Pope Hadrian's renovations, and there are also stylistic similarities to the mural depicting Hadrian in Santa Maria Antiqua.[52] The surviving section of the middle register includes two standing bishops, one with a Latin pallium and one with a Greek *omophorion*, both garments correctly rendered, but with no identifying inscriptions.

---

[47] *CBCR* II: 306. [48] Davis 2007: 162. [49] Bartoli 1963.
[50] Mancini 1968; Bordi 2000; and Bordi 2001. [51] Osborne 1992: 337–9.
[52] Mancini 1968: 201–7; Bordi 2000: 23–4; and Bordi 2001: 481.

Fig. 9.3. Sant'Adriano, Rome: murals now in the Museo Nazionale Crypta Balbi.

Of considerable interest, however, are the fragmentary narrative scenes in the uppermost register, where some painted captions do survive. Here we find a narrative cycle of the influential fourth-century Cappadocian theologian, Saint Basil of Caesarea, apparently the first such cycle known anywhere in Christian art.[53] As Giulia Bordi has noted, Pseudo-Amphilocius' life of Basil must have been available in Rome at this time, although no Latin translation is recorded until that of the papal librarian Anastasius a full century later. This suggests the presence of a Greek-speaking community, as is apparently confirmed by the graffiti written in Greek found inside the church.[54] Also in the interior, in the central niche on the left wall, are the remnants of a painted image of Christ, flanked by saints and kneeling donors, two of whom sport 'square haloes' signifying portraits. One of them is identified by a painted inscription as 'CONSTANTINUS CONSUL'. Although this Constantine is not otherwise recorded, Bordi has suggested that he belongs to the same aristocratic group as Theodotus and other holders of this honorific title, many of whom seem to have played an important role in the provision for and management of the city's welfare stations.[55]

In addition to architecture and its painted decoration the pontificate of Hadrian I also witnessed a blossoming in other aspects of church furnishing, and the media of stone sculpture, metalwork, and textiles may be singled out for special attention. All three can be documented through some combination of surviving remains and the extensive documentation of papal patronage provided by the *Liber pontificalis*.

The preceding decades had not witnessed much work in marble, at least not that has survived or been recorded; and this change did not escape the attention of the compiler of Hadrian's *vita*, who in discussing the pope's repairs and additions to the Lateran patriarchate comments that 'he adorned ... all his new constructions with painting and marble'.[56] As noted previously, this 'marble' mainly took the form of furniture intended to facilitate the performance of the liturgy, including screens to define the spaces reserved for clergy, pulpits, *fastigia*,[57] and altar canopies (*ciboria*); and Hadrian's rebuilding of Santa Maria in Cosmedin provides evidence for this apparent revival of work in stone on a substantial scale.[58]

---

[53] Bordi 2000: 13.   [54] Ibid., 14.   [55] Bordi 2011: 423–7.

[56] *LP* 97.56, ed. Duchesne I: 503, 'et picturis atque marmoribus ... cuncta aedificia ab eo noviter constructa decoravit.' English trans. Davis 2007: 147.

[57] A *fastigium* (also sometimes called a *pergula*) was an honorific arched structure separating the nave from the sanctuary; see De Blaauw 1994: 119–26.

[58] Melucco Vaccaro 1974: 146–53, pls XL–XLII; Macchiarella 1976a: 268–75; and Paroli 1998: 102–3.

One piece bears part of an inscription naming Hadrian as the reigning pope, although listing the (presumably lay?) donor as a 'Gregorius no[tarius?]'.[59] Curiously, perhaps, if this inscription were the only evidence we had of epigraphy in these years, then its impoverished quality would attest to a rapid decline from the situation only a generation or so earlier. Gone are the elegant capital letters of uniform size and shape, now replaced by a script of inconsistent height and also utilizing some uncial forms, for example, for 'M' and 'D'. But such a view would be erroneous. Other contemporary fragments similarly bearing parts of dedication inscriptions have been found in the churches of Sant'Adriano and Santa Martina, both located in the Roman Forum. In both instances they formed part of architraves from what were presumably *fastigia* (the architectural screens separating the nave from the sanctuary), and the similarities in decoration and epigraphy suggest that both were products of the same workshop.[60] By contrast, here the lettering is somewhat closer to earlier examples, with uniform sizing and no uncial intrusions, although the capitals are higher than they are wide, no longer employing the 'square' module of Luca Cardin's '*capitale di papa*'. And given that the patron in both cases is likely to have been the pope himself, in the differences between these fragments and those from Santa Maria in Cosmedin we can perhaps find evidence for his contention that access to expert epigraphers was reserved for those with high clerical status.[61]

Many dozens of analogous fragments have been found elsewhere in Rome, albeit without inscriptions, all loosely dated to the 'Carolingian' period. Such pieces are notoriously difficult to date precisely, particularly in the absence of an inscription naming the donor or reigning pope, or some other documented patronage; but the sculpture of the late eighth and early ninth century is in general easily distinguishable, by the form and the subject matter of the carved designs, from material dating from the previous flowering of church furnishings in the first half of the sixth century.[62] Also perhaps to be associated with Santa Maria in Cosmedin, on the basis

---

[59] Silvagni 1943a I: pl. XIV.5; Gray 1948: 54, no. 14; Melucco Vaccaro 1974: 152–3, no. 106; Cardin 2008: 36, and pl. 50a; and Ballardini 2010: 141–2, and fig. 167.

[60] De Rubeis and Bordi 2001; Ballardini 2010: 141–2, and figs. 161–6. Immediately adjacent to Sant'Adriano, Santa Martina was the former '*secretarium Senatus*'. The date of its conversion to a church is unknown, but the first secure documentation occurs in the life of Hadrian I: *LP* 97.96; ed. Duchesne I: 514. The fragments from both churches are now exhibited in the Museo Nazionale Romano at the Crypta Balbi.

[61] Cardin 2008: 82–4. For a discussion of the difference in the levels of workmanship, see also Ballardini 2010: 141–2.

[62] For the latter, mostly imported from Constantinople, see the overview by Guiglia Guidobaldi 2002.

of style and decorative vocabulary, is a remarkable episcopal throne with lavishly carved panels, currently housed in a private collection but recently published by Marco Aimone.[63]

Churches were not the only focus of Hadrian's activity. The new era of external peace ushered in by the alliance with the Franks, coupled with the return to some semblance of stability within Rome itself following the period of civil strife which engulfed the city following the death of Paul I, created the conditions under which time and energy could also be devoted profitably to repairing the city's crumbling infrastructure. As had been demonstrated all too frequently, the security of the city was contingent on the existence of defensible walls, and its inhabitants required an adequate provision of both food and water. Hadrian turned his attention to all three issues.

Not surprisingly, perhaps, the most immediate project was the restoration of the urban perimeter, a project that may have been as much symbolic as practical since it also served to cast the pope in a role previously exercised by the emperors.[64] At the time of Hadrian's pontificate the Aurelian walls had been in service for some 500 years. Over the course of the intervening centuries repairs had been necessary and not infrequent, initially undertaken by the imperial administration, but most recently in the first half of the eighth century by Popes Gregory II and Gregory III, both of whom are given credit for this activity in the *Liber pontificalis* (*LP* 91.2, 92.15; ed. Duchesne I: 396, 420). The walls had successfully withstood the lengthy siege of King Aistulf in 756, and no doubt had been hastily reinforced as part of the preparations made for the defence of the city when the last of the Lombard kings, Desiderius, approached in 773 (*LP* 97.24, ed. Duchesne I: 493). But Charlemagne's annexation of the Lombard kingdom in 774 removed any immediate physical threat, thus permitting a more systematic and better organized campaign; and this project began almost immediately, necessitating considerable expense for both materials and labour.

The *Liber pontificalis* reports that Hadrian 'renewed the walls and towers of this city of Rome that had been demolished and destroyed to their foundations, and restored everything around as required; to which he devoted much money, both to pay for those who built the wall and on their sustenance, also on limestone and various requirements, and spent up to 100 lb. gold'.[65] De Rossi and Duchesne believed that this activity may

---

[63] Aimone 2019.   [64] Dey 2011: 255–7.

[65] *LP* 97.52, ed. Duchesne I: 501, 'Verum etiam et muros atque turres huius Romane urbis quae diruti erant et usque ad fundamenta destructi renovavit atque utiliter omnia in circuitu restauravit; ubi et multa stipendia tribuit, tam in mercedes eorum qui ipsum murum

have prompted the detailed description appended to the Einsiedeln Itinerary, enumerating the number of towers, battlements, postern gates, latrines, and both large and small windows in the stretch between each of the major gates.[66] Further repairs were undertaken about fifteen years later, when we are told that responsibility for providing the labour required for each section was assigned to a different group, including the towns in the surrounding regions of Tuscia and Campania (*LP* 97.92; ed. Duchesne I: 513). While the format of the defences followed the now centuries-old late imperial model, the precise areas of early medieval repair and rebuilding can be determined from their technique, which employed large square-cut blocks of *tufa* coupled with undulating courses of brickwork, a practice also paralleled in contemporary church construction.[67] For example, very similar *tufa* blocks may be observed in the foundations of Sant'Angelo in Pescheria (755), and the undulating courses of brickwork appear at Santa Maria in Cosmedin. The similarity in construction technique across the second half of the eighth century does not make it easy to distinguish between the work undertaken by different pontiffs, nor even to separate this from the repairs made in the mid-ninth century under Pope Leo IV (847–55); but Robert Coates-Stephens has proposed that the rebuilding of the sixth tower south of the Porta Tiburtina, on the east side of the city, may have been undertaken by Gregory II, based on the *Liber pontificalis* passage which cites this stretch of the wall as the focus of his activity.[68]

The second area requiring papal attention was the water supply,[69] and here the *Liber pontificalis* provides some explicit detail. For example, the right bank of the Tiber, including both the church of Saint Peter's and the grain mills on the slope of the Janiculum hill, had been supplied by the Aqua Sabbatina which brought water from Lake Bracciano (in antiquity called Lake Sabbatinus), some 40 km to the north. It was also known as the Aqua Traiana, after the Emperor Trajan who had been responsible for the project in the year 109 CE. The aqueducts were always among the first casualties when a city was under siege, either damaged by the attackers in an attempt to cut off the supply of water to those inside or by the defenders in an attempt to stop the besiegers from gaining passage through the walls; and for this latter

---

fabricaverunt, quamque in ipsorum alimentis, simulque et in calce atque diversis utilitatibus usque ad centum auri libras expendit.' English trans. Davis 2007: 143.

[66] *CT* II: 202–7.
[67] Coates-Stephens 1998: 167–71; Coates-Stephens 1999; Meneghini 2004a: 54–65; Santangeli Valenzani 2004c: 135–7; Dey 2011: 63–7; and Dey 2019.
[68] Coates-Stephens 1999: 213.
[69] Coates-Stephens 1998: 171–6; Coates-Stephens 1999; Coates-Stephens 2001–2; Coates-Stephens 2003a; Coates-Stephens 2003b; and De Francesco 2017: 81–4.

reason the Sabbatina and others had been blocked by Belisarius during the Ostrogothic siege in 537.[70] One of what were presumably multiple channels, still blocked by rubble for a distance of more than six metres, was discovered in excavations at the end of the twentieth century beneath the parking lot of the American Academy on the Janiculum, just inside the circuit of the walls.[71] In the first half of the seventh century, Honorius I (625–38) undertook necessary repairs, presumably to a different channel, and constructed a new mill at the Porta San Pancrazio (*LP* 72.5, ed. Duchesne I: 324). Hadrian's biographer relates that the '*forma*' (aqueduct) 'had now been badly broken for a period of twenty years',[72] which suggests that it had again been cut by Aistulf in the siege of 756. The restoration was not a simple undertaking, since we are told that some 100 arches had been 'demolished and destroyed from their foundations'; and it was also necessary to install a new lead pipe to bring water from the top of the hill down to the fountain in the atrium of Saint Peter's, as well as to supply the adjacent bathhouses for pilgrims. But the task was accomplished successfully, such that water once again ran 'abundantly, as it had of old'.[73]

In addition to the Aqua Sabbatina, Hadrian also restored the courses of three other aqueducts: the Jovia, the Claudia, and the Virgo (*LP* 97.61, 97.62, 97.65; ed. Duchesne I: 504–5). The Aqua Virgo ran mostly underground, entering from the north and serving the centre of the city, in the area of the Campus Martius and the Via Lata.[74] We are told that the flow had not ceased entirely, but after repair 'there gushed forth a great abundance of water, which satisfied almost the whole city'.[75] The Einsiedeln Itinerary mentions the Virgo on two occasions;[76] and today its modern replacement supplies what is perhaps the most famous of Rome's fountains, the Trevi.

Rome's longest aqueduct, the Claudia, came from the south and served the Lateran Palace and baptistery.[77] Again we are told that previously the flow had been reduced to a trickle, but that the pope 'gathered a crowd of people from the districts of Campania' and 'renewed and restored it afresh

---

[70] Procopius, *History of the Wars* 5.19.18, trans. Dewing III: 189–91. In November 536 Belisarius had gained entry to the city of Naples by precisely such a stratagem: *ibid.*, 5.10.1–20, trans. Dewing III: 93–7.

[71] Wilson 2000.   [72] *LP* 97.59, ed. Duchesne I: 503; English trans. Davis 2007: 148–9.

[73] Davis 2007: 149. It is not clear whether a subsequent reference to repairs to the Aqua Sabbatina (*LP* 97.81, ed. Duchesne I: 510) is a duplication or a record of a second separate project; see Davis 2007: 162 note 177.

[74] Coates-Stephens 2003a: 91–5.   [75] Davis 2007: 152–3.

[76] *CT* II: 181, 186. Davis (2007: 153 note 131) observes that the second mention states that the aqueduct was broken, and suggests on this basis that Hadrian's restoration may provide a *terminus ante quem* for the compilation of this text.

[77] Coates-Stephens 2003a: 95–9.

from its foundations'.[78] A section of this aqueduct may still be seen in the *piazza* adjacent to the north transept of the Lateran basilica.

As had been the case with the Sabbatina, we are informed by the *Liber pontificalis* that the Aqua Jovia had also been dysfunctional for some twenty years, so presumably it too had been blocked during the siege of Aistulf. This is another aqueduct which seems not to have retained its ancient name, and it has been usually identified as the Aqua Antoniana, which supplied the Baths of Caracalla, based on two passages in the Einsiedeln Itinerary which refer to a '*forma Jobia*' in relation to the Via Appia.[79] Robert Coates-Stephens, however, prefers to identify it as the Aqua Alexandrina, built in the third century to supply Alexander Severus's expansion of the baths of Nero, which entered the city at the Porta Maggiore.[80]

One final infrastructure project of note involved the pilgrims' route under a covered portico leading from the bridge across the Tiber at the Castel Sant'Angelo, the ancient *pons Aelius*, to the church of Saint Peter's. Hadrian's biographer records that the pope restored the riverbank passage with some 12,000 blocks of tufa, and rebuilt the portico all the way to the steps of Saint Peter's (*LP* 97.72, ed. Duchesne I: 507). Repairs were also undertaken to similar covered passages leading from gates in the Aurelian walls to the shrine churches of San Lorenzo fuori le mura and San Paolo (*LP* 97.74, ed. Duchesne, I: 508).

Papal activity was not confined to the *urbs* alone. The freedom from Lombard aggression enjoyed by the Roman *campagna* resulted in a revival of the project to establish papal agricultural estates: the *domuscultae* initiated in the time of Pope Zacharias, perhaps at the instigation of Theodore and Theodotus, Hadrian's father and uncle respectively. Early in Hadrian's reign the network was expanded substantially with the addition of four new groupings of properties: Capracorum, north of Rome in the territory of Veii; Galeria, northwest of the city on the Via Aurelia; a second Galeria, on the Via Portuensis near the ancient harbour of Portus and including parts of Isola Sacra at the mouth of the Tiber; and Calvisianum, south of the city on the Via Ardeatina. These are described in the *Liber pontificalis* in substantial detail, and apparently comprised existing farms which were amalgamated through gift, bequest, and purchase. They included grain fields (wheat and barley are specified), olive groves, vineyards, pig farms, and even a lettuce garden (*LP* 97.54–55; ed. Duchesne I: 501–2). In some instances, we are provided with information

[78] Davis 2007: 151.   [79] *CT* II:173, 199.   [80] Coates-Stephens 2003a: 99–101.

about how the properties were acquired. Capracorum, for example, began with an estate owned by the pope himself, part of his inheritance from his parents, and the *Liber*'s readers are reassured that the adjacent lands added to this core were purchased by paying 'fair compensation'.[81] It is also stressed that these changes of ownership were deemed to be irreversible, under pain of excommunication, and that their produce was intended for the sustenance of 'Christ's poor'. Specific instructions are even provided for the daily ration to be accorded to each person in the portico of the Lateran Palace.

In a subsequent passage we are given further details about the church built by Hadrian on the Capracorum estate (*LP* 97.69; ed. Duchesne I: 506–7). Dedicated initially to Saint Peter, it received relics of Christ, Mary and the apostles; and in what can only be described as a deliberate attempt to utilize the cult of the saints in order to extend the authority of the Roman church into the hinterland, the pope and his court travelled out from the city for its dedication, bringing with them from the catacombs the bodies of four early pontiffs, three martyrs of the mid-third century CE (Cornelius, Lucius, Felix), and one *confessor* from the early fifth century (Innocent). From the first of these, Cornelius, the site would later be known as Santa Cornelia, a name which has survived to the present day.

A few years later, two more estates would be added to the growing list of properties managed by the church and intended to help meet its evident need to acquire foodstuffs; and once again we are given copious details. Both follow a pattern similar to the earlier examples. The *domusculta* of Saint Hedistus, also south of the city on the via Ardeatina, was initiated with a legacy gift from Leoninus *consul et dux*, to which Hadrian added lands donated by others from the ranks of the military aristocracy and senior papal administration. Three such individuals are named: the *comes* (count) Peter; Agnes, widow of the *scrinarius* Agatho; and Theodota, widow of the *praefectorius* Dominic (*LP* 97.63; ed. Duchesne I: 505). And the *domusculta* of Saint Leucius, situated at the fifth mile of the Via Flaminia, grew from another posthumous legacy bequest, this time from the *primicerius* Mastalus (*LP* 97.77; ed. Duchense I: 509).

What makes these *domuscultae* of more than passing interest in a study focussing on material culture is that each was centred around one or more churches, presumably intended at one level to serve the religious needs of

---

[81] '*iusta reconpensatione*': *LP* 97.54; ed. Duchesne I: 501; trans. Davis 2007: 145. We may well agree with Davis that this sounds suspiciously like 'special pleading' (*ibid.*, note 95), although the same phrase had been used in the record of the establishment of the first *domuscultae* by Pope Zacharias (*LP* 93.25, ed. Duchesne I: 434). See also Christie 1995: 651.

the resident population, and at another to reinforce the bonds of loyalty to the papacy. A number of these sites were identified in the British School at Rome's South Etruria Survey, a project initiated by John Ward-Perkins in the early 1950s,[82] and subsequently have been excavated.

The first to be explored was Santa Cornelia at the *domusculta* of Capracorum, situated some 3 km northeast of Veii, excavated by Charles Daniels in the years 1962–4.[83] The site comprised a church, a baptistery, and numerous other buildings all enclosed by a perimeter wall, and the archaeology produced considerable evidence of marble furnishings. This was followed in 1965 by Santa Rufina, some 9 km northwest of Rome, the site identified in the *Liber pontificalis* as the nucleus of the first of the *domuscultae* named Galerius, where the dedication has also remained a toponym into the modern age.[84] Both sites provided evidence of the new type of glazed pottery known as Forum Ware, as well as fragments of their early medieval marble church furnishings. Those from Santa Cornelia were particularly elaborate, comprising portions of choir and chancel screens, a pulpit, and a *fastigium* or *ciborium*, all carved with the same design vocabulary (interlace and plaited patterns, interlocking circles, peacocks, etc.) that characterize late-eighth-century production inside the city in churches such as Santa Maria in Cosmedin.[85]

A third site, Mola di Monte Gelato, on the Treia river south of Nepi and thought to have been another primary centre of the Capracorum estate, was excavated by Timothy Potter and Anthony King between 1986 and 1990, sponsored by the British School and the British Museum.[86] This excavation also produced fragments of church furnishings, including an elaborately carved marble slab featuring the 'lamb of God' ('*agnus Dei*'), perhaps originally the frontal for an altar, which in a later period has been broken and reused in a floor pavement with its carved surface turned downwards (Fig. 9.4).[87]

Apart from serving as an explicit illustration of the text of the canon of the mass, the presence of the apocalyptic Lamb provides useful evidence for a larger iconographic issue. The Quinisext Council of 692 had specifically prohibited the depiction of Christ in the form of a lamb, and many have considered that Pope Sergius I's insertion into the liturgy of John the Baptist's words '*Ecce agnus Dei* ... ' was a direct response, indicating Roman opposition to Constantinopolitan attempts to control visual culture.

---

[82] Ward-Perkins 1955; and Potter 1979: 146–55.
[83] Christie and Daniels 1991; and Christie 1995.   [84] Cotton, Wheeler and Whitehouse 1991.
[85] Christie and Daniels 1991: 105–8; Paroli 1995: 245–92; and Paroli 1998: 94, 104–13.
[86] Potter and King 1997.   [87] Osborne 1994; and Osborne 1997c: 219–20.

Fig. 9.4. Mola di Monte Gelato: marble altar frontal (?) with 'Agnus Dei'.

There can be little doubt that the Roman church continued to use lamb imagery, as we have encountered in the painted decorations of San Lorenzo fuori le mura and Santa Susanna. The Mola di Monte Gelato fragment provides further corroboration of the Roman decision not to enforce the provisions of canon 82, and other examples of 'agnus Dei' images have been documented in the contemporary sculpture of northern Italy.[88]

[88] Brunet 2007.

Unfortunately, it is simply not possible to determine whether this would have been interpreted in the late eighth century as a conscious 'anti-Greek' political statement, or simply a normal choice for the decoration of altars and altar niches.[89]

The ultimate fate of the *domuscultae* has not yet been determined, although all seem to have disappeared by the second half of the ninth century.[90] Capracorum was still functioning in the late 840s, when it provided labour to assist in building the walls around Saint Peter's, the 'Leonine City' project of Pope Leo IV;[91] but the insecurity of the Roman hinterland occasioned by Arab raiders was not propitious for their continued survival. A monastery on the site, dedicated to Saint Cornelius, can be documented from the eleventh century, but it too had been abandoned by the middle of the fifteenth.[92]

Finally, no discussion of the 'material culture' associated with this pope could be complete without some mention of Hadrian's elaborate funerary inscription, a sizeable slab of greyish-black marble quarried in the valley of the Meuse in what is today Belgium, elegantly inscribed with verses composed in a classicizing style by Alcuin of York, that was commissioned by Charlemagne himself to honour his steadfast partner in the new political system governing western Europe. When Old Saint Peter's was demolished, this stone was salvaged from its position on the western wall of the south transept, where Hadrian's tomb had joined those of Leo I and Paul I on the line of the pilgrims' approach to the tomb of Peter; and in 1619 it was placed in the portico of the new church, where it remains today.[93] Joanna Story has presented a case for 'embedded cultural messages' that include 'the imperial ambition of the patron'.[94] But at a more prosaic level we can perhaps see it simply as an important witness to the new relationship which had been established between the papacy and the Franks by the time of Hadrian's death in December 795, one that would provide the model for the entire period of the subsequent Middle Ages. The church of Saint Peter's would quickly become the single most important setting for the manifestation and public display of this new political reality, and the Carolingian links to Peter's shrine were extensive, including numerous royal gifts of golden liturgical vessels for use at the high altar, as well as an altar cloth for the Chapel of Saint Peter the Shepherd (*Oratorium Pastoris*).[95] Many earlier popes had been the recipients of funerary

---

[89] Opie 2002 argues that canon 82 was largely observed in Rome until the early ninth century, but the surviving murals and sculpture suggest otherwise.
[90] Partner 1966: 70.   [91] Gibson and Ward-Perkins 1979: 33.   [92] Christie 1995: 651–2.
[93] De Rossi 1888; Story *et al.* 2005.   [94] Story *et al.* 2005, 190.   [95] Story 2013.

inscriptions, but none had ever been as grand nor supplied by such a significant political figure, who 'speaks' in the verses in the first person. That this epitaph alone has been carefully preserved through to the present day constitutes further evidence of the importance accorded to the new relationship over the following twelve centuries. The alliance developed by Hadrian and Charlemagne would resonate for a long time afterwards.

At the same time, however, this political shift did not mean that Rome simultaneously rejected its deeply rooted hellenophone culture. Indeed, to the contrary – politics and culture were separate realms. As earlier noted, at least two abbots of the Greek monastery of San Saba, Pardus and Peter, served Hadrian as senior ambassadors, leading Roman delegations to the Lombard king, Desiderius, to Charlemagne, and to the Second Council of Nicaea. And it was also in the first year of his pontificate, at the monastery of Saint Agatha, that a liturgical inscription in Greek was written on the inner face of a consular diptych of Clementinus (513 CE), now in Liverpool.[96] Nor was 'Greek culture' restricted to monasteries. The subject matter of the Sant'Adriano murals, including the earliest-known narrative cycle of Saint Basil anywhere in Christian art, constitutes evidence of a much broader diffusion; and the 'non-Roman' nature of Santa Maria in Cosmedin has also been noted.

With Hadrian, the process of reimagining the role of the bishops of Rome was brought to a full and successful conclusion, with the pope assuming the range of responsibilities that would previously have been undertaken by the secular administration and the *dux*; and this might have been an easy transition for someone whose adoptive father had once held that precise title. But it was no longer some higher earthly political power to whom he 'reported'. Just as Gregory I had styled himself as 'God's consul', so too we might perhaps think of Hadrian as 'God's duke' (*dux Dei*), although there is no evidence for the use of that particular expression at the time. Previous popes had taken steps in this direction, but there was no sense that it formed part of a deliberate plan. With Hadrian that seems to change, with the language of his correspondence to Charlemagne and his actions to repair Rome's infrastructure suggesting that the process had become more self-conscious. There remained only a few final steps to tidy up the political transition from constituent element of the 'Roman' Empire to autonomous 'republic' under Frankish military protection, and these would fall to his successor, Pope Leo III.

---

[96] Sansterre 1984b.

10 | Leo III and Charlemagne

One of the very last acts of a century that had witnessed so much change in Rome took place in the church of Saint Peter's on 25 December 800, namely the coronation of Charlemagne as 'emperor of the Romans', although what precisely that phrase was intended to mean is not specified.[1] Perhaps most importantly, the ceremony was performed by the pope, establishing a practice that would endure for a millennium. In political terms, the transition from the old order was now fully complete: the bishops of Rome had emerged victorious. And it seems somehow fitting that the pontiff who presided over this triumph bore the name Leo, Leo III (795–816), given that the campaign to establish the hegemony of the see of Rome had been launched almost four centuries earlier by Pope Leo I. Having seen off all external enemies, most recently both the Byzantine exarchs and the Lombards, and under the powerful protection of the Franks, the most significant dangers now facing the Roman pontiffs were all internal, as factions in the Roman aristocracy competed for control of the papal throne ... a reality that Leo himself would quickly discover.

The *Liber pontificalis* relates at length the dramatic events which began on 25 April 799 and their aftermath (*LP* 98.11–24, ed. Duchesne II: 4–7). While traversing the city from the Lateran to the church of San Lorenzo in Lucina, the starting point for the annual *Letania maior*, the pope was waylaid outside Paul I's monastery of Saint Stephen and Saint Silvester (the modern San Silvestro in Capite), in a plot apparently hatched by members of the family of the previous pope, Hadrian I, including Hadrian's nephew, Paschal. The location of the ambush is perhaps no coincidence, given that this family is known to have resided in this very region of Rome, the Via Lata. Leo was severely beaten, and attempts were made, unsuccessfully as it turned out, to remove his eyes and tongue. Badly injured, and apparently bleeding profusely, he was imprisoned first in the adjacent monastery, and later in the monastery of Sant'Erasmo; but the pope did not succumb to his wounds, and he was eventually rescued by his

---

[1] The Latin title stated is '*imperator Romanorum*'; *LP* 98.23, ed. Duchesne II: 7.

supporters, who brought him to Saint Peter's, and then, with the assistance of Duke Winichis of Spoleto, to safety in Umbria. Leo would later journey northwards across the Alps to meet with Charlemagne at Paderborn, eventually returning to Rome under Frankish protection to triumph over his erstwhile opponents. Charlemagne would also come to Rome the following year, to hear the charges of perjury and adultery brought against the pope. But the senior clergy declined to sit in judgement, and Leo himself took an oath attesting his innocence on all charges. This set up the dramatic moment of the imperial coronation on Christmas Day.

Leo's biographer describes him as '*ecclesiasticarum rerum defensor*', translated insightfully by Raymond Davis as 'a defender of the church establishment'.[2] The phrase seems apt, although not original as it had been used previously to describe Pope Gregory II (*LP* 91.1, ed. Duchesne I: 396). For the years following 800 there is no mention whatsoever in the *Liber pontificalis* of any political events, not even of the death of Charlemagne in 814, but instead the reader is treated to an exceptionally detailed account of papal repairs and improvements to churches both inside the city and beyond, including Sant'Apollinare in Classe near Ravenna, as well as lengthy enumerations of the pope's extraordinary largesse in the form of gifts of gold, silver, and precious silks. As Herman Geertman has demonstrated, these are organized chronologically by indiction year, the fiscal year running from September to August,[3] with a special distribution of largesse in the year 807 that touched almost every ecclesiastical institution in the city, all named and usefully grouped by category (*LP* 98: 69–81, ed. Duchesne II: 18–25).[4] Clearly there was an enormous quantity of wealth available to dispense, and Leo did indeed take good care of the churches of the papal state for which he was responsible.

Some of the building projects survive, or are at least documented in some way, and these demonstrate Leo's efforts to build on the work of previous pontiffs with a view to creating a courtly setting and infrastructure worthy of a secular magnate, not simply a bishop. Among the earliest, probably dating to the indiction year 797–8, and arguably the most overtly political in terms of the statement conveyed by its decorations, was the new triclinium which Leo constructed in the Lateran patriarchate.[5] This dining

---

[2] *LP* 98.2, ed. Duchesne II: 1; trans. Davis 2007: 176.   [3] Geertman 1975: 37–70.
[4] For analysis, Geertman 1975: 82–129; and Davis 2007: 172–5.
[5] The extensive bibliography includes Lauer 1911: 105–19; Ladner 1941a: 113–26; Davis-Weyer 1965; Davis-Weyer 1966; Walter 1970; Davis-Weyer 1974; Belting 1976; Belting 1978; Iacobini 1989; Engemann 1995; Herklotz 1995; Luchterhandt 1999d; Noble 2001b: 68–72; Luchterhandt 2006: 179–84; Moretti 2006; Ballardini 2015; and D'Onofrio 2016.

hall was, in the words of his biographer, 'greater than all other such, adorned on a wondrous scale'.[6] We are told that it featured three apses, the main one decorated in mosaic and the other two in paint, and columns of porphyry and other marbles, while the walls and floors were also covered in marble.[7] There was even 'lily-shaped ornamentation' on the doorposts! This is probably the hall in the patriarchate in which Leo received Charlemagne and his retinue on the feast of Saint Andrew (November 30) in the year 800, and in the following month it was used by the Carolingian episcopal tribunal charged with investigating the assassination attempt made on the pontiff the previous year (*LP* 98.20, ed. Duchesne II: 6–7).

The 'Aula Leonina' had become an abandoned ruin by the middle of the sixteenth century, when it was seen and described by Onofrio Panvinio (1530–68), who uses that term.[8] The main apse would survive the demolition of the medieval papal palace by Pope Sixtus V in the 1580s; and parts of its mosaic decoration were still intact in the early seventeenth century when they caught the attention of Cardinal Francesco Barberini, nephew of Pope Urban VIII (1623–44), and also archpriest of the Lateran. He funded a restoration of the apse and its decorations aimed to coincide with the celebrations of the 1625 Jubilee.[9] The mosaic in the conch of the apse depicted the 'Mission of the Apostles', with a central figure of Christ flanked by eleven apostles, illustrating his command to his followers to 'Go and teach all nations ... ' (Matthew 28:19), and this Biblical text was inscribed beneath. The '*missio apostolorum*' was a theme of considerable topicality at the end of the eighth century given the Carolingian campaign to evangelize central Europe following their final military defeat of the Avars in 796, and the same text is invoked on multiple occasions in the contemporary correspondence of Alcuin, who urged the Franks to be 'preachers not predators' ('*praedicatores non praedatores*').[10]

But possibly of greater political importance were the mosaics on the arch framing the apse. Modern visitors to the Lateran may admire a full-scale replica of the apse and arch from Leo's triclinium, situated to the northeast of the basilica, adjacent to the Scala Santa and chapel of the Sancta

---

[6] *LP* 98.10, ed. Duchesne II: 3–4; trans. Davis 2007: 180.
[7] For the imperial connotations of triconch triclinia in Late Antiquity and the early Middle Ages: Lavin 1961.
[8] Panvinio, ed. Lauer: 481–2; English trans. in Davis-Weyer 1986: 89.
[9] Herklotz 1995; and Russo 2014.
[10] The text of Matthew 28:19 is invoked by Alcuin in letters to Charlemagne, Arno of Salzburg, and Megenfridus: Alcuin, *Epistolae* 100, 111, 113, ed. Dümmler pp. 158, 160, 164. For the context, Sullivan 1956 and Osborne 1999: 382–3; and Costambeys 2014: 269–71.

Fig. 10.1. Lateran Palace, Rome: Triclinium of Leo III, facsimile of original apse mosaic.

Sanctorum (Fig. 10.1). This depicts, on the left, Christ enthroned, flanked by two kneeling figures: Saint Peter, who receives the keys to the church, and Emperor Constantine, who receives the military banner of Christianity, or *labarum*. And balancing this composition on the right side of the arch, in a typological parallel reflecting the situation at the end of the eighth century, Saint Peter offers the papal pallium to Leo III and the *labarum* to Charlemagne. The two latter figures, both identified by inscriptions, bear 'square haloes' framing their heads, indicating portraits. The political message appears explicit: it is Peter, and by analogy his papal successors, who wield the authority to invest secular rulers, thus echoing the message of the *Constitutum Constantini* and anticipating the events of December 800.

Unfortunately, however, not a single *tessera* of this mosaic is original, nor is it even on the original site.[11] What we see today was commissioned as a full-scale 'facsimile' by Pope Benedict XIV in 1743, and it copies the Barberini restoration of the original in 1624–25. The latter was the work of the mosaicist Giovan Battista Calandra (1586–1644), and should itself be viewed in terms of the fierce debate about papal primacy which engaged that age. Moreover, the iconography that it presents must also be regarded as at least partially suspect. Antiquarian descriptions and drawings from the second half of the sixteenth century indicate that, already by that time, the mosaics on the left side of the arch had all but vanished, with the result that the subject matter was completely illegible,[12] and thus what appears there today is entirely the invention of Calandra and the Barberini circle. Much of their thinking is reflected in a treatise written by Nicolò Alemanni, the Vatican librarian, published in 1625: *De lateranensibus parietinis*.[13]

But even if the precise typological parallel may not have been present in the original, there is no question that the right side did portray Leo III and Charlemagne being invested by Saint Peter, and all three figures along with their identifying inscriptions are recorded by Onofrio Panvinio. The earliest antiquarian drawing (Vatican City, BAV, Barb. Lat. 2738, fol. 104r), to be linked to Panvinio or the Spanish church historian Alonso Chacón (Ciacconio), and certainly made well before the Barberini restoration of the mosaic, shows all three figures.[14]

But this is not the only record. Among other useful pieces of documentation, there is also a sketch of the triclinium by Pompeo Ugonio, made prior to the restructuring undertaken by Pope Sixtus V (Vatican City, BAV, Barb. Lat. 2160, 55r),[15] and an annotated watercolour copy of the surviving right side of the arch in another Ciacconio manuscript: BAV, Barb. Lat.

---

[11] The possible site of the original apse has recently been identified using ground penetrating radar, see Piro *et al.* 2020. I am grateful to Ian Haynes for sharing the text of this study with me prior to publication.

[12] Waetzoldt 1964: 40.   [13] Herklotz 1985b: 35–6; and Herklotz 1995.

[14] This drawing is discussed and illustrated by Ladner 1935: 267–9 and fig. 1; Waetzoldt 1964: 40, no. 208 and fig. 120; Davis-Weyer 1965 and fig. 1; Iacobini 1989: 189 and fig. 3; and Herklotz 1995: fig. 7.

[15] Published images include Lauer 1911: 104, fig. 40; and Iacobini 1989: fig. 2.

Fig. 10.2. Lateran Triclinium of Leo III: BAV, cod. Barb. Lat. 5407, fol. 97r. © 2020 Biblioteca Apostolica Vaticana

5407, fol. 97r (Fig. 10.2);[16] so at least some details of the original can be confirmed. Numerous other drawings circulated immediately before and after 1600, mostly copies of copies,[17] and additional versions and a written description were included in the documentation prepared by Giacomo Grimaldi for Pope Paul V.[18] The main inscription requested that Peter grant life to Pope Leo and victory to King Charles, and one possible

---

[16] Published images include Lauer 1911: 106, fig. 43; Waetzoldt 1964: 40, no. 218 and fig. 121; Osborne and Claridge 1996–8 II: 59; Luchterhandt 1999c: 49; and Moretti 2006: fig. 2.

[17] See for example Osborne and Claridge 1996–8 II: 56–9, no. 168.   [18] Grimaldi 1972: 353–7.

measure of its authenticity can be found in the initial letter of the word 'victoria', a 'B',[19] which is among the very last eighth-century instances of 'betacism' in Rome. Similarly, the papal pallium is depicted without shoulder crosses, lending credence to both its authenticity and that of the copy. Presumably Charlemagne is receiving the banner of the *patricius Romanorum*, the title conferred on him by Pope Hadrian, and not that of *imperator*, as the inscription gives him the title 'rex'. The imperial coronation was still a year or two away.

There can be little doubt that the original decoration was intended as an overt statement engaging contemporary politics, and thus one must agree with Richard Krautheimer, Antonio Iacobini and others that, even if the mosaic on the left side cannot be documented before 1625, it must originally have depicted something very similar to what we see today,[20] perhaps with Pope Silvester as Constantine's episcopal counterpart, instead of Saint Peter. It is certainly in keeping with papal attempts to characterize Charlemagne as the 'new Constantine', for example, in Pope Hadrian's letter to Charlemagne of May 778 where he is called explicitly '*novus christianissimus Dei Constantinus imperator*'.[21]

How all of this was understood in 798 is of course a matter of conjecture, as too is the subsequent imperial coronation.[22] Parts of the original composition, or more accurately its Barberini restoration, survived into the second quarter of the eighteenth century, but were lost in an unsuccessful attempt made under Pope Clement XII (1730–40) to move the mosaic, thus prompting the copy by the mosaicist Pier Leone Ghezzi in the time of Clement's successor. Two small fragments are preserved today at the Vatican, probably acquired by Pope Pius VII with the Mariotti collection of Christian antiquities in 1819.[23] Both depict heads of apostles from the apse conch: the second figure to the left of Christ and the first on his right, the latter apparently entirely the work of Calandra's seventeenth-century restoration. The first head, however, does appear to be original, although even this piece has received some subsequent repair.[24] Unlike the mosaicists of John VII at the beginning of the eighth century, those employed by Leo III worked entirely with glass tesserae, even for flesh areas, a practice

---

[19] Lauer 1911: 113.   [20] Krautheimer 1942: 36–7, and 1980: 115; and Iacobini 1989: 192.
[21] *Codex epistolaris carolinus* 60, ed. Gundlach, pp. 587, lines 16–17.
[22] Krautheimer 1980: 114–17. An attempt to view the Frankish king as the 'new Constantine' has been downplayed by Emerick (2017), who sees it as running counter to Carolingian attempts to characterize him as the 'new David'.
[23] Davis-Weyer 1974; Iacobini 1989: 195; Luchterhandt 1999a; and Luchterhandt 1999b.
[24] Lauer 1911: 116, fig. 49; Iacobini 1989: pl. 34; and Moretti 2006: fig. 5.

that would continue into the ninth century in the mosaic projects of Pope Paschal I (817–24).[25]

The banqueting hall was not Pope Leo's only project at the Lateran. In the early ninth century he added a second triclinium, this time with eleven apses (five on each side, and one on the end), a room which subsequently came to be called the *Sala del Concilio*.[26] The *Liber pontificalis* once again provides a number of details. The main apse was decorated in mosaic, and those on the side were equipped with dining couches ('*accubita*') and painted with scenes illustrating the apostles preaching. The floor was covered in marble, and in the centre was a fountain featuring a porphyry shell.[27] Lauer suggests, probably with good reason, that the model was the great triclinium in the imperial palace at Constantinople, known as the 'hall of the nineteen couches', and this idea was further developed by Richard Krautheimer.[28] Once again there is a description by Panvinio.[29] The only pictorial record is a sixteenth-century drawing by Ugonio preserved in the Vatican Library (Vatican City, BAV, Barb. Lat. 2160, fol. 157r);[30] and as had been the case in the first triclinium, once again Leo's monogram was placed at the apex of the apse. Although restored by Pope Julius II in preparation for the Fifth Lateran Council in 1512, it did not survive the demolitions of Sixtus V in the 1580s.

And finally, Leo later rebuilt the portico joining the two sections of the papal residence, known as the *macrona* (from the Greek word for 'long'), complete with a 'veranda' (*solarium*), and he also added a chapel dedicated to Saint Michael, the latter decorated with mosaics and murals.[31]

Leo's biography in the *Liber pontificalis* provides plenty of evidence, should such be needed, that important events, for example, Charlemagne's imperial coronation, were now increasingly taking place at the shrine of Saint Peter, and not at the papal palace or adjacent cathedral church of San Giovanni. And thus Saint Peter's was also the beneficiary of Leo's energetic plan to create appropriate spaces for non-liturgical activities, anticipating by some six centuries the eventual move of the official residence from the Lateran to the Vatican. These projects were undertaken primarily in two locations. The first was on the south flank of the church, adjacent to the circular mausoleum that had been

---

[25] Davis-Weyer 1974: 38–9; and Iacobini 1989: 195.   [26] Lauer 1911: 103–5.
[27] *LP* 98.39, ed. Duchesne II: 11. For reconstruction drawings, see Belting 1978: 60 fig. 2 (hall), and 69 fig. 3 (apse mosaic), both discussed *ibid.*, 67–72.
[28] Lauer 1911: 102–3; and Krautheimer 1966.
[29] Panvinio, ed. Lauer: 483–4; English trans. in Davis-Weyer 1986: 89–90.
[30] Published images include Lauer 1911: 101 fig. 38; Belting 1976: fig. 183; and Luchterhandt 2006: 199 fig. 21.
[31] *LP* 98.92, ed. Duchesne II: 28–9; trans. Davis 2007: 220; see also Lauer 1911: 118.

converted by Pope Symmachus (498–514) into the chapel of Saint Andrew (*LP* 53.6, ed. Duchesne I: 261). This was a primary point of entry for pilgrims and visitors who, as we have seen, passed through the two late Roman funerary rotundas and then entered the basilica via the south transept on their way to the crypt. This was also the location of the Egyptian obelisk, which still stood where it had been erected back in the first century CE, on the *spina* of the Vatican circus, and where it would indeed remain until moved by Domenico Fontana in 1586 to its present location in the Piazza San Pietro; and from the latter monument the location became known as the 'Agulia', or 'Needle'.[32] The *Liber pontificalis* relates that Leo constructed a triclinium 'close to St Peter's, at the Needle',[33] and this would later come to be known as the 'House of the Needle' ('*Domus Aguliae*'). Again there were three apses, mirroring the first triclinium in the Lateran, and lavish decorations in mosaic and marble. Some years later he would also add a bath, 'placed on the higher level close to the great column, a round construction marvellously decorated'.[34] One of his ninth-century successors, Pope Gregory IV (827–44), would further elaborate this cluster '*iuxta Accolam*' by building 'a hospice, small yet becomingly constructed, for the pontiff to rest in when after morning prayers or the offices of mass his limbs are liable to fatigue'.[35]

The second entrance to Saint Peter's, through the atrium, also received Leo's attention. First he repaired the steps, both those to the gatehouse and those leading from the atrium into the church; and then on the right side of the atrium he added yet another reception building ('*domus*'), 'beautifully decorated on a wondrous scale' and complete with 'dining couches'. And there was also a bath 'for the benefit of Christ's poor and pilgrims'.[36] But of all these various endeavours at the shrine of Saint Peter not a single brick now remains.

Another project which similarly hasn't survived, but for which we have some documentation, was the church of Santa Susanna, where Leo had served as cardinal priest prior to his election as pope. Very early in his reign, in the indiction year 797–8, he rebuilt this church on a much larger scale (*LP* 98.9, ed. Duchesne II: 3), complete with galleries[37] and an

---

[32] The term 'Agulia' is possibly a corruption of 'Acus Iulii', or 'Julius's Needle', since it was believed through the Middle Ages that the bronze orb at its top contained the cremated remains of Julius Caesar: Magister Gregorius, *Narracio de mirabilibus urbis Romae*, ed. Huygens, cap. 29; *The Marvels of Rome*, trans. Osborne: 34–5, 88–94; and Osborne 2013: 279–84.

[33] *LP* 98.27, ed. Duchesne II: 8; trans. Davis 2007: 189–90.

[34] *LP* 98.89, ed. Duchesne II: 27–28; trans. Davis 2007: 218.

[35] *LP* 103.35, ed. Duchesne II: 81; trans. Davis 1995: 66.

[36] *LP* 98.89, ed. Duchesne II: 28; trans. Davis 2007: 218.

[37] The *LP* text uses a Greek word: *caticuminia*, presumably deriving from the original use of such spaces for catechumens.

adjacent baptistery. Richard Krautheimer's analysis of the architecture suggests that more of the previous structure may have been salvaged and incorporated into the new church than the *Liber pontificalis* passage suggests,[38] but at a minimum the church was widened, and to facilitate this process the builders reused large blocks from the adjacent Servian wall. He notes that while it is tempting to view the galleries as a 'Byzantine' feature, it is possible that they were already present in the earlier church.[39] It is certainly a curious feature, not required by the liturgy, and the only known parallel in Rome is Santa Maria in Cosmedin, built by Leo III's immediate predecessor. One cannot help but wonder whether Leo may also have been the one responsible for carefully preserving the fragments of painting, illustrating the 'Maria *regina*' and the two saints Johns flanking the '*agnus Dei*', that were placed in a sarcophagus and then buried beneath the floor of the new structure.

As seems to have been the case with all of this pope's projects, the decorations of Santa Susanna were lavish, and comprised both mosaics and marble. Unfortunately, the medieval church was demolished and rebuilt in 1595, and no trace of Leo III's images now remain. The pre-demolition description of the apse mosaic by Pompeo Ugonio (Vatican City, BAV, Barb. Lat. 2160, fols 177r–177v) indicates that it followed the traditional formula of Christ between Peter, Paul, and (unusually) Mary, flanked by additional saints and contemporary figures. At the far left, Susanna presented the papal donor, shown holding a model of the church, and at the far right, Saint Gabinus (Susanna's father) presented Charlemagne. Slightly complicating our understanding of the original, the sixteenth-century antiquarian drawings that purport to preserve details of the figures of Pope Leo III and Charlemagne have been shown by Caecilia Davis-Weyer to be at least partially based not on the original mosaic but rather on the 'Aula Leonina' drawings then in circulation, and thus some hesitation may be required in using them unreservedly.[40] Transcriptions of the original dedication inscription record examples of 'betacism', suggesting some degree of accuracy in that regard: Leo was named, and credited with having '*ornabit atque decorabit*' the basilica.

Leo's other major building project which has survived is the church of Santi Nereo ed Achilleo, on the south side of the city and constructed in part with *spolia* from the adjacent Baths of Caracalla, but this dates from the second decade of the ninth century, so will be excluded from the

---

[38] Krautheimer and Frankl 1939: 398–400; and *CBCR* IV: 254–78.   [39] *CBCR* IV: 277–8.
[40] Ladner 1941a: 126–8; Davis-Weyer 1965; Osborne and Claridge 1996–8 II: 60–3; Luchterhandt 1999d; and Nilgen 1999a.

present discussion.[41] The mosaics surviving on the apsidal arch presage the substantial revival of work in that medium undertaken under Pope Paschal I (817–24).[42] Once again there were galleries, in addition to a second distinctly 'non-Roman' architectural feature: the twin towers flanking the apse, for which the closest parallels may be found in Syria.

Following the dramatic events in the early years of his reign, Leo III would occupy the papal throne well into the new century, outliving Charlemagne; and the account of his life in the *Liber pontificalis* is the longest of all the papal biographies. As was the case with the life of Pope Hadrian before him, this mostly comprises an extensive list of gifts to Roman churches. For textiles we are given detailed information concerning both the material and the nature of their decoration, and for objects of precious metal their weight. The sheer quantity of wealth available for distribution was extraordinary. The 807 distribution of silver crowns and canisters totalled well over 700 pounds, so clearly silver was available in very significant quantities. As Raymond Davis has observed, these lists 'provide a remarkable insight into the non-political activities of the papacy in Carolingian times'.[43]

And there was one final category of 'wealth' which made an impact on material culture. Like almost all of his predecessors, Leo III was deeply engaged with the cult of relics, although with less of an emphasis on the translations of saintly bodies from the catacombs, an activity championed by Paul I and Hadrian I before him, and Paschal I after him. Leo seems to have preferred objects or bits, as opposed to complete bodies, and he was responsible for placing the papal collection of more than 100 such items, complete with identifying labels or 'authentics', in a cypress-wood chest bearing his name. Further additions to the collection were made by subsequent popes. At some point, either in Leo's own time or later, this chest was placed in the private papal chapel in the Lateran Palace, known as the 'Sancta Sanctorum' ('Holy of Holies'), where it was rediscovered in 1903 when the altar was opened. The reliquaries themselves were transported to the Vatican in 1905, where they remain.[44] The core of the collection comprises some 57 bits of stone, wood, and textiles from sites in the Holy Land, plus a few saintly relics, again mostly from the eastern Mediterranean. There is no suggestion that

---

[41] Krautheimer and Frankl 1939: 392–4; *CBCR* III: 135–52; Sacchi 1987–8; Curzi 1993; Turco 1994; Nilgen 1999b; Osborne and Claridge 1996–8 I: 264–5; and Utro 2004.
[42] For Paschal's churches of Santa Prassede, Santa Cecilia in Trastevere and Santa Maria in Domnica, see Goodson 2010.
[43] Davis 2007: 170.
[44] O'Connor 2013; Smith 2014: 195–204; Luchterhandt 2017; and Maskarinec 2018: 133–7. For the context of the 1903 reopening, Noreen 2011.

this was amassed in any sort of systematic fashion, and the objects may have reached Rome as diplomatic gifts from the patriarch of Jerusalem and other prelates, with whom the papacy was in regular contact. There are, for example, some nine pieces of rock identified as coming from Golgotha, the site of the Crucifixion.[45] Maya Maskarinec's recent comment about the interior of Saint Peter's, that it had become 'a dense web of Christian memory',[46] also applies not only to the Lateran but by the year 800 to the entire city. Rome had forged its new role in the world as the primary centre of the expanding Christian faith, and the principal repository of tangible sacrality.

---

[45] Luchterhandt 2017: 49–52.   [46] Maskarinec 2018: 127.

Afterword

With the advantage of hindsight, the political transformation of Rome over the course of the eighth century can be seen to have been substantial, charting the city's future. Popes such as Sergius I and John VII had taken the first steps towards increased papal autonomy from imperial rule and the creation of a new independent identity, and this process then accelerated under their successors, driven by the necessity for survival in the face of a looming Lombard threat. A hostile enemy was quite literally at their door. Stephen II and Paul I had first constructed, and then Hadrian I and Leo III had thoroughly cemented, a new alliance with the Franks, creating a political dynamic in which each side legitimized and reinforced the other: the papacy offered the sacralization of political authority, ultimately including imperial coronation, and in return the Franks extended much needed military protection. In one form or another, this model would endure for the next millennium; and in the process, Rome's political 'gaze' increasingly and unsurprisingly turned away from Byzantium and the eastern Mediterranean. The last pontiff to visit Constantinople was Constantine I in 710–11, and all the major journeys undertaken by his medieval successors were northwards across the Alps. But it should also be noted that a 'pro-Byzantine' political faction seems to have remained active in Rome well into the ninth century. Following the shock of the Arab attack on Rome in 846, and the sack of Saint Peter's, a return to the former political arrangement may have seemed desirable in some quarters. In the reign of Pope Leo IV (847–55), the *Liber pontificalis* reports that the papal *superista* Gratian was charged with plotting with Constantinople to restore imperial rule, although eventually he was exonerated (*LP* 105.110, ed. Duchesne II: 134). And later in the century when Rome was once again threatened in this fashion, it was the Byzantine fleet that came to the city's rescue; and Pope John VIII (872–82) would write to the Emperor Basil I to offer his thanks.[1]

---

[1] See Osborne 2011a: 226–7. McCormick (1995: 372) speaks in terms of a political 'rapprochement'.

Although the *Liber pontificalis*, along with the papal letters preserved in the *Codex epistolaris carolinus* and a handful of surviving inscriptions, together paint a fairly straightforward picture of Roman (read 'papal') triumphalism, if we view the eighth century through the lens of archaeology and material culture we find a somewhat more variegated scenario. Yes, there was change, but scratch the surface and one also finds a remarkable degree of cultural continuity. If we examine what popes such as Zacharias or noblemen such as Theodotus did with their time and money, we can perhaps gain greater insight into their thinking.

Much of the 'change' involved agency. In the eighth century Rome finally became a 'city of the church',[2] with the pope and his growing administrative bureaucracy absorbing most of the functions previously exercised by secular authority, including feeding the population and maintaining civic infrastructure. In many respects it is difficult to ascertain how much of this transition was conscious and deliberate, and how much simply a necessary reaction to the prevailing circumstances, brought on by a dramatic decline of imperial engagement with matters Italian; but there can be little doubt that a visitor to the city in 800 would have seen newly repaired walls and a restored public water supply, in addition to a construction boom that had produced dozens of new or refurbished churches, monasteries, and *diaconiae*, not to mention *xenodochia* and the infrastructure needed to accommodate pilgrims. Furthermore, many of these buildings were sumptuously decorated with marble furnishings, objects of gold and silver, and imported silk curtains and altar cloths. Important visitors were treated to meals in the new spacious papal dining halls, resplendent with decorations in the costly medium of mosaic; and even ordinary pilgrims would have witnessed colourful processions through the streets, in which the entire hierarchical structure of Roman society was placed on public display as the pope and his entourage moved through the physical spaces of what had become *his* city. Factions might contest for control of the papal throne, but there was no doubt that it was now the pope who was in charge. By the last quarter of the eighth century the Byzantine emperor's image had disappeared from the coinage, and his name from the dating formula used in official documents. At the same time, the popes were redefining themselves as the legitimate inheritors of imperial *potestas*, a claim made explicitly in the forged 'Donation of Constantine' and implicitly in the collection of bronze statues set up outside the Lateran Palace.

[2] Noble 2001b: 49.

In terms of the city's geography, the previous locus of authority on the Palatine was abandoned in favour of the Lateran and, increasingly, the shrine church of Saint Peter. These twin poles would now dominate urban life until the fifteenth century, when the balance would swing decisively to the Vatican. But civic politics and administration were only the tip of the proverbial iceberg for the beginnings of a profound cultural shift, and one that would ultimately divide Christendom into two separate families. That broader break was still in the future, but the seeds were sown when the inhabitants of Rome began to regard the 'Greeks' as being different from themselves, as the 'other'.

On a year-by-year basis, the changes apparent to the average inhabitant of Rome might have been almost imperceptible, with many innovations more likely to have been responses to specific events rather than part of some organized and coherent grand plan. But given the political shift, what is perhaps most intriguing about the eighth century is the remarkable degree of residual continuity with the world of the eastern Mediterranean, in other words with 'Byzantium' in the broader non-political sense of that term. This continuity was most prevalent in the sphere of material culture, where it was manifested in everything from building types and their decoration to fashions in media as varied as painting, sculpture, textiles, and ceramics. The inhabitants of north-western Europe might look to Rome to set the standards for liturgical and other practices, as well as regarding the city as the place to do their 'shopping' for books and images, but Rome's own gaze in this regard remained pointedly eastwards.

This balance between continuity and change may also be observed in the composition of Roman élite society. In the seventh century the old Roman senatorial families had been replaced by a new aristocracy comprised primarily of military officers and bureaucrats who had settled and become major landowners, many of them of eastern Mediterranean origin. And they shared those broad Byzantine cultural roots with much of the city's ecclesiastical hierarchy. Perhaps the most interesting phenomenon is the process in which this new aristocracy sought to re-identify themselves as 'Roman' after the middle of the century when the adjective 'Greek' began to be used pejoratively in papal documents. In 700 the pope and his court chatted to one another in Greek, and the Greek language featured prominently in many painted or carved inscriptions, as well as in graffiti; but we have rather scant evidence for such practices a century later. That said, however, the knowledge and use of Greek never disappeared entirely. As Michael McCormick has noted, 'the person who forged the Donation of Constantine wrote a Greek-accented Latin, the Lateran Palace probably had a library of Greek manuscripts and Pope Paul I supplied Pippin III with Greek books'.[3]

Trade across the Mediterranean continued to flourish, probably after a slight hiatus at the beginning of the century in the aftermath of the Arab conquest of North Africa. But the items traded had shifted perceptibly. Rome no longer imported food or pottery; those were now sourced locally, and this is reflected in the establishment of the papal agricultural estates (the *domuscultae*) and the development of a local ceramics industry producing glazed jugs. On the other hand, an apparent abundance of disposable wealth fuelled an unprecedented and almost insatiable demand for silks and other luxury fabrics, imported from Byzantium and the Muslim Middle East. And there was at least one new commodity going in the other direction, slaves, with the trade carried primarily by Venetian and Arab merchants.[4]

There was also considerable continuity in the arts and in some artistic practices. Mosaic remained the medium of choice for the decoration of churches and banqueting halls. We have evidence for very substantial mosaic production from both the beginning and the end of the eighth century, plus knowledge that the craft continued to be practised through the decades in between. Paul I's facade of the gatehouse entrance to the atrium of Saint Peter's must have glittered brightly in the morning sun; and his funerary chapel in the south transept was no doubt equally impressive, even if we can't now determine whether the mosaicists used glass or marble tesserae for the hands and faces. Painting and sculptural techniques remained largely unaltered, as did the use of artificial pigments such as Egyptian blue. One apparently new addition was another blue pigment, lapis lazuli, mined in Afghanistan, not previously documented in Rome, and probably introduced by artists from the eastern Mediterranean. And while there were some changes to the subjects painted and in the vocabulary of carved ornament, almost certainly reflecting current theological debates and liturgical practices, as well as new patrons with different tastes, the overall impression is of a city that remained closely in touch with contemporary fashions emanating from Byzantium.

In fact, this observation will also continue to hold true for much of the following century. Just as the mosaic decorations of John VII need to be placed in the broader context of Byzantine art, so too do the ninth-century mosaic projects of Pope Paschal I (817–24) or the mural decorations in

---

[3] McCormick 1995: 362. For the gift of Greek books, *Codex epistolaris carolinus* 24, ed. Gundlach, p. 529.

[4] McCormick 1995: 358; McCormick 2001: 622–6; McCormick 2002; and Rio 2017: 35–6.

churches such as San Clemente *c.* 850 and Santa Maria de Secundicerio *c.* 875. It is telling, for example, that there remains a lively and completely unresolved debate regarding a profusely illustrated deluxe manuscript known as the *Sacra Parallela* (Paris, BNFr cod. gr. 923), a compendium of patristic passages, organized alphabetically by topic, whose initial compilation is usually associated with the anti-Iconoclast theologian John of Damascus. While few now doubt that this particular manuscript copy dates from approximately the middle of the ninth century, as yet there is no consensus whether it was written in Rome or Constantinople.[5]

Another change which emerges from our examination of the eighth century occurs in the cult of the saints. While there is no evidence of any diminution of interest in saints or their relics, there does seem to have been a rather dramatic shift in the identities of the specific saints whose cults were celebrated. This may have been abetted to some extent by the growth of 'religious tourism', as well as the possibility that Rome would lose some of the remains of its saintly protectors, but there were also strong political overtones. In the sixth and seventh centuries, the most popular cults had been eastern imports, for example, Cosmas and Damian, Sergius and Bacchus, or Abbacyrus and John. By the year 800, however, the focus was primarily, indeed almost exclusively, on indigenous 'Roman' saints: the early popes and martyrs, whose remains were increasingly being translated from the suburban catacombs into the city as part of a process of creating an *urbs sacra*. Their bodies assisted the city in the process of fulfilling its manifest destiny to have been chosen by God as the primary centre of Christianity. Rome now traded on both its name and its physical landscape, the latter pregnant with historic resonances of both antiquity and early Christianity. Ancient statues and buildings were given a new political spin, echoing the narrative by which Constantine had conveyed imperial authority to Pope Silvester. The shrine of Peter quickly became western Europe's top draw. One other aspect of Byzantine devotional practice remained deeply embedded, however: devotion to the 'Mother of God'. Images of Mary were everywhere, and many if not most depicted her with imperial regalia, seated on a sumptuous throne.

This survey of one of the most pivotal moments in Rome's long history will close with one final 'document' that can be associated with the city in the very last year of the eighth century: a manuscript of Pope Zacharias's Greek translation of the *Dialogues* of Pope Gregory I. As was noted in Chapter Six, this translation is singled out for mention in the *Liber*

---

[5] Osborne 2011a: 234–5.

pontificalis because it made an important papal text accessible to the 'many who do not know Latin' ('*plures qui Latinam ignorant*'), and it enjoyed a broad distribution; for example, it can be documented as reaching at least as far as Constantinople. The earliest surviving copy of the Greek version, BAV cod. gr. 1666, has a colophon on folio 185 v stating that the book was completed on 21 April of the year 6308, in other words 800 CE. The place of writing is not specified, but various clues, including invocations expressed in Latin but written in Greek characters, induced Pierre Battifol to suggest an origin in Rome or environs, a view that has never been challenged.[6]

What can Vat. gr. 1666 tell us about life in or near Rome in that year? To begin with, it constitutes additional evidence, should such be needed, that there was still a sufficient demand for Greek texts to make it worth someone's time, trouble, and expense to produce a book of this sort. Secondly, and perhaps much more importantly, it also provides our first indication that a new wave of cultural influence had started to reach central Italy, and its impact was being felt even in Greek-language scriptoria. This new impulse came not from the east, but instead from the north, from beyond the Alps.

As the name implies, the *Dialogues* is constructed as a conversation between Gregory and a deacon named Peter. It is divided into four books, and each opens with an enlarged and decorated initial. The first three – an 'M' (mu) on folio 3r (Fig. 11.1), an 'A' (alpha) on folio 42v, and an 'E' (epsilon) on folio 83r – are rather unexciting, all featuring the replacement of one or more of the strokes of the letter by a stylized fish, a practice common in Latin manuscripts produced in Italy since at least the sixth century.[7] But the fourth initial, the 'M' (mu) on folio 136v, is not only very much larger, but also uses an unprecedented ornamental vocabulary as well as a different palette, including the colour green. The central curve of the letter is formed by the body of a two-headed dragon, with each mouth grasping a wriggling snake that in turn is in the process of swallowing a fish; and the posts of the letter are decorated with interlaced knotwork reminiscent of the designs on contemporary sculpture (Fig. 11.2). It is quite unlike anything known to have been produced previously in any central Italian scriptorium, either Greek or Latin, although a Latin manuscript thought to have been written in Rome in the early years of the ninth century, the Codex Juvenianus (Rome, Bib. Vallicelliana MS B 25²), provides plentiful evidence of the same new direction.[8] The use of elaborately

---

[6] Battifol 1888; Grabar 1972: 30–1; Cavallo 1979; Spatharakis 1981: 6; Sansterre 1983 I: 169–70; and Osborne 1990: 77–80.
[7] Nordenfalk 1970: 166–70.
[8] Lowe 1934–71: no. 430; Mütherich 1976; and Osborne 1990: 82–4.

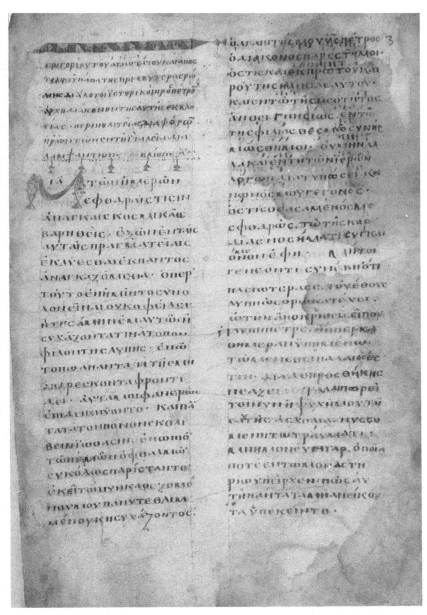

Fig. 11.1. Initial introducing Book I of the Greek translation of the *Dialogues* of Pope Gregory I, BAV, cod. gr. 1666, fol. 3r. © 2020 Biblioteca Apostolica Vaticana

decorated initials, a practice first developed in north-western Europe, may well have made the jump from Latin to Greek book culture in Rome. By the middle of the ninth century they were also beginning to appear in

Fig. 11.2. Initial introducing Book IV of the Greek translation of the *Dialogues* of Pope Gregory, BAV, cod. gr. 1666, fol. 136v. © 2020 Biblioteca Apostolica Vaticana

Constantinople;[9] and a similar west-to-east trajectory has been posited for the production of cloisonné enamel.[10]

Clemens Gantner has proposed that Rome, and more specifically the papacy, at this time became what he styles in anthropological terms a 'cultural broker'. The city stood on the frontier between two languages, Greek and Latin, two cultures, East and West, and also between the world of the past and that of the present. It was not simply the ideal place for interaction between all of these disparate components, but perhaps the only place where this process of cohabitation and intermingling could happen.

The flow of history is of course a never-ending stream of actors and events. But as we look backwards over the city's last 1200 years, the eighth century stands out as the moment when those who became the bishops of Rome, and their colleagues both clerical and secular, laid the groundwork for much of that subsequent millennium and beyond. And of course the papal state, even if much diminished after the Italian *Risorgimento*, still remains intact today, as too does the notion, albeit certainly disputed, of a universal Christian church with Rome at its centre.

[9] Brubaker 1991. [10] Buckton 1988.

Bibliography

Primary sources

Agnellus, *Liber pontificalis ecclesiae Ravennatis*, D. Mauskopf Deliyannis (ed.) (Corpus Christianorum Continuatio Mediaevalis 199) (Turnhout: Brepols, 2006); English translation, D. Mauskopf Deliyannis, *The Book of Pontiffs of the Church of Ravenna* (Washington: Catholic University of America Press, 2004).

Alcuin, *De pontificibus et sanctis ecclesiae Eboracensis*, J.-P. Migne (ed.), *PL* 101, 812–46; English translation, P. Godman, *The Bishops, Kings, and Saints of York* (Oxford: Clarendon Press, 1982).

Alcuin, *Epistolae*, E. Dümmler (ed.), MGH Epistolae IV: Epistolae Karolini aevi II (Berlin: Weidmann, 1895), 1–481.

Anon., *De locis sanctis martyrum quae sunt foris civitatis Romae*, R. Valentini and G. Zucchetti (eds.), *Codice Topografico della Città di Roma* II (Rome: Istituto Storico Italiano per il Medio Evo, 1942), 101–31; and *Itineraria et alia geographica*, CCSL 175 (Turnhout: Brepols, 1965), 313–22.

Anon., *Laudes mediolanensis civitatis*, E. Dümmler (ed.), MGH Poetae Latini aevi Carolini I (Berlin: Weidmann, 1881), 24–6.

Anon., *Libellus de imperatoria potestate in urbe Roma*, G. Zucchetti (ed.) (Fonti per la Storia d'Italia 55) (Rome: Istituto Storico Italiano per il Medio Evo, 1920).

Anon., *Notitia ecclesiarum urbis Romae*, R. Valentini and G. Zucchetti (eds.) *Codice Topografico della Città di Roma* II (Rome: Istituto Storico Italiano per il Medio Evo, 1942), 67–99; and *Itineraria et alia geographica*, CCSL 175 (Turnhout: Brepols, 1965), 303–11.

Bede, *De temporum ratione*, T. Mommsen (ed.), MGH Auctores Antiquissimi XIII (Berlin: Weidmann, 1898), 247–327; English translation, F. Wallis, *Bede: The Reckoning of Time* (Liverpool: Liverpool University Press, 1999).

Benedict of Monte Soratte, *Chronicon*, G. Zucchetti (ed.) (Fonti per la Storia d'Italia 55) (Rome: Istituto Storico Italiano per il Medio Evo, 1920).

Codex epistolaris carolinus, W. Gundlach (ed.), MGH Epistolae III: Epistolae Merowingici et Karolini aevi I (Berlin: Weidmann, 1892, repr. 1957), 469–657.

Codice topografico della città di Roma, R. Valentini and G. Zucchetti (eds.), 4 vols. (Rome: Istituto Storico Italiano per il Medio Evo, 1940–53).

Constitutum Constantini, H. Fuhrmann (ed.), *Das Constitutum Constantini*, MGH Fontes iuris Germanici antiqui in usum scholarum separatim editi X (Hanover: Hahn, 1968).

Gregory I, Pope, *Dialogi*, U. Moricca (ed.) (Fonti per la Storia d'Italia 57) (Rome: Istituto Storico Italiano per il Medio Evo, 1924).

Gregory I, Pope, *Homiliae in Ezechielem*, J. P. Migne (ed.), *PL* 76, 786–1074; English translation, T. Gray, *The Homilies of Saint Gregory the Great on the Book of the Prophet Ezekiel* (Etna, CA: Center for Traditionalist Orthodox Studies, 1990).

Gregory I, Pope, *Registrum Epistolarum Libri I–VII*, P. Ewald and L. Hartmann (eds.), MGH Epistolae I (Berlin: Weidmann, 1891).

Gregory of Tours, *De gloria martyrum*, B. Krusch (ed.) MGH Scriptores rerum Merovingicarum I, pt. 2 (Hanover: Hahn, 1885, repr. 1969), 34–111; English translation, R. Van Dam, *Glory of the Martyrs* (Liverpool: Liverpool University Press, 1988).

Gregory of Tours, *Historia Francorum*, B. Krusch and W. Levison (eds.), MGH Scriptores rerum Merovingicarum I, pt. 1 (rev. ed., Hanover: Hahn, 1965); English translation, O.M. Dalton, *The History of the Franks*, 2 vols. (Oxford: The Clarendon Press, 1927).

Le Liber Pontificalis: texte, introduction, et commentaire, L. Duchesne (ed.), 2 vols. (Paris: Ernest Thorin, 1886–92). *Tome troisième. Additions et corrections par Cyrille Vogel* (Paris: E. de Boccard, 1955).

[Magister] Gregorius, *Narracio de mirabilibus urbis Romae*, R. B. C. Huygens (ed.) (Leiden: Brill, 1970); English translation, J. Osborne, *Master Gregorius: The Marvels of Rome* (Toronto: Pontifical Institute of Mediaeval Studies, 1987).

Moduin of Autun, *Ecloga*, E. Dümmler (ed.), MGH Poetae Latini aevi Carolini I (Berlin: Weidmann, 1881), 382–92; English translation, P. Godman, *Poetry of the Carolingian Renaissance* (London: Duckworth, 1985), pp. 190–6.

Les 'Ordines Romani' du Haut Moyen Age, M. Andrieu (ed.), 5 vols. (Louvain: Spicilegium sacrum Lovaniense, 1931–61).

Panvinio, Onofrio, *De sacrosancta basilica, baptisterio et patriarchio Lateranensi*, P. Lauer (ed.), *Le palais du Latran: étude historique et archéologique* (Paris: Ernest Leroux, 1911), 410–90.

Patrologiae cursus completus, Series Latina (Patrologia Latina), J. -P. Migne (ed.), 221 vols. (Paris: Garnier, 1841–64).

Paul the Deacon, *Historia Langobardorum*, L. Bethmann and G. Waitz (eds.), MGH Scriptores Rerum Langobardicarum et Italicarum saec. VI–IX (Hanover: Hahn, 1878), 7–192.

Photios, *Bibliothèque*, trans. R. Henry, 9 vols. (Paris: Belles lettres, 1959–91).

Pliny the Elder, *Natural History*, trans. H. Rackham, 10 vols. (Cambridge, MA: Harvard University Press, 1949–62).

Procopius, *History of the Wars*, trans. H. B. Dewing, 5 vols. (London: William Heinemann, 1914–28).

Stephanus, *Vita Wilfridi I. Episcopi Eboracensis*, W. Levison (ed.), MGH Scriptores rerum Merovingicarum VI (Hanover: Hahn, 1913), 163–263.

Venantius Fortunatus, *Vita Sancti Martini*, F. Leo (ed.), MGH Auctores Antiquissimi IV, pt. 1 (repr. Berlin: Weidmann, 1961), 293-370.

Walahfrid Strabo, *Carmina*, E. Dümmler (ed.), MGH Poetae Latini aevi Carolini II (Berlin: Weidmann, 1884), 259-473.

Zosimus, *New History. A translation with commentary by Ronald T. Ridley* (Byzantina Australiensia 2) (Sydney: Australian Association for Byzantine Studies, 1982).

Secondary sources

Acconci, A. 2002 'Note sulla decorazione pittorica altomedievale del nartece pelagiano di San Lorenzo fuori le mura', in F. Guidobaldi and A. Guiglia Guidobaldi (eds.), *Ecclesiae Urbis. Atti del Congresso Internazionale di Studi sulle Chiese di Roma (IV-X secolo). Roma, 4-10 settembre 2000* (Vatican City: Pontificio Istituto di Archeologia Cristiana), 1789-1812.

Aimone, M. 2019 'A Roman *cathedra episcopalis* from the era of Pope Hadrian I', *Gesta* 58: 27-54.

Amato, P. 1988 *'De Vera Effigie Mariae': Antiche Icone Romane* (Milan: Arnoldo Mondadori).

Amato, S. R., D. Bersani, P. P. Lottici, P. Pogliani and C. Pelosi 2017 'A multi-analytical approach to the study of the mural paintings in the presbytery of Santa Maria Antiqua al Foro Romano in Rome', *Archaeometry* 59: 1050-64.

Andaloro, M. 1972-3 'La datazione della tavola di S. Maria in Trastevere', *Rivista dell'Istituto Nazionale di Archeologia e Storia dell'Arte* 19-20:138-215.

Andaloro, M. 1976 'Il *Liber Pontificalis* e la questione delle immagini da Sergio I a Adriano I', in *Roma e l'Età Carolingia. Atti delle giornate di studio, 3-8 maggio 1976* (Rome: Multigrafica Editrice), 69-77.

Andaloro, M. 1986 'I mosaici parietali di Durazzo o dell'origine costantinopolitana del tema iconografico di Maria Regina', in O. Feld and U. Peschlow (eds.), *Studien zur spätantiken und byzantinischen Kunst: Friedrich Wilhelm Deichmann gewidmet*, 3 vols. (Bonn: Rudolf Habelt), III, 103-12.

Andaloro, M. 1989 'I mosaici dell'oratorio di Giovanni VII', in M. Andaloro, A. Ghidoli, A. Iacobini, S. Romano, and A. Tomei (eds.), *Fragmenta picta: Affreschi e mosaici staccati del Medioevo romano* (Rome: Argos edizioni), 169-77.

Andaloro, M. 2001 'S. Susanna. Gli affreschi frammentati', in M. S. Arena, P. Delogu, L. Paroli, M. Ricci, L. Saguì, and L. Vendittelli (eds.), *Roma dall'Antichità al Medioevo. Archeologia e Storia nel Museo Nazionale Romano Crypta Balbi* (Milan: Electa), 643-5.

Andaloro, M. 2001-2 'Immagine e immagini nel Liber Pontificalis da Adriano I a Pasquale I', in H. Geertman (ed.), *Atti del Colloquio Internazionale Il 'Liber Pontificalis' e la storia materiale (Roma, 21-22 febbraio 2002)* (= Mededelingen van het Nederlands Instituut te Rome 60-61), 45-103.

Andaloro, M. 2002 'Le icone a Roma in età preiconoclasta', *Roma fra Oriente e Occidente*, Settimane di Studio del CISAM 49 (Spoleto: Centro Italiano di Studi sull'Alto Medioevo), 719–53.

Andaloro, M. 2003 'I dipinti murali depositati nel sarcofago dell'area di Santa Susanna a Roma', in E. Russo (ed.), *1983-1993: dieci anni di archeologia cristiana in Italia. Atti del VII Congresso nazionale di archeologia cristiana (Cassino, 20-24 settembre 1993)* (Cassino: Edizioni dell'Università degli Studi di Cassino), 377–83.

Andaloro, M. 2004 'La parete palinsesto: 1900, 2000', in J. Osborne, J. R. Brandt, and G. Morganti (eds.), *Santa Maria Antiqua cento anni dopo* (Rome: Campisano), 97–111.

Andaloro, M. 2005 'I papi e l'immagine prima e dopo Nicea', in A. C. Quintavalle (ed.), *Medioevo: immagini e ideologie (Atti del Convegno internazionale di studi, Parma, 23-27 settembre 2002)* (Milan: Electa), 525–40.

Andaloro, M. 2016a 'L'*imago antiqua* e il ritorno nella sua chiesa', in M. Andaloro, G. Bordi, and G. Morganti (eds.), *Santa Maria Antiqua tra Roma e Bisanzio* (Milan: Electa), 190–6.

Andaloro, M. 2016b 'L'Adorazione dei Magi', in M. Andaloro, G. Bordi, and G. Morganti (eds.), *Santa Maria Antiqua tra Roma e Bisanzio* (Milan: Electa), 256–9.

Andaloro, M. 2020 'The icon of S. Maria Nova after S. Maria Antiqua', in E. Rubery, G. Bordi, and J. Osborne (eds.), *Santa Maria Antiqua: the Sistine Chapel of the Eighth Century* (Turnhout: Brepols), in press.

Andaloro, M., E. Anselmi, and C. D'Angelo 2017 'Antica Basilica di San Pietro, Oratorio di Giovanni VII. Il mosaico con la Vergine dalla scena della Natività (705-707): Le vicende e l'attività del cantiere musivo', in M. Andaloro and C. D'Angelo (eds.), *Mosaici medievali a Roma attraverso il restauro dell'ICR. 1991-2004* (Rome: Gangemi), 187–94.

Andaloro, M. and G. Matthiae 1987 *Pittura Romana del medioevo: secoli IV-X. Aggiornamento scientifico e bibliografia* (Rome: Fratelli Palombi).

Angelova, D. 2004 'The ivories of Ariadne and ideas about female imperial authority in Rome and early Byzantium', *Gesta* 43: 1–15.

Ansaldi, G. R. 1953 'Un'antica icone della Vergine', *Studi bizantini e neoellenici* 8: 63–72.

Aronen, J. 1989 'La sopravvivenza dei culti pagani e la topografia cristiana dell'area di Giuturna e nelle sue adiacenze', in E. M. Steinby (ed.), *Lacus Iuturnae* (Rome: De Luca), 148–74.

Augenti, A. 1996 *Il Palatino nel Medioevo: archeologia e topografia (secoli VI-XIII)* (Rome: L'Erma di Bretschneider).

Augenti, A. 2000 'Giacomo Boni, gli scavi di Santa Maria Antiqua e l'archeologia medievale a Roma all'inizio del Novecento', *Archeologia Medievale* 27: 39–46. Also published in J. Osborne, J. R. Brandt, and G. Morganti (eds.) *Santa Maria*

Antiqua al Foro Romano cento anni dopo. Atti del colloquio internazionale, Roma, 5–6 maggio 2000 (Rome: Campisano, 2004), 31–9.

Augenti, A. 2016 *Archeologia dell'Italia medievale* (Rome: Edizioni Laterza).

Auzépy, M.-F. 1990 'La destruction de l'icône de la Chalké par Léon III: propagande ou réalité?', *Byzantion* 60: 445–92.

Baldovin, J. 1987 *The Urban Character of Christian Worship. The Origins, Development, and Meaning of Stational Liturgy* (Rome: Pontificio Istituto Orientale).

Ballardini, A. 2010 'Scultura a Roma: standards qualitivi e committenza (VIII secolo)', in V. Pace (ed.), *L'VIII secolo: un secolo inquieto. Atti del Convegno internazionale di studi, Cividale del Friuli, 4–7 dicembre 2008* (Cividale del Friuli: Comune di Cividale del Friuli), 141–8.

Ballardini, A. 2011 'Un oratorio per la *Theotokos*: Giovanni VII (705–707) committente a San Pietro', in A. C. Quintavalle (ed.), *Medioevo: i committenti. Atti del Convegno internazionale di studi, Parma, 21–26 settembre 2010* (Milan: Electa), 94–116.

Ballardini, A. 2015 '"In antiquissimo ac venerabilis Lateranensi palatio": la residenza dei pontefici secondo il *Liber Pontificalis*', in *Le Corti nell'Alto Medioevo*, Settimane di Studio del CISAM 62 (Spoleto: Centro Italiano di Studi sull'Alto Medioevo), 889–927.

Ballardini, A. 2016a 'Il perduto Oratorio di Giovanni VII nella basilica di San Pietro in Vaticano. Architettura e scultura', in M. Andaloro, G. Bordi, and G. Morganti (eds.), *Santa Maria Antiqua tra Roma e Bisanzio* (Milan: Electa), 220–7.

Ballardini, A. 2016b 'Piattaforma di ambone in Santa Maria Antiqua', in M. Andaloro, G. Bordi, and G. Morganti (eds.), *Santa Maria Antiqua tra Roma e Bisanzio* (Milan: Electa), 228–30.

Ballardini, A. 2016c 'Titulus dell'Oratorio di Giovanni VII', in M. Andaloro, G. Bordi, and G. Morganti (eds.), *Santa Maria Antiqua tra Roma e Bisanzio* (Milan: Electa), 231–3.

Ballardini, A. and P. Pogliani 2013 'A reconstruction of the oratory of John VII (705–707)', in R. McKitterick, J. Osborne, C. Richardson, and J. Story (eds.), *Old Saint Peter's, Rome* (Cambridge: Cambridge University Press), 190–213.

Barber, C. 1991 'The Koimesis church, Nicaea. The limits of representation on the eve of Iconoclasm', *Jahrbuch der österreichischen Byzantinistik* 41: 43–60.

Barral i Altet, X. 2016 'L'VIII secolo: da Giovanni VI (701–705) ad Adriano I (772–795)', in M. D'Onofrio (ed.), *La committenza artistica dei papi a Roma nel Medioevo* (Rome: Viella), 181–212.

Bartlett, R. 1994 'Symbolic meanings of hair in the Middle Ages', *Transactions of the Royal Historical Society*, 6th ser., 4: 43–60.

Bartoli A. 1947–9 'L'ultimo relitto dell'archivio imperiale sul Palatino', *Atti della Pontificia Accademia Romana di Archeologia. Rendiconti* 23–4: 269–75.

Bartoli, A. 1963 *Curia Senatus. Lo scavo e il restauro* (Rome: Istituto di Studi Romani).

Bartolini, D. 1879 *Di S. Zaccaria papa e degli anni del suo pontificato* (Ratisbon [Regensburg]: Pustet).

Bartoloni, G. (ed.) 2010 *La Lupa Capitolina: Nuove prospettive di studio* (Rome: 'L'ERMA' di Bretschneider).

Battifol, P. 1888 'Librairies byzantines à Rome', *Mélanges d'Archéologie et d'Histoire* 8: 297–308.

Bauer, F. A. 1997 'Das Bild der Stadt Rom in karolingischer Zeit: Der Anonymous Einsidlensis', *Römische Quartalschrift für christliche Altertumskunde und Kirchengeschichte* 92: 190–228.

Bauer, F. A. 1997–8 'Papst Hadrian I und die Krypta von S. Maria in Cosmedin', *Römisches Jahrbuch der Bibliotheca Hertziana* 32: 135–78.

Bauer, F. A. 1999a 'La frammentazione liturgica nella chiesa romana del primo medioevo', *Rivista di Archeologia Cristiana* 75: 385–446.

Bauer, F. A. 1999b 'Die Bau- und Stiftungspolitik der Päpste Hadrian I. (772–795) und Leo III. (795–816)', in C. Stiegemann and M. Wemhoff (eds.), *799. Kunst und Kultur der Karolingerzeit. Karl der Große und Papst Leo III. in Paderborn. Beiträge zum Katalog der Ausstellung* (Mainz: Philipp von Zabern), 514–28.

Bauer, F. A. 2001–2 'Il rinnovamento di Roma sotto Adriano I alla luce del Liber Pontificalis', in H. Geertman (ed.), *Atti del colloquio internazionale Il Liber Pontificalis e la storia materiale (Roma, 21–22 febbraio 2002)* (= Mededelingen van het Nederlands Instituut te Rome 60–61), 189–203.

Bauer, F. A. 2004 *Das Bild der Stadt Rom im Frühmittelalter: Papststiftungen im Spiegel des Liber Pontificalis von Gregor dem Dritten bis zu Leo dem Dritten* (Wiesbaden: Ludwig Reichert).

Bavant, B. 1979 'Le duché byzantin de Rome. Origine, durée et extension géographique', *Mélanges de l'École Française de Rome. Moyen Age – Temps Modernes* 91: 41–88.

Baynes, N. 1949 'The supernatural defenders of Byzantium', *Analecta Bollandiana* 67: 165–77.

Beckwith, J. 1975 'Some early Byzantine rock crystals', in G. Robertson and G. Henderson (eds.), *Studies in Memory of David Talbot Rice* (Edinburgh: Edinburgh University Press), 1–5.

Bellardini, D. and P. Delogu 2002 'Liber Pontificalis e altre fonti: la topografia di Roma nell'VIII secolo', in H. Geertman (ed.), *Atti del colloquio internazionale Il 'Liber Pontificalis' e la storia materiale (Roma, 21–22 febbraio 2002)* (= Mededelingen van het Nederlands Instituut te Rome 60–61), 205–23.

Bellini, M. and P. Brunori 2016 'Nota sull'ipotesi ricostruttiva dell'ambone di Giovanni VII in Santa Maria Antiqua', in M. Andaloro, G. Bordi, and G. Morganti (eds.), *Santa Maria Antiqua tra Roma e Bisanzio* (Milan: Electa), 234–9.

Belting, H. 1961 'Das Fassadenmosaik des Atriums von Alt St. Peter in Rom', *Wallraf-Richartz-Jahrbuch* 23: 37–54.

Belting, H. 1968 *Studien zur beneventanischen Malerei* (Wiesbaden: F. Steiner).

Belting, H. 1976 'I mosaici dell'aula Leonina come testimonianza della prima "renovatio" nell'arte medievale di Roma', in *Roma e l'Età Carolingia. Atti delle giornate di studio, 3–8 maggio 1976* (Rome: Multigrafica Editrice), 167–82.

Belting, H. 1978 'Die beiden Palastaulen Leos III. im Lateran und die Entstehung einer päpstlichen Programmkunst', *Frühmittelalterliche Studien* 12: 55–83.

Belting, H. 1987 'Eine Privatkapelle im frühmittelalterlichen Rom', *Dumbarton Oaks Papers* 41: 55–69.

Beneš, C. 1999 'Cola di Rienzo and the "Lex regia"', *Viator* 30: 231–51.

Bernabò, M. 2008 'Miniature e decorazione', in M. Bernabò (ed.), *Il Tetravangelo di Rabbula (Firenze, Biblioteca Medicea Laurenziana, Plut. 1.56): l'illustrazione del Nuovo Testamento nella Siria del VI secolo* (Rome: Edizioni di Storia e Letteratura), 79–112.

Bernabò, M. 2014 'The miniatures of the Rabbula Gospels: Postscripta to a Recent Book', *Dumbarton Oaks Papers* 68: 343–58.

Bertelli, C. 1961 *La Madonna di Santa Maria in Trastevere: storia, iconografia, stile di un dipinto romano dell'ottavo secolo* (Rome: [publisher not identified]).

Bertelli, C. 1970 'Caput Sancti Anastasii', *Paragone* 247: 12–25.

Bertelli, C. 2016 'Un frammento di affresco strappato con Sant'Agata', in M. Andaloro, G. Bordi, and G. Morganti (eds.), *Santa Maria Antiqua tra Roma e Bisanzio* (Milan: Electa), 197–9.

Bertolini, O. 1947 'Per la storia delle Diaconie romane nell'alto Medio Evo sino alla fine del secolo VIII', *Archivio della Società Romana di Storia Patria* 70: 1–145.

Bertolini, O. 1973 'Le origini del potere temporale e del dominio temporale dei papi', *I problemi dell'Occidente nel secolo VIII*, Settimane di Studio del CISAM 20 (Spoleto: Centro Italiano di Studi sull'Alto Medioevo), 231–55.

Bischoff, B. 1998–2017 *Katalog der festländischen Handschriften des neunten Jahrhunderts*, 4 vols. (Wiesbaden: Harrassowitz).

Bisconti, F. 2004 'L'affresco di Sant'Agostino', in P. Liverani (ed.), *Giornata di studio tematica dedicata al Patriarchio Lateranense* (= Mélanges d'Archéologie et d'Histoire. Antiquité 116.1), 51–78, and discussion, 112–14.

Boholm, Å. 1997 'Reinvented histories: medieval Rome as memorial landscape', *Ecumene* 4: 247–72.

Bolgia, C. 2006 'The mosaics of Gregory IV at S. Marco, Rome: papal response to Venice, Byzantium and the Carolingians', *Speculum* 81: 1–34.

Bonifay, M., L. Paroli, and M. Picon 1986 'Ceramiche a vetrina pesante scoperte a Roma e a Marsiglia: resultati delle prime analisi fisico-chimiche', *Archeologia Medievale* 13: 79–95.

Borchardt, P. 1936 'The sculpture in front of the Lateran as described by Benjamin of Tudela and Magister Gregorius', *Journal of Roman Studies* 26: 68–70.

Bordi, G. 2000 'L'affresco *staccato* dalla Chiesa di S. Adriano al Foro Romano. Una nuova lettura', *Studi Romani* 48: 5–25.

Bordi, G. 2001 'Sant'Adriano al Foro Romano e gli affreschi altomedievale', in M. S. Arena, P. Delogu, L. Paroli, M. Ricci, L. Saguì, and L. Vendittelli (eds.), *Roma dall'Antichità al Medioevo. Archeologia e Storia nel Museo Nazionale Romano Crypta Balbi* (Milan: Electa), 478–83.

Bordi, G. 2006a 'San Clemente, basilica inferiore', in M. Andaloro (ed.), *Pittura Medievale a Roma, 312–1431. Atlante I: Suburbio, Vaticano, Rione Monti* (Milan: Jaca Book), 177–90.

Bordi, G. 2006b 'San Lorenzo fuori le mura', in M. Andaloro (ed.), *Pittura Medievale a Roma, 312–1431. Atlante I: Suburbio, Vaticano, Rione Monti* (Milan: Jaca Book), 77–94.

Bordi, G. 2008 *Gli affreschi di San Saba sul piccolo Aventino. Dove e come erano* (Milan: Jaca Book).

Bordi 2009a 'Giuseppe Wilpert e la scoperta della pittura altomedievale a Roma', in S. Heid (ed.), *Giuseppe Wilpert archeologo cristiano: Atti del convegno (Roma, 16–19 maggio 2007)* (Vatican City: Pontificio Istituto di Archeologia Cristiana), 323–58.

Bordi, G. 2009b 'Copie, fotografie, aquerelli. Documentare la pittura medievale a Roma in Otto e Novecento', in A. C. Quintavalle (ed.), *Medioevo: immagine e memoria. Atti del Convegno internazionale di studi, Parma, 23–28 settembre 2008* (Milan: Electa), 454–62.

Bordi, G. 2011 'Committenza laica nella Chiesa di Sant'Adriano al Foro romano nell'alto Medioevo', in A. C. Quintavalle (ed.), *Medioevo: i committenti. Atti del Convegno internazionale di studi, Parma, 21–26 settembre 2010* (Milan: Electa), 420–33.

Bordi, G. 2014 'Santa Maria Antiqua. Prima di Maria Regina', in G. Bordi, I. Carlettini, M.L. Fobelli, M. R. Menna, and P. Pogliani (eds.), *L'officina dello sguardo: scritti in onore di Maria Andaloro* 2 vols. (Rome: Gangemi), I, 285–90.

Bordi, G. 2015 'Tra pittura e parete. Palinsesti, riusi e obliterazioni nella diaconia di Santa Maria in Via Lata tra VI e XI secolo', in A. Molinari, R. Santangeli Valenzani, and L. Spera (eds.), *L'archeologia della produzione a Roma (secoli V–XV). Atti del Convegno internazionale di studi, 27–29 marzo 2014* (Collection de l'École française de Rome 516) (Bari: Edipuglia), 395–410.

Bordi, G. 2016a 'Santa Maria Antiqua attraverso i suoi palinsesti pittorici', in M. Andaloro, G. Bordi, and G. Morganti (eds.), *Santa Maria Antiqua tra Roma e Bisanzio* (Milan: Electa), 34–53.

Bordi, G. 2016b 'La cappella del "primicerius" Theodoto', in M. Andaloro, G. Bordi, and G. Morganti (eds.), *Santa Maria Antiqua tra Roma e Bisanzio* (Milan: Electa), 260–9.

Bordi, G. 2016c 'Frammenti inediti dal ciclo pittorico dei Quaranta Martiri di Sebaste', in M. Andaloro, G. Bordi, and G. Morganti (eds.), *Santa Maria Antiqua tra Roma e Bisanzio* (Milan: Electa), 362–3.

Bordi, G. 2016d 'Laïcs, nobles et parvenus dans la peinture murale à Rome du VIIIe au XIIe siècle', *Les Cahiers de Saint-Michel de Cuxa* 47: 37–44.

Bordi, G. and A. Guiglia Guidobaldi 2016 'Elementi di opus sectile parietale in marmo e in vetro', in M. Andaloro, G. Bordi, and G. Morganti (eds.), *Santa Maria Antiqua tra Roma e Bisanzio* (Milan: Electa), 364–5.

Bordino, C. 2016 'Nella cappella dei santi *anargyroi* in Santa Maria Antiqua', in M. Andaloro, G. Bordi, and G. Morganti (eds.), *Santa Maria Antiqua tra Roma e Bisanzio* (Milan: Electa), 200–11.

Borgolte, M. 1989 *Petrusnachfolge und Kaiserimitation. Die Grablegen der Päpste, ihre Genese und Traditionsbildung* (Göttingen: Vandenhoeck and Ruprecht).

Bosio, A. 1632 *Roma sotteranea* (Rome: Facciotti).

Bowes, K. and J. Mitchell 2009 'The main chapel of the Durres amphitheater: decoration and chronology', *Mélanges de l'École française de Rome. Antiquité* 121: 569–95.

Brandenburg, H. 1968–69 'Das Grab des Papstes Cornelius und die Lucinaregion der Calixtus-Katakombe', *Jahrbuch für Antike und Christentum* 11–12: 42–54.

Breckenridge, J. D. 1959 *The Numismatic Iconography of Justinian II* (New York: American Numismatic Society).

Breckenridge, J. D. 1972a 'Evidence for the nature of relations between Pope John VII and the Byzantine Emperor Justinian II', *Byzantinische Zeitschrift* 65: 364–74.

Breckenridge, J. D. 1972b 'The Iconoclasts' Image of Christ', *Gesta* 11: 3–8.

Bréhier, L. 1903 'Les colonies d'orientaux en occident au commencement du moyen-âge', *Byzantinische Zeitschrift* 12: 1–39.

Brenk, B. 2004 'Papal patronage in a Greek church in Rome', in J. Osborne, J. R. Brandt, and G. Morganti (eds.), *Santa Maria Antiqua al Foro Romano cento anni dopo. Atti del colloquio internazionale, Roma, 5–6 maggio 2000* (Rome: Campisano Editore), 67–81.

Brenk, B. 2010 *The Apse, the Image, and the Icon: An Historical Perspective of the Apse as a Space for Images* (Wiesbaden: Reichert).

Brogiolo, G. P. 1999 'La nuova sequenza architettonica e il problema degli affreschi del S. Salvatore di Brescia', in A. Cadei, M. Righetti Tosti-Croce, and A. Segagni Malacart (eds.), *Arte d'Occidente: temi e metodi. Scritti in onore di Angiola Maria Romanini* (Rome: Sintesi Informazione), 25–34.

Brogiolo, G. P. 2014 'Dalla fondazione del monastero al mito di Ansa e Santa Giulia', in G.P. Brogiolo and F. Morandini (eds.), *Dalla corte regia al monastero di San Salvatore-Santa Giulia di Brescia* (Mantua: SAP Società Archeologica), 17–33.

Brown, P. 1973 'A Dark-Age crisis: aspects of the Iconoclastic controversy', *English Historical Review* 88: 1–34.

Brown, T. S. 1984 *Gentlemen and Officers. Imperial Administration and Aristocratic Power in Byzantine Italy A.D. 554–800* (London: British School at Rome).

Brown, T. S. 1988 'The interplay between Roman and Byzantine traditions and local sentiment in the Exarchate of Ravenna', *Bisanzio, Roma e l'Italia nell'Alto Medioevo*, Settimane di Studio del CISAM 34 (Spoleto: Centro Italiano di Studi sull'Alto Medioevo), 127–60.

Brown, T. S. 1995a 'Byzantine Italy, *c*.680–*c*.876', in R. McKitterick (ed.), *The New Cambridge Medieval History. Volume II: c.700–c.900* (Cambridge: Cambridge University Press), 320–48.

Brown, T. S. 1995b 'Justinian II and Ravenna', *Byzantinoslavica* 56: 29–36.

Brubaker, L. 1991 'The introduction of painted initials in Byzantium', *Scriptorium* 45: 22–46.

Brubaker, L. 2004 '100 years of solitude: Santa Maria Antiqua and the history of Byzantine Art History', in J. Osborne, J.R. Brandt, and G. Morganti (eds.), *Santa Maria Antiqua al Foro Romano cento anni dopo. Atti del colloquio internazionale, Roma, 5–6 maggio 2000* (Rome: Campisano Editore), 41–7.

Brubaker, L. 2010 'The visualization of gift giving in Byzantium and the mosaics of Hagia Sophia', in W. Davies and P. Fouracre (eds.), *The Languages of Gift in the Early Middle Ages* (Cambridge: Cambridge University Press), 33–61.

Brubaker, L. and J. Haldon 2001 *Byzantium in the Iconoclast Era (ca. 680–850): The Sources* (Aldershot: Ashgate).

Brunet, E. 2007 'Note circa l'uso del simbolo dell'*Agnus Dei* nella scultura altomedievale (Italia centro-settentrionale)', *Venezia Arti* 21: 5–18.

Buckton, D. 1988 'Byzantine enamel and the West', *Byzantinische Forschungen* 13: 235–44.

Buddensieg, T. 1965 'Gregory the Great, the destroyer of Pagan idols. The history of a medieval legend concerning the decline of ancient art and literature', *Journal of the Warburg and Courtauld Institutes* 28: 44–65.

Buddensieg, T. 1983 'Die Statuenstiftung Sixtus' IV im Jahre 1471', *Römisches Jahrbuch für Kunstgeschichte* 20: 33–73.

Bullough, D. 1977 'Roman books and Carolingian "Renovatio"', in D. Baker (ed.), *Renaissance and Renewal in Christian History* (Oxford: Blackwell), 23–50.

Burgarella, F. 2001 'Il Senato', *Roma nell'Alto Medioevo*, Settimane di Studio del CISAM 48 (Spoleto: Centro Italiano di Studi sull'Alto Medioevo), 121–75.

Burgarella, F. 2002 'Presenze greche a Roma: aspetti culturali e religiosi', in *Roma fra Oriente e Occidente*, Settimane di Studio dell CISAM 49 (Spoleto: Centro Italiano di Studi sull'Alto Medioevo), 943–88.

Cagiano de Azevedo, M. 1949 'Il restauro di una delle pitture di S. Maria Antiqua', *Bollettino d'arte* 24: 60–2.

Calabria, P. and G. De Spirito 1995 'La zecca di Roma tra fine VII ed VIII secolo: una vexata quaestio', in *Akten des XII. internationalen Kongresses für christliche Archäologie (Bonn, 22–28 September 1991)* (= *Jahrbuch für Antike und Christentum*, Ergänzungsband 20) (Münster: Aschendorff), 603–8.

Calvelli, L. 2012 'Pociora legis precepta. Considerazioni sull'epigrafia giuridica esposta in Laterano fra Medioevo e Rinascimento', in J.-L. Ferrary (ed.), *Leges publicae. La legge nell'esperienza giuridica romana* (Pavia: IUSS Press), 593–625.

Cameron, A. 1978 'The Theotokos in sixth-century Constantinople', *Journal of Theological Studies* N.S. 29: 79–108.

Cannizzaro, M. E. 1901 'Nuove scoperte nella città e nel suburbio', *Notizie degli scavi di antichità*: 10–14.

Cannizzaro, M. E. and I. C. Gavini 1902 'Nuove scoperte avvenute nella Chiesa di S. Saba sul falso Aventino', *Notizie degli scavi di antichità*: 270–3, 465–6.

Capo, L. 2009 *Il 'Liber Pontificalis', i Longobardi e la nascita del dominio territoriale della chiesa di Roma* (Spoleto: Centro Italiano di Studi sull'Alto Medioevo).

Carboni, F. 2016 'Un complesso altomedievale nel cuore della *Domus Tiberiana*', in M. Andaloro, G. Bordi, and G. Morganti (eds.), *Santa Maria Antiqua tra Roma e Bisanzio* (Milan: Electa), 86–95.

Cardin, L. 2008 *Epigrafia a Roma nel primo medioevo (secoli IV–X): modelli grafici e tipologie d'uso* (Rome: Jouvence).

Carletti, C. 1986 'I graffiti sull'affresco di S. Luca nel Cimitero di Commodilla. Addenda et corrigenda', *Atti della Pontificia Accademia Romana di Archeologia, Rendiconti* 57: 129–43.

Carletti, C. 2002 '"Scrivere i santi": epigrafia del pellegrinaggio a Roma nei secoli VII–IX', *Roma fra Oriente e Occidente*, Settimane di Studio del CISAM 49 (Spoleto: Centro Italiano di Studi sull'Alto Medioevo), 323–60.

Carruba, A. M. 2006 *La Lupa Capitolina. Un bronzo medievale* (Rome: De Luca Editori d'Arte).

Cavallo, G. 1979 'Interazione tra scrittura greca e scrittura latina a Roma tra VIII e IX secolo', in P. Cockshaw, M.-C. Garand, and P. Jodogne (eds.), *Miscellanea Codicologica F. Masai dicata* (Ghent: Story-Scientia) I, 23–9.

Cavallo, G. 1988 'Le tipologie della cultura nel riflesso delle testimonianze scritte', *Bisanzio, Roma e l'Italia nell'Alto Medioevo*, Settimane di Studio del CISAM 34 (Spoleto: Centro Italiano di Studi sull'Alto Medioevo), 467–516.

Cecchelli, M and A. Milella, R. Varoli-Piazza, C. d'Angelo, P. Bianchetti, M. Marabelli, P. Santopadre, P. Cini, F. Mallegni, and B. Lippi 2004 'Santa Susanna', in L. Paroli and L. Vendittelli (eds.), *Roma dall'antichità al medioevo II: contesti tardoantichi e altomedievali* (Milan: Electa), 328–41.

Cellini, P. 1950 'Una Madonna molto antica', *Proporzioni* 3: 1–6.

Chastagnol, A. 1996 'La fin du Sénat de Rome', in C. Lepelley (ed.), *La fin de la cité antique et le début de la cité médiévale de la fin du IIIe siècle à l'évènement de Charlemagne* (Bari: Edipuglia), 345–54.

Chiesa, P. 2002 'Traduzioni e traduttori a Roma nell'alto medioevo', *Roma fra Oriente e Occidente*, Settimane di Studio dell CISAM 49 (Spoleto: Centro Italiano di Studi sull'Alto Medioevo), 455–87.

Christie, N. 1987 'Forum ware, the duchy of Rome, and incastellamento: problems in interpretation', *Archeologia Medievale* 14: 451–66.

Christie, N. 1995 'Popes, Pilgrims and Peasants. The rôle of the domusculta Capracorum', in *Akten des XII. internationalen Kongresses für christliche Archäologie (Bonn, 22–28 September 1991)* (= *Jahrbuch für Antike und Christentum*, Ergänzungsband 20) (Münster: Aschendorff), 650–7.

Christie, N. and C. Daniels 1991 'Santa Cornelia: the excavation of an early medieval papal estate and a medieval monastery', in N. Christie (ed.), *Three South Etrurian Churches: Santa Cornelia, Santa Rufina and San Liberato* (London: The British School at Rome), 1–209.

Claridge, A. 1998 *Rome: An Oxford Annotated Guide* (Oxford: Oxford University Press).

Claussen, P. C. 2002 *Die Kirchen der Stadt Rom in Mittelalter 1050–1300*, 3 vols. (Stuttgart: Franz Steiner).

Coates-Stephens 1996 'Housing in early medieval Rome, 500–1000 AD', *Papers of the British School at Rome* 64: 239–59.

Coates-Stephens, R. 1997 'Dark age architecture in Rome', *Papers of the British School at Rome* 65: 177–232.

Coates-Stephens, R. 1998 'The walls and aqueducts of Rome in the early Middle Ages, A.D. 500–1000', *Journal of Roman Studies* 88: 166–78.

Coates-Stephens, R. 1999 'Le ricostruzioni altomedievali delle mura aureliane e degli acquedotti', *Mélanges de l'École française de Rome. Moyen Âge* 111: 209–225.

Coates-Stephens, R. 2001–2 'Gli impianti ad acqua e la rete idrica urbana', in H. Geertman (ed.), *Atti del colloquio internazionale Il Liber Pontificalis e la storia materiale (Roma, 21–22 febbraio 2002)* (= Mededelingen van het Nederlands Instituut te Rome 60–61), 135–53.

Coates-Stephens, R. 2003a 'The water-supply of early medieval Rome', in C. Bruun and A. Saastamoinen (eds.), *Technology, Ideology, Water: From Frontinus to the Renaissance and Beyond* (= Acta Instituti Romani Finlandiae 31) (Rome: Institutum Romanum Finlandiae), 81–113.

Coates-Stephens, R. 2003b 'The water-supply of Rome from late Antiquity to the early Middle Ages', *Acta ad archaeologiam et artium historiam pertinentia* 17: 165–86.

Coates-Stephens, R. 2006 'Byzantine building patronage in post-reconquest Rome', in M. Ghilardi, C. Goddard, and P. Porena (eds.), *Les cités de l'Italie tardo-antique (IVe–VIe siècle): institutions, économie, société, culture et religion*, Collection de l'École française de Rome 369 (Rome: École française de Rome), 155–66.

Coates-Stephens, R. 2007 'San Saba and the *xenodochium de via Nova*', *Rivista di Archeologia Cristiana* 83: 223–56.

Coates-Stephens, R. 2017 'The Byzantine sack of Rome', *Antiquité Tardive* 25: 191–212.

Coates-Stephens, R. 2018 '*Inde lupae fulvo nutricis tegmine laetus / Romulus excipiet gentem*: The Vergilian inscription of the Scala Santa', in S. Pedone and

A. Paribeni (eds.), *'Di Bisanzio dirai ciò che è passato, che passa e che sarà'*: *Scritti in onore di Alessandra Guiglia* (Rome: Bardi Edizioni), 281–97.

Coates-Stephens, R. 2020 'The "Oratory of the Forty Martyrs of Sebaste"', in E. Rubery, G. Bordi, and J. Osborne (eds.), *Santa Maria Antiqua: the Sistine Chapel of the Eighth Century* (Turnhout: Brepols), in press.

Coleman, C. 1922 *The Treatise of Lorenzo Valla on the Donation of Constantine* (New Haven: Yale University Press).

Colgrave, B. 1969 'Pilgrimage to Rome in the seventh and eighth centuries', in E. B. Atwood and A. Hill (eds.), *Studies in Language, Literature and Culture of the Middle Ages and Later* (Austin: University of Texas Press), 156–72.

Collins, A. 1998 'Cola di Rienzo, the Lateran basilica, and the *Lex de imperio* of Vespasian', *Mediaeval Studies* 60: 159–83.

Corbett, S. 1970 'SS Quirico e Giulitta', in R. Krautheimer (ed.), *Corpus Basilicarum Christianarum Romae* (Vatican City: Pontificio Istituto di Archeologia Cristiana), IV: 37–50.

Cormack, R. 1985 *Writing in Gold: Byzantine Society and Its Icons* (London: George Philip).

Corrigan, K. 1988 'The witness of John the Baptist on an early Byzantine icon in Kiev', *Dumbarton Oaks Papers* 42: 1–11.

Cosentino, S. 1996–2000 *Prosopografia dell'Italia bizantina (493–804)*, 2 vols. (Bologna: Lo Scarabeo).

Costambeys, M. 2000 'Review article: Property, ideology and the territorial power of the papacy in the early Middle Ages', *Early Medieval Europe* 9: 367–96.

Costambeys, M. 2001 'Burial topography and the power of the church in fifth- and sixth-century Rome', *Papers of the British School at Rome* 69: 169–189.

Costambeys, M. 2002 'The culture and practice of burial in and around Rome in the sixth century', in F. Guidobaldi and A. Guiglia Guidobaldi (eds.), *Ecclesiae Urbis. Atti del Congresso Internazionale di Studi sulle Chiese di Roma (IV–X secolo). Roma, 4–10 settembre 2000* (Vatican City: Pontificio Istituto di Archeologia Cristiana), 721–31.

Costambeys, M. 2014 'Alcuin, Rome, and Charlemagne's imperial coronation', in F. Tinti (ed.), *England and Rome in the Early Middle Ages: Pilgrimage, Art, and Politics* (Turnhout: Brepols), 255–89.

Costambeys, M. 2018 'Paul the Deacon and Rome', in E. Screen and C. West (eds.), *Writing the Early Medieval West: Studies in Honour of Rosamond McKitterick* (Cambridge: Cambridge University Press), 49–63.

Costambeys, M. 2020 'Pope Hadrian I and Santa Maria Antiqua: liturgy and patronage in the late eighth century', in E. Rubery, G. Bordi, and J. Osborne (eds.), *Santa Maria Antiqua: The Sistine Chapel of the Eighth Century* (Turnhout: Brepols), in press.

Costambeys, M. and C. Leyser 2007 'To be the neighbour of St Stephen: patronage, martyr cult, and Roman monasteries, *c*.600–*c*.900', in K. Cooper and J. Hillner (eds.), *Religion, Dynasty, and Patronage in Early Christian Rome, 300–900* (Cambridge: Cambridge University Press), 262–87.

Coste, J. 1984 'La *Domusculta Sanctae Caeciliae*. Méthode et portée d'une localisation', *Mélanges de l'École française de Rome. Moyen Age-Temps Modernes* 96: 727–75.

Cotton, M., M. Wheeler, and D. Whitehouse 1991, 'Santa Rufina: a Roman and medieval site in South Etruria', in N. Christie (ed.), *Three South Etrurian Churches: Santa Cornelia, Santa Rufina and San Liberato* (London: The British School at Rome), 211–312.

Coupland, S. 2018 'The Formation of a European Identity: Revisiting Charlemagne's Coinage', in E. Screen and C. West (eds.), *Writing the Early Medieval West: Studies in Honour of Rosamond McKitterick* (Cambridge: Cambridge University Press), 213–29.

Croisier, J. 2006a 'La decorazione pittorica dei sotterranei del Sancta Sanctorum', in S. Romano (ed.), *La Pittura Medievale a Roma, 312–1431. IV: Riforma e Tradizione 1050–1198* (Milan: Jaca Book), 224–32.

Croisier, J. 2006b 'La perduta decorazione dell'Oratorio di San Nicola al patriarchio lateranense', in S. Romano (ed.), *La Pittura Medievale a Roma, 312–1431. IV: Riforma e Tradizione 1050–1198* (Milan: Jaca Book), 290–3.

Croquison, J. 1964 'L'iconographie chrétienne à Rome d'après le *Liber Pontificalis*', *Byzantion* 34: 535–606.

Curzi, G. 1993 'La decorzazione musiva della basilica dei SS. Nereo e Achilleo in Roma: materiali ed ipotesi', *Arte Medievale* 7.2: 21–45.

Curzi, G. 1999 'La decorazione medievale del c.d. oratorio del SS. Salvatore sotto la basilica dei SS. Giovanni e Paolo a Roma', in A. Cadei, M. Righetti Tosti-Croce, and A. Segagni Malacart (eds.), *Arte d'Occidente: temi e metodi. Scritti in onore di Angiola Maria Romanini* (Rome: Sintesi Informazione), 607–16.

Curzi, G. 2018 'Reflexes of Iconoclasm and Iconophilia in the Roman wall paintings and mosaics of the 8th and 9th centuries', *IKON: Journal of Iconographic Studies* 11: 9–20.

D'Acunto, N. 2015 'Evergetismo monastico e stabilizzazione del 'regnum langobardorum': il caso di Desiderio e Ansa', in G. Archetti (ed.) *Desiderio: il progetto politico dell'ultimo re longobardo. Atti del Primo convegno internazionale di studio (Brescia, 21–24 marzo 2013)* (Spoleto: Centro Italiano di Studi sull'Alto Medioevo), 315–26.

Dagron, G. 1988 'Rome et l'Italie vues de Byzance (IVe–VIIe siècles)', *Bisanzio, Roma e l'Italia nell'Alto Medioevo*, Settimane di Studio del CISAM 34 (Spoleto: Centro Italiano di Studi sull'Alto Medioevo), 43–64.

D'Amico, R. 1976 'L'organizzazione assistenziale: le diaconie', *Roma e l'Età Carolingia. Atti delle giornate di studio, 3–8 maggio 1976* (Rome: Multigrafica Editrice), 229–36.

Davis, R. 1995 *The Lives of the Ninth-Century Popes (Liber Pontificalis)*, Translated Texts for Historians 20 (Liverpool: Liverpool University Press).

Davis, R. 2007 *The Lives of the Eighth-Century Popes (Liber Pontificalis)*, 2nd ed., Translated Texts for Historians 13 (Liverpool: Liverpool University Press).

Davis, R. 2010 *The Book of Pontiffs (Liber Pontificalis): The Ancient Biographies of the First ninety Roman Bishops to AD 715*, 3rd ed., Translated Texts for Historians 6 (Liverpool: Liverpool University Press).
Davis-Weyer, C. 1965 'Das Apsismosaik Leos III. in S. Susanna. Rekonstruktion und Datierung', *Zeitschrift für Kunstgeschichte* 28: 177–94.
Davis-Weyer, C. 1966 'Die Mosaiken Leos III. und die Anfänge der karolingischen Renaissance in Rom', *Zeitschrift für Kunstgeschichte* 29: 111–32.
Davis-Weyer, C. 1974, 'Karolingisches und nicht Karolingisches in zwei Mosaikfragmenten der Vatikanischen Bibliothek', *Zeitschrift für Kunstgeschichte* 37: 31–9.
Davis-Weyer, C. 1986 *Early Medieval Art, 300–1150. Sources and Documents* (repr. Toronto: University of Toronto Press).
Davis-Weyer, C. 1989 'S. Stefano Rotondo in Rome and the Oratory of Theodore I', in W. Tronzo (ed.), *Italian Church Decoration of the Middle Ages and Early Renaissance. Functions, Forms and Regional Traditions* (Bologna: Nuova Alfa Editoriale), 61–80.
De Benedictis, E. 1981 'The Senatorium and Matroneum in the early Roman church', *Rivista di Archeologia Cristiana* 57: 69–85.
De Blaauw, S. 1991 'Architecture and Liturgy in Late Antiquity and the Middle Ages. Traditions and trends in modern scholarship', *Archiv für Liturgiewissenschaft* 33: 1–34.
De Blaauw, S. 1994 *Cultus et Decor: Liturgia e architettura nella Roma tardoantica e medievale* (Vatican City: Biblioteca Apostolica Vaticana).
De Blaauw, S. 2016 'Die Gräber der frühen Päpste', in B. Schneidmüller, S. Weinfurter, M. Matheus, and A. Wieczorek (eds.), *Die Päpste: Amt und Herrschaft in Antike, Mittelalter und Renaissance* (Regensberg: Schnell und Steiner), 77–99.
De Blaauw, S. 2017 'Urban Liturgy: the Conclusive Christianization of Rome', in I. Foletti and A. Palladino (eds.), *Ritualizing the City: Collective Performances as Aspects of Urban Construction from Constantine to Mao* (Rome: Viella), 15–28.
Deckers, J. G., G. Mietke and A. Weiland 1994 *Die Katakombe 'Commodilla'. Repertorium der Malereien* (Vatican City: Pontificio Istituto di Archeologia Cristiana).
Declerck, J. 2017 'Le Parisinus gr. 923: un manuscrit destiné à l'empereur Basile Ier (867–886)', *Byzantion* 87: 181–206.
De Francesco, D. 2004 *La proprietà fondiaria nel Lazio, secoli IV–VIII: storia e topografia* (Rome: Edizioni Quasar).
De Francesco, D. 2017 *Il papato e l'approvvigionamento idrico e alimentare di Roma tra la tarda anichità e l'alto medioevo* (Rome: Edizioni Quasar).
de Grüneisen, W. 1911 *Sainte-Marie-Antique* (Rome: Max Bretschneider).
De Jerphanion, G. 1913 'Le nimbe rectangulaire en Orient et en Occident', *Études* 134: 85–93.

De Lachenal, L. 1990 'Il gruppo equestre di Marco Aurelio e il Laterano. Ricerche per una storia della fortuna del monumento dall'età medievale sino al 1538', *Bollettino d'Arte* ser. VII, 61: 1–52; 62–63:1–56.

Del Duca, L. and C. Falcucci 2010 'Riflessioni sulle novità e le persistenze tecniche nell'alto Medio Evo', in C. Tempesta (ed.), *L'icona murale di Santa Sabina all'Aventino* (Rome: Gangemi), 35–41.

Delehaye, H. 1911 'Les saints d'Aboukir', *Analecta Bollandiana* 30: 448–50.

Dell'Acqua, F. 2018 'Iconophilia in Italy, c. 680–880. A European project and its method', *IKON: Journal of Iconographic Studies* 11: 31–46.

Dell'Acqua, F. and C. Gantner 2019 'Resenting Byzantine Iconoclasm. Its early reception in Italy through an inscription from Corteolona', *Medieval Worlds* 9: 160–86.

Delle Rose, M. 1991 'Il Patriarchio: note storicho-topografiche', in C. Pietrangeli (ed.), *Il Palazzo apostolico lateranense* (Florence: Nardini), 18–35.

Del Lungo, S. 2004 *Roma in età carolingia e gli scritti dell'anonimo Augiense* (Rome: Società Romana di Storia Patria).

Delogu, P. 1988a 'The rebirth of Rome in the 8th and 9th centuries', in R. Hodges and B. Hobley (eds.), *The Rebirth of Towns in the West, AD 700–1050* (London: Council for British Archaeology), 32–42.

Delogu, P. 1988b 'Oro e argento in Roma tra il VII e il IX secolo', in *Cultura e società nell'Italia medievale: studi per Paolo Brezzi* (Rome: Istituto storico italiano per il Medio Evo, 1988), I, 273–93.

Delogu, P. 1998 'L'importazione di tessuti preziosi e il sistema economico romano nel IX secolo', in P. Delogu (ed.), *Roma medievale: aggiornamenti* (Florence: All'Insegna del Giglio), 123–41.

Delogu, P. 2000 'Zaccaria', Enciclopedia dei Papi, 3 vols. (Rome: Istituto della Enciclopedia Italiana), I: 656–60.

Delogu, P. 2001 'Il papato tra l'impero bizantino e l'Occidente nel VII e VIII secolo', in G. De Rosa and G. Cracco (eds.), *Il Papato e l'Europa* (Soveria Mannelli: Rubbettino), 55–79.

Delogu, P. 2015 'I Romani e l'Impero (VII–X secolo)', in V. West-Harling (ed.), *Three Empires, Three Cities: Identity, Material Culture and Legitimacy in Venice, Ravenna and Rome, 750–1000* (Turnhout: Brepols), 191–225.

Delogu, P. 2017 'The popes and their town in the time of Charlemagne', in J. Mitchell, J. Moreland and B. Leal (eds.), *Encounters, Excavations and Argosies. Essays for Richard Hodges* (Oxford: Archaeopress), 105–15.

Demacopoulos, G. 2013 *The Invention of Peter: Apostolic Discourse and Papal Authority in Late Antiquity* (Philadelphia: University of Pennsylvania Press).

De Nie, G. 2014 '"Whatever mystery may be given to my heart": A latent image in Arator's *History of the Apostles*', in V. Garver and O. Phelan (eds.), *Rome and Religion in the Mediterranean World. Studies in Honor of Thomas F.X. Noble* (Farnham: Ashgate), 1–19.

De Rossi, G. B. 1864 *La Roma Sotterranea Cristiana* (Roma: Cromo-litografia pontificia).

De Rossi, G.B. 1857–88 *Inscriptiones Christianae urbis Romae septimo saeculo antiquiores*, 2 vols. (Rome: Ex Officina Libraria Pontificia).

De Rossi, G.B. 1888 'L'inscription du tombeau d'Hadrien I', *Mélanges d'Archéologie et d'Histoire* 8: 478–501.

De Rubeis, F. 2001 'Epigrafi a Roma dall'età classica all'alto medioevo', in M. S. Arena, P. Delogu, L. Paroli, M. Ricci, L. Saguì, and L. Vendittelli eds., *Roma dall'Antichità al Medioevo: archeologia e storia nel Museo Nazionale Romano Crypta Balbi* (Milan: Electa), 104–21.

De Rubeis, F. and G. Bordi 2001 '*Pergulae* di Adriano I (772–795)', in M. S. Arena, P. Delogu, L. Paroli, M. Ricci, L. Saguì, and L. Vendittelli (eds.), *Roma dall'Antichità al Medioevo. Archeologia e Storia nel Museo Nazionale Romano Crypta Balbi* (Milan: Electa), 483–6.

De Waal, A. 1888 'Figürliche Darstellungen auf Teppichen und Vorhängen in römischen Kirchen bis zur Mitte des IX. Jahrhunderts nach dem Liber Pontificalis', *Römische Quartalschrift für christliche Altertumskunde und Kirchengeschichte* 2: 313–21.

Dey, H. 2008 '*Diaconiae, xenodochia, hospitalia* and monasteries: "social security" and the meaning of monasticism in early medieval Rome', *Early Medieval Europe* 16: 398–422.

Dey, H. 2011 *The Aurelian Walls and the Refashioning of Imperial Rome, AD 271-855* (Cambridge: Cambridge University Press).

Dey, H. 2019 'Politics, patronage and the transmission of construction techniques in early medieval Rome, c.650–750', *Papers of the British School at Rome* 87: 177–205.

Dodd, E. 1980 'The Sion treasure: problems of dating and provenance', *Byzantine Studies Conference, Abstracts of Papers* 6: 3–4.

D'Onofrio, M. 2002 'Aspetti inediti e poco noti del Patriarchio lateranense', in A. C. Quintavalle (ed.), *Medioevo: I modelli. Atti del Convegno internazionale di studi. Parma, 27 settembre-1 ottobre 1999* (Milan: Electa), 221–36.

D'Onofrio, M. 2016 'Leone III (795–816)', in M. D'Onofrio (ed.), *La committenza artistica dei papi a Roma nel Medioevo* (Rome: Viella), 213–8.

Duchesne, L. 1897 'S. Maria Antiqua', *Mélanges d'Archéologie et d'Histoire* 17: 13–37.

Dumville, D. 1995 'The importation of Mediterranean manuscripts into Theodore's England', in M. Lapidge (ed.), *Archbishop Theodore: Commemorative Studies on his Life and Influence* (Cambridge: Cambridge University Press), 96–119.

Durliat, J. 1990 *De la ville antique à la ville byzantine: Le problème des subsistences*, Collection de l'École française de Rome 136 (Rome: École française de Rome).

Dyer, J. 2007 'Roman processions of the Major Litany (*litaniae maiores*) from the Sixth to the Twelfth century', in É. Ó Carragáin and C. Neuman de Vegvar (eds.), *Roma Felix - Formation and Reflections of Medieval Rome* (Aldershot: Ashgate), 113-37.

Ekonomou, A. 2007 *Byzantine Rome and the Greek Popes: Eastern Influences on Rome and the Papacy from Gregory the Great to Zacharias, A.D. 590-752* (Lanham, MD: Rowland and Littlefield).

Emerick, J. 2017 'Charlemagne: a new Constantine?', in M. S. Bjornlie (ed.), *The Life and Legacy of Constantine: Traditions through the Ages* (London and New York: Routledge), 133-61.

Engemann, J. 1995 'Skizzen zu Bedeutungsgrösse und Seitenwertigkeit in frühmittelalterlichen und mittelalterlichen Bildwerken', in D. Mouriki, C. Moss, and K. Kiefer (eds.), *Byzantine East, Latin West: Art Historical Studies in Honor of Kurt Weitzmann* (Princeton: Princeton University Press), 142-52.

Erler, A. 1972 *Lupa, Lex und Reiterstandbild im mittelalterlichen Rom* (Wiesbaden: Franz Steiner).

Etinhof, O. 1991 'I mosaici di Roma nella raccolta di P. Sevastjanov', *Bollettino d'Arte* ser. VI, 66: 29-38.

Falkenstein, L. 1966 *Der 'Lateran' der karolingischen Pfalz zu Aachen* (Cologne: Bühlau).

Federici, V. 1899 'Regesto del monastero di S. Silvestro de Capite', *Archivio della R. Società Romana di Storia Patria* 22: 213-300, 489-538.

Fehl, P. 1974 'The placement of the equestrian statue of Marcus Aurelius in the Middle Ages', *Journal of the Warburg and Courtauld Institutes* 37: 362-7.

Ferrari, G. 1957 *Early Roman monasteries: Notes for the History of the Monasteries and Convents at Rome from the V through the X Century* (Vatican City: Pontificio Istituto di Archeologia Cristiana).

Folgerø, P. O. 2009 'The lowest, lost zone of "The Adoration of the Crucified" scene in S. Maria Antiqua in Rome: a new conjecture', *Journal of the Warburg and Courtauld Institutes* 72: 207-19.

Folgerø, P. O. 2020 'Expressions of dogma: text and imagery in the apsidal arch decoration of S. Maria Antiqua', in E. Rubery, G. Bordi and J. Osborne (eds.), *Santa Maria Antiqua: The Sistine Chapel of the Eighth Century* (Turnhout: Brepols), in press.

Forsyth, G. H. and K. Weitzmann 1973 *The Monastery of Saint Catherine at Mount Sinai: The Church and Fortress of Justinian. Plates* (Ann Arbor: University of Michigan Press).

Fortini, P. and G. Bordi 2016 'Cronaca dello scavo e della sua documentazione. 1900-1907', in M. Andaloro, G. Bordi, and G. Morganti (eds.), *Santa Maria Antiqua tra Roma e Bisanzio* (Milan: Electa), 300-15.

Franses, R. 2018 *Donor Portraits in Byzantine Art. The Vicissitudes of Contact between Human and Divine* (Cambridge: Cambridge University Press).

Freeman, A. 1985 'Carolingian orthodoxy and the fate of the *Libri Carolini*', *Viator* 16: 65-108.

Fried, J. 2007 *'Donation of Constantine' and 'Constitutum Constantini': The Misinterpretation of a Fiction and Its Original Meaning* (Berlin: Walter de Gruyter).
Fusciello, G. 2011 *Santa Maria in Cosmedin a Roma* (Rome: Edizioni Quasar).
Gaetani, M. C., U. Santamaria and C. Seccaroni 2004 'The Use of Egyptian Blue and Lapis Lazuli in the Middle Ages – The Wall Paintings of the San Saba Church in Rome', *Studies in Conservation* 49.1: 13–22.
Galletti, P. 1776 *Dal primicero della Santa Sede Apostolica e di altri uffiziali maggiori del sacro palagio Lateranense* (Rome: Salomoni).
Gandolfo, F. 1989 'Gli affreschi di San Saba', in M. Andaloro, A. Ghidoli, A. Iacobini, S. Romano, and A. Tomei (eds.), *Fragmenta Picta: Affreschi e mosaici staccati del Medioevo romano* (Rome: Argos Edizioni), 183–7.
Gantner, C. 2013a 'The Lombard recension of the *Liber Pontificalis*', *Rivista di Storia del Cristianesimo* 10: 65–114.
Gantner, C. 2013b 'The label "Greeks" in the papal diplomatic repertoire in the eighth century', in W. Pohl and G. Heydemann (eds.), *Strategies of Identification: Ethnicity and Religion in Early Medieval Europe* (Turnhout: Brepols), 303–49.
Gantner, C. 2014a *Freunde Roms und Völker der Finsternis. Die päpstliche Konstruktion von Anderen im 8. und 9. Jahrhundert* (Vienna, Cologne and Weimar: Böhlau).
Gantner, C. 2014b '*Romana urbs*: levels of Roman and imperial identity in the city of Rome', *Early Medieval Europe* 22: 461–75.
Gantner, C. 2015 'The eighth-century papacy as cultural broker', in C. Gantner, R. McKitterick and S. Meeder (eds.), *The Resources of the Past in Early Medieval Europe* (Cambridge: Cambridge University Press), 245–61.
Ganz, D. 2002 'Roman manuscripts in *Francia* and Anglo-Saxon England', *Roma fra Oriente e Occidente*, Settimane di Studio del CISAM 49 (Spoleto: Centro Italiano di Studi sull'Alto Medioevo), 607–47.
Gasbarri, G. 2015 *Riscoprire Bisanzio: lo studio dell'arte bizantina a Roma e in Italia tra Ottocento e Novecento* (Rome: Viella).
Gatto, L. 1998 'Riflettendo sulla consistenza demografica della Roma altomedievale', in P. Delogu (ed.), *Roma medievale: aggiornamenti* (Florence: All'Insegna del Giglio), 143–57.
Geary, P. 1978 *Furta Sacra: Thefts of Relics in the Central Middle Ages* (Princeton: Princeton University Press).
Geertman, H. 1975 *More Veterum: il 'Liber pontificalis' e gli edifici ecclesiastici di Roma nella tarda anichità e nell'alto medioevo* (Groningen: H.D. Tjeenk Willink).
Gem, R., and E. Howe 2008 'The ninth-century polychrome decoration at St Mary's church, Deerhurst', *The Antiquaries Journal* 88: 109–64.
Germano di S. Stanislao, P. 1894 *La Casa Celimontana dei SS. Martiri Giovanni e Paolo* (Rome: Tipografia della Pace di F. Cuggiani).

Gianandrea, M. 2010 'Lettura iconografica e stilistica del dipinto murale', in C. Tempesta (ed.), *L'icona murale di Santa Sabina all'Aventino* (Rome: Gangemi), 25–30.

Gianandrea, M. 2011 'Un'inedita committenza nella Chiesa romana di Santa Sabina all'Aventino: il dipinto altomedievale con le "Vergine e il Bambino, santi e donatori"', in A.C. Quintavalle (ed.), *Medioevo: i committenti. Atti del Convegno internazionale di studi, Parma, 21–26 settembre 2010* (Milan: Electa), 399–410.

Gianandrea, M. 2014 'Politica delle immagini al tempo di Papa Costantino (708–715): Roma *versus* Bisanzio?', in G. Bordi, I. Carlettini, M.L. Fobelli, M. R. Menna, and P. Pogliani (eds.), *L'officina dello sguardo: scritti in onore di Maria Andaloro*, 2 vols. (Rome: Gangemi), I, 335–42.

Gianandrea, M. 2020 'The fresco with the Three Mothers and the paintings of the right aisle in the church of Santa Maria Antiqua', in E. Rubery, G. Bordi and J. Osborne (eds.), *Santa Maria Antiqua: The Sistine Chapel of the Eighth Century* (Turnhout: Brepols), in press.

Gibson, S. and B. Ward-Perkins 1979 'The surviving remains of the Leonine wall', *Papers of the British School at Rome* 47: 30–57.

Goodson, C. 2007 'Building for Bodies: the architecture of saint veneration in early medieval Rome', in É. Ó Carragáin and C. Neuman de Vegvar (eds.), *Roma Felix – Formation and Reflections of Medieval Rome* (Aldershot: Ashgate), 51–79.

Goodson, C. 2010 *The Rome of Pope Paschal I: Papal Power, Urban Renovation, Church Rebuilding and Relic Translation, 817–824* (Cambridge: Cambridge University Press).

Goodson, C. 2015 'To be the daughter of Saint Peter: S. Petronilla and forging the Franco-Papal alliance', in V. West-Harling (ed.) *Three empires, three cities: identity, material culture and legitimacy in Venice, Ravenna and Rome, 750–1000* (Turnhout: Brepols), 159–84.

Goodson, C. 2018 'Garden cities in early medieval Italy', in R. Balzaretti, J. Barrow, and P. Skinner (eds.) *Italy and Early Medieval Europe. Papers for Chris Wickham* (Oxford: Oxford University Press), 339–55.

Goodson, C. and J. Nelson 2010 'The Roman contexts of the "Donation of Constantine"', *Early Medieval Europe* 18: 446–67.

Grabar, A. 1936 *L'empereur dans l'art byzantine: recherches sur l'art officiel de l'empire d'Orient* (Paris: Belles Lettres).

Grabar, A. 1968 'L'imago clipeata chrétienne', in *L'art de la fin de l'Antiquité et du Moyen Age*, 3 vols. (Paris: Collège de France), I, 607–613.

Grabar, A. 1972 *Les manuscrits grecs enluminés de provenance italienne (IXe–XIe siècles)* (Paris: Klincksieck).

Grafova, M. 2020 'The decoration in the left aisle of S. Maria Antiqua within the context of the political history of the iconoclastic era', in E. Rubery, G. Bordi, and

J. Osborne (eds.), *Santa Maria Antiqua: The Sistine Chapel of the Eighth Century* (Turnhout: Brepols), in press.

Gray, N. 1948 'The paleography of Latin inscriptions in the eighth, ninth and tenth centuries in Italy', *Papers of the British School at Rome* 16: 38–167.

Grierson, P. and M. Blackburn 1986 *Medieval European Coinage with a catalogue of the coins in the Fitzwilliam Museum, Cambridge. I: The Early Middle Ages (5th–10th centuries)* (Cambridge: Cambridge University Press).

Grimaldi, G. 1972 *Descrizione della basilica antica di S. Pietro in Vaticano: Codice Barberini latino 2733*, R. Niggl (ed.) (Vatican City: Biblioteca Apostolica Vaticana).

Grossi Gondi, F. 1920 'La "cripta confessionis" del sec. VIII nella Chiesa di S. Angelo in Pescheria', *La Civiltà cattolica* 71.3: 524–32.

Grotz, H. 1980 'Beobachtungen zu den zwei Briefen Papst Gregors II. an Kaiser Leo III.', *Archivum Historiae Pontificiae* 18: 9–40.

Grumel, V. 1958 *Traité d'Études byzantines. 1. La Chronologie* (Paris: Presses universitaires de France).

Guidobaldi, F. 1986 'L'ediliza abitativa unifamiliare nella Roma tardoantica', in A. Giardina (ed.), *Società Romana e Impero Tardoantico. 2: Roma: Politica, economia, paesaggio urbano* (Bari: Laterza), 165–237.

Guidobaldi, F. 2007 'Una *domus* tardoantica e la sua trasformazione in chiesa dei SS Quirico e Giulitta', in A. Leone, D. Palombini, and S. Walker (eds.), *Res bene gestae. Ricerche di storia urbana su Roma antica in onore di Eva Margareta Steinby* (Rome: Edizioni Quasar), 55–78.

Guiglia Guidobaldi, A. 2002 'La scultura di arredo liturgico nelle chiese di Roma: il momento bizantino', in F. Guidobaldi and A. Guiglia Guidobaldi (eds.), *Ecclesiae Urbis. Atti del Congresso Internazionale di Studi sulle Chiese di Roma (IV–X secolo). Roma, 4–10 settembre 2000* (Vatican City: Pontificio Istituto di Archeologia Cristiana), 1479–1524.

Guiglia Guidobaldi, A. 2004 'La decorazione marmorea dell'edificio di Santa Maria Antiqua fra tarda antichità e alto medioevo', in J. Osborne, J.R. Brandt, and G. Morganti (eds.), *Santa Maria Antiqua al Foro Romano cento anni dopo. Atti del colloquio internazionale, Roma, 5–6 maggio 2000* (Rome: Campisano), 48–65.

Haldon, J. and B. Ward-Perkins 1999 'Evidence from Rome for the Image of Christ on the Chalke Gate in Constantinople', *Byzantine and Modern Greek Studies* 23: 286–96.

Hallenbeck, J. 1978 'Rome under attack: an estimation of King Aistulf's motives for the Lombard siege of 756', *Mediaeval Studies* 40: 190–222.

Hallenbeck, J. 1982 *Pavia and Rome: The Lombard Monarchy and the Papacy in the Eighth Century* (Philadelphia: American Philosophical Society).

Hallenbeck, J. 1989 'King Desiderius as surrogate *patricius Romanorum*: the politics of equilibrium, 757–768', *Studi medievali*, 3rd ser. 30: 49–64.

Halphen, L. 1907 *Études sur l'administration de Rome au moyen âge* (Paris: Librairie Honoré Champion).

Handley, M. 2003 *Death, Society and Culture: Inscriptions and Epitaphs in Gaul and Spain, AD 300–750*, BAR International Series 1135 (Oxford: Archaeopress).

Harper, K. 2011 *Slavery in the Late Roman World, AD 275–425* (Cambridge: Cambridge University Press).

Hartmann, F. 2006 *Hadrian I. (772–795): Frühmittelalterliches Adelspapsttum und die Lösung Roms vom byzantinischen Kaiser*, Päpste und Papsttum 34 (Stuttgart: Anton Hersemann).

Heckscher, W. S. 1955 *Sixtus IIII aeneas insignes statuas Romano populo restituendas censuit* (The Hague: M. Nijhoff).

Hennessy, C. 2003 'Iconic Images of children in the church of St Demetrios, Thessaloniki', in A. Eastmond and L. James (eds.), *Icon and Word: The Power of Images in Byzantium. Essays presented to Robin Cormack* (Aldershot: Ashgate), 157–72.

Herklotz, I. 1985a *'Sepulcra' e 'Monumenta' del Medioevo* (Rome: Edizioni Rari Nantes).

Herklotz, I. 1985b 'Historia sacra und mittelalterliche Kunst während der zweiten Hälfte des 16. Jahrhunderts in Rom', in R. De Maio, A. Borromeo, L. Gulia, G. Lutz, and A. Mazzacane (eds.), *Baronio e l'arte. Atti del convegno internazionale di studi. Sora, 10–13 ottobre 1984* (Sora: Centro di Studi Sorani 'Vincenzo Patriarca'), 21–74.

Herklotz, I. 1995 'Francesco Barberini, Nicolò Alemanni, and the Lateran Triclinium of Leo III: An Episode in Restoration and Seicento Medieval Studies', *Memoirs of the American Academy in Rome* 40: 175–96. Italian translation with *postscriptum* in I. Herklotz, *'Apes urbanae': Eruditi, mecenati e artisti nella Roma del Seicento* (Città di Castello: LuoghInteriori, 2017), 71–104.

Herklotz, I. 2000 *Gli eredi di Costantino. Il papato, il Laterano e la propaganda visiva nel XII secolo* (Rome: Viella).

Hermes, R. 1996 'Die stadtrömischen Diakonien', *Römische Quartalschrift für christliche Altertumskunde und Kirchengeschichte* 91: 1–120.

Hilliard, P. 2018 'Bede and the changing image of Rome and the Romans', in E. Screen and C. West (eds.), *Writing the Early Medieval West: Studies in Honour of Rosamond McKitterick* (Cambridge: Cambridge University Press), 33–48.

Hillner, J. 2006 'Clerics, property and patronage: the case of the Roman titular churches', *Antiquité tardive* 14: 59–68.

Hillner, J. 2007 'Families, patronage, and the titular churches of Rome, c.300–c.600', in K. Cooper and J. Hillner (eds.), *Religion, Dynasty, and Patronage in Early Christian Rome, 300–900* (Cambridge: Cambridge University Press), 225–61.

Hodges, R. 1993 'The riddle of St Peter's Republic', in L. Paroli and P. Delogu (eds.), *La storia economica di Roma nell'alto Medioevo alla luce dei recenti scavi archeologici: atti del seminario, Roma, 2–3 aprile 1992* (Florence: All'Insegna del Giglio), 353–66.

Hülsen, C. 1907 *La Roma antica di Ciriaco d'Ancona* (Rome: E. Loescher).

Hülsen, C. 1927 *Le Chiese di Roma nel Medio Evo* (Florence: Leo S. Olschki).

Humphries, M. 2007 'From emperor to pope? Ceremonial, space, and authority at Rome from Constantine to Gregory the Great', in K. Cooper and J. Hillner (eds.), *Religion, Dynasty, and Patronage in Early Christian Rome, 300–900* (Cambridge: Cambridge University Press), 21–58.

Huyghebaert, N. 1979 'Une légende de fondation: le *Constitutum Constantini*', *Le Moyen Age* 85: 177–209.

Iacobini, A. 1989 'Il mosaico del triclinio Lateranense', in M. Andaloro, A. Ghidoli, A. Iacobini, S. Romano, and A. Tomei (eds.), *Fragmenta Picta: Affreschi e mosaici staccati del Medioevo romano* (Rome: Argos Edizioni), 189–96.

Iosi, E. 1924 'Il cimitero di Panfilo', *Rivista di Archeologia Cristiana* 1: 15–119.

Ippoliti, A. 1991 'La sistemazione Sistina della Scala Santa', in C. Pietrangeli (ed.), *Il Palazzo apostolico lateranense* (Florence: Nardini), 120–37.

Izzi, L. 2014 'Anglo-Saxons Underground: early medieval *graffiti* in the catacombs of Rome', in F. Tinti (ed.), *England and Rome in the Early Middle Ages: Pilgrimage, Art, and Politics* (Turnhout: Brepols), 141–77.

James, L. 2017 *Mosaics in the Medieval World from Late Antiquity to the Fifteenth Century* (Cambridge: Cambridge University Press).

James, M.R. 1924 *The Apocryphal New Testament* (Oxford: Clarendon Press).

Jessop, L. 1999 'Pictorial cycles of non-biblical saints: the seventh- and eighth-century mural cycles in Rome and contexts for their use', *Papers of the British School at Rome* 67: 233–79.

Johnson, M. 1991 'On the burial places of the Theodosian dynasty', *Byzantion* 61: 330–9.

Johnson, M. 2009 *The Roman Imperial Mausoleum in Late Antiquity* (Cambridge: Cambridge University Press).

Jones, H. S. 1926 *A Catalogue of the Ancient Sculptures Preserved in the Municipal Collections of Rome. 2: The Sculptures of the Palazzo dei Conservatori* (Oxford: The Clarendon Press).

Kalas, G. 2017 'The divisive politics of Phocas (602–610) and the last imperial monument of Rome', *Antiquité tardive* 25: 173–90.

Kalas, G. 2018 'Acquiring the antique in Byzantine Rome: the economics of architectural reuse at Santa Maria Antiqua', in D. Ng and M. Swetnam-Burland (eds.), *Reuse and Renovation in Roman Material Culture: Functions, Aesthetics, Interpretations* (Cambridge: Cambridge University Press), 186–207.

Kalavrezou, I. 1990 'Images of the Mother: When the Virgin Mary became "Meter Theou"', *Dumbarton Oaks Papers* 44: 165–72.

Kartsonis, A. 1986 *Anastasis: The Making of an Image* (Princeton: Princeton University Press).

Kinney, D. 2002 'The Horse, the King and the Cuckoo: medieval narrations of the statue of Marcus Aurelius', *Word & Image* 18: 372–98.

Kinney, D. 2005 'Spolia', in W. Tronzo (ed.), *St Peter's in The Vatican* (New York: Cambridge University Press), 16–47.

Kitzinger, E. 1934 *Römische Malerei vom Beginn des 7. bis zur Mitte des 8. Jahrhunderts* (Munich: R. Warth and Co).

Kitzinger, E. 1958 'Byzantine art in the period between Justinian and Iconoclasm', *Berichte zum XI. Internationalen Byzantinisten-Kongress, München 1958*, IV/1, 1–50; repr. in E. Kitzinger, *The Art of Byzantium and the Medieval West: Selected Studies* (Bloomington: Indiana University Press, 1976), 157–206.

Kitzinger, E. 1977 *Byzantine Art in the Making: Main Lines of Stylistic Development in Mediterranean Art, 3rd–7th Century* (Cambridge, MA: Harvard University Press).

Klein, H. 2006 'Sacred relics and imperial ceremonies at the Great Palace of Constantinople', in F. A. Bauer (ed.), *Visualisierungen von Herrschaft. Frühmittelalterliche Residenzen – Gestalt und Zeremoniell. Internationales Kolloquium 3./4. Juni 2004 in Istanbul* (Istanbul: Deutsches Archäologisches Institut Istanbul), 79–99.

Knipp, D. 2002 'The Chapel of Physicians at Santa Maria Antiqua', *Dumbarton Oaks Papers* 56: 1–23.

Knipp, D. 2012 'Coptic stuccoes at Santa Maria Antiqua', *Acta ad archaeologiam et artium historiam pertinentia* 25: 159–75.

Knipp, D. 2020 'Richard Delbrueck and the Reconstruction of a "Ceremonial Route" in Domitian's Palace Vestibule', in E. Rubery, G. Bordi and J. Osborne (eds.), *Santa Maria Antiqua: the Sistine Chapel of the Eighth Century* (Turnhout: Brepols), in press.

Kramer, R. and C. Gantner 2016 '"Lateran Thinking": building on the idea of Rome in the Carolingian Empire', *Viator* 47.3: 1–26.

Krautheimer, R. et al., *Corpus Basilicarum Christianarum Romae*, 5 vols. (Vatican City: Pontificio Istituto di Archeologia Cristiana, 1937–77).

Krautheimer, R. 1942 'The Carolingian revival of Early Christian Architecture', *The Art Bulletin* 24: 1–38.

Krautheimer, R. 1966 'Die Decanneacubita in Konstantinopel. Ein kleiner Beitrag zur Frage Rom und Byzanz', in W. Schumacher (ed.), *Tortulae: Studien zu altchristlichen und byzantinischen Monumenten* (Rome and Freiburg im Breisgau: Herder), 195–9.

Krautheimer, R. 1980 *Rome: Profile of a City, 312–1308* (Princeton: Princeton University Press).

Krautheimer, R. and W. Frankl 1939 'Recent discoveries in churches in Rome', *American Journal of Archeology* 43: 388–400.

Krueger, D. 2015 'Liturgical time and Holy Land reliquaries in early Byzantium', in C. Hahn and H. Klein (eds.), *Saints and Sacred Matter: The Cult of Relics in*

Byzantium and Beyond (Washington: Dumbarton Oaks Center for Byzantine Studies), 111–31.

Kupfer, M. 1994 'Medieval world maps: embedded images, interpretive frames', *Word & Image* 10: 262–88.

Ladner, G. 1935 'I mosaici e gli affreschi ecclesiastico-politici nell'antico palazzo Lateranense', *Rivista di Archeologia Cristiana* 12: 265–92.

Ladner, G. 1941a *I Ritratti dei Papi nell'Antichità e nel Medioevo. I: Dalle origini fino alla fine della lotta per le investiture* (Vatican City: Pontificio Istituto di Archeologia Cristiana).

Ladner, G. 1941b 'The so-called square nimbus', *Mediaeval Studies* 3: 15–45.

Ladner, G. 1984 *Die Papstbildnisse des Altertums und des Mittelalters*, vol. 3 (Vatican City: Pontificio Istituto di Archeologia Cristiana).

Lai, A. 2017 'Nuove osservazioni a proposito dell'origine romana del ms. Oxford, Bodleian Library, Laud. gr. 35', *Byzantinische Zeitschrift* 110: 673–90.

La Mantia, S. 2010 '"Santi su misura": la parete di Paolo I a Santa Maria Antiqua', in V. Pace (ed.), *L'VIII secolo: un secolo inquieto. Atti del Convegno internazionale di studi, Cividale del Friuli, 4–7 dicembre 2008* (Cividale del Friuli: Comune del Cividale del Friuli), 149–61.

Lanciani, R. 1883 'L'atrio di Vesta', *Notizie degli scavi di Antichità*, 434–514.

Lanciani, R. 1891 *L'itinerario di Einsiedeln e l'ordine di Benedetto Canonico* (Rome: Accademia dei Lincei).

Lapidge, M. 1995 'The career of Archbishop Theodore', in M. Lapidge (ed.), *Archbishop Theordore. Commemorative Studies on His Life and Influence* (Cambridge: Cambridge University Press), 1–29.

Latham, J. 2009 'The making of a papal Rome: Gregory I and the *letania septiformis*', in A. Cain and N. Lenski (eds.), *The Power of Religion in Late Antiquity* (Farnham: Ashgate), 293–304.

Lauer, P. 1900 'Les fouilles du "Sancta Sanctorum" au Latran', *Mélanges d'Archéologie et d'Histoire* 20: 251–87.

Lauer, P. 1911 *Le palais de Latran: étude historique et archéologique* (Paris: Ernest Leroux).

Laurent, V. 1965 'L'oeuvre canonique du concile "in Trullo" (691–692), source primaire du droit de l'Église orientale', *Revue des études byzantines* 23: 7–41.

Lavin, I. 1962 'The House of the Lord: aspects of the role of palace triclinia in the architecture of Late Antiquity and the early Middle Ages', *The Art Bulletin* 44: 1–27.

Lawrence, M. 1924–5 'Maria Regina', *The Art Bulletin* 7: 150–61.

Lestocquoy, J. 1929 'Notes sur l'église de St Saba', *Rivista di Archeologia Cristiana* 6: 313–57.

Lestocquoy, J. 1930 'Administration de Rome et diaconies du VIIe au IXe siècle', *Rivista di Archeologia Cristiana* 7: 261–98.

Lexicon Topographicum Urbis Romae, E. M. Steinby (ed.), 6 vols. (Rome: Edizioni Quasar, 1993–2000).

Leyser, C. 2000 'The temptations of cult: Roman martyr piety in the age of Gregory the Great', *Early Medieval Europe* 9: 289–307.

Lidova, M. 2016 'Empress, Virgin, "Ecclesia". The icon of Santa Maria in Trastevere in the early Byzantine context', *IKON: Journal of Iconographic Studies* 9: 109–28.

Lidova, M. 2017 '"Maria Regina" on the "palimpsest wall" in S. Maria Antiqua in Rome: historical context and imperial connotations of the early Byzantine image', *Iconographica* 16: 9–25.

Liverani, P. 1991 'Monumenti di epoca classica nel Patriarchio e nel Campo Lateranense', in C. Pietrangeli (ed.), *Il Palazzo apostolico lateranense* (Florence: Nardini), 106–17.

Liverani, P. 1999 'Dalle *aedes Laterani* al patriarchio Lateranense', *Rivista di Archeologia Cristiana* 75: 521–49.

Liverani, P. 2008 'Saint Peter's, Leo the Great and the leprosy of Constantine', *Papers of the British School at Rome* 76: 155–72.

Liverani, P. 2012 'L'episcopio Lateranense dalle origini all'Alto Medioevo', in S. Balcon-Berry, F. Baratte, J.-P. Caillet, and D. Sandron (eds.), *Des 'Domus ecclesiae' aux palais épiscopaux. Actes du colloque tenu à Autun du 24 au 28 novembre 2009* (Turnhout: Brepols), 119–31.

Liverani, P. 2013 'Saint Peter's and the city of Rome between Late Antiquity and the early Middle Ages', in R. McKitterick, J. Osborne, C. Richardson, and J. Story (eds.), *Old Saint Peter's, Rome* (Cambridge: Cambridge University Press), 21–34.

Llewellyn, P. 1993 *Rome in the Dark Ages*, rev. ed. (London: Constable).

Lowe, E. A. 1934–71 *Codices Latini antiquiores: a palaeographical guide to Latin manuscripts prior to the ninth century*, 10 vols. (Oxford: Clarendon Press).

Lowe, E. A. 1955 'An unknown Latin psalter on Mount Sinai', *Scriptorium* 9: 177–99.

Lucey, S. J. 2007 'Art and Socio-Cultural Identity in Early Medieval Rome: The Patrons of Santa Maria Antiqua', in É. Ó Carragáin and C. Neuman de Vegvar (eds.), *Roma Felix – Formation and Reflections of Medieval Rome* (Aldershot: Ashgate), 139–58.

Luchterhandt, M. 1999a 'Kopf eines Apostels aus dem Lateranstriklinium Leos III', in C. Stiegemann and M. Wemhoff (eds.), *799. Kunst und Kultur der Karolingerzeit. Karl der Große und Papst Leo III. in Paderborn. Katalog der Ausstellung* (Mainz: Philipp von Zabern), 47–8 (Kat. II.8).

Luchterhandt, M. 1999b 'Kopf eines Apostels aus dem Lateranstriklinium Leos III', in C. Stiegemann and M. Wemhoff (eds.), *799. Kunst und Kultur der Karolingerzeit. Karl der Große und Papst Leo III. in Paderborn. Katalog der Ausstellung* (Mainz: Philipp von Zabern), 48 (Kat. II.9).

Luchterhandt, M. 1999c 'Alfonso Ciacconio, Kopie der rechten Stirnseite des Trikliniumsmosaik im Lateran', in C. Stiegemann and M. Wemhoff (eds.), *799. Kunst und Kultur der Karolingerzeit. Karl der Große und Papst Leo III. in*

Paderborn. Katalog der Ausstellung (Mainz: Philipp von Zabern), 48–50 (Kat. II.10).

Luchterhandt, M. 1999d '"Famulus Petri" – Karl der Große in den römischen Mosaikbildern Leos III.', in C. Stiegemann and M. Wemhoff (eds.), *799. Kunst und Kultur der Karolingerzeit. Karl der Große und Papst Leo III. in Paderborn. Beiträge zum Katalog der Ausstellung* (Mainz: Philipp von Zabern), 55–70.

Luchterhandt, M. 2006 'Stolz und Vorurteil. Der Westen und die byzantinische Hofkultur im Frühmittelalter', in F.A. Bauer (ed.), *Visualisierungen von Herrschaft. Frühmittelalterliche Residenzen – Gestalt und Zeremoniell. Internationales Kolloquium 3./4. Juni 2004 in Istanbul* (Istanbul: Deutsches Archäologisches Institut Istanbul), 171–211.

Luchterhandt, M. 2017 'The popes and the loca sancta of Jerusalem: relic practice and relic diplomacy in the Eastern Mediterranean after the Muslim conquest', in R. Bartal, N. Bodner, and B. Kühnel (eds.), *Natural Materials of the Holy Land and the Visual Translation of Place, 500–1500* (Abingdon: Routledge), 36–63.

Macchiarella, G. (ed.) 1976a 'Seminario sulla tecnica e il linguaggio della scultura a Roma tra VIII e IX secolo', *Roma e l'Età Carolingia. Atti delle giornate di studio, 3–8 maggio 1976* (Rome: Multigrafica Editrice), 267–88.

Macchiarella, G. 1976b 'Note su la scultura in marmo a Roma tra VIII e IX secolo', *Roma e l'Età Carolingia. Atti delle giornate di studio, 3–8 maggio 1976* (Rome: Multigrafica Editrice), 289–99.

Mackie, G. 1996 'The San Venanzio Chapel in Rome and the Martyr Shrine Sequence', *RACAR* 23: 1–13.

Mackie, G. 2003 *Early Christian Chapels in the West: Decoration, Function, and Patronage* (Toronto: University of Toronto Press).

Manacorda, D. 2001 *Crypta Balbi: Archeologia e storia di un paesaggio urbano* (Milan: Electa).

Manacorda, D. 2017 'A proposito di archeologia della produzione a Roma nel medioevo', *Archeologia medievale* 44: 291–5.

Mancini, A. 1968 'La chiesa medioevale di S. Adriano nel Foro Romano', *Atti della Pontificia Accademia Romana di Archeologia. Rendiconti* 40: 191–245.

Mango, C. 1959 *The Brazen House: a study of the vestibule of the imperial palace in Constantinople* (Copenhagen: i kommission hos Ejnar Munksgaard).

Mango, C. 1973 'La culture grecque et l'Occident au VIIIe siècle', *I problemi dell'Occidente nel secolo VIII*, Settimane di Studio del CISAM 20 (Spoleto: Centro Italiano di Studi sull'Alto Medioevo), 683–721.

Mango, C. 1976 'Historical Introduction', in A. Bryer and J. Herrin (eds.), *Iconoclasm: Papers given at the Ninth Spring Symposium of Byzantine Studies* (Birmingham: Centre for Byzantine Studies, University of Birmingham), 1–6.

Mango, C. 1990 'Constantine's Mausoleum and the Translation of Relics', *Byzantinische Zeitschrift* 83: 51–62.

Mango, C. 2000, 'Constantinople as Theotokoupolis', in M. Vassilaki (ed.), *Mother of God. Representations of the Virgin in Byzantine Art* (Milan: Skira), 16–25.

Mansi, G. D. 1759–98 *Sacrorum conciliorum nova et amplissima collectio*, 31 vols. (Florence: Antonio Zatta).

Marazzi, F. 1991 'Il conflitto fra Leone III Isaurico e il papato fra il 725 e il 733, e il "definitivo" inizio del medioevo a Roma', *Papers of the British School at Rome* 59: 231–57.

Marazzi, F. 1998 *I 'patrimonia sanctae Romanae ecclesiae' nel Lazio (secoli IV–X): Strutture amministrative e prassi gestionali* (Rome: Istituto Storico Italiano per il Medio Evo).

Marazzi, F. 2000 'Rome in Transition: Economic and political change in the fourth and fifth centuries', in J. M. H. Smith (ed.), *Early Medieval Rome and the Christian West. Essays in Honour of Donald A. Bullough* (Leiden: Brill), 21–41.

Marazzi, F. 2001 'Aristocrazia e società (secoli VI–XI)', in A. Vauchez (ed.), *Roma medievale* (Rome: Laterza), 41–69.

Marazzi, F. 2001–2 'Il "Liber Pontificalis" e la fondazione delle "domuscultae"', in H. Geertman (ed.), *Atti del colloquio internazionale Il Liber Pontificalis e la storia materiale (Roma, 21–22 febbraio 2002)* (= Mededelingen van het Nederlands Instituut te Rome 60–61), 167–88.

Marcelli, M. 1989 'Su alcune tombe tardo-antiche di Roma: nota preliminare', *Archeologia Medievale* 16: 525–40.

Marinis, V. 2009 'Tombs and burials in the Monastery *tou Libos* in Constantinople', *Dumbarton Oaks Papers* 63: 147–66.

Marinis, V. 2014 *Architecture and Ritual in the Churches of Constantinople: Ninth to Fifteenth Centuries* (Cambridge: Cambridge University Press).

Markus, R. A. 1997 *Gregory the Great and his World* (Cambridge: Cambridge University Press).

Marrou, H.-I. 1940 'L'origine orientale des diaconies romaines', *Mélanges d'Archéologie et d'Histoire* 57: 95–142.

Martiniani-Reber 1986 'Nouveau regard sur les soieries de l'Annonciation et de la Nativité du Sancta Sanctorum', *Bulletin de Liaison du Centre International d'Étude des Textiles Anciens* 63–4:12–19.

Martiniani-Reber, M. 1999 'Tentures et textiles des églises romaines au haut Moyen Âge d'après le *Liber pontificalis*', *Mélanges de l'École française de Rome: Moyen Âge* 111: 289–305.

Marucchi, O. 1900 'Scoperte nell'antica chiesa di S. Saba', *Nuovo Bollettino di Archeologia Cristiana* 6: 175–6.

Maskarinec, M. 2013 'Who were the Romans? Shifting scripts of Romanness in Early Medieval Italy', in W. Pohl and G. Heydemann (eds.), *Post-Roman Transitions: Christian and Barbarian Identities in the Early Medieval West* (Turnhout: Brepols), 297–363.

Maskarinec, M. 2017 'Saints for all Christendom: naturalizing the Alexandrinian saints Cyrus and John in seventh- to thirteenth-century Rome', *Dumbarton Oaks Papers* 71: 337–65.

Maskarinec, M. 2018 *City of Saints: Rebuilding Rome in the Early Middle Ages* (Philadelphia: University of Pennsylvania Press).

Massimo, G. 2003 'Papa Zaccaria e i lavori di rinnovamento del Patriarchio Lateranense (741–752)', *Arte Medievale* N.S. 2.1: 17–37.

Matthews, J. F. 1970 'Olympiodorus of Thebes and the history of the West (A.D. 407–425)', *Journal of Roman Studies* 60: 79–97.

Mazzucato, O. 1993 *Tipologie e techniche della ceramica a vetrina pesante, IX-X secolo* (Rome: CNR Edizioni).

McClendon, C. 2013 'Old Saint Peter's and the Iconoclastic Controversy', in R. McKitterick, J. Osborne, C. Richardson, and J. Story (eds.), *Old Saint Peter's, Rome* (Cambridge: Cambridge University Press), 214–28.

McCormick, M. 1991 'Proskynesis', in *ODB*, 1738–9.

McCormick, M. 1995 'Byzantium and the West, 700–900', in R. McKitterick (ed.), *The New Cambridge Medieval History. Volume II: c.700–c.900* (Cambridge: Cambridge University Press), 349–80.

McCormick, M. 2001 *Origins of the European Economy. Communications and Commerce, A.D. 300–900* (Cambridge: Cambridge University Press).

McCormick, M. 2002 'New light on the "Dark Ages": How the slave trade fuelled the Carolingian economy', *Past & Present* 177: 17–54.

McCulloh, J. M. 1976 'The cult of relics in the letters and "Dialogues" of Pope Gregory the Great: a lexicographical study', *Traditio* 32: 145–84.

McEvoy, M. 2013 'The mausoleum of Honorius: Late Roman imperial Christianity and the city of Rome in the fifth century', in R. McKitterick, J. Osborne, C. Richardson, and J. Story (eds.), *Old Saint Peter's, Rome* (Cambridge: Cambridge University Press), 119–36.

McKinnon, J. 2000 *The Advent Project: The Late-Seventh-Century Creation of the Roman Mass Proper* (Berkeley and Los Angeles: University of California Press).

McKitterick, R. 1989 *The Carolingians and the Written Word* (Cambridge: Cambridge University Press).

McKitterick, R. 2004 *History and Memory in the Carolingian World* (Cambridge: Cambridge University Press).

McKitterick, R. 2006 *Perceptions of the Past in the Early Middle Ages* (Notre Dame, IN: University of Notre Dame Press).

McKitterick, R. 2008 *Charlemagne: The Formation of a European Identity* (Cambridge: Cambridge University Press).

McKitterick, R. 2011 'Roman texts and Roman history in the early Middle Ages', in C. Bolgia, R. McKitterick, and J. Osborne (eds.), *Rome across Time and Space c.500–c.1400: Cultural Transmission and Exchange of Ideas* (Cambridge: Cambridge University Press), 19–34.

McKitterick, R. 2013 'The representation of Old Saint Peter's basilica in the *Liber Pontificalis*', in R. McKitterick, J. Osborne, C. Richardson, and J. Story (eds.), *Old Saint Peter's, Rome* (Cambridge: Cambridge University Press), 95–118.

McKitterick, R. (ed.) 2014 *Being Roman after Rome*, themed edition of *Early Medieval Europe* 22: 387–505.

McKitterick, R. 2015 'Transformations of the Roman past and Roman identity in the early Middle Ages', in C. Gantner, R. McKitterick and S. Meeder (eds.), *The Resources of the Past in Early Medieval* Europe (Cambridge: Cambridge University Press), 225–44.

McKitterick, R. 2016 'The papacy and Byzantium in the seventh- and early eighth-century sections of the *Liber pontificalis*', *Papers of the British School at Rome* 84: 241–73.

McKitterick, R. 2018 'The *damnatio memoriae* of Pope Constantine II (767–768)', in R. Balzaretti, J. Barrow, and P. Skinner (eds.) *Italy and Early Medieval Europe. Papers for Chris Wickham* (Oxford: Oxford University Press), 231–48.

McKitterick, R. 2020a 'The Constantinian basilica in the early medieval *Liber pontificalis*', in L. Bosman, I. Haynes, and P. Liverani (eds.), *St John Lateran to 1600* (Cambridge: Cambridge University Press), forthcoming.

McKitterick, R. 2020b 'The Church and the Law in the early Middle Ages', in *The Church and the Law,* Studies in Church History 56, in press.

McNally, R. 1978 'Gregory the Great and his declining world', *Archivum Historiae Pontificiae* 16: 7–26.

Mei, O. 2020 '1702: the discovery of Santa Maria Antiqua', in E. Rubery, G. Bordi and J. Osborne (eds.), *Santa Maria Antiqua: the Sistine Chapel of the Eighth Century* (Turnhout: Brepols), in press.

Melograni, A. 1990 'Le pitture del VI e VIII secolo nella basilica inferiore di S. Crisogono in Trastevere', *Rivista dell'Istituto Nazionale di Archeologia e Storia dell'Arte* ser. III, 13: 139–78.

Melucco Vaccaro, A. (ed.) 1974 *Corpus della Scultura Altomedievale. VII. La Diocesi di Roma. Tomo III: La II Regione Ecclesiastica* (Spoleto: Centro Italiano di Studi sull'Alto Medioevo).

Melucco Vaccaro, A. 1999 'Le officine marmorarie romane nei secoli VIII-IX. Tradizione ed apporti', in A. Cadei, M. Righetti Tosti-Croce, and A. Segagni Malacart (eds.), *Arte d'Occidente: temi e metodi. Scritti in onore di Angiola Maria Romanini* (Rome: Sintesi Informazione), 299–308.

Melucco Vaccaro, A. 2001 'Le botteghe dei lapicidi: dalla lettura stilistica all'analisi delle tecniche di produzione', *Roma nell'Alto Medioevo*, Settimane di Studio del CISAM 48 (Spoleto: Centro Italiano di Studi sull'Alto Medioevo), 393–420.

Mende, U. 1999 'Die Aachener *Lupa*', in C. Stiegemann and M. Wemhoff (eds.), *799. Kunst und Kultur der Karolingerzeit. Karl der Große und Papst Leo III. in Paderborn. Band 1: Katalog der Ausstellung* (Mainz: Philipp von Zabern), 112–13.

Meneghini, R. 1997 'Edilizia pubblica e riuso di monumenti classici a Roma nell'alto medioevo: l'area dei templi di Apollo Sosiano e Bellona e la diaconia di S. Angelo in Pescheria', in S. Gelichi (ed.), *I Congresso nazionale di archeologia medievale (Pisa, 29–31 maggio 1997)* (Florence: All'Insegna del Giglio), 51–7.

Meneghini, R. 2004a 'Edilizia pubblica', in R. Meneghini and R. Santangeli Valenzani (eds.), *Roma nell'alto medioevo: topografia urbanistica della città dal V al X secolo* (Rome: Libreria dello Stato), 53–101.

Meneghini, R. 2004b 'Sepolture urbane', in R. Meneghini and R. Santangeli Valenzani (eds.), *Roma nell'alto medioevo: topografia urbanistica della città dal V al X secolo* (Rome: Libreria dello Stato), 103–25.

Meneghini, R. 2013 'Le vicende del 408–410 e la comparsa delle sepulture urbane a Roma', in J. Lipps, C. Machado, and P. von Rummel (eds.), *The Sack of Rome in 410 AD: the event, its context and its impact. Proceedings of the conference held at the German Archaeological Institute at Rome, 04–06 November 2010* (Wiesbaden: Dr. Ludwig Reichert Verlag), 403–9.

Meneghini, R. and R. Santangeli Valenzani 1993 'Sepolture intramuranee e paesaggio urbano a Roma tra V e VII secolo', in L. Paroli and P. Delogu (eds.), *La storia economica di Roma nell'alto medioevo alla luce dei recenti scavi archeologici (Atti del seminario, Roma 2–3 aprile 1992)* (Florence: All'Insegna del Giglio), 89–111.

Meneghini, R. and R. Santangeli Valenzani 1995 'Sepolture intermuranee a Roma tra V e VII secolo d.C. – Aggiornamenti e considerazioni', *Archeologia Medievale* 22: 283–90.

Mercati, S. G. 1919 'Sull'epigramma acrostico. Premesso alla versione greca di S. Zaccaria papa del "Liber Dialogorum" di S. Gregorio Magno', *Bessarione* 35: 67–72.

Michalsky, T. 2015 '*Grata pictura* and *mapa duplex*. Paolino Minorita's late medieval map of Rome as an epistemological instrument of a historiographer', *Convivium* 2.1: 38–58.

Milella, A. 2004 'San Teodoro alle pendici del Palatino: considerazioni sulle origini della diaconia', *Archeologia Classica* 55: 203–34.

Miller, D. 1974 'The Roman revolution of the eighth century. A study of the ideological background of the papal separation from Byzantium and alliance with the Franks', *Mediaeval Studies* 36: 79–133.

Miller, D. 1975 'Byzantine-papal relations during the pontificate of Paul I: confirmation and completion of the Roman revolution of the eighth century', *Byzantinische Zeitschrift* 68: 47–62.

Miller, M. 2000 *The Bishop's Palace: Architecture and Authority in Medieval Italy* (Ithaca and London: Cornell University Press).

Miller, M. 2014 'The sources of textiles and vestments in early medieval Rome', in V. Garver and O. Phelan (eds.), *Rome and Religion in the Medieval World: Studies in Honor of Thomas F.X. Noble* (Farnham: Ashgate), 83–99.

Minasi, M. 2009 *La Tomba di Callisto: appunti sugli affreschi altomedievali della cripta del papa martire nella Catacomba di Calepodio* (Vatican City: Pontificia Commissione di Archeologia Sacra).

Mitchell, J. and B. Leal 2013 'Wall paintings in S. Maria *foris portas* (Castelseprio) and the tower at Torba. Reflections and reappraisal', in P. M. De Marchi (ed.),

Castelseprio e Torba: Sintesi delle ricerche e aggiornamenti (Mantua: Soprintendenza per i Beni Archeologici della Lombardia), 311–44.

Mommsen, T. 1942 'Petrarch's conception of the "Dark Ages"'. *Speculum* 17: 226–42.

Moretti, F. R. 2006 'Triclinio di Leone III', in M. Andaloro (ed.), *La pittura medievale a Roma, 312-1431. Atlante I* (Milan: Jaca Book), 217–20.

Moretti, S. 1997 'Appunti di lettura del *Liber pontificalis*: valenza dei termini "imago", "effigies", "figura", icona ed entità dei doni dall'impero bizantino', *Arte Medievale* 11: 61–73.

Morey, C. R. 1926 'The painted panel from the Sancta Sanctorum', *Festschrift zum sechzigsten Geburtstag von Paul Clemen 31. Oktober 1926* (Düsseldorf: K. Schwann).

Morganti, G. 2004 'Giacomo Boni e i lavori di Santa Maria Antiqua: un secolo di restauri', in J. Osborne, J. R. Brandt, and G. Morganti (eds.), *Santa Maria Antiqua cento anni dopo. Atti del colloquio internazionale, Roma, 5-6 maggio 2000* (Rome: Campisano editore), 11–30.

Morganti, G. 2016 'Lo spazio di Santa Maria Antiqua', in M. Andaloro, G. Bordi, and G. Morganti (eds.), *Santa Maria Antiqua tra Roma e Bisanzio* (Milan: Electa), 54–69.

Morrisson, C. and J.-N. Barrandon 1988 'La trouvaille de monnaies d'argent byzantines de Rome (VII–VIII siècles): analyse et chronologie', *Revue numismatique* 30: 149–65.

Mosino, F. 1983 'I grecismi del *Liber Pontificalis*', *Bollettino della Badia greca di Grottaferrata* N.S. 37: 61–73.

Motta, G. 2015 'Desiderio e il papato', in G. Archetti (ed.) *Desiderio: il progetto politico dell'ultimo re longobardo. Atti del Primo convegno internazionale di studio (Brescia, 21-24 marzo 2013)* (Spoleto: Centro Italiano di Studi sull'Alto Medioevo), 305–13.

Mütherich, F. 1976 'Manoscritti romani e miniatura carolingia', *Roma e l'Età Carolingia. Atti delle giornate di studio, 3-8 maggio* 1976 (Rome: Multigrafica Editrice), 79–85.

Neil, B. 2013 'The papacy in the age of Gregory the Great', in B. Neil and M. Del Santo (eds.), *A Companion to Gregory the Great* (Leiden: Brill), 3–27.

Neri, E. 2017 'The mosaics of Durres amphitheatre: an assessment using technical observations', *Antiquité tardive* 25: 353–74.

Nestori, A. 1971 'La catacomba di Calepodio al III miglio dell'Aurelia vetus e i sepolcri dei papi Callisto I e Giulio I', *Rivista di Archeologia Cristiana* 47: 169–278; 48: 193–233.

Neuman de Vegvar, C. 2007 'Gendered Spaces: the placement of imagery in Santa Maria Maggiore', in É. Ó Carragáin and C. Neuman de Vegvar (eds.), *Roma Felix – Formation and Reflections of Medieval Rome* (Aldershot: Ashgate), 97–111.

Nilgen, U. 1981 'Maria Regina – Ein politischer Kultbildtypus?', *Römisches Jahrbuch für Kunstgeschichte* 19: 35–83.

Nilgen, U. 1999a 'Papst Leo III. und Karl der Große aus dem Apsismosaik von S. Susanna', in C. Stiegemann and M. Wemhoff (eds.), *799. Kunst und Kultur der Karolingerzeit. Karl der Große und Papst Leo III. in Paderborn. Katalog der Ausstellung* (Mainz: Philipp von Zabern), 637–8 (Kat. IX.23).

Nilgen, U. 1999b 'Apsismosaik von SS. Nereo ed Achilleo', in C. Stiegemann and M. Wemhoff (eds.), *799. Kunst und Kultur der Karolingerzeit. Karl der Große und Papst Leo III. in Paderborn. Katalog der Ausstellung* (Mainz: Philipp von Zabern), 638–40 (Kat. IX.24).

Nilgen, U. 2002 'Eine neu aufgefundene Maria Regina in Santa Susanna, Rom', in K. Möseneder and G. Schüssler (eds.), *'Bedeutung in den Bildern': Festschrift für Jörg Traeger zum 60. Geburtstag* (Regensburg: Schnell und Steiner), 231–45.

Nilgen, U. 2004 'The Adoration of the Crucified Christ at Santa Maria Antiqua and the tradition of triumphal arch decoration in Rome', in J. Osborne, J. R. Brandt, and G. Morganti (eds.), *Santa Maria Antiqua cento anni dopo. Atti del colloquio internazionale, Roma, 5–6 maggio 2000* (Rome: Campisano editore), 129–35.

Nobiloni, B. 1999 'I pilastri marmorei dell'Oratorio di Giovanni VII nella vecchia basilica di San Pietro', *Xenia Antiqua* 8: 69–128.

Noble, T. F. X. 1984 *The Republic of St Peter: The Birth of the Papal State, 680–825* (Philadelphia: University of Pennsylvania Press).

Noble, T. F. X. 1985 'The declining knowledge of Greek in eighth- and ninth-century papal Rome', *Byzantinische Zeitschrift* 78: 56–62.

Noble, T. F. X. 1990 'Literacy and the papal government in late antiquity and the early middle ages', in R. McKitterick (ed.), *The Uses of Literacy in Early Medieval Europe* (Cambridge: Cambridge University Press), 82–108.

Noble, T. F. X. 1995 'Rome in the seventh century', in M. Lapidge (ed.), *Archbishop Theodore: Commemorative Studies on His Life and Influence* (Cambridge: Cambridge University Press), 68–87.

Noble, T. F. X. 2000 'Paradoxes and possibilities in the sources for Roman society in the early Middle Ages', in J. M. H. Smith (ed.), *Early Medieval Rome and the Christian West: Essays in Honour of Donald A. Bullough* (Leiden: Brill), 55–83.

Noble, T. F. X. 2001a 'The intellectual culture of the early medieval papacy', *Roma nell'Alto Medioevo*, Settimane di Studio del CISAM 48 (Spoleto: Centro Italiano di Studi sull'Alto Medioevo), 179–213.

Noble, T. F. X 2001b 'Topography, celebration, and power: the making of a papal Rome in the eighth and ninth centuries', in M. de Jong and F. Theuws (eds.), *Topographies of Power in the Early Middle Ages* (Leiden: Brill), 45–91.

Noble, T. F. X. 2003 'The Roman elite from Constantine to Charlemagne', *Acta ad archaeologiam et artium historiam pertinentia* 17: 13–25.

Noble, T. F. X. 2009 *Images, Iconoclasm and the Carolingians* (Philadelphia: University of Pennsylvania Press).

Noble, T. F. X. 2013 'The reception of visitors in early medieval Rome', in C. Chandler and S. Stofferahn (eds.), *Discovery and Distinction in the early Middle Ages: Studies in Honor of John J. Contreni* (Kalamazoo: Western Michigan University), 205–17.

Noble, T. F. X. 2014 'Greek Popes: Yes or No, and did it matter?', in A. Fischer and I. Wood (eds.), *Western Perspectives on the Mediterranean: Cultural Transfer in Late Antiquity and the Early Middle Ages, 400–800 A.D.* (London: Bloomsbury Academic), 77–86.

Noble, T. F. X. 2015 'A court without courtiers: the Roman church in Late Antiquity and the Early Middle Ages', *Le Corti nell'Alto Medioevo*, Settimane di Studio del CISAM 62 (Spoleto: Centro Italiano di Studi sull'Alto Medioevo), 235–57.

Nordenfalk, C. 1970 *Die spätantiken Zierbuchstaben* (Stockholm: Röder).

Nordhagen, P. J. 1961 'The origin of the Washing of the Child in the Nativity scene', *Byzantinische Zeitschrift* 54: 333–7.

Nordhagen, P. J. 1962 'The earliest decorations in Santa Maria Antiqua and their date', *Acta ad archaeologiam et artium historiam pertinentia* 1: 53–72.

Nordhagen, P. J. 1965 'The mosaics of John VII (705–707 A.D.)', *Acta ad archaeologiam et artium historiam pertinentia* 2: 121–66.

Nordhagen, P. J. 1967 'John VII's "Adoration of the Cross" in S. Maria Antiqua', *Journal of the Warburg and Courtauld Institutes* 30: 388–90.

Nordhagen, P. J. 1968 'The Frescoes of John VII (A.D. 705–707) in S. Maria Antiqua in Rome' = *Acta ad archaeologiam et artium historiam pertinentia* 3.

Nordhagen, P. J. 1969 'A carved marble pilaster in the Vatican Grottoes: Some remarks on sculptural technique of the early Middle Ages', *Acta ad archaeologiam et artium historiam pertinentia* 4: 113–19.

Nordhagen, P. J. 1972a 'The integration of the Nativity and the Annunciation to the Shepherds in Byzantine art', *Acts of the XXIInd International Congress of the History of Art* (Budapest): 253–7; repr. in P. J. Nordhagen, *Studies in Byzantine and Early Medieval Painting* (London: The Pindar Press, 1990), 318–25.

Nordhagen, P. J. 1972b '"Hellenism" and the frescoes in Santa Maria Antiqua', *Konsthistorisk Tidskrift* 41: 73–80.

Nordhagen, P. J. 1978 'S. Maria Antiqua: the frescoes of the seventh century', *Acta ad archaeologiam et artium historiam pertinentia* 8: 89–142.

Nordhagen, P. J. 1982 'The Harrowing of Hell as imperial iconography. A note on its earliest use', *Byzantinische Zeitschrift* 75: 345–8.

Nordhagen, P. J. 1983 'The use of palaeography in the dating of early medieval frescoes', *Jahrbuch der Österreichischen Byzantinistik* 32.4: 167–73; repr. in P.J. Nordhagen, *Studies in Byzantine and Early Medieval Painting* (London: The Pindar Press, 1990), 386–90.

Nordhagen, P. J. 1985 'Working with Wilpert. The Illustrations in *Die römischen Mosaiken und Malereien* and their source value', *Acta ad archaeologiam et artium historiam pertinentia. Series altera* 5: 247–57.

Nordhagen, P. J. 1987 'Icons designed for the display of sumptuous votive gifts', *Dumbarton Oaks Papers* 41: 453–60.

Nordhagen, P. J. 1996 [untitled response to article by Natalia Teteriatnikov] *Cahiers Archéologiques* 44: 182–3.

Nordhagen, P. J. 2000 'Constantinople on the Tiber: the Byzantines in Rome and the Iconography of their Images', in J. M. H. Smith (ed.), *Early Medieval Rome and the Christian West: Essays in Honour of Donald A. Bullough* (Leiden: Brill), 113–34.

Nordhagen, P. J. 2002 'Early medieval church decoration in Rome and "The Battle of Images"', in F. Guidobaldi and A. Guiglia Guidobaldi (eds.), *Ecclesiae Urbis. Atti del Congresso internazionale di studi sulle chiese di Roma (IV–X secolo), Roma, 4–10 settembre 2000* (Vatican City: Pontificio Istituto di Archeologia Cristiana), 1749–62.

Nordhagen, P. J. 2004 'Iconoclasm: rupture or interlude? A reassessment of the evidence', *Acta ad archaeologiam et artium historiam pertinentia* 18: 205–15.

Nordhagen, P. J. 2007 'The Use of Antiquity in Early Byzantium. Ernst Kitzinger's thesis on the "perennial Hellenism" of Constantinople', *Bizantinistica: Rivista di Studi Bizantini e Slavi* 9: 61–71.

Nordhagen, P. J. 2012 'The presence of Greek artists in Rome in the early Middle Ages: a puzzle solved', *Bizantinistica: Rivista di Studi Bizantini e Slavi* 14: 183–91.

Nordhagen, P. J. 2014 'Form and function in the mosaic Maria Regina from the oratory of John VII (A.D. 705–707) in the Old St Peter's', *Musiva & Sectilia* 8: 193–205.

Nordhagen, P. J. 2015 'In the Iconographer's Studio. The fashioning of new motif types in pre-Iconoclastic art', *Acta ad archaeologiam et artium historiam pertinentia* 28: 95–110.

Nordhagen, P. J. 2017 'The Frescoes of Pope John VII (705–707 A.D.) in S. Maria Antiqua in Rome. Supplementum', *Acta ad archaeologiam et artium historiam pertinentia* 29: 163–75.

Nordhagen, P. J. 2018a 'Byzantium, the enigmatic seventh century', in T. A. Bács, A. Bollók, and T. Vida (eds.), *Across the Mediterranean – Along the Nile. Studies in Egyptology, Nubiology and Late Antiquity dedicated to László Török on the occasion of his 75th birthday* (Budapest: Hungarian Academy of Sciences and Museum of Fine Art), 901–13.

Nordhagen, P. J. 2018b 'The art of recycling fresco-icons at the roots of the cult of images', *Acta ad archaeologiam et artium historiam pertinentia* 30: 237–47.

Noreen, K. 2011 'Opening the Holy of Holies: early twentieth-century explorations of the Sancta Sanctorum (Rome)', *Church History* 80: 520–46.

Ó Carragáin, É. 2013 'Interactions between liturgy and politics in Old Saint Peter's, 670–741', in R. McKitterick, J. Osborne, C. Richardson, and J. Story (eds.), *Old Saint Peter's, Rome* (Cambridge: Cambridge University Press), 177–89.

O'Connor, L. 2013 'The late antique wooden reliquaries from the chapel of the "Sancta Sanctorum"', *Bollettino dei Monumenti Musei e Gallerie Pontificie* 31: 201–29.

O'Hara, M. 1985 'A find of Byzantine silver from the Mint of Rome for the period A.D. 641–752', *Revue suisse de numismatique* 64: 105–40.

Opie, J. 2002 'Agnus Dei', in F. Guidobaldi and A. Guiglia Guidobaldi (eds.), *Ecclesiae Urbis. Atti del Congresso Internazionale di Studi sulle Chiese di Roma (IV–X secolo). Roma, 4–10 settembre 2000* (Vatican City: Pontificio Istituto di Archeologia Cristiana), 1813–40.

Osborne, J. 1979 'The portrait of Pope Leo IV in San Clemente, Rome: a re-examination of the so-called 'square' nimbus in medieval art', *Papers of the British School at Rome* 47: 58–65.

Osborne, J. 1981a 'Early medieval wall-paintings in the Catacomb of San Valentino, Rome', *Papers of the British School at Rome* 49: 82–90.

Osborne, J. 1981b 'Early medieval painting in San Clemente, Rome: the Madonna and Child in the niche', *Gesta* 20: 299–310.

Osborne, J. 1981c 'The painting of the Anastasis in the lower church of San Clemente, Rome: a re-examination of the evidence for the location of the tomb of St. Cyril', *Byzantion* 51: 255–87.

Osborne, J. 1982 'Early medieval wall-painting in the church of San Clemente, Rome: the Libertinus cycle and its date', *Journal of the Warburg and Courtauld Institutes* 45: 182–5.

Osborne, J. 1984a *Early medieval wall-paintings in the lower church of San Clemente Rome* (New York: Garland Press).

Osborne, J. 1984b 'Death and burial in sixth-century Rome', *Echos du Monde Classique/Classical Views* 28: 291–9.

Osborne, J. 1985 'The Roman catacombs in the Middle Ages', *Papers of the British School at Rome* 53: 278–328.

Osborne, J. 1987 'The atrium of S. Maria Antiqua, Rome: a history in art', *Papers of the British School at Rome* 55: 186–223.

Osborne, J. 1990 'The use of painted initials by Greek and Latin scriptoria in Carolingian Rome', *Gesta* 29: 76–85.

Osborne, J. 1992 'Textiles and their painted imitations in early medieval Rome', *Papers of the British School at Rome* 60: 309–51.

Osborne, J. 1994 'A Carolingian "Agnus Dei" relief from Mola di Monte Gelato, near Rome', *Gesta* 33: 73–8.

Osborne, J. 1996 'Einsiedeln Itinerary', in N. Thomson de Grummond (ed.), *An Encyclopedia of the History of Classical Archeology* (Westport, CT: Greenwood Press), 386–7.

Osborne, J. 1997a 'The sources of ornamental motifs in the mural decorations of early medieval Rome: some preliminary observations', in *L'ornement dans la peinture murale du Moyen Age (Actes du Colloque internationale tenu à Saint-Lizier du 1er au 4 juin 1995)* (Poitiers: Université de Poitiers, Centre d'études supérieures de civilisation médiévale), 27–34.

Osborne, J. 1997b 'The "Cross-under-Arch" motif in ninth-century Venetian sculpture: an imperial reading', *Thesaurismata* 27: 7–18.

Osborne, J. 1997c 'The early medieval sculpture', in T. W. Potter and A. C. King (eds.), *Excavations at the Mola di Monte Gelato: A Roman and Medieval Settlement in South Etruria* (London: The British School at Rome in association with The British Museum), 217–28.

Osborne, J. 1999 'Politics, diplomacy and the cult of relics in Venice and the northern Adriatic in the first half of the ninth century', *Early Medieval Europe* 8: 369–86.

Osborne, J. 2003 'Images of the Mother of God in Early Medieval Rome', in L. James and A. Eastmond (eds.), *Icon and Word: The Power of Images in Byzantium. Studies presented to Robin Cormack* (Aldershot: Ashgate), 135–56.

Osborne, J. 2004 'Framing sacred space. Eleventh-century mural painting in the churches of Rome', *Analecta Romana Instituti Danici* 30: 137–51.

Osborne, J. 2008 'The cult of Maria Regina in early medieval Rome', *Acta ad archaeologiam et artium historiam pertinentia* 21: 95–106.

Osborne, J. 2011a 'Rome and Constantinople in the ninth century', in C. Bolgia, R. McKitterick, and J. Osborne (eds.), *Rome Across Time and Space: Cultural Transmission and the Exchange of Ideas, c. 500–1400* (Cambridge: Cambridge University Press), 222–36.

Osborne, J. 2011b 'The early medieval painting of St Augustine in the Lateran palace', in O. Brandt and P. Pergola (eds.), *Marmoribus vestita: miscellanea in onore di Federico Guidobaldi*, Studi di Antichità Cristiana 63 (Vatican City: Pontificio Istituto di Archeologia Cristiana), 993–1002.

Osborne, J. 2013 '*Plus Caesare Petrus*: the Vatican obelisk and the approach to Saint Peter's', in R. McKitterick, J. Osborne, C. Richardson, and J. Story (eds.), *Old Saint Peter's, Rome* (Cambridge: Cambridge University Press), 274–86.

Osborne, J. 2014 'Rome and Constantinople about the year 700: the significance of the recently uncovered mural in the narthex of Santa Sabina', in G. Bordi, I. Carlettini, M. L. Fobelli, M. R. Menna, and P. Pogliani (eds.), *L'officina dello sguardo: scritti in onore di Maria Andaloro*, 2 vols. (Rome: Gangemi), I, 329–34.

Osborne, J. and A. Claridge 1996–8 *The Paper Museum of Cassiano dal Pozzo, Series A, Part II: Early Christian and Medieval Antiquities*, 2 vols. (London: Harvey Miller).

Oxford Dictionary of Byzantium, A. Kazhdan (ed.) (New York and Oxford: Oxford University Press, 1991).

Pace, V. 2003 'Mosaici e pittura in Albania (VI–XIV secolo). Stato degli studi e prospettive di ricerca', *Antichità Altoadriatiche* 53: 93–128.

Pace, V. 2004 'Immagini sacre a Roma fra VI e VII secolo. In margine al problema "Roma e Bisanzio"', *Acta ad archaeologiam et artium historian pertinentia* 18: 139–56.

Pace, V. 2015 'Alla ricerca di un'identità: affreschi, mosaici, tavole dipinte e libri a Roma fra VI e IX secolo', in C. Carbonetti Vendittelli, S. Lucà, and M. Signorini (eds.), *Roma e il suo territorio nel medioevo. Le fonti scritte fra tradizione e innovazione* (Spoleto: Centro Italiano di Studi sull'Alto Medioevo), 471–98.

Page, C. 2010 *The Christian Singers in the West. The First Thousand Years* (New Haven and London: Yale University Press).

Panciera, S. 1986 '"His ego nec metas rerum nec tempora pono". Virgilio in un'inedita iscrizione romana', *Studi tardoantichi* 2: 191–210.

Pani Ermini, L. 1976 'Il ciborio della basilica di S. Ippolito all'Isola Sacra', *Roma e l'Età Carolingia. Atti delle giornate di studio, 3–8 maggio 1976* (Rome: Multigrafica Editrice), 337–44.

Paribeni, A. 2011 'Giacomo Boni e il mistero delle monete scomparse', in O. Brandt and P. Pergola (eds.), *Marmoribus vestita: miscellanea in onore di Federico Guidobaldi*, Studi di Antichità Cristiana 63 (Vatican City: Pontificio Istituto di Archeologia Cristiana), 1003–23.

Parisi Presicce, C. 2000 *La Lupa Capitolina* (Milan: Electa).

Paroli, L. 1990 'Ceramica a vetrina pesante altomedievale (Forum Ware) e medievale (Sparse Glazed). Altre invetriate tardo-antiche e altomedievali', in L. Saguì and L. Paroli (eds.), *Archeologia urbana a Roma: il progetto della Crypta Balbi. 5. L'esedra della Crypta Balbi nel medioevo (XI–XV secolo)* (Florence: All'Insegna del Giglio), 314–56.

Paroli, L. 1995 'I reperti extraurbani', in A. Melucco Vaccaro and L. Paroli (eds.), *Corpus della scultura altomedievale VII: La Diocesi di Roma, tomo 6: Il Museo dell'Alto Medioevo* (Spoleto: Centro Italiano di Studi sull'Alto Medioevo), 199–299.

Paroli, L. 1998 'La scultura in marmo a Roma tra l'VIII e il IX secolo', in P. Delogu (ed.), *Roma medievale: aggiornamenti* (Florence: All'Insegna del Giglio), 93–122.

Paroli, L. 2004 'Roma dal V al IX secolo: uno sguardo attraverso le stratigrafie archeologiche', in L. Paroli and L. Vendittelli (eds.), *Roma dall'antichità al medioevo II: contesti tardoantichi e altomedievali* (Milan: Electa), 11–40.

Partner, P. 1966 'Notes on the lands of the Roman church in the early Middle Ages', *Papers of the British School at Rome* 34: 68–78.

Patlagean, E. 2002 'Variations impériales sur le thème romain', *Roma fra Oriente e Occidente*, Settimane di Studio del CISAM 49 (Spoleto: Centro Italiano di Studi sull'Alto Medioevo), 1–47.

Peers, G. 2001 *Subtle Bodies. Representing Angels in Byzantium* (Berkeley and Los Angeles: University of California Press).

Pennesi, S. 2006 'Ambienti sotteranei del Sancta Sanctorum', in M. Andaloro (ed.), *La pittura medievale a Roma, 312–1431. Atlante I* (Milan: Jaca Book), 231–8.

Petriaggi, R. 1984 'Utilizzazione, decorazione e diffusione dei tessuti nei corredi delle basiliche cristiane secondo il Liber Pontificalis (514–795)', *Prospettiva* 39: 37–46.

Petrucci, A. 1972 'Libro, scrittura e scuola', *La Scuola nell'Occidente latino nel Alto Medioevo*, Settimane di Studio del CISAM 19 (Spoleto: Centro Italiano di Studi sull'Alto Medioevo), 313–37. Reprinted in English translation in Armando Petrucci, *Writers and Readers in Medieval Italy. Studies in the History of Written Culture*, trans. C. Radding (New Haven: Yale University Press, 1995), 59–76.

Picard, J.-C. 1969 'Étude sur l'emplacement des tombes des papes du IIIe au Xe siècle', *Mélanges d'Archéologie et d'Histoire* 81: 725–82.

Piro, S. and I. Haynes, P. Liverani, and D. Zamuner 2020. 'Ground Penetrating Radar Survey in the St. John Lateran Basilica Complex', in L. Bosman, I. Haynes, and P. Liverani (eds.), *St John Lateran to 1600* (Cambridge: Cambridge University Press), forthcoming.

Pogliani, P. 2006 'San Pietro', in M. Andaloro (ed.), *La pittura medievale a Roma, 312-1431. Atlante I* (Milan: Jaca Book), 21–44.

Pogliani, P. 2014 'Pittori e mosaicisti nei cantieri di Giovanni VII', in G. Bordi, I. Carlettini, M. L. Fobelli, M. R. Menna, and P. Pogliani (eds.), *L'officina dello sguardo: scritti in onore di Maria Andaloro*, 2 vols. (Rome: Gangemi), II, 443–50.

Pogliani, P. 2016a 'Il perduto Oratorio di Giovanni VII nella basilica di San Pietro in Vaticano. I mosaici', in M. Andaloro, G. Bordi, and G. Morganti (eds.), *Santa Maria Antiqua tra Roma e Bisanzio* (Milan: Electa), 240–7.

Pogliani, P. 2016b 'Il ritratto di Giovanni VII', in M. Andaloro, G. Bordi, and G. Morganti (eds.), *Santa Maria Antiqua tra Roma e Bisanzio* (Milan: Electa), 248–9.

Pogliani, P. 2016c 'La lavanda del Bambino', in M. Andaloro, G. Bordi, and G. Morganti (eds.), *Santa Maria Antiqua tra Roma e Bisanzio* (Milan: Electa), 252–3.

Pogliani, P., C. Pelsosi and G. Agresti, 2020 'Eyes fixed on the palimpsests of Santa Maria Antiqua', in E. Rubery, G. Bordi and J. Osborne (eds.), *Santa Maria Antiqua: The Sistine Chapel of the Eighth Century* (Turnhout: Brepols), in press.

Pohl, W. 2014 'Romanness: a multiple identity and its changes', *Early Medieval Europe* 22: 406–18.

Pohl, W. 2018 'Social cohesion, breaks, and transformation in Italy: 535–600', in R. Balzaretti, J. Barrow, and P. Skinner (eds.) *Italy and Early Medieval Europe. Papers for Chris Wickham* (Oxford: Oxford University Press), 19–38.

Pohl W. and C. Gantner, C. Grifoni, and M. Pollheimer-Mohaupt (eds.) 2018 *Transformations of Romanness: Early Medieval Regions and Identities*, Millennium Studies 71 (Berlin: Walter de Gruyter).

Potter, T. W. 1979 *The Changing Landscape of South Etruria* (New York: St Martin's Press).

Potter, T. W., and A. C. King (eds.) 1997 *Excavations at the Mola di Monte Gelato: A Roman and Medieval Settlement in South Etruria* (London: The British School at Rome in association with The British Museum).

Price, R. 2014 *The Acts of the Lateran Synod of 649. Translated with notes by Richard Price, with contributions by Phil Booth and Catherine Cubitt*, Translated Texts for Historians 61 (Liverpool: Liverpool University Press).

Price, R. 2020 'The frescoes in Santa Maria Antiqua, the Lateran Synod of 649, and Pope Vitalian', in E. Rubery, G. Bordi, and J. Osborne (eds.), *Santa Maria Antiqua: The Sistine Chapel of the Eighth Century* (Turnhout: Brepols), in press.

Prigent, V. 2004 'Les empereurs isauriens et la confiscation des patrimoines pontificaux d'Italie du sud', *Mélanges de l'École française de Rome. Moyen Âge* 116: 557–94.

Pugliesi, L. 2008 'Alcuni osservazioni sulle fasi più antiche della Chiesa di S. Angelo in Pescheria', *Rivista di Archeologia Cristiana* 84: 377–414.

Quattrocchi, A. 2002 'Le processioni stazionali: cerimoniale papale, fonti e topografia', in F. Guidobaldi and A. Guiglia Guidobaldi (eds.), *Ecclesiae Urbis. Atti del Congresso internazionale di studi sulle chiese di Roma (IV–X secolo), Roma, 4–10 settembre 2000* (Vatican City: Pontificio Istituto di Archeologia Cristiana), 85–95.

Queijo, K. 2012 'Le "Storie di san Pietro e san Paolo" nell'oratorio di Giovanni VII in San Pietro in Vaticano', in S. Romano (ed.), *La pittura medievale a Roma, 312–1431. Corpus V: Il Duecento e la Cultura Gotica, 1198–1287 ca.* (Milan:Jaca Book), 51–3.

Rea, R. 1993 'Roma: l'uso funerario della valle del Colosseo tra tardo antico e alto medioevo', *Archeologia Medievale* 20: 645–58.

Rebillard, É. 2003 *Religion et sépulture. L'Église, les vivants et les morts dans l'Antiquité tardive* (Paris: Éditions de l'École des Hautes Études en Sciences Sociales).

Redig de Campos, D. 1963 'Il "Sant'Agostino" della Scala Santa restaurato', *Römische Quartalschrift für christliche Altertumskunde und Kirchengeschichte* 58: 101–4.

Reekmans, L. 1964 *La tombe du pape Corneille et sa région cémétériale* (Vatican City: Pontificio Istituto di Archeologia Cristiana).

Rettner, A. 1995 'Dreimal Theodotus? Stifterbild und Grabstiftung in der Theodotus-Kapelle von Santa Maria Antiqua in Rom', in H.-R. Meier, C. Jäggi, and P. Büttner (eds.), *Für irdischen Ruhm und himmlischen Lohn: Stifter und Auftraggeber in der mittelalterlichen Kunst* (Berlin: Dietrich Reimer), 31–46.

Reynolds, R. E. 1991 'Leonard Boyle and Mediaeval Studies in Canada', in C. Brown, J. Osborne, and C. Kirwin (eds.), *Rome: Tradition, Innovation and Renewal* (Victoria: University of Victoria), 23–38.

Ricci, C. 2013 'Gregory's missions to the barbarians', in B. Neil and M. Del Santo (eds.), *A Companion to Gregory the Great* (Leiden: Brill), 29–56.

Ricci, M. 1997 'Relazioni culturali e scambi commerciali nell'Italia centrale romano-longobarda alla luce della Crypta Balbi in Roma', in L. Paroli (ed.), *L'Italia centro-settentrionale in età longobarda (Atti del Convegno Ascoli Piceno 6–7 ottobre 1995)* (Florence: All'Insegna del Giglio), 239–73.

Richards, J. 1979 *The Popes and the Papacy in the Early Middle Ages, 476–752* (London: Routledge and Kegan Paul).

Richards, J. 1980 *Consul of God: The Life and Times of Gregory the Great* (London: Routledge and Kegan Paul).

Richardson, L. 1992 *A New Topographical Dictionary of Ancient Rome* (Baltimore and London: Johns Hopkins University Press).

Righetti Tosti-Croce, M. 1991 'Il Sancta Sanctorum: architettura', in C. Pietrangeli (ed.), *Il Palazzo apostolico lateranense* (Florence: Nardini), 50–7.

Rio, A. 2017 *Slavery after Rome, 500–1100* (Oxford: Oxford University Press).

Rocca, A. 1609 *De particula ex pretioso et vivifico ligno sacratissimae crucis salvatoris Iesu Christi* (Rome: Guglielmo Facciotti).

Romanelli, P. and P. J. Nordhagen 1964 *S. Maria Antiqua* (Rome: Istituto poligrafico dello Stato).

Romano, J. 2014 *Liturgy and Society in Early Medieval Rome* (Farnham: Ashgate).

Romei, D. 2004 'Produzione e circolazione dei manufatti ceramici a Roma nell'alto medioevo', in L. Paroli and L. Vendittelli (eds.), *Roma dall'antichità al medioevo II: contesti tardoantichi e altomedievali* (Milan: Electa), 278–311.

Rossi, M. 2010 'Il problema Castelseprio', in V. Pace (ed.), *L'VIII secolo: un secolo inquieto. Atti del Convegno internazionale di studi, Cividale del Friuli, 4–7 dicembre 2008* (Cividale del Friuli: Comune del Cividale del Friuli), 131–7.

Rossi, P. 1993 'Elementi per l'individuazione di una tipologia di ambone "romano" in epoca altomedievale', *Arte Medievale* 7.1: 1–13.

Rovelli, A. 1998 'La circolazione monetaria a Roma nei secoli VII e VIII. Nuovi dati per la storia economica di Roma nell'alto medioevo', in P. Delogu (ed.), *Roma medievale: aggiornamenti* (Florence: All'Insegna del Giglio), 79–91.

Rovelli, A. 2000 'Monetary circulation in Byzantine and Carolingian Rome: a reconsideration in the light of recent archaeological data', in J. M. H. Smith (ed.), *Early Medieval Rome and the Christian West. Essays in Honour of Donald A. Bullough* (Leiden: Brill), 85–99.

Rubery, E. 2009 'Christ and the Angelic Tetramorphs: the meaning of the eighth-century apsidal conch at Santa Maria Antiqua in Rome', in S. Neocleous (ed.), *Papers from the First and Second Postgraduate Forums in Byzantine Studies: Sailing to Byzantium* (Newcastle: Cambridge Scholars Publishing), 183–220.

Rushforth, G. 1902 'The church of S. Maria Antiqua', *Papers of the British School at Rome* 1: 1–123.

Russo, E. 1985 'La recinzione del presbiterio di S. Pietro in Vaticano dal VI all'VIII secolo', *Atti della Pontificia Accademia Romana di Archeologia. Rendiconti* 55–6: 3–33.

Russo, A. 2014 'Francesco Barberini e la "restauratione" del Triclinio Leoniano: il cantiere e un progetto inedito', *Bollettino d'Arte* ser.VII, 24: 111–24.

Sacchi, G. 1987–8 'Elementi dell'architettura carolingia ed affreschi medievali rinvenuti nella chiesa dei SS. Nereo ed Achilleo in Roma', *Atti della Pontificia Accademia Romana di Archeologia. Rendiconti* 60: 103–44.

Saguì, L. 1998 'Indagini archeologiche a Roma: nuovi dati sul VII secolo', in P. Delogu (ed.), *Roma medievale: aggiornamenti* (Florence: All'Insegna del Giglio), 63–78.

Salzman, M. R. 2013 'Leo's Liturgical Topography: contestations for space in fifth-century Rome', *Journal of Roman Studies* 103: 208–32.
Sanfilippo, I. L. 1994 'Un "luoco famoso" nel Medioevo, una chiesa oggi poco nota. Notizie extravaganti su S. Angelo in Pescheria', *Archivio della Società Romana di Storia Patria* 117: 231–68.
Sansterre, J.-M. 1982 'Jean VII (705–707): idéologie pontificale et réalisme politique', in L. Hadermann-Misguich and G. Raepsaet (eds.), *Rayonnement grec. Hommages à Charles Delvoye* (Brussels: Editions de l'Université de Bruxelles), 377–88.
Sansterre, J.-M. 1983 *Les moines grecs et orientaux à Rome aux époques byzantine et carolingienne (milieu du VIe s. – fin du IXe s.)*, 2 vols. (Brussels: Palais des Académies).
Sansterre, J.-M. 1984a 'Le pape Constantin Ier (708–715) et la politique religieuse des empereurs Justinien II et Philippikos', *Archivum Historiae Pontificiae* 22: 7–29.
Sansterre, J.-M. 1984b 'Où le diptyque consulaire de Clementinus fut-il employé à une fin liturgique?', *Byzantion* 54: 641–7.
Sansterre, J.-M. 1987 'À propos de la signification politico-religieuse de certaines fresques de Jean VII à Sainte-Marie-Antique', *Byzantion* 57: 434–40.
Sansterre, J.-M. 1988 'Le monachisme byzantin à Rome', *Bisanzio, Roma e l'Italia nell'Alto Medioevo*, Settimane di Studio del CISAM 34 (Spoleto: Centro Italiano di Studi sull'Alto Medioevo), 701–46.
Sansterre, J.-M. 2002 'Entre deux mondes? La vénération des images à Rome et en Italie d'après les textes des VIe–XIe siècles', *Roma fra Oriente e Occidente*, Settimane di Studio del CISAM 49 (Spoleto: Centro Italiano di Studi sull'Alto Medioevo), 993–1050.
Santangeli Valenzani, R. 1997 'Edilizia residenziale e aristocrazia urbana a Roma nell'altomedioevo', in S. Gelichi (ed.), *I Congresso nazionale di archeologia medievale (Pisa, 29–31 maggio 1997)* (Florence: All'Insegna del Giglio), 64–70.
Santangeli Valenzani, R. 2003 'Struttura economica e ruoli sociali a Roma nell'alto medioevo: una lettura archeologica', *Acta ad archaeologiam et artium historiam pertinentia* 17: 115–26.
Santangeli Valenzani, R. 2004a 'Strutture demografiche, economiche e sociali', in R. Meneghini and R. Santangeli Valenzani (eds.), *Roma nell'alto medioevo: topografia urbanistica della città dal V al X secolo* (Rome: Libreria dello Stato), 21–7.
Santangeli Valenzani, R. 2004b 'Coltivare in città', in R. Meneghini and R. Santangeli Valenzani (eds.), *Roma nell'alto medioevo: topografia urbanistica della città dal V al X secolo* (Rome: Libreria dello Stato), 127–32.
Santangeli Valenzani, R. 2004c 'Techniche edilizie', in R. Meneghini and R. Santangeli Valenzani (eds.), *Roma nell'alto medioevo: topografia urbanistica della città dal V al X secolo* (Rome: Libreria dello Stato), 133–42.

Santangeli Valenzani, R. 2004d 'Abitare a Roma nell'alto medioevo', in L. Paroli and L. Vendittelli (eds.), *Roma dall'antichità al medioevo II: contesti tardoantichi e altomedievali* (Milan: Electa), 41–59.

Santangeli Valenzani, R. 2014 'Hosting foreigners in early medieval Rome: from *xenodochia* to *scholae peregrinorum*', in F. Tinti (ed.), *England and Rome in the Early Middle Ages: pilgrimage, art, and politics* (Turnhout: Brepols), 69–88.

Sauget, J.-M. 1973 'Saint Grégoire le Grand et les reliques de Saint Pierre dans la tradition arabe chrétienne', *Rivista di Archeologia Cristiana* 49: 301–9.

Saxer, V. 2001 'Le chiese di Roma dal V al X secolo: amministrazione centrale e organizzazione territoriale', *Roma nell'Alto Medioevo*, Settimane di Studio del CISAM 48 (Spoleto: Centro Italiano di Studi sull'Alto Medioevo), 493–637.

Schieffer, R. 2000 'Charlemagne and Rome', in J. M. H. Smith (ed.), *Early Medieval Rome and the Christian West: Essays in Honour of Donald A. Bullough* (Leiden: Brill), 279–95.

Schmid, W. 2014 'I primi due strati dipinti della parete-palinsesto di Santa Maria Antiqua: nuove osservazioni di carattere tecnico-esecutivo', in G. Bordi, I. Carlettini, M. L. Fobelli, M. R. Menna, and P. Pogliani (eds.), *L'officina dello sguardo: scritti in onore di Maria Andaloro*, 2 vols. (Rome: Gangemi), II, 437–42.

Schmid, W. 2016 'Il lungo restauro di Santa Maria Antiqua e delle sue pitture, 2000-2015', in M. Andaloro, G. Bordi, and G. Morganti (eds.), *Santa Maria Antiqua tra Roma e Bisanzio* (Milan: Electa), 386–95.

Schmid, W. 2020 'Diary of a long conservation campaign', in E. Rubery, G. Bordi and J. Osborne (eds.), *Santa Maria Antiqua: The Sistine Chapel of the Eighth Century* (Turnhout: Brepols), in press.

Schmid, W. and V. Valentini 2013 'Alcune considerazioni sulle techniche pittoriche dei dipinti murali altomedievali di S. Maria Antiqua al Foro Romano', in P. M. De Marchi (ed.), *Castelseprio e Torba: Sintesi delle ricerche e aggiornamenti* (Mantua: Soprintendenza per i Beni Archeologici della Lombardia), 415–21.

Serlorenzi, M. 2016 'Sette casse dello scavo', in M. Andaloro, G. Bordi, and G. Morganti (eds.), *Santa Maria Antiqua tra Roma e Bisanzio* (Milan: Electa), 358–60.

Severini, G. 2015 'Il ciborio di Santa Maria Antiqua: analisi comparativa di rilievo 3D per un'ipotesi di ricostruzione', *Temporis Signa* 10: 135–62.

Sharpe, R. 2005 'King Caedwalla's Roman Epitaph', in K. O'Brien O'Keeffe and A. Orchard (eds.), *Latin Learning and English Lore: Studies in Anglo-Saxon Literature for Michael Lapidge*, 2 vols. (Toronto: University of Toronto Press), I, 171–93.

Silvagni, A. 1908 'Per la datazione di una iscrizione romana medievale di S. Saba', *Archivio della R. Società Romana di Storia Patria* 31: 433–45.

Silvagni, A. 1943a *Monumenta Epigraphica Christiana saeculo XIII antiquiora quae in Italiae finibus adhuc exstant*, 4 vols. (Vatican City: Pontificio Istituto di Archeologia Cristiana).

Silvagni, A. 1943b 'La Silloge epigrafica di Cambridge', *Rivista di Archeologia Cristiana* 20: 49–112.

Sinthern, P. 1908 'Der römische Abbacyrus in Geshichte, Legende und Kunst', *Römische Quartalschrift für christliche Altertumskunde und Kirchengeschichte* 22: 196–239.

Smiraglia, E. 1989 'Donazione di libri sacri alla chiesa di S. Clemente', *Vetera Christianorum* 26: 351–60.

Smith, J. M. H. 2000 'Old Saints, New Cults: Roman relics in Carolingian Francia', in J. M. H. Smith (ed.), *Early Medieval Rome and the Christian West. Essays in Honour of Donald A. Bullough* (Leiden: Brill), 317–39.

Smith, J. M. H. 2014 'Care of relics in early medieval Rome', in V. Garver and O. Phelan (eds.), *Rome and Religion in the Medieval World: Studies in Honor of Thomas F.X. Noble* (Farnham: Ashgate), 179–205.

Smith, J. M. H. 2018 'Cursing and curing, or the practice of Christianity in eighth-century Rome', in R. Balzaretti, J. Barrow, and P. Skinner (eds.) *Italy and Early Medieval Europe. Papers for Chris Wickham* (Oxford: Oxford University Press), 460–75.

Snow-Smith, J. 1989 'Brunelleschi's competition panel: the Spinario and the sin of heresy', *Gazette des Beaux-Arts* 113: 159–69.

Soavi, A., F. Di Cosimo, F. Fumelli, C. Longo, G. Galotta, M. R. Giuliani, and E. Giani 2016 'Il restauro dell'icona di Santa Maria Nova', *Bollettino ICR* N.S. 32: 49–76.

Solin, H. 2003 'Le trasformazioni dei nomi personali tra antichità e medioevo', in F. De Rubeis and W. Pohl (eds.), *Le Scritture dai Monasteri* (= *Acta Instituti Romani Finlandiae*, 29), 15–45.

Spatharakis, I. 1981 *Corpus of dated Illuminated Greek Manuscripts to the Year 1453* (Leiden: Brill).

Spera, L. 1997 'Cantieri edilizi a Roma in età carolingia. Gli interventi di papa Adriano I (772–795) nei santuari delle catacombe. Strategie e modalità di intervento', *Rivista di Archeologia Cristiana* 73: 185–254.

Spera, L. 2016 'Il papato e Roma nell'VIII secolo. Rileggere la "svolta" istituzionale attraverso la documentazione archeologica', *Rivista di Archeologia Cristiana* 92: 393–430.

Sternberg, T. 1988 'Der vermeintliche Ursprung der westlichen Diakonien in Ägypten und die Consolationes des Johannes Cassian', *Jahrbuch für Antike und Christentum* 31: 173–209.

Story, J. 2010 'Aldhelm and Old St Peter's, Rome', *Anglo-Saxon England* 39: 7–20.

Story, J. 2013 'The Carolingians and the oratory of Saint Peter the Shepherd', in R. McKitterick, J. Osborne, C. Richardson, and J. Story (eds.), *Old Saint Peter's, Rome* (Cambridge: Cambridge University Press), 257–273.

Story, J. 2018 'Lands and lights in early medieval Rome', in R. Balzaretti, J. Barrow, and P. Skinner (eds.), *Italy and Early Medieval Europe: Papers for Chris Wickham* (Oxford: Oxford University Press), 315–38.

Story, J., J. Bunbury, A. C. Felici, G. Fronterotta, M. Piacentini, C. Nicolais, D. Scacciatelli, S. Sciuti, and M. Vendittelli 2005 'Charlemagne's black marble: the origin of the epitaph of Pope Hadrian I', *Papers of the British School at Rome* 73: 157–90.

Stroll, M. 1997 'Maria Regina: papal symbol', in A.J. Duggan (ed.), *Queens and Queenship in Medieval Europe* (Woodbridge: Boydell and Brewer), 173–203.

Styger, P. 1914 'Die Malereien in der Basilika des hl. Sabas auf dem kl. Aventin in Rom', *Römische Quartalschrift für christliche Altertumskunde und Kirchengeschichte* 28: 49–96.

Succurro, M. C. 2015 'Una politica della memoria? Fondazioni monastiche e traslazioni reliquiali di re Desiderio', in G. Archetti (ed.) *Desiderio: il progetto politico dell'ultimo re longobardo. Atti del Primo convegno internazionale di studio (Brescia, 21–24 marzo 2013)* (Spoleto: Centro Italiano di Studi sull'Alto Medioevo), 607–29.

Sullivan, R. 1956 'Carolingian missionary theories', *The Catholic Historical Review* 42: 273–95.

Taddei, A. 2014a 'Smaragdos "patrikios", la colonna dell'imperatore Foca e la chiesa di Roma. Committenze artistiche e Realpolitik', in M. Gianandrea, F. Gangemi, and C. Costantini (eds.), *Il potere dell'arte nel medioevo: studi in onore di Mario D'Onofrio* (Rome: Campisano), 531–50.

Taddei, A. 2014b 'A journey of men and names. Constantinople's Kosmidion and its Italian replicas', *Convivium* 1.1: 20–30.

Tea, E. 1937 *La Basilica di Santa Maria Antiqua* (Milan: Società Editrice 'Vita e Pensiero').

Testini, P. 1980 *Archeologia cristiana: nozioni generali dalle origini alla fine del sec. VI*, 2nd ed. (Bari: Edipuglia).

Teteriatnikov, N. 1993 'For whom is Theodotus praying? An interpretation of the program of the private chapel in S. Maria Antiqua', *Cahiers Archéologiques* 41: 37–46.

Thacker, A. 1998 'Memorializing Gregory the Great: the origin and transmission of a papal cult in the seventh and early eighth centuries', *Early Medieval Europe* 7: 59–84.

Thacker, A. 2007 'Rome of the Martyrs: saints, cults and relics, fourth to seventh centuries', in É. Ó Carragáin and C. Neuman de Vegvar (eds.), *Roma Felix – Formation and Reflections of Medieval Rome* (Aldershot: Ashgate), 13–49.

Thacker, A. 2014 'Rome: the Pilgrims' City in the Seventh Century', in F. Tinti (ed.), *England and Rome in the Early Middle Ages: Pilgrimage, Art, and Politics* (Turnhout: Brepols), 89–139.

Themelly, A. 2008 'Immagini di Maria nella pittura e nei mosaici romani dalla crisi monotelita agli inizi della seconda iconoclastia (640–819)', *Acta ad archaeologiam et artium historiam pertinentia* 21: 107–38.

Thierry, N. 1968 'Une mosaïque à Dyrrachium', *Cahiers Archéologiques* 18: 227–29.

Thunø, E. 2015 *The Apse Mosaic in Early Medieval Rome: Time, Network, and Repetition* (New York: Cambridge University Press).

Thürlemann, F. 1977 'Die Bedeutung der Aachener Theoderich-Statue für Karl den Großen (801) und bei Walahfrid Strabo (839). Materialen zu einer Semiotik visueller Objekte im frühen Mittelalter', *Archiv für Kulturgeschichte* 59: 25–65.

Tomea, P. 2001 'Intorno a S. Giulia. Le traslazioni e la "rapina" dei corpi santi nel regno longobardo (Neustria e Austria)', in G. Ardenna (ed.), *Culto e Storia in Santa Giulia* (Brescia: Grafo), 29–101.

Tomei, A. 1991 'I mosaici e gli affreschi della cappella del Sancta Sanctorum', in C. Pietrangeli (ed.), *Il Palazzo apostolico lateranense* (Florence: Nardini), 58–79.

Toubert, P. 2001 '"Scrinium" et "Palatium": la formation de la bureaucratie romano-pontificale aux VIIIe–IXe siècles', *Roma nell'Alto Medioevo*, Settimane di Studio del CISAM 48 (Spoleto: Centro Italiano di Studi sull'Alto Medioevo), 57–117.

Toynbee, J. M. C. and J. B. Ward Perkins 1950 '"Peopled scrolls": a Hellenistic motif in imperial art', *Papers of the British School at Rome* 18: 1–43.

Tronzo, W. 1985 'The Prestige of Saint Peter's: Observations on the Function of Monumental Narrative Cycles in Italy', in H. Kessler and M. Shreve Simpson (eds.), *Pictorial Narrative in Antiquity and the Middle Ages*, Studies in the History of Art 16 (Washington: National Gallery of Art), 93–112.

Tronzo, W. 1987 'Setting and structure in two Roman wall decorations of the early Middle Ages', *Dumbarton Oaks Papers* 41: 477–92.

Trout, D. 2015 *Damasus of Rome: The Epigraphic Poetry* (Oxford: Oxford University Press).

Turco, M. G. 1994 'Osservazioni e considerazioni sulla fabbrica medievale della chiesa dei Santi Nereo e Achilleo', *Bollettino d'Arte* 88: 93–112.

Ullmann, W. 1960 'Leo I and the theme of papal primacy', *Journal of Theological Studies* N.S. 11: 25–51.

Underwood, P. 1959 'The evidence of restorations in the sanctuary mosaics of the Church of the Dormition at Nicaea', *Dumbarton Oaks Papers* 13: 235–43.

Urbani, G. 1964 'Le condizioni del dipinto ed i provvedimenti adottati', in C. Brandi (ed.), *Il Restauro della Madonna della Clemenza* (= *Bollettino dell'Istituto Centrale del Restauro* 41–44), 15–24.

Utro, U. 2004 'Una "falsa testimonianza": il dipinto della Biblioteca Vaticana e il mosaico absidale perduto dei SS. Nereo e Achilleo', in C. Angelelli (ed.), *Atti del IX Congresso dell'Associazione Italiana per lo Studio e la Conservazione del Mosaico (Aosta, 20–22 febbraio 2003)* (Ravenna: AISCOM), 507–18.

Valenti, M. 2018 'Changing rural settlements in the early Middle Ages in central and northern Italy: towards the centralization of rural property', in R. Balzaretti, J. Barrow, and P. Skinner (eds.) *Italy and Early Medieval Europe. Papers for Chris Wickham* (Oxford: Oxford University Press), 123–39.

Valentini, V. 2016 'Il cantiere pittorico della Cappella di Teodoto', in M. Andaloro, G. Bordi, and G. Morganti (eds.), *Santa Maria Antiqua tra Roma e Bisanzio* (Milan: Electa), 270–7.

Valesio, F. 1977–9 *Diario di Roma*, G. Scano (ed.), 6 vols. (Milan: Longanesi).

van Dijk, A. 1995 'The Oratory of Pope John VII (705–707) in Old St Peter's'. Unpublished Ph.D. dissertation, The Johns Hopkins University.

van Dijk, A. 1999 'The Angelic Salutation in Early Byzantine and Medieval Annunciation Imagery', *The Art Bulletin* 81: 420–36.

van Dijk, A. 2001 'Jerusalem, Antioch, Rome, and Constantinople: The Peter Cycle in the Oratory of Pope John VII (705–707)', *Dumbarton Oaks Papers* 55: 305–28.

van Dijk, A. 2004 'Type and Antitype in Santa Maria Antiqua: the Old Testament scenes on the transennae', in J. Osborne, J. R. Brandt, and G. Morganti (eds.), *Santa Maria Antiqua cento anni dopo. Atti del colloquio internazionale, Roma, 5–6 maggio 2000* (Rome: Campisano editore), 113–27.

van Dijk, A. 2006 'Reading medieval mosaics in the seventeenth century: the preserved fragments from Pope John VII's oratory in Old St Peter's', *Word & Image* 22: 285–91.

Vendittelli, L. 2004 '*Crypta Balbi*: stato e prospettive della ricerca archeologica nel complesso', in L. Paroli and L. Vendittelli (eds.), *Roma dall'antichità al medioevo II: contesti tardoantichi e altomedievali* (Milan: Electa), 222–30.

Verzone, P. 1976 'La distruzione dei palazzi imperiali di Roma e di Ravenna e la ristrutturazione del Palazzo Lateranense nel IX secolo nei rapporti con quello di Costantinopoli', in *Roma e l'Età Carolingia: atti delle giornate di studio 3–8 maggio 1976* (Rome: Multigrafica editrice), 39–54.

Vileisis, B. 1979 'The Genesis Cycle of Santa Maria Antiqua', Unpublished Ph.D. dissertation, Princeton University.

Viscontini, M. 2014 'I cicli cristologici del presbitero d Santa Maria Antiqua', in G. Bordi, I. Carlettini, M. L. Fobelli, M. R. Menna, and P. Pogliani (eds.), *L'officina dello sguardo: scritti in onore di Maria Andaloro*, 2 vols. (Rome: Gangemi), I: 291–6.

Vlad Borelli, L. 1954, 'Il restauro di una Crocifissione di S. Maria Antiqua', *Bollettino dell'Istituto Centrale del Restauro* 19–20:123–9.

Von Duhn, F. 1928 'Dante e la Lupa Capitolina', *Studi Etruschi* 2: 9–14.

Von Falkenhausen, V. 2015 'Roma greca. Greci e civiltà greca a Roma nel medioevo', in C. Carbonetti Vendittelli, S. Lucà, and M. Signorini (eds.), *Roma e il suo territorio nel medioevo. Le fonti scritte fra tradizione e innovazione* (Spoleto: Centro Italiano di Studi sull'Alto Medioevo), 39–72.

Waetzoldt, S. 1964 *Die Kopien des 17. Jahrhunderts nach Mosaiken und Wandmalereien in Rom* (Vienna: Schroll).

Walser, G. 1987 *Die Einsiedler Inschriftensammlung und der Pilgerführer durch Rom (Codex Einsidlensis 316: Facsimile, Umschrift, Übersetzung und Kommentar* (Stuttgart: Franz Steiner).

Walter, C. 1970 'Papal political imagery in the medieval Lateran palace', *Cahiers Archéologiques* 20: 155–76.

Ward-Perkins, J. B. 1955 'Notes on Southern Etruria and the Ager Veientanus', *Papers of the British School at Rome* 23: 44–72.

Weitzmann, K. 1951 *The Fresco Cycle of S. Maria di Castelseprio* (Princeton: Princeton University Press).

Weitzmann, K. 1976 *The Monastery of Saint Catherine at Mount Sinai, the Icons. Volume One: From the Sixth to the Tenth Century* (Princeton: Princeton University Press).

Weitzmann, K. 1979 *The Miniatures of the Sacra Parallela: Parisinus graecus 923* (Princeton: Princeton University Press).

Whitehouse, D. 1982 'Medieval pottery from South Etruria', in D. Andrews, J. Osborne, D. Whitehouse, *Medieval Lazio: Studies in Architecture, Painting and Ceramics*, BAR International Series 125 (Oxford: BAR), 299–344.

Whitehouse, D. 1988 'Rome and Naples: survival and revival in central and southern Italy', in R. Hodges and B. Hobley (eds.), *The Rebirth of Towns in the West, AD 700–1050* (London: Council for British Archaeology), 28–31.

Whitehouse, D. 2002 'The Transition from Natron to Plant Ash in the Levant', *Journal of Glass Studies* 44: 193–6.

Wickham, C. 1999 'Early medieval archeology in Italy; the last twenty years', *Archeologia Medievale* 26: 7–19.

Wickham, C. 2005 *Framing the Early Middle Ages: Europe and the Mediterranean, 400–800* (Oxford: Oxford University Press).

Wickham, C. 2015 *Medieval Rome: Society and Crisis of a City, 900–1150* (Oxford: Oxford University Press).

Wilpert, J. 1903 *Le pitture delle catacombe romane* (Rome: Desclée, Lefebvre et C.).

Wilpert, J. 1905 'Appunti sulle pitture della chiesa di S. Maria Antiqua', *Byzantinische Zeitschrift* 14: 578–83.

Wilpert, J. 1906 'Le pitture dell'Oratorio di S. Silvia', *Mélanges d'Archéologie et d'Histoire* 26: 15–26.

Wilpert, J. 1910 'Sancta Maria Antiqua', *L'Arte* 13: 1–20, 81–107.

Wilpert, J. 1916 *Die römischen Mosaiken und Malereien der kirchlichen Bauten vom IV. bis XIII. Jahrhundert* (Freiburg im Breisgau: Herder).

Wilson, A. 2000 'The water mills on the Janiculum', *Memoirs of the American Academy in Rome* 45: 219–46.

Wiseman, T. P. 1985–6 'Con Boni nel Foro. I diari romani di W. St Clair Baddeley', *Rivista dell'Istituto Nazionale di Archeologia e Storia dell'Arte* ser. III, 8–9:119–49.

Wolf, G. 2005 'Icons and sites. Cult images of the Virgin in medieval Rome', in M. Vassiliki (ed.), *Images of the Mother of God: Perceptions of the Theotokos in Byzantium* (Aldershot: Ashgate), 23–49.

Wortley, J. 1982 'Iconoclasm and leipsanoclasm: Leo III, Constantine V and the relics', *Byzantinische Forschungen* 8: 253–79.

Zucchetti, G. 1953 'Marco Aurelio', *Capitolium* 28: 328–32.

Index

Aachen, Charlemagne's 'Lateran', 156
Abbacyrus, saint, 56, 57, 125, 126
Ælberht, 138
Agnellus of Ravenna, 157
agnus Dei iconography, 202, 215
Aimone, Marco, 210
Aistulf, king, 20, 159, 177, 179, 210
Akathistos hymn, 33
Ambrose, *primicerius notariorum*, 121, 141
anargyroi, 56
Anastasis, 59, 61
Anastasius Sinaites, 61
Anastasius the Persian, St, 10
Andaloro, Maria, 202
Anna and Joachim, saints, 190
annus mundi dating, 116
Arator, 88
Augenti, Andrea, 40
Augustine of Hippo, relics of, 179

Ballardini, Antonella, 38, 126
Barberini, Francesco, 221
Bartoli, Alfonso, 206
Basil of Caesarea, scenes from the life of, 208
Battifol, Pierre, 236
Bauer, Franz Alto, 166, 194, 204
Bavant, Bernard, 123
Bede, 24, 78, 179
Belisarius, 3, 212
Belting, Hans, 127
Benedict Biscop, 138
Benedict II, pope, 117
Benedict of Monte Soratte, 125, 150
Benjamin of Tudela, 153, 155
Bertelli, Carlo, 64, 65
Bertolini, Ottorino, 117
betacism, 83, 115, 189, 196, 228
Blaise, saint, 126
Boni, Giacomo, 33, 37
Boniface IV, pope, 7
Bordi, Giulia, 75, 77, 111
Bosio, Antonio, 79
Brenk, Beat, 42
Brescia
  San Salvatore, 179

Brown, Thomas, 11, 130, 131, 134, 136
Brubaker, Leslie, 135, 192
Burgarella, Filippo, 139
Byzantine artists in Rome, 27, 62

Calandra, Giovanni Battista, 223
Callixtus I, pope, 85
Cambridge sylloge, 23
Cappadocia, 98
Capracorum, *domusculta* of, 132, 213–217
Cardin, Luca, 120, 209
Castelseprio
  Santa Maria *foris portas*, 31
Cavallo, Guglielmo, 45
Cecilia, saint, 178
Cecilia, saint, *domusculta* of, 124, 131, 138
Celestine, pope, 67
Chacón, Alonso, 223
Charlemagne, king, 161, 162, 203, 210, 219
Charles Martel, 91
Christopher, *dux*, 122
Christopher, *primicerius*, 122, 160
Coates-Stephens, Robert, 157, 158, 211, 213
Codex epistolaris carolinus, 91, 139
Codex Juvenianus (Rome, Bib. Vallicelliana MS B 25^2), 236
Conon, pope, 117
Constans II, emperor, 7, 38, 55, 157
Constantina, empress, 176
Constantine I, emperor, 23, 141, 151, 183
Constantine I, pope, 56, 68–71, 86, 89, 121, 122
Constantine II, pope, 160
Constantine V, emperor, 162, 172, 180, 187
Constantine, consul, 208
Constantine, father of popes Stephen II and Paul I, 159
Constantinople
  imperial palace, *Chalke* gate, 147
consular diptych of Clementinus, 218
Cornelius, pope, 79
Cosmas and Damian, saints, 13
Costambeys, Marios, 9, 197
Croquison, Jean, 168
Crucifixion, 107, 133

cult of Isis *medica*, 57
Curzi, Gaetano, 187
Cyprian, bishop of Carthage, 80
Cyrus and John, saints, 13

Damasus, pope, 174
David, Joseph, 196
Davis, Raymond, 171, 220
Davis-Weyer, Caecilia, 228
De Grüneisen, Wladimir, 82, 133, 134, 192, 195
De locis sanctis martyrum, 10, 64, 65, 78, 80, 174
De Rossi, Giovanni Battista, 79, 80
Delogu, Paolo, 130, 169
Desiderius, king, 74, 122, 159, 160, 161, 179, 203, 210
diaconiae, 116, 117
Dionysius, pope, 173
domuscultae, 118, 213
Donation of Constantine, 17, 155, 164, 180, 181, 183, 196, 223
Donus, pope, 10
Duchesne, Louis, 37, 178
Durrës, 35

Egyptian blue, 77
Einsiedeln Itinerary, 37, 205, 211, 212, 213
Ekonomou, Andrew, 134
Eugenia, saint, 199, 200
Eugenius II, pope, 166
Eustathius, *dux*, 119, 120, 158

Farfa abbey, 162
Felix IV, pope, 58
fictive curtains (*vela*), 49, 97, 146, 206
Forum Ware, 165, 215
Fried, Johann, 164

Gantner, Clemens, 17, 156, 163, 238
Geertman, Herman, 167, 220
Gelasius I, pope, 117
George, saint, 138
Gianandrea, Manuela, 72, 191
Goodson, Caroline, 164, 180
Gowans, Alan, xiv
Grafova, Maria, 189
Graphia aureae urbis, 152
Gratian, papal superista, 231
Gray, Nicolette, 126, 147, 180
Greek translation of Gregory I's *Dialogues* (BAV, cod. gr. 1666), 84, 139, 236
Gregory I, pope, 5–7, 74, 78, 116, 117, 121, 139, 152, 176, 197

Gregory II, pope, 71, 89, 91, 93, 118, 139, 141, 210, 211, 220
Gregory III, pope, 18, 41, 71, 77, 81, 85, 90, 91, 93, 117, 118, 129, 141, 159, 167, 184, 210
Gregory IV, pope, 84, 129, 227
Gregory of Tours, 12
Gregory, priest of San Clemente, 140
Grimaldi, Giacomo, 25, 27, 30, 126, 143, 185, 224

Hadrian I, pope, xix, 18, 20, 74, 93, 119, 120, 123, 126, 128, 156, 157, 160, 161, 166, 168, 184, 192, 194–218, 219
Harper, Kyle, xiv
Hedistus, saint, domusculta of, 214
Heraclius, emperor, 9
Hilarus, pope, 146
Hodges, Richard, xiii, 5
Honorius I, pope, 7, 12, 78, 131, 206, 212
Huyghebaert, Nicolas, 164

Iacobini, Antonio, 225
Iconoclasm, 2, 90, 147, 187
incubation, practice of, 57

Jessop, Lesley, 128
John III, pope, 80
John IV, pope, 175, 196
John of Damascus, 74
John V, pope, 117
John VI, pope, 14, 24, 89
John VII, pope, 11, 22–66, 98, 106, 130, 141, 184, 198
John VIII, pope, 231
John XIII, pope, 151
John XIV, pope, 151
Justin II, emperor, 41
Justinian I, emperor, 147
Justinian II, emperor, 13, 16, 54, 55, 69, 88, 198

Kalas, Gregor, 40
Kartsonis, Anna, 61
Kitzinger, Ernst, 77, 82, 135, 192
Knipp, David, 57
Kramer, Rutger, 156
Krautheimer, Richard, xiv, 4, 41, 162, 166, 206, 225, 226, 228

La Mantia, Serena, 189
Lai, Andrea, 84
Lanciani, Rodolfo, 37
Lateran, Council of 649, 28, 43, 82
Laudes mediolanensis civitatis, 178
Lauer, Philippe, 144, 151
Lawrence, Marion, 32, 197

lazurite (lapis lazuli), 73, 77
Leo I, pope, 24, 48, 79, 183
Leo II, pope, 176
Leo III, emperor, 14, 89, 90, 118, 139, 147
Leo III, pope, xvii, xviii, 20, 26, 74, 79, 80, 84, 119, 125, 148, 156, 161, 219–230
Leo IV, emperor, 162, 172
Leo IV, pope, 106, 211, 231
Leoninus *consul et dux*, 214
Leontius, abbot of San Silvestro in Capite, 172, 177
Lestocquoy, Jean, 117
Libellus de imperatoria potestate in urbe Roma, 150
Liutprand, king, 18, 91, 123, 137, 179
Liverani, Paolo, 151
Lombard hairstyle, 18
Lombard interest in relics, 178
Lombard sculpture, sources of, 167
Lucey, Stephen, 136, 191
Lucius II, pope, 75

Madonna della Clemenza icon, 63, 64
Magister Gregorius, 149, 151, 152, 153, 155
Manacorda, Daniele, 92
Marazzi, Federico, 93, 118, 130
Marcelli, Marina, 8
Maria *regina*, 27, 32, 33, 43, 63, 107, 197, 200
Martin I, pope, 48
Mary, cult of, 16, 198
Mary, scenes from the life of, 75
Maskarinec, Maya, 13, 117, 125, 138, 230
Mastalus, *primicerius*, 214
McCormick, Michael, 169
Megistus Cataxanthus, 124
Melograni, Anna, 77
Meneghini, Roberto, 9
Milix and Pumenius, saints, 79
Mirabilia urbis Romae, 153
Moduin of Autun, 170
Mola di Monte Gelato, 215
Monotheletism, 2, 27, 56, 72
Moschus, John, 9
Mount Sinai, Crucifixion icon, 133

natron use in mosaics, 35
Nelson, Janet, 164
Nestori, Aldo, 85
Nicaea
    Church of the Dormition, 2, 26
Nicaea, Second Council of, 74, 163, 203
Nicholas, saint, 126
Nilgen, Ursula, 53

Noble, Thomas, 89, 130, 131, 136, 161, 164, 169, 203
Nordhagen, Per Jonas, xvi, 25, 44, 49, 51, 53, 55, 59, 61, 62, 82, 128, 192
Notitia ecclesiarum urbis Romae, 78, 80, 174

Old Testament events, depictions of, 58
Optatus, 80
Orbetello inscription, 139
Ordines Romani, 15, 20, 71, 121, 129
Ostia
    Sant'Aurea, 15

palaeography as a dating tool, 82
Palatine hill, 36, 38, 40
pallium, decoration of, 196
Panvinio, Onofrio, 221, 223
Pardus, abbot of San Saba, 74
Paroli, Lidia, 167
Paschal I, pope, 26, 61, 111, 177, 178, 184
Paschal, nephew of Hadrian I, 219
Passionei, Domenico, 45, 186
Paul Afiarta, 122, 160, 162
Paul I, pope, 17, 19, 26, 49, 72, 111, 139, 141, 157, 159, 171–193
Paul the Deacon, 17
Pelagius II, pope, 12, 78
Peter and Marcellinus, saints, 79
Peter, abbot of San Saba, 74
Peter, *dux*, 122
Petronilla, saint, 182
Pippin III, king, 17, 91, 159, 172, 177, 182
Plato, father of John VII, 40
Polion, saint, 79
Prigent, Vivian, 118
primicerius defensorum, 121
primicerius sanctae sedis apostolicae, 121, 132
Primus and Felicianus, saints, 176
Procopius, 3, 9
Protoevangelium of James, 30, 75

Quinisext Council, 16, 54, 70, 88, 202, 215
Quiricus and Julitta, saints, 95, 99–104

Rabbula Gospels, 134
Rea, Rossella, 9
Reekmans, Louis, 82
Rettner, Arno, 128
Robigalia festival, 6
Roman Senate, 6
Romanelli, Pietro, 192
Romanitas, 17
Rome
    Aqua Claudia, 212
    Aqua Jovia, 213

Rome (cont.)
    Aqua Sabbatina, 211
    Aqua Virgo, 212
    Aurelian walls, 210
    Baths of Caracalla, 228
    Catacomb of Calepodius, 85
    Catacomb of Commodilla, 128
    Catacomb of Pontianus, 79
    Catacomb of Priscilla, 173
    Catacomb of San Callisto, 78–85, 114, 147, 173
    Catacomb of San Valentino, 31, 53, 134
    catacombs, 8
    Cemetery of Generosa, 176
    Crypta Balbi, 13, 19, 86, 92, 165, 206
    Forum of Caesar, 92
    importation of silk textiles, 167
    Lateran baptistery, San Venanzio chapel, 26, 32, 82, 176, 195
    Lateran Palace, 6, 138, 140–158, 166, 212, 220–226
    Lateran Palace, Aula Leonina, 221
    Lateran Palace, Aula Leonina replica, 222
    Lateran Palace, bronze statuary, 148–155
    Lateran Palace, *macrona*, 226
    Lateran Palace, mural of Saint Augustine (?), 144
    Lateran Palace, *Sala del Concilio*, 226
    Lateran Palace, Sancta Sanctorum, 229
    Palatine hill, 22
    Pantheon, 7, 160
    Porta San Pancrazio, 212
    Porta Tiburtina, 211
    San Clemente, 61, 106, 133, 140, 198–200
    San Crisogono, 77, 80
    San Giorgio in Velabro, 138
    San Lorenzo fuori le mura, 104, 199, 213
    San Lorenzo in Lucina, 6
    San Marco, 84
    San Paolo fuori le mura, 15, 54, 166, 184, 204, 213
    San Pietro in Vincoli, 175
    San Saba, 10, 73–78
    San Silvestro in Capite, 26, 111, 160, 161, 172–181, 219
    San Teodoro, 117
    Sant'Adriano, 7, 16, 84, 106, 111, 119, 206–208, 209
    Sant'Agnese fuori le mura, 26
    Sant'Anastasia, 40
    Sant'Angelo in Pescheria, 114–116, 126, 132, 135, 165, 206, 211
    Sant'Euphemia, 15
    Sant'Eusebio, 137
    Santa Bibiana, 176
    Santa Maria Antiqua, 9, 14, 19, 32–35, 36–63, 76, 95–136, 175, 185–193, 194–197
    Santa Maria de Secundicerio, 76
    Santa Maria in Aquiro, 117
    Santa Maria in Cosmedin, 25, 119, 120, 158, 165, 204–206, 208, 209, 211, 228
    Santa Maria in Domnica, 111
    Santa Maria in Trastevere, 63, 111, 129
    Santa Maria Maggiore, 16, 204
    Santa Maria Nova, 37
    Santa Maria Nova, icon, 41
    Santa Martina, 209
    Santa Passera, 126
    Santa Prassede, 166
    Santa Pudenziana, 204
    Santa Sabina, 51, 67–73, 105, 111, 133, 166
    Santa Susanna, 15, 200–202, 227–229
    Santi Cosma e Damiano, 54, 104, 119
    Santi Giovanni e Paolo, 134, 175
    Santi Nereo ed Achilleo, 228
    Santi Sergio e Bacco, 117, 120, 196
    Santo Stefano Rotondo, 26, 176
    slave market, 169
    Saint Peter's, 12, 15, 23–36, 61, 71, 90, 122, 126, 130, 134, 137, 138, 168, 181–185, 203, 212, 217, 227
    Saint Peter's, Chapel of Santa Petronilla, 182
    Saint Peter's, funerary inscription of Pope Hadrian I, 217
    Saint Peter's, Santa Maria in Turri, 185
    Vatican obelisk, 227
    water supply, 211–213
Rome as a bilingual city, 14
Rome as a source of books, 138
Rome as the city of Romulus, 158
Rubery, Eileen, 187
Rushforth, Gordon, 42, 53, 58, 95, 97, 100, 128, 192, 194, 195, 196
Russo, Eugenio, 167

Sacra Parallela (Paris, BNFr cod. gr. 923), 235
Sansterre, Jean-Marie, 11, 203
Santa Cornelia, excavation of, 215
Santa Rufina, excavation of, 215
Santangeli Valenzani, Riccardo, xiii, 4, 9, 14, 92
Schmid, Werner, 42, 43
Sebastian, saint, 75
Sergius and Bacchus, saints, 196
Sergius I, pope, xvii, 15, 16, 24, 54, 88, 142, 183, 215
Sergius, *sacellarius*, 160
Silvester I, pope, 173, 196
Sisinnius, pope, 71
Sixth Ecumenical Council, 28, 69, 72

Sixtus II, pope, 80
Sophronius, 10
square halo, 31, 64, 72, 194
Stephen I, pope, 173
Stephen II, pope, 17, 92, 120, 121, 126–129, 141, 159, 172, 177, 179, 182
Stephen III, pope, 142, 160
Stephen, *patricius et dux*, 122
Story, Joanna, 184, 217
Styger, Paul, 75
Sutri, 91
Sylvester I, pope, 155
Symmachus, pope, 23, 227

Tea, Eva, 41, 128, 192
Teteriatnikov, Natalia, 128, 129
tetramorphs, iconography of, 187
Theodelinda, queen, 178
Theodora, empress, 199
Theodore of Tarsus, 86
Theodore, archpriest, 69, 106
Theodore, father of Hadrian I, 123, 124, 128, 131
Theodore, pope, 10, 142, 176, 195
Theodotus, 20, 94, 95, 113–124, 126–127, 208
Theophanes, 118
Thessaloniki
  Saint Demetrios, 26, 113
Totila, king of Ostrogoths, 3

Toto, duke of Nepi, 160, 184
Transfiguration, 76
translations of relics into Rome, 174
Tronzo, William, 36, 53

Ugonio, Pompeo, 223, 226, 228

Valesio, Francesco, 45, 186
van Dijk, Ann, 36, 58
Venantius Fortunatus, 109
Verzone, Paolo, 148
Vespignani, Virginio, 200
Vileisis, Birute, 190
Vitalian, pope, 143

Walahfrid Strabo, 157
Wandelbert of Prüm, 146
Ward-Perkins, John, 215
Weitzmann, Kurt, 113, 133
Wickham, Chris, xiv, 5
Wilfrid, 14
Wilpert, Joseph, 42, 80, 82, 186, 192, 194, 197
Winichis, duke of Spoleto, 220
world map, 143

Zacharias, pope, 84, 91, 93, 104, 137–140, 159
Zacharias, *spatharius*, 16, 89
Zosimus, 8, 9

CPSIA information can be obtained
at www.ICGtesting.com
Printed in the USA
LVHW060854030821
694401LV00007B/491